Shaping the Normative Land

Shaping the Normative Landscape is an investigation of the value of obligations anu of rights, of forgiveness, of consent and refusal, and of promise and request. David Owens shows that these are all instruments by which we exercise control over our normative environment. Philosophers from Hume to Scanlon have supposed that when we make promises and give our consent, our real interest is in controlling (or being able to anticipate) what people will actually do and that our interest in rights and obligations is a by-product of this more fundamental interest. In fact, we value for its own sake the ability to decide who is obliged to do what, to determine when blame is appropriate, to settle whether an act wrongs us. Owens explores how we control the rights and obligations of ourselves and of those around us. We do so by making friends and thereby creating the rights and obligations of friendship. We do so by making promises and so binding ourselves to perform. We do so by consenting to medical treatment and thereby giving the doctor the right to go ahead. The normative character of our world matters to us on its own account. To make sense of promise, consent, friendship, and other related phenomena we must acknowledge that normative interests are amongst our fundamental interests. We must also rethink the psychology of agency and the nature of social convention.

David Owens is Professor of Philosophy at the University of Reading.

Shaping the Normative Landscape

DAVID OWENS

OXFORD
UNIVERSITY PRESS

OXFORD
UNIVERSITY PRESS

Great Clarendon Street, Oxford, OX2 6DP,
United Kingdom

Oxford University Press is a department of the University of Oxford.
It furthers the University's objective of excellence in research, scholarship,
and education by publishing worldwide. Oxford is a registered trade mark of
Oxford University Press in the UK and in certain other countries

First Edition published in 2012
First published in paperback 2014

Published in the United States of America by Oxford University Press
198 Madison Avenue, New York, NY 10016, United States of America

British Library Cataloguing in Publication Data
Data available

Library of Congress Cataloging in Publication Data
Data available

ISBN 978-0-19-969150-0 (Hbk)
ISBN 978-0-19-870804-9 (Pbk)

For Sam

Preface

This book contributes to a tradition of thought according to which facts about what people have a right to, or what obligations they have, or what they are to be blamed for, depend on facts about human interests. I depart from (or develop) this tradition in postulating *normative* interests.

The phrase 'normative interest' can be given either a broad or a narrow construal. On the broader construal a normative interest is any interest with normative significance, any interest that affects the normative situation, any interest that is normative for us, which should guide how we think, feel, and act. On the narrower construal a normative interest is an interest that takes normative phenomena as its object, an interest *in* which thoughts, feelings, and actions are obligatory, blameworthy, appropriate, or even intelligible. I'll be using 'normative interest' in this second sense. In particular, I shall urge that a wide range of normative phenomena can be explained only by supposing that human beings have interests in controlling the distribution of rights and obligations, the appropriate objects of blame, etc., interests distinct from their non-normative interests. Our interests in the normative are often normative for us.

This book is concerned with what I call choice-dependent obligations, a varied category which includes obligations of reciprocation and due care for expectations, obligations implicated in relationships like friendship, obligations which can be abolished by consent, as well as promissory obligations. The book also considers forgiveness. To explain these phenomena, I construct and deploy an account of their value. The same approach may cast light on aspects of our social lives that lie on the periphery of the present work such as property rights, political authority, positive law, and linguistic assertion.

My account of these matters differs from many others in that it makes no use of notions with a special moralized sense. I am thinking of 'autonomy', 'respect', 'recognition', and 'equality', as well 'moral obligation 'moral value', 'moral right', 'moral reason', 'moral principle', and so forth. I worry that (at least in their intended sense) these notions cannot be understood independently of the deontic phenomena we are trying to explain. My own foundational notions—'interest', 'value', 'habit', 'practice', 'appropriate', 'intelligible', and so forth—are of very broad application and so offer an explanatory purchase on the deontic. Even a complete sceptic about the deontic would need to employ them in other domains.

To my mind recent writing about morality presents us with a false dilemma. Some think 'moral' norms are to be established by practical reasoning and that our adherence to them is an expression of our nature as free and rational beings. Within this camp there is a lively debate about what constitutes practical reasoning but relatively little discussion of whether morality is generated by practical reasoning. Others insist that 'moral' norms are the products of those drives, reflexes, and instincts which enabled us to prevail in the evolutionary struggle, that they express our animal nature. On this view, guilt, blame, and even conscientious agency are more sophisticated versions of something that occurs throughout the animal world. Perhaps the rationalist and the naturalist approach are each suited to explain some aspect of what is generally called morality but I doubt they cover the field. Our normative niche is moulded by habits, customs, and practices. These social phenomena are the products of rational choices but to subscribe to a practice or to act out of habit is to act neither on reason nor on impulse.

In the past decade, I have acquired many debts to persons and institutions. As to the latter, I owe thanks to the University of Sheffield for granting me sabbatical leave in 2001 and again in 2005 and to the Arts and Humanities Research Council for supporting my work on both occasions through their Research Leave Scheme. I also thank the School of Advanced Study in the University of London for enabling me to spend the autumn of 2005 in London as a Visiting Professorial Fellow. During that first phase of work I managed to write several papers on promising and obligation. That I was able to turn these papers into this book is down to the Leverhulme Foundation who awarded me a two-year Major Research Fellowship for 2008–9. I am deeply grateful for that opportunity. I spent the autumn of 2009 revising the manuscript in Oxford, thanks to the award of a Visiting Fellowship at All Souls College. The final version of the book was prepared in the autumn of 2011 during a term of sabbatical leave from the University of Reading and whilst I was a Visiting Fellow at the New York University Institute of Philosophy. I was also the recipient of a British Academy Research Development Award for a project on 'Telling and Trusting' between 2009 and 2011. This award financed a number of workshops that aided the development of these ideas.

My interest in many of the issues discussed here grew out of a seminar on promissory obligation run by Liam Murphy back in 2001. Daniel Markovits, Joseph Raz, Nishi Shah, and David Velleman all played an important role in bringing the project to completion, by reading drafts and discussing the issues as well supporting my work in other ways. Jonathan Adler, who died whilst this book was in press, was a constant source of help and encouragement. I am also grateful for the comments of Jody Azzouni, Ralph Bader, Chris Bennett, Curtis Bridgeman, Tim Clarke, Jules Coleman, Troy Cross, Veronique Munoz-Darde, Stephen Darwall, Alex Gregory, Matt Evans, Kati Farkas, John Gardner, Zoltan Szabo Gendler, Michael Gibb, Andrew Gold, Pete Graham, Peter Goldie, Leslie Green, Edward Harcourt, Alison Hills, Brad Hooker, Chris Hookway, Robert Hopkins, Ulrike Heuer, Mike Huemer, Shelly Kagan, Francis Kamm, Rosanna Keefe, Gregory Klass, Niko Kolodny, Jody Kraus, Noa Leibowitz, Jimmy Lenman, Michael Martin, Mike Otsuka, Richard

Parkhill, Ian Phillips, Tom Pink, Michael Pratt, Andrew Simester, Jennifer Saul, Tim Scanlon, Sam Scheffler, Seana Shiffrin, Jonathan Smith, Matt Smith, Nic Southwood, Michael Stocker, Galen Strawson, Sharon Street, John Tasioulas, Roger Teichmann, Peter Vallentyne, Daniel Viehoff, Gary Watson, Ralph Wedgwood, and Leif Wenar.

I thank Oxford University Press for permission to quote from Hume's *Treatise on Human Nature*, 2nd edn., ed. P. Nidditch. Parts of Chapter 3 are taken from 'Rationalism about Obligation', *European Journal of Philosophy* 16(3) (December 2008): 403–31. Chapter 5 is based on 'The Problem with Promising', in H. Sheinman (ed.): *Understanding Promises: Philosophical Essays* (Oxford: Oxford University Press 2011): 58–79. Most of Chapter 8 appears as 'Promising Without Intending', *Journal of Philosophy* 105(12) (December 2008): 737–55, and parts of Chapter 10 derive from 'Duress, Deception and the Validity of a Promise', *Mind* 116(462) (April 2007): 293–315. In Chapters 6 and 9, I reproduce sections of 'A Simple Theory of Promising', *Philosophical Review* 115(1) (January 2006): 51–77, and passages in Chapters 1 and 4 appear in 'The Value of Duty', *Proceedings of the Aristotelian Society, Supplementary Volume* LXXVI (July 2012). Finally, an abbreviated version of Chapter 7 was published as 'The Possibility of Consent' *Ratio* 24 (December 2011): 402–21.

I am grateful to Sam Ishii-Gonzales for the front cover and for fifteen years of support and encouragement.

Contents

Introduction

In the final section of his *Enquiry Concerning the Principles of Morals*, Hume raises a familiar issue: is it good for us to be good?

Having explained the moral *approbation* attending merit or virtue, there remains nothing but briefly to consider our interested *obligation* to it, and to enquire whether every man, who has any regard to his own happiness and welfare, will not best find his account in the practice of every moral duty.   (Hume 1975: 278)

Here Hume is addressing a question about *compliance*. He is asking whether it is in our interests to fulfil our duties, to behave well rather than to behave badly. Within Hume's own framework, it is possible to formulate a rather different question. It is possible to ask whether it is in our interests that we are subject to certain duties, whether it is good for us that certain actions count as virtuous or vicious. This is possible because Hume recognized the category of what he called artificial virtue, virtues which are (in part) the product of social convention, virtues which exist because we have an interest in those conventions being in force. Nothing counts as an artificial *virtue* unless our interests are served by the relevant social conventions and so we may ask what interest these conventions serve, what *value* there is in the obligations or the rights they engender.[1]

The compliance question arises whenever we might fail to conform to those norms. The value question arises whenever we might fail to create or sustain those norms. In Hume's eyes, fidelity to promises and respect for property are artificial virtues and so we can ask after the value of these virtues. Almost everyone will allow that at least some practical norms are a product of social practices (e.g. positive law) but many will take issue with Hume's own list of artificial virtues.

We find considerable disagreement about where and when the value question can sensibly be raised. For some, asking whether it is in our interests that promises ought to be kept or stealing avoided would be like asking whether it is in our interests

---

[1] I use 'convention' to mean 'social rule' or 'social practice'. Some conventions may be arbitrary (e.g. rules about word meaning) but many others are not.

that $2 + 2 = 4$.[2] There is much more agreement on the terms in which it should be answered where it can be raised. The consensus is that it is in our interest to have positive law because the existence of law renders human social life predictable. For Hume, the same is true of the rules of property and contract: adherence to such rules facilitates social co-ordination and these rules are in force only in so far as they are generally adhered to.

Answers of this sort resolve the value question by appealing to purely non-normative interests. We can state our interest in social co-ordination without recourse to normative notions. For Hume, social institutions like property ownership help us to control our own lives by granting us a certain amount of control over how others behave towards us. I agree that human beings need to control their social environment but I wonder why this need shouldn't extend to its normative aspects. Suppose we have normative interests, that normative phenomena can be good (or bad) for us quite apart from their impact on our non-normative concerns. Since we generally have an interest in controlling things that matter to us, wouldn't we wish to exercise control over these normative phenomena also? For example, facts about what we are obliged to do are an important part of our social world. Wouldn't it matter to us whether we control such facts and not just because of their impact on what people actually do? If so, we have normative interests alongside our non-normative interests.

Some writers take duty and obligation and the like to be a bad thing, both constraining us and creating opportunities for 'negative' emotions like blame and guilt. Any positive value they possess is purely instrumental. On this view, human beings do indeed have a (negative) interest in whether or not a certain range of normative facts obtains and thus an interest in controlling whether they obtain. But such an aversion can't explain why such normative phenomena exist. I will urge that duty and obligation (for instance) can be valuable for their own sake, that they often make a positive contribution to our lives, e.g. to valuable relationships like friendship. We have an interest in such normative phenomena where these norms would be good for us and our normative interests can explain the existence of various obligations by delivering a positive answer to the value question. They also explain both our need and our ability to control those obligations and I shall use the phrase 'normative interest' to cover these control interests also.[3]

The first item of business is to delineate the scope of my inquiry. My main focus will be on *interested obligations*, which I now define as obligations whose existence is

---

[2] For example (Ross 1930: 29–30), (Prichard 1968: 8), (Reid 1969: 444).

[3] A utilitarian may allow that obligations can be a source of pleasure or that we can have a non-derivative preference for obligation. On this view obligation has a value which it derives from the value of certain non-normative phenomena, namely that of pleasure or of preference satisfaction. My thought is that (in certain contexts) obligation as such is good for us and that this fact explains why we want it and/or derive pleasure from it (if we do).

to be explained (at least in part) by reference to our interest in the existence of those very obligations. Here I am co-opting Hume's terminology to express a rather un-Humean idea. How does this notion of an interested obligation relate to other more familiar ways of categorizing obligations?

1. Choice-dependent obligations

Some obligations are chosen in that they exist in part because of our choices but this remark fails to delineate any very definite subject matter for there are many different ways in which what we are obliged to do can depend upon the choices we have made. Relatively few obligations are completely independent of our choices. In this section, I shall describe the various roles that an individual's choice can play in determining who is obliged to do what at a given moment.[4]

There are at least four grades of choice-dependence. The null grade applies where the obligation is independent of choice. If I'm obliged to refrain from filling in the Grand Canyon, that obligation is rooted in the natural beauty of the Canyon and not in any choice of mine. Some interpersonal duties may fall into the same category. When I encounter the proverbial child drowning in the pond I must rescue the child regardless of my past choices. I may have done everything I could to avoid such encounters. I might have moved to the proverbial desert island where the child was then abandoned by a passing ship. Still I am obliged to rescue the child.[5]

Very often the fact that someone chose to do something is an important element in the story of how they came to acquire a certain obligation. For example, should I choose to drive a car, I am obliged to be sober and the fact that I chose to drive is an important part of the story as to why I have this obligation. Because I can avoid this burden by choosing not to drive, it is fair to insist on my being sober should I drive. The distinctive feature of this *first* grade of choice-dependence is that I incur this obligation in choosing to drive the car whether or not I am aware that my choice will have this consequence. Where I know of the consequent obligation, I intentionally incur it by starting my car. I may even intend to incur it (e.g. to stop myself drinking) but none of this matters to whether I actually do incur it.[6]

Another type of obligation with the first grade of choice-dependence (and one which appears regularly in what follows) is an obligation of reciprocation, a duty to help someone who has helped you. Most such obligations arise only because the recipient has chosen to accept the help. It is usually unfair to expect a return where

---

[4] See (Raz 1999: 98–104) and (Raz 1982: 928–31) for a helpful discussion of choice-dependent obligation. My notion of normative power is narrower than Raz's (1999: 103).

[5] It may be thought that even these obligations can be affected by choice, e.g. if I invited the child onto my desert island, I have a greater obligation to rescue them. Since, for my purposes, it will not matter whether any forms of obligations are entirely choice-independent, I shall ignore this complication.

[6] Though ignorance of the fact that I have incurred it *may* still furnish me with an excuse for violation.

the aid was neither requested nor taken advantage of once offered. There may be exceptions to this. For example, those with devoted parents may feel a special obligation to take care of them in their old age, a feeling that does not depend on the idea that they *accepted* their parent's generosity[7] but mostly we wouldn't require someone to take on the burdens of reciprocation unless they had accepted the gift in the first place (p. 140). My concern is with cases where acceptance *is* crucial to whether you are obliged to reciprocate. Again one can choose to accept the help and thereby incur the obligation to reciprocate without choosing to take on the conse-quent obligation. Obtusely, I may not realize that I am obliged to reciprocate but I remain so obliged. Where obligations of reciprocation are choice-dependent, they have the first grade of choice-dependence.

A second grade of choice-dependence is present where someone's choice puts them under an obligation only when they make this choice in the knowledge that it might have the effect of putting them under this obligation. As just noted, this is not required for you to be under an obligation to reciprocate but it is required when we are dealing with what I shall call obligations of involvement. Take friendship for example. Someone becomes my friend by spending time with me, by sharing various activities and experiences, by expressing interest and affection. And there are duties of friendship, things one is obliged to do for one's friends but not for other people. Still, one ignorant of the prevailing forms friendship (perhaps newly arrived in the country and simply 'being friendly') could not be held to these expectations. This outsider must deal with the resulting hurt and disappointment but that is a quite different matter from fulfilling the obligations of friendship.[8] There may be forms of friendship of which this isn't true, relationships which can be entered into unknow-ingly and which impose their obligations regardless. I maintain only that there are forms of friendship familiar to us all of which this is true. These I call involvements.

The third grade of choice-dependence is exhibited by the exercise of a *normative power*, where I change what someone is obliged to do by intentionally communicat-ing the intention of hereby so doing. Suppose I intentionally communicate the intention of hereby imposing an obligation on you. Since this communication is

---

[7] One might accommodate some such obligations by allowing that acceptance can be retrospective (as when I'm grateful that you rescued me from my suicide bid) but this won't acquit children who renounce their parents at the first opportunity of the 'horrid and unnatural' crime of ingratitude (Hume 1978: 466). In this area, mores have changed considerably and it is unclear to me what responsibilities children have to care for their parents and whether the notion of reciprocation is their basis. What seems clear is that one can normally avoid an obligation to reciprocate by refusing (or evading) the offer. People often decline a gift precisely to avoid 'being obliged'.

[8] Note this point does not turn on the conventional character of friendship. There might be relation-ships created by convention (e.g. forms of neighbourliness which apply to you simply in virtue of physical proximity) that include you regardless of your choices. Here ignorance would not exempt you from the relevant obligations, though it might help to excuse your violations if you couldn't be expected to have discovered the relevant conventions.

intentional, the imposition of the obligation presupposes a choice and since the intention communicated is to change the normative situation, I must at least purport to believe that this choice can affect your obligations. So the products of an exercise of normative power possess both of the elements of choice-dependence so far identified. I give them a yet higher grade because, when a normative power is exercised, the speaker must present himself as intending to *hereby* change the normative situation, to change the normative situation by means of this very communication. Thus, at least where the speaker is sincere, this change in the normative situation is either an end in itself or a means to some other end. This need not be so when he accepts a gift, nor when he makes a friend; obligations of reciprocation or friendship may be unintended side effects of what we do, and no part of our plan of action (p. 102).[9]

Promise, command, and consent all involve the exercise of normative power. A promise is made where the promisor communicates the intention of hereby putting himself under an obligation to perform the promised act. And a promissory obligation is an obligation created by means of the very mechanism envisaged in the making of the promise. Similarly, the commands of a legitimate authority create obligations because they communicate the authority's intention to hereby place its subordinates under an obligation, while consent removes a prior obligation by communicating the intention so to do. For brevity's sake, I shall say that obligations subject to normative power are created or abolished *by declaration*, meaning that they are created or abolished by the communication of the relevant intention. (Friendships are not created simply by declaration.) Hume's discussion of artificial virtue focuses on four sources of normative power: ownership, political authority, contract, and consent. All will be mentioned in the course of the book but promise will get the lion's share of our attention.

I have distinguished three grades of choice-dependence amongst obligations. Some of these differences are widely appreciated. For example the difference between the highest grade (the products of normative power) and the rest is generally marked, sometimes by calling promises, consents, etc., *performatives*. But obligations of the first and the second grade are often assimilated.[10] This conflation matters because it obscures a further and deeper division between these two forms of obligation, namely that between interested and non-interested obligations.

Consider the first grade of choice-dependence. In order to account for the role that choice plays in generating obligations of reciprocation (for instance) we need not suppose that people have any interest in the existence of the obligations themselves. The interests in play here may all be non-normative interests, e.g. in the goods and services being exchanged. The role of choice (i.e. the acceptance of a benefit) is to

---

[9] The choices discussed in this section are all 'voluntary' choices but obligations with different grades of choice-dependence also differ in regards to what constitutes a 'voluntary' choice (Sec. 47).

[10] Perhaps in an attempt to reduce the obligations of friendship to obligations of reciprocation (pp. 107–9).

ensure that such obligations are avoidable. By requiring choice we remove an objection of unfairness to our incurring an obligation to reciprocate, we don't provide a positive reason for our incurring it.

I shall argue that things are rather different when it comes to the obligations of the second grade such as those constitutive of an involvement like friendship. Part of the value of friendship is that it serves our interest in being able to control the normative landscape. In particular it serves our *deontic interest* in being able to determine what does and does not constitute a wronging (Sec. 21). Because we choose our friends and friendship involves obligations (and permissions) the cultivation of friendship serves this normative interest, an interest in controlling our normative environment, and this interest is a ground of these obligations. It also explains why obligations of both the second and third grade are incurred only by those who know that their choices may lead to this result. The creation of an obligation can hardly serve one's interest in controlling whether a certain obligation exists if one is unaware of creating it.

In Part II, I shall argue that normative powers exist because they serve further normative interests: an *authority interest* in the case of promise, a *permissive interest* in the case of consent. Thus our second and third grades of choice-dependent obligation are usefully classified together as different forms of interested obligation, as obligations that exist and are taken seriously because people have a normative interest, an interest in both the existence of and control over such obligations. Nevertheless, as we shall see, choice underwrites interested obligations in two quite different ways. With obligations of involvement, choice matters because the obligations are constitutive of a relationship whose value is choice-dependent. With promissory obligation and the like, there need be no valuable relationship; rather what gives choice its significance here is our interest in the ability to be able to create (or waive) obligations by declaration.

2. Normative interests

I'm out to explain the influence of choice on our normative situation by postulating normative interests. Such an explanation contains three elements. First, it has *presuppositions*, concepts whose significance and claims whose truth it takes for granted. For example, in Part I, I simply presuppose that human beings have interests, that their lives can go better or worse, that things can be good or bad for them. I also assume that human beings feel anger and that our anger can be more or less appropriate. In developing my argument I will elaborate some of these presuppositions. For example, I'll make some claims about what is involved in feeling anger and what makes anger appropriate but those remarks are not intended to remove doubts about whether there is such thing as appropriate anger. An explanatory project also has *explananda*, things which are *prima facie* problematic prior to the inquiry but, given the theory's intelligibility and credibility, are no longer so problematic at its end. For example, Part II shows why it might make sense to fulfil a promise even when no human interest would be served by its fulfilment.

There is a third element in an inquiry of this sort which is neither simply taken for granted in the explanations it generates nor explained by them. Consider the claim that human beings have normative interests. This is not meant to be playing the role of a presupposition. Many will find it to be problematic and their puzzlement should not bar them from our inquiry. Indeed, my explanations are intended to dispel their puzzlement. But normative interests are not *explananda* either. I'm not seeking to allay these misgivings by accounting for our possession of normative interests in other terms (e.g. by reference to some of our more obvious non-normative interests). Rather I establish the existence and content of our normative interests by describing how they hang together with other elements of a theory that has a certain overall explanatory power. This involves specifying a range of normative interests, showing how they relate to one another and then describing how our possession of these interests helps to explain the existence and character of a whole range of normative phenomena.

Thus I'll contrast the *postulates* of our theory both with its presuppositions and with its *explananda*. A presupposition is assumed to be available to us regardless of the success of the explanatory project. Success may reinforce that presupposition but failure will not undermine it. Success also explains our theory's *explananda* but not its postulates. Its postulates stand in need of justification and they depend for it on the success of the project but a successful inquiry justifies its postulates without explaining them. The crucial postulate in my theory is that of a normative interest and I'll first discuss the notion of an interest that it presupposes.

At least one way of making sense of an action is to show that the action was (or appeared to be) in the interests of the agent. Something is in the interests of an agent when it is good for the agent, when it makes that agent's life go better. For example, it is good for me to have friends, my life is enriched by friendship and this fact makes sense of my choosing to have friends rather than remain alone. In this book, I presuppose that there are objective facts about human interests, that it is an objective fact that friendship enriches human life and so forth. We take an interest in friendship because friendship is in our interests, not vice versa. People's interests are not constituted by their opinions or judgements about what is in their interest, though the fact that they have opinions on these points may affect what is objectively good for them (e.g. by influencing their chances of enjoying it). Their opinions may also determine what it makes sense for them to do. Nevertheless, these opinions concern an objective matter of fact, namely what is in their own (or someone else's) interests.

Beyond this, I mean to avoid controversial assumptions about what sort of thing can make a person's life go well. In particular, I don't wish my argument to depend on taking too narrow a view of what is relevant to that question. For example, I maintain that possession of a normative power must make some difference to a person's life if it is to count as a benefit to them but I am not assuming that it must make a difference to the quality of the person's *experience* of their own life. On the other hand, were a narrowly experientialist view of human well-being correct, my argument could proceed on that basis also. In the body of the book, I shall make frequent use of the notion of a *bare wronging*. A bare wronging is an action which is a wronging but not in virtue of its being an action against any human interest. It requires some care to identify such wrongings precisely because I am not adopting a restrictive conception of the scope of human interests.

Some maintain that the only way to make sense of action is to show that the action was (or appeared to be) in the interests of its agent but most writers allow that it makes sense to act on the interests of others, even at one's own expense. For example, one might do something because it is in one's friend's interests even though it would make one's own life go worse. I can sensibly take an interest in things that are not in my interests. I shall assume that we can make sense of choice by reference to human interests, by reference to the fact that the thing chosen would be good for someone, not necessarily one's self. Human interests make sense of human choice.[11] Is this the *only* way of making sense of human choice? Postponing that question until the next section, I'll first identify the objects of our normative interests.

The ascription of a normative interest requires normative notions. Which normative notions? We've already employed one such, namely *making sense*. For example, I have an interest in whether John's asking for help would make sense of my helping him. The notion of *appropriateness* is also required. For example, I have an interest in whether it would be appropriate for me to blame my friend were he disloyal to me. I'll say something about making sense (and its terminological variant *intelligibility*) in the next section and I'll say more about appropriateness (and its terminological variant *aptness*) in Chapter 1 but neither notion will be explained in other terms. Where it either makes sense for me to feel or do something or is appropriate for me to feel or do it, it is often said that I possess some *reason* to feel or do it. On this usage facts about what I have reason to feel or do will also be objects of my normative interests.

Our interest in what actions and attitudes make sense or else are appropriate underlies further normative interests and especially our concern with who is obliged to do what and with who has a right to do what. For example, part of our interest in friendship is our interest in the existence of certain bonds of loyalty between ourselves and our friends, bonds involving obligations to perform certain actions

---

[11] For ease of exposition I ignore the interests of non-human animals.

and refrain from others. Now where we are obliged to ϕ, it makes sense for us to ϕ. Furthermore, where we are obliged to ϕ it tends to be the case that blame and guilt are apt should we fail to ϕ. So our interest in who is obliged to do what involves an interest both in which actions make sense and in which attitudes are appropriate. No doubt further normative notions are needed in order to formulate the full range of normative interests possessed by the average human being. I make no claim to a comprehensive treatment but the normative interests that concern me in this book can be specified in the terms just employed.

The possible objects of our normative interests comprise what it makes sense for us to do or feel, what it is appropriate for us to do or feel as well as deontic phenomena like permissions, rights, and obligations. Facts about what is good for us cannot be the object of normative interests. Such values do of course possess normative significance, in that they help to determine what we are justified in doing, what it is reasonable for us to do, what we ought to do, and so forth. But whilst at least some of our obligations, rights, etc. depend on the fact that we have an interest in having those obligations and rights, nothing is good for us because we have an interest in its being good for us. In so far as these things are a function of what is good for us, nothing is justified, or reasonable, or is such that it ought to be done simply because we have an interest in this being so.

I'm postulating normative interests in the hope of explaining various normative phenomena but I doubt that the mere possession of such normative interests ensures that we can create obligations of friendship, promissory obligations, and so forth. Nagel suggests that we have certain rights simply because, were this so, this would be a good thing (Nagel 1995: 92). One might say the same of normative powers, that we can make promises, offer our consent, and so forth simply because it would be good for us to have these powers. I shall argue that the mere fact that our possession of certain rights or powers would be good for its own sake does not ensure that we actually possess these rights or powers (p. 151). Though the value of the right or the power helps to explain its existence, we need the idea of a social convention to complete the story.

Few people will deny that at least some of the norms which govern our lives are set by social convention—they are in force only because those around us are in the habit of recognizing their authority and rather different norms would be in force were their authority recognized instead. How far does this observation extend? I shall argue that breach of promise, disloyalty in friendship, and even rape (in abstraction from the harm it causes) constitute wrongs only against a background of social convention. These claims will stoke controversy but the idea of a normative interest provides us with a middle way, one that should give both conventionalists and their opponents all they can reasonably ask for.

On the one hand, the notion of a norm embedded in the idea of a normative interest involves a conventional element. For it to be a good thing for us that we are subject to a norm, that norm must have a certain social reality, its authority must be recognized by the people around us. How could it be in our interests that we are subject to a norm if this fact made no difference to our lives?[12] Whether what is in question is the ability to make friends or forgive wrongdoers, or else a normative power like the power to promise or to consent, possession of this ability or power does us no good unless it is recognized in some form. It would make no sense for us to bother to exercise such abilities or powers unless their exercise had some social significance.[13] So rights and powers grounded in our normative interests exist only where the relevant social conventions are in force.

On the other hand, the notion of an interest implicit in the idea of a normative interest is pre-conventional. Pre-conventional facts about which norms would be good for us constrain the normative situation in various ways. First, they ensure that certain social conventions have no authority despite being recognized as authoritative by those around us. For example, the conventions that constitute exploitative or demeaning forms of involvement (like henchmanship or hero worship) have no authority because they serve no normative interest (Raz 1986: 310). Second, our normative interests ensure that it is a bad thing when certain norms are not in force, e.g. a bad thing for there to be no practice of promising, or no forms of involvement like friendship. This can be bad whether or not anyone is to blame for the situation. In certain cases, it may be such a bad thing that it rises to the level of a wrong, a lack for which we are all to blame unless we strive to eliminate it. The absence of any conventional recognition of the wrong of rape and other assaults on bodily integrity may be such a case.

Having discussed the main postulate of my theory, the idea of a normative interest, I shall briefly review the theory's principal *explananda* and note how the postulation of various normative interests is intended to account for a range of normative phenomena. In Part I, we introduce two normative interests, two interests in controlling some aspect of the normative situation. The *remissive* interest, an interest in controlling when blame is an appropriate reaction to a wronging, underwrites our ability to forgive the wrongs we suffer. Our remissive interest focuses on the significance of a wronging once it has occurred. By contrast, the *deontic* interest concerns what should count as a wronging in the first place. Part of what we seek in friendship is people who are bound to us and to whom we are bound in certain ways, as well as

---

[12] (Nagel 1995: 92–3) maintains that we are all better off simply in virtue of being possessors of 'moral' rights and regardless of whether these rights are recognized but he does not explain how the fact that we are wronged by torture and so forth could make our lives better. He says that the relevant notion of well-being presupposes the possession of moral status but that implies only that nothing counts as better or worse for us unless we have moral status, not that possession of moral status makes things go any better.

[13] I am not here assuming that our exercise of these powers must change our *experience* of the social world, merely that they must change our social situation in way that might intelligibly matter to us whether or not we happen to be aware of that change.

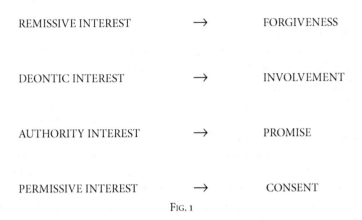

REMISSIVE INTEREST $\rightarrow$ FORGIVENESS

DEONTIC INTEREST $\rightarrow$ INVOLVEMENT

AUTHORITY INTEREST $\rightarrow$ PROMISE

PERMISSIVE INTEREST $\rightarrow$ CONSENT

Fig. 1

people with a special license for intimacy. We thereby open up new possibilities of wronging and close down others. So our deontic interests underlie the obligations constitutive of friendship and other forms of involvement like acquaintanceship, neighbourliness, relations of hospitality, and so forth. These are obligations with the second grade of choice-dependence.

In Part II of the book, I turn to normative powers generating interested obligations with the third grade of choice-dependence. Some writers are sceptical of the whole idea of a normative power, of the thought that we can shape the normative landscape by declaration. Others respond to this sceptical worry by seeking to ground our normative powers in our non-normative interests. I argue that attempts to show how possession of normative powers would further our non-normative interests (in particular our interest in being informed what others are going to do so we can co-ordinate our activities with them) miss what is distinctive about promise and consent. These powers exist to serve our interest in being able to shape the normative landscape by declaration, an interest that takes at least two forms: the *authority* interest, which underwrites promissory obligation and the *permissive* interest that underwrites the power of consent.

By the end of Part II, we will have connected various social phenomena to various normative interests in the way summed up in Figure 1. Part III descends to the details of the social practice of promising and asks how much of this detail can be explained on the basis of the normative interest underlying promissory obligation. It turns out that many features of promising are fixed by the underlying interest, at least when that interest is taken to be an authority interest rather than any interest in informa-tion. I consider three aspects of the practice: first, the act of promising and what it communicates; second, the constitutive structure of the resulting promissory bond; third, how a promise can fail to create such a bond, how a promise can be rendered invalid. Our hypothesis that human beings have normative interests is bolstered by its ability to explain these features of the social practice of promising.[14] Promising occupies Part III of the book simply because it is the social practice I have thought about the most but if the apparatus deployed in Parts I and II of the book is well conceived, it should cast light on a range of social practices and institutions, e.g. those surrounding ownership and social authority.

All of the above normative interests are *human* interests. I leave it open whether human beings possess normative interests simply in virtue of being persons, i.e. agents who are capable of controlling what they do by thinking about what they ought to do.[15] Perhaps there are non-human agents without normative interests, rational agents whose lives are made no better by rights and obligations and who thus have no (intrinsic) interest in controlling the normative landscape they inhabit. Some human beings may fit this description. If so they would be as different from the rest of us as human beings devoid of aesthetic concerns. Promising, consent, forgiveness, and friendship could not exist among them. Their dealings with one another would still be governed by obligations with the first degree of choice-dependence but the world of artificial virtue would be closed to them.

3. Making sense

In this section, I say more about one of the normative phenomena in which we have an interest, namely the phenomenon of one thing's *making sense* of another. This is a good place to begin because the making sense relation is the basic normative relation. No attitude or action can be apt, obligatory, and so forth unless it also makes sense, whilst attitudes and actions can make sense or (in phrases I shall use interchangeably) *be intelligible* or *have a point* without being either apt or obligatory. Much contemporary moral philosophy begins with the notion of a *reason* (or cognate notions like 'rational intelligibility'). This may be mere variation on my own terminology but it might also involve buying into a set of assumptions some of which I reject. The task of this section is to make it clear what I am presupposing in this area, what I am rejecting, and what I am seeking to establish.

---

[14] Treatments of promissory obligation come in two varieties: *practice* theories and *expectation* theories. The details must wait but it is worth briefly noting how my position relates to these familiar alternatives. In maintaining that promising is not here to serve our information interests, I am rejecting an assumption commonly made by both parties to this debate. Nevertheless I side with the practice theory and against the expectation theory in maintaining that promises bind only where people are in the habit of recognizing the authority of a promise. Part II engages with the practice theory as it is found in the works of Hume and Rawls. Part III engages with the expectation theory as it is found in the writings of Scanlon.

[15] Hegel argues that the rights of contract and property derive simply from our nature as persons, i.e. they are aspects of what he calls Abstract Right. See (Hegel 1991: 65–114). And since, for Kant, we cannot coherently will that promises be breached, our rationality alone will ensure that we respect them (Kant 1996: 74).

Talk of making sense might just connote explicability but I have something much more specific in mind. Behaviour can be predictable and indeed explicable without making much sense, without being intelligible in the way that intentional action is intelligible.[16] And only actions intelligible in that way are under the agent's direct control. The distinction between mere explicability and real intelligibility applies also to thoughts and feelings but I'll give the reader a sense of what I have in mind by focusing on a case of action.[17]

A man is eating sawdust. His bodily movements have a physiological explanation sure enough but so does the beating of his heart and the fact his eyelids close when an object moves towards his face. The latter bodily movements are not intentional, they are not under his direct control. Our man might have some way of ensuring that his heart does not beat or his eyelids do not close, there might be something he can do to bring this about. But, absent the possibility of such self-manipulation, he is not in control of the beating of his heart or the closing of his eyelids.

Is his eating sawdust in the same case? Our man probably doesn't believe that sawdust is either tasty or nutritious. Still he craves it and eats it because he craves it. Does that make sense of what he does? It would if he foresaw enjoying the sawdust. It would if he foresaw at least relief from his painful craving for sawdust. But suppose nothing like this is true. Suppose he sees no point in eating sawdust. This fact throws doubt on the claim that he is intentionally eating it. His relationship to these bodily movements now looks like his relationship to the beating of his heart or the closing of his eyelids, in that whether they occur does not depend on whether he sees any point in them.[18]

What is required to render this man's behaviour intelligible? Here is one answer: there must be a *reason* for what he does, where a reason for ϕ-ing is a consideration which supports the proposition that he ought to ϕ by recommending ϕ-ing.[19] This *Rationalist* answer opens the way for practical deliberation, for reasoning about what to do. At least where you are aware of your reasons, you will often be able to reason from them to conclusions about what you ought to do. But the Rationalist also makes room for the possibility of intentionally failing to comply with the verdict of your own practical deliberation, of intelligibly doing what you (know you) ought not to be

---

[16] My notion of 'making sense' is close to Weber's *Verstehen*. As Weber notes, no degree of regularity in a pattern of behaviour will render it intelligible if 'adequacy with respect to meaning' is lacking (Weber 1947: 99).

[17] The issue of control of thoughts and feelings is more tricky (pp. 88–9).

[18] It might be said that there is an alternative explanation of why his heart does not beat intentionally, namely that he could not have done otherwise. But (a) it is controversial whether the truth of a 'could have done otherwise' counterfactual is required for action to be intentional and (b) in any case the counterfactual must be spelt out as 'could have done otherwise had he chosen to' which raises the question of what it is to *choose* to do otherwise.

[19] This formulation is not meant as an analysis of any of the notions contained in it. It merely provides some information about the relationship between them.

doing. For your action to make sense, it is required only that there be *some* point in behaving as you do, some consideration that counts in favour of doing it. It need not also establish that you ought to be doing it.[20]

My characterization of Rationalism leaves two important issues open. First, we have yet to be told how a given consideration might constitute a reason to ϕ, how it might support the proposition that one ought to ϕ by *recommending* ϕ-ing. Second, we have yet to be told how this recommending consideration must connect to the ϕ-ing that it recommends in order to make sense of that ϕ-ing. If a reason for our man's eating the sawdust is to render eating intelligible, it can't be a complete accident that he eats the sawdust in the presence of this reason. How must the reason for eating be connected to his eating for that reason to make sense of his eating?

According to the version of Rationalism I shall consider in this book, a reason recommends an action by identifying some good, desirable, or valuable feature of the proposed action.[21] On this view, what makes sense of our actions is the desirability of what is done. For a Rationalist, all rationalizing considerations must connect with what is good or desirable and so the actions of our man are rendered intelligible by making that connection.[22] Other Rationalists (intuitionists, coherentists) have rather different conceptions of a practical reason but I shall set these doctrines to one side.[23] I'll further simplify matters by confining my attention to those sources of goodness or value that have their roots in human interests. Perhaps values having nothing to do with human interests can make sense of human action but since the values underlying the social phenomena to be discussed in this book are rooted in human interests, I shall ignore this possibility. We don't keep our promises or discharge the obligations of friendship out of respect for some cosmic value.

---

[20] I am not imputing to the Rationalist any view about the epistemological (or metaphysical) status of claims about what ought to be done.

[21] An important function of decision-making is to break ties between options that are equally valuable. In such a case one can intelligibly choose to pick one tin of biscuits rather than another even though there is nothing to tell them apart. (The same should be said when the options are incommensurable in value.) Here (a) one needs to make a decision and (b) there is nothing to be said against picking as one does rather than choosing the alternative. The truth of (a) and (b) should be enough to make one's choice intelligible in the eyes of the Rationalist (by establishing that it is rationally permissible) even though there is no good in choosing this tin rather than that. (b) does not hold in cases that create real difficulties for the Rationalist: see below.

[22] Some Rationalists deny that facts about which attitudes make sense (or are appropriate) are *grounded in* facts about value; rather it is the other way around (Scanlon 1998: 95–8). On their view, what it is for something to have value is for it to make sense of (or render appropriate) certain attitudes and reactions. I shall largely ignore this variation in what follows since, for my purposes, the kernel of Rationalism is the nexus it postulates between value and normative relations rather than the priority it accords to value.

[23] Nearly all of the most considerable writers on agency have endorsed the value-based form of Rationalism. I am unable to find any pre-modern writer who explicitly rejects it (at least in respect of terrestrial agents). Among the moderns (Hume 1978: 439) and (Kant 1996: 186) both endorse it. Among contemporaries the list includes Anscombe, Davidson, Raz, and many others.

Let's now return to the issue of how a reason must be connected to the action it makes sense of. Distinguish *complying* with a reason from *conforming* to a reason (Raz 1999: 178). One who complies with a reason is motivated by their awareness of the reason with which they comply. Our man complies with no reason unless he is aware of something that recommends doing what he is doing. But one can conform to a reason, in the sense of doing what it recommends, without complying with it. And one's conformity can be non-accidental without being a case of compliance. Perhaps our man's craving is a symptom of some nutritional deficiency that will be met by eating sawdust. There is now a reason that recommends eating and further-more it is no accident that he does what this reason recommends. Is that enough for his action to make sense?

Here are two forms of Rationalism which return different answers:[24]

Subjective Rationalism: An action makes sense in so far as its performance involves compliance with a reason that identifies a desirable feature of this action.

Objective Rationalism: An action makes sense in so far as its performance involves (non-accidental) conformity to a reason that identifies a desirable feature of this action.

The nutritional deficiency gives the Objective Rationalist what he wants, whilst the Subjective Rationalist remains unsatisfied unless our man is aware of the desirability of eating sawdust. If his behaviour is unintelligible to the agent, it must remain unintelligible to us also.

The Subjective Rationalist is right that the beneficial character of a behavioural disposition does not suffice to make that disposition a source of intelligible agency. For example, it may be desirable that my eyes automatically shut when an object approaches my face at high speed but that fact does not render this bodily movement intelligible in the way that intentional action is intelligible. It does not put me in control of my eye movements as I am of the books that I write. But this observation fails to resolve the matter in favour of the Subjective Rationalist for there are other cases in which it makes perfect sense for me to behave in a certain way even though I know of nothing which recommends my acting in that way. For example, it may be that no human interest, whether the promisor's, the promisee's, or the interests of a third party, would be served by the fulfilment of a promise. Yet I can be obliged to keep a promise, and held responsible for keeping it, even though nothing recom-mends keeping it. When one is obliged to perform, it still makes sense to perform. Since neither compliance nor conformity with reason would be secured, both the Subjective and the Objective Rationalist are confounded.

Where breach of promise constitutes action against no human interest, breach of promise is a *bare wronging*. Philosophers have adopted various attitudes to the

---

[24] I shall simplify the discussion of both forms of Rationalism by ignoring cases in which the agent falsely believes that they have a reason.

phenomenon of bare wronging. Some maintain that deontic considerations can make sense of action all by themselves and regardless of whether any connection can be made between our rights or our obligations on the one hand and what is good for us (or anyone else) on the other (Prichard 1968: 158–63). For them, bare wronging is unproblematic. Others, more attached to the Rationalist idea, have insisted that deontic considerations must be grounded in facts about human good if they are to make sense of human agency. For them, taking promises seriously is unintelligible unless there is some good in the making and keeping of promises. They go on to identify various human interests that a conscientious attitude to promises might serve even in those cases where fulfilment of a promise appears completely undesirable but, in the end, they maintain that if an action cannot be made sense of in this way then it cannot be made sense of at all. To be anything more than a conditioned reflex, promise keeping must involve either compliance with and/or conformity to reason.

Suppose human beings have normative interests, interests that can be formulated only in normative language. And suppose that such normative interests are fundamental in that they are neither based on nor grounded in any non-normative interest. Such normative interests open up a middle way between the Rationalists and their opponents. We can agree with the Rationalist that facts about obligation make sense of acts (and attitudes) only because they are grounded in facts about our good, whilst agreeing with their opponents that deontic notions like right and obligation make an independent contribution to intelligible agency because we have interests which can be formulated only in deontic terms.

It might, for example, make sense for us to fulfil a promise because it is in our interests that such a thing should make sense. And, given the autonomy of such normative interests, it might be in our interests for fulfilment to make sense even if the actual fulfilment of the promise would further no interest (either normative or non-normative, either of ours or of anyone else's), even if it would involve neither compliance with nor conformity to any reason. The value that makes sense of our discharging this obligation lies in the power to create the obligation rather than in the act that discharges it. And where it is a good thing that we would be wronging X by breaking our promise to X, it makes sense for us to keep our promise to X whether or not there is any good in keeping it. Since it is possible to make sense of a human action other than by reference to the fact that it furthers a human interest, both Objective and Subjective Rationalism must be rejected as accounts of intentional agency. Nevertheless, what it makes sense for us to do is always determined by human interests, where these include normative interests.

In this section, I have attempted no analysis of the making sense relation. Rather I have indicated, largely by means of examples, what notion of making sense is in play and differentiated it from various notions of rational intelligibility. Reasons do make sense of action but action can make sense without them. In what follows I shall defend the idea that whether an action, thought, or feeling makes sense often depends on whether we have an interest in its making sense. This idea will puzzle anyone inclined to assume that the intelligibility of an action is a function of its value. As noted in section 2, we cannot suppose that an action is good for us in virtue of our interest in its being good for us. So if practical intelligibility is just value in action, the intelligibility of an action cannot depend on our interest in its intelligibility. The rejection of Rationalism removes this difficulty.

4. Deontic value

If there are normative interests then normative phenomena must have value and if these interests are basic rather than derived, normative phenomena must be valuable for their own sake. It must be good (or bad) for certain things to count as wrongs, as wrongings, as obligations, as appropriate objects of blame. It must be good (or bad) for us. In this book, I offer an account *not* of what deontic phenomena are, *not* of what it is for an act to be wrongful, a wronging, or an obligation but rather an account of what is would be for these phenomena to be of value, to be worthy of choice.

This section sketches the theory of deontic value to be developed in Part I. Like more familiar accounts of value, mine is focused on certain characteristic reactions provoked by the things whose value is in question. But these reactions play a non-standard role in my theory. I trace the value of deontic phenomena like wrongfulness and obligation to the value of its being appropriate for us to react in certain ways, rather than to the value of our actually reacting in those ways. Thus the value of one normative phenomenon is explained in terms of the value of another.

Deontic value is the value of something's constituting a wrong, a wronging, an obligation, and so forth. How might one construct a *reaction-based* theory of deontic value? Blame and guilt are often appropriate where a wronging has occurred. Furthermore, where something is obligatory it is appropriate for an agent to ignore certain relevant considerations in their deliberations about whether to discharge that obligation. Though these sentimental and deliberative reactions are indicative of the presence of certain deontic phenomena, they don't seem a plausible source of the value of such phenomena, however appropriate they might be. Neither guilt nor blame nor the exclusion of relevant considerations from one's deliberation look like reactions valuable for their own sake. So how can these reactions be a source of the value of anything else?

I shall propose that the value of deontic phenomena lies in the fact that they give these reactions a certain normative status. Whether or not the actual occurrence of a reaction on a particular occasion is of value, the fact that such reactions possess a certain normative status may well be of value. Any plausible account of deontic value will, I think, appeal to more than one type of reaction and to more than one form of normative status. Take the value of a certain deed's constituting a wrong. The reactions in question are various and include our deliberating in a certain way about whether to commit it (when the wrong is an action rather than an attitude) as well as feeling guilt or suffering blame where the wrong is not avoided. The forms of normative status involved are also various. The reaction in question may make some sense or no sense. Furthermore, it may also be appropriate or inappropriate.

Take blame and guilt. Such reactions seem not to be valuable for their own sake (as say pleasure is). If so, we shouldn't seek to create opportunities for guilt and blame by getting people to commit wrongs (as we do seek to create opportunities for aesthetic pleasure by creating beautiful things). Nevertheless, blame and guilt are the kind of thing whose normative status is of interest to us. Blame is a form of anger, anger can be more or less appropriate and, in Chapter 1, I shall argue that the potential appropriateness of anger can be a positive thing, e.g. within a relationship like friendship. It is often good for us to render anger a potentially appropriate reaction to the attitudes or behaviour of another by becoming their friend. Furthermore, the fact that it renders anger a potentially appropriate reaction is part of what makes friendship valuable for its own sake. Appropriate anger is anger that we should (tend to) feel, though the good is in its being appropriate rather than in our feeling it.[25]

Where the wrong in question is an act rather than an attitude, its wrongfulness indicates that we are under an obligation and this brings a further reaction into play. When one feels under an obligation to do something, one deliberates about whether to do it in a special way. In Chapter 3, I argue that this is a matter of excluding from one's practical deliberation certain considerations which count in favour of violating one's obligation. Now excluding relevant considerations from our deliberations is not an activity valuable for its own sake. Nevertheless, we may have an interest in being able to ensure that such exclusion would be appropriate in certain circumstances. In Chapter 4, I maintain that it is a valuable aspect of many valuable relationships that, within such a relationship it is potentially appropriate to exclude such considerations from one's deliberations.

Mine is a reaction-based theory of deontic value but reaction-based theories normally take a rather different form; they explain the value of something by tracing its value to the value of certain reactions. For example, many writers have thought that beautiful things are of value to us because and in so far as we can enjoy their beauty, because and in so far as their beauty gives us pleasure. That is a plausible story in that pleasure is surely valued for its own sake and so could be the source of beauty's

---

[25] Someone attracted by Moore's doctrine of organic unities (Moore 1959: 27–31) might maintain that appropriate blame is a good thing even though the two components of appropriate blame, namely the blameworthy action and the blaming reaction to it, are both bad things. This is not my view. For me, what has value is the normative fact that such blame would count as appropriate (or inappropriate) and not the actual occurrence of appropriate blame. Thus it can make sense to feel a certain way even though there is nothing desirable about the occurrence of such a feeling.

value. I introduce this theory of aesthetic value not to defend it but because it offers an illuminating contrast with my own approach to deontic value.

Let us see exactly what is implied by the view that that pleasure is the source of beauty's value. Pleasure is not just the means whereby we can appreciate the value of beauty; our enjoyment gives beautiful things their value. It follows that in a world devoid of creatures that could enjoy their beauty, the beauty of the Alps, say, would lack any value. Were there no one around to appreciate the beauty of the Alps, this beauty would not matter, it would not be worth anything because the Alps can matter in that way only if someone can enjoy the sight of them.[26]

That much does follow from this reaction-based theory of aesthetic value. Much else does not. For one thing, the Alps might still be beautiful in such a world. Perhaps beauty is not itself a value but rather something which makes beautiful things valuable in the right circumstances, namely when there are creatures capable of appreciating their beauty. A theory of the value of beauty need not be a theory of beauty. Neither does our reaction-based theory imply that the value of beauty is instrumental, that beautiful things are valuable simply as generators of pleasurable experiences, experiences whose value is quite independent of the character of the items experienced. Some things do have purely hedonistic value, e.g. a pill worth nothing in itself but valuable as a means to pleasurable sensation. But in the case of beauty, we can distinguish appropriate and inappropriate pleasure. An ecstatic reaction to Bach Cantata might be appropriate when a similar reaction to elevator music is not. And *appropriate* pleasure is the source of the distinctive aesthetic value of music. Such value is conditional on the occurrence, or the possible occurrence, of appropriate pleasure without being valuable simply as a means to such pleasure.[27]

My account of deontic value partially resembles this account of aesthetic value. Whilst (as we hypothesized) aesthetic value derives from the value of certain reactions, deontic value derives from the value of certain reactions being potentially appropriate, etc. One important consequence of the reaction-based character of aesthetic value is that there is no such value in a world devoid of these reactions. I allowed that beauty might exist without anyone who could enjoy it but such beauty would lack all value. Something similar is true of deontic phenomena. At least some forms of wrong, wronging, and obligation might exist in a world in which these deontic phenomena went unrecognized, in which the just mentioned reactions never occurred (p. 65). Nevertheless, in such a world there would be no good in the fact that the relevant actions and attitudes constitute wrongings, etc. and there would be no

---

[26] I'm inclined to endorse Sidgwick's observation that 'no one would consider it rational to aim at the production of beauty in external nature, apart from any possible contemplation of it by human beings' (Sidgwick 1981: 114). Moore disagrees (Moore 1959: 83–5).

[27] For discussion of conditional value that is not instrumental value, see (Korsgaard 1996: esp. 250–3 and 264–5).

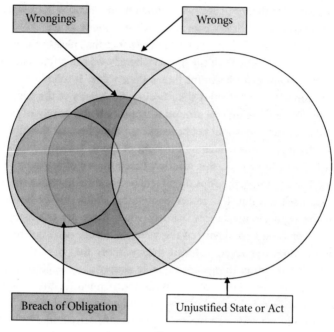

Fig. 2

point in choosing to create such forms of wronging (at least for their own sake). There may be forms of wronging which can exist even though we have no interest in their existence (just as there may be forms of beauty that can exist even though they mean nothing to us) but this isn't true of the wrongings generated by friendships and promises, wrongings which depend for their existence on there being some point in our bringing them into existence.[28]

If what I have just said is correct, it would be bad were instances of blame and particular acts of deliberative exclusion *never* to occur. The world is a better place because people do sometimes feel blame or guilt, for instance, even though each instance of blame or guilt may be regrettable. True, we can value the fact that these reactions are appropriate without valuing their occurrence even when appropriate. But the fact that such reactions are appropriate could be a good thing only where their appropriateness is a social reality, only when it is recognized to some extent in

---

[28] Do we need a theory of deontic value in order to explain how obligations (etc.) can be chosen? Have we not rejected the Rationalist idea that only value makes sense of choice? The objector is right in that, on a given occasion, one might choose to become someone's friend or make them a promise simply because one feels obliged so to do. And where this is so, one need see no good in the friendship or the promise. Nevertheless, one usually makes friends and promises because one sees some good in so doing. And where one does so regardless, there must be a story about how the obligation to make a promise or a friend serves some normative interest, i.e. a story about deontic value.

our acts and attitudes (pp. 9–10). And that requires a practice of recognition, i.e. a propensity to feel guilt and blame and so forth that is manifested on at least some occasions (pp. 150–1). Hence the complete absence of these reactions would be bad.

The business of Part I is to expound and apply my theory of deontic value. In Chapter 1, I offer a theory of guilt and blame, one which makes it clear that they are suited to play their role in a reaction-based account of wrong, wrongings, rights, and obligations. I begin with guilt and blame because they are implicated in all of the deontic phenomena which interest us. Treatments of wronging and obligation will follow in Chapters 2 and 3, while Chapter 4 will bring the whole apparatus to bear in an account of the deontic aspect of valuable relationships like friendship. Figure 2 depicts the logical relations between the crucial notions. The occupants of the various sectors of the Venn diagram will be introduced course of Chapters 1–3 and it might help readers to refer back to Figure 2.

Part I
Interests

1

Blame and Guilt

Neither guilt nor blame tops the standard list of human goods. Indeed, philosophical writing about blame in particular is largely motivated by the apparent *disvalue* of blame. Isn't blame intrinsically undesirable? And isn't it especially hard to justify when inflicted upon others rather than upon ourselves? Much reflection on blame starts from the premise that blame is problematic because it entails a wounding judgement, hard feelings, a punitive reaction, or some combination of these. Yet, it seems, blame (and guilt) can be a positive feature of our lives. For one thing, certain valuable relationships involve obligation and breach of an obligation often renders one vulnerable to blame. These obligation-involving relationships exist only where people are in the habit of blaming certain kinds of action. Since our lives are enriched once we enjoy these relations with others, the habits of blame that help to constitute such bonds are good for us. Our interest in these habits of blame is one aspect of our interest in enjoying those relationships.

How could it be that we should value the habit of feeling guilt and blame whilst the actual occurrence of guilt and blame is a cause for regret? Leaving it open whether the occurrence of blame and guilt could, in itself, be a good thing, I shall urge that habits of blaming are a positive aspect of certain relationships even if blame (as such) is regrettable. When two people become friends, reactions like guilt and blame are now appropriate where they would otherwise have been inappropriate. And, I maintain, it can be a good thing for certain reactions to count as appropriate (or inappropriate) even if it is not a good thing for these reactions to actually occur. We may affirm that habits of blame are good in as much as they make it the case that guilt and blame can be more or less appropriate without implying that blame, whether appropriate or inappropriate, is in any individual instance a good thing.

Here is one way in which the fact that blame can be appropriate might have a value that the occurrence of appropriate blame lacks. Suppose (contrary to what I shall argue) that relationships like friendship have blame-independent value, that we can specify what makes them valuable *qua* friendship (etc.) without reference to the fact that they render blame appropriate. Still the capacity to blame might add to the value of friendship as follows. Appropriate blame might be blame that accurately represents or at least tracks the blame-independent value of the relationship within which it occurs. For example, where the relationship has been impaired by certain behaviour, accurate blame will register the consequent diminution in its value. On this *value-tracking* model of the appropriateness of blame, the relationship in question has a blame-independent value and blame reflects that blame-independent value more or less accurately. Where habits or tendencies of feeling have evolved and established a correlation between the occurrence of blame and the value of certain relationships, blame constitutes a more or less accurate representation (or at least tracker) of that value. And, we may suppose, a relationship is better if those so related are sensitive to its value in this way.

This value-tracking model allows it to be a good thing that blame can occur appropriately (or inappropriately) without implying that appropriate blame is good. Appropriateness is, we are supposing, accuracy. It is a good thing to have ways of representing the worth of your relationships, whether correctly or incorrectly, and blame enables you to do so, given that blame may be assessed as accurate or inaccurate. Nevertheless, the sheer accuracy of your blame reactions would not render them any the less regrettable, since it implies that you are accurately registering the degradation of a valuable relationship. So it may be a good thing that blame can occur appropriately (i.e. that blame is subject to this form of normative assessment) and better when it occurs appropriately rather than inappropriately, without appropriate blame being a good thing.[1]

As we shall see, the value-tracking hypothesis can take various forms (of which the above is only one) depending on how we think blame or guilt tracks the value of a relationship. Blame and guilt involve elements of three sorts. First, to one who is guilty or blames, it seems as if something has gone wrong (where, as I shall argue, this need not involve that something's being represented as *a* wrong, i.e. as being wrongful). This is the representational element of blame. Second, there are feelings of guilt and blame. This is the emotional element of blame. Finally, those who feel guilt or blame behave in certain characteristic ways. This is the practical element of blame. Each of these elements is a medium in which the value of a relationship could be tracked. But, on all versions of the value-tracking hypothesis, blame is appropriate in so far as it reflects fluctuations in the blame-independent value of relationships like friendship.

I shall oppose to the value-tracking hypothesis the *value-constituting* hypothesis according to which when friendships are valuable as friendships (rather than as relations of benefaction for instance), they are valuable as the sort of relationship in

---

[1] If, as I suppose, where the appropriateness of blame is a good thing, that appropriateness is constituted by the existence of habits of appropriate blame, then it will not be reasonable to regret the existence of these habits. Since there can be such habits only where appropriate blame has actually occurred, it cannot be reasonable to regret that appropriate blame has ever occurred. Nevertheless, it may be true of each instance of blame that it is reasonable to regret its occurrence, however appropriate it may be (pp. 20–1).

which it is appropriate for one party to blame the other. The appropriateness of blame within friendship does not consist in the ability to track some blame-independent value possessed by friendship. Rather the value of the friendship (*qua* friendship) derives, in part, from the (norm-constituting) tendency of friends to blame one another. A valuable aspect of friendship is the fact that it renders certain (disloyal, etc.) actions wrongful and where it is a good thing that these actions are wrongful, this is so, in part, in virtue of the fact that it is a good thing that they would render blame appropriate.

To adjudicate these various claims, we must have some notion of what blame is and of what makes it appropriate but I shall say no more on this score than is needed to explain why the aptness of blame might be a good thing. In Section 5, I suggest that blame is neither regret, nor sorrow, nor a critical judgement but a form of anger. One way in which blame as anger might track the value of relationships like friendship is by representing it more or less accurately. In Sections 5 and 6, I argue that blame as anger can be perfectly accurate whilst being quite inappropriate. Therefore, the appropriateness of blame can't be grounded solely in the accuracy of its representational content. In Section 7, I consider Scanlon's view according to which blame is not a form of anger at all. Scanlon's view opens up the possibility that appropriate blame might track the value of friendship without representing that value, thus avoiding the above objection. Having rejected Scanlon's view, I conclude that we should not attempt to explain the appropriateness of blame as anger in other terms. It matters to us whether blame is appropriate and this helps to explain why it matters to us that we have relations with others that render blame appropriate or inappropriate. In the final section, I widen my focus to include both guilt and the other 'reactive attitudes' like indignation and resentment.

5. Blame as anger

His virtues notwithstanding, my friend is a bit of a charming rascal. He can be thoughtless, let me down, and take my affection for granted. When he does I tend not hold it against him. Of course, I'm saddened by his failings and fervently wish that he were different but I'm hardly ever furious with nor even mildly annoyed by him. Where he is at fault, I rarely feel either outrage or hurt. His charm prevents it. In one way, I have no illusions about this man: I know I am indulging or even condoning his roguish behaviour. I know that he is *to blame* for what he does but I'm insufficiently inclined to blame my friend for his transgressions. Though I regret them, I rarely get worked up about them, I rarely 'take them personally' as we say. What's missing here is a kind of anger (Wallace 1993: 76–7).[2] That anger may take the form of outrage or

---

[2] It is often said that anger involves either a desire to hurt the object of your anger or at least the wish that they should suffer (e.g. Mill 1991: 186–7 and Rawls 1999: 423). I want to remain agnostic on this point.

fury or else appear in a more defensive guise as hurt feelings.[3] But, at least the context of friendship, such anger is an *appropriate* reaction.

That blame as anger is an appropriate reaction does not imply that I should feel it whenever my friend misbehaves.[4] For one thing, we must husband our limited supply of emotional energy. For another, we have a certain latitude here: one need not always rise to the bait. But the appropriateness of anger means more than anger's merely making sense. Where anger is appropriate I should have some inclination to feel it, to be somewhat irascible on the point. And there may be occasions on which I must feel angry because the offence is so egregious. Compare charitable giving; whilst one need not give to every worthy cause (one must husband one's financial resources), one ought to give to a sufficient number of causes on a sufficient number of occasions. That is what it means to say that giving to charity is fitting or appropriate. Perhaps the need can be so pressing that one *must* give but normally one has some choice in the matter.

I should not want people to be in need of my charity, nor should I wish to have occasion to blame my friend. Rather what I should wish for is that, where blame would be appropriate, I have some tendency to go in for it. Blaming my friend's disloyalty is like feeling distress or even devastation at his misfortune. Whether or not such feelings are valuable for their own sake, they are appropriate within relationships like friendship and, since this appropriateness is part of what it is to be involved with someone, perhaps their appropriateness is part of what makes such relationships valuable for their own sake. How I react to a distressing occasion will rightly depend on all sorts of factors, like what else is happening in my life but there is something wrong with a friendship in which these feelings have no place.[5]

Someone might agree that feelings of anger or distress are appropriate within friendship and agree that these feelings are appropriate because of the valuable bonds of friendship whilst denying that their appropriateness is any part of what makes either friendship or its bonds valuable. Rather the appropriateness of these emotions is a by-product of whatever does give friendship its value. On this view, even a good

---

True, anger can be assuaged when its object suffers but it does not follow that anger involves a desire for revenge. Anger is also placated by apology, compensation, or even by some unrelated good behaviour on the part of its object. These remarks (and the fact that I treat hurt feelings as a form of anger) may show that I'm operating with a rather loose conception of anger. That would serve my wider purposes well enough. Indeed treating blame as a *sui generis* feeling would suffice provided what I say of blame as anger (e.g. the difference between aptness and accuracy) is also true of that feeling.

[3] One need not boil with anger nor seethe with resentment. One might remain unaware of one's own anger or hurt feelings (i.e. of one's blame). There is also the phenomenon of cold anger that is fully conscious and can even be savoured ('revenge is a dish best eaten cold').

[4] The fact that we are friends sometimes makes forgiveness a more appropriate reaction than continued blame.

[5] It is not just blame between friends that friendship renders appropriate. When one friend betrays another, third parties share the victim's outrage and friendship could not have the sort of value that it does if nobody other than its victim ever reacted to a betrayal of friendship with anger.

friend of mine might well regret the fact that were I to suffer some tragedy it would be appropriate for him to feel distress, or else that were I to betray him it would be appropriate for him to blame me. After all, we need not value the by-products of things we value, only those features that give them value. But to have such regrets would manifest a peculiar attitude to our friendship. Surely, one who values the bonds of friendship in the way a good friend does cannot regret the (purely normative) fact that these emotions *would be* appropriate, however much he might regret it when they actually become appropriate.

There are valuable relationships other than friendship within which blame understood as anger is not especially fitting. These relationships bring constitutive norms and standards with them but anger is not in general an appropriate reaction to their breach. Consider rivalry. It would be odd to maintain that two people vying for the same house or even the same lover are locked in a valuable relationship. But where such competition is valued for its own sake, as in a sport, things are different: here a rivalry enriches the lives of its participants and not just because it makes them run faster or jump higher. Life is better, is more enjoyable both for them and for onlookers where these results are achieved in competition. Indeed in a society governed by a chivalric ethic, even having a rival in love might be a contribution rather than an obstacle to a successful life, to a life that goes well.

Good rivals feel and act a certain way towards one another in virtue of their rivalry. It is appropriate to rise to my rival's challenge, to feel sadness or disappointment should I lose and increased respect for them should they win. On the other hand, if they lose because they don't try hard enough to win, as a good rival I may hold them in contempt. By not really trying, my rival has spoiled a valuable relationship and to that extent impoverished our lives, a matter for regret. But there need be nothing fitting about my also being angry with my dilatory rival. Indeed such anger may tarnish the rivalry by introducing an element of rancour.

The last point requires careful statement. Anger or at least annoyance is a very natural reaction to a rival who does not give of his best. Nevertheless it is not an appropriate reaction to a violation of the norms of rivalry. The rivalry would be no less valuable (*qua* rivalry) if you were quite incapable of such anger, if you never 'took it personally' and confined yourself to disappointment on your own behalf, contempt for your rival, and so forth. Anger is much like envy on this point. Nothing is more usual than to envy the acclaim accorded to one's successful rival and this reaction to their triumph might be accurate.[6] All I maintain is that the value of rivalry is not enhanced and may be diminished by a tendency to envy one's rival.

---

[6] Envy represents the advantage envied as undeserved and a triumph may indeed be underserved. That need not imply that there is anything wrong with the triumph. It might legitimately be a matter of luck that one's rival wins the race (Rawls 1999: 466–7). Here envy of their victory would be accurate without being appropriate.

One might respond that anger at a dilatory rival is in fact inaccurate because it misrepresents the rival as someone who has *wronged* you by not being a good rival, by betraying your rivalry. And perhaps this inaccuracy suffices to explain the inappropriateness of anger. I agree that a dilatory rival probably has not wronged us but I doubt this is why anger is inapt. My doubts are twofold. First, I wonder whether anger need represent its object as wronging us.[7] True, human anger is not just a bite-back response: the world looks annoying to the angry person and the world looks annoying because something has gone wrong, some relevant standard or norm has been violated, some expectation confounded (Williams 1995: 40). Accurate anger requires that something has gone wrong but things can go wrong without anyone being wronged or any wrong being committed. For example, a rivalry can go wrong without anyone being wronged as when my rival declines to push himself to the limit of his abilities. If so, anger at a dilatory rival is accurate though inappropriate.[8]

I'll return to the issue of whether anger (and thus blame as anger) must represent a wronging in the last section. But even if my anger does misrepresent my dilatory rival as wronging me, a second doubt emerges: is this misrepresentation really the source of its inappropriateness? Suppose I instead feel sorrow or regret because I think my rival has wronged me. Given that he hasn't, that reaction *would* be inapt because inaccurate yet it wouldn't be inapt in just the same way as my anger. There is some further element of inaptness in getting angry about it.

It is worth noting that the norms of both friendship and rivalry are embedded in a wider set of norms governing interactions between those who are neither rivals nor friends. I would deny that the norms of either friendship or rivalry can be *derived* from this wider set of norms (even when combined with a specification of the circumstances that give rise to friendship and rivalry). To my mind the norms of friendship and rivalry derive their force from the way they contribute to the distinctive value of the relationships in question and, in Chapter 4, I shall argue this point for the case of friendship. But the fact that the norms distinctive of friendship and rivalry are embedded in more generic norms does blur the sharp contrast I have drawn between them.

Many ways of wronging one's rival are not wrongs of rivalry, rather they are generic wrongs committed in the context of a rivalry. For example, cheating someone or verbally abusing them are ways of wronging them both inside and outside a

---

[7] (Gibbard 1990: ch. 7) and (Rawls 1999: 427) both deny that anger represents its object as a wronging. On the other hand, (Gardner and Shute 2007: 161–2) claim that in anger one feels one has been wronged and defends this by noting (like Rousseau 2004: 128) that people tend to attribute malevolent agency to the objects of their anger. If people have this tendency this may be because they wish their anger to be appropriate as well as accurate.

[8] Anger's focus on mistake and malfunction is one thing that distinguishes it from contempt. You can feel contempt for something simply because of what it is and regardless of whether it has gone wrong.

rivalry. Nevertheless it *may* be that such wrongs acquire extra significance when they occur in the context of rivalry. Cheating a rival might be a more serious matter than cheating a mere competitor. If so, blame as anger is implicated in the norms of rivalry. The waters are further muddied by the fact that blame is not implicated in many aspects of friendship. There are deeds which my friendship for John renders appropriate without making it the case that I would wrong him by not performing them, e.g. acceding to a non-urgent request for help. I would have been a better friend had I helped John out here and he might regret my attitude but John would be a worse friend if he were angry with me about it. Though the contrast between friendship and rivalry is less clear cut than it might be, the following point stands: *the central and distinctive norms of rivalry need not be buttressed by hard feelings whilst many of the central and distinctive norms of friendship depend upon such feelings.*

6. Aptness and accuracy

Let's suppose that blame is a form of anger. Were appropriate anger the same thing as accurate anger, were appropriate anger simply anger that correctly represents an action (attitude) as violating the norms of (and thereby diminishing the value of) a relationship, the value-tracking hypothesis would be the right story about what makes blame appropriate. I've already suggested that accuracy and appropriateness come apart in the case of rivalry: the inaptness of anger at one's dilatory rival is not to be traced to its inaccuracy. In this section, I want to reinforce that conclusion by considering cases, within the sphere of friendship, of inappropriateness without inaccuracy. In fact, I'll distinguish three dimensions in which blame, like other emotions, may be assessed: first *accuracy*, second *aptness* (or *appropriateness, or fittingness*), and third *desirability*.

Let's start with accuracy. Getting angry with the messenger is a very natural reaction to the bad news he brings. It is natural to conflate the source of the harm or the injury with the person who informs you of it. But this conflation is just that, an error, a mistake; call this mistake *transference*. You might not be making this mistake at the level of your beliefs, it might just *seem* to you as if the messenger is harming you. Nevertheless you are under some sort of illusion and that is why you feel as you do.

An emotion is inaccurate when it involves a mistake or an illusion, when it misrepresents the world in some way. What is called *overreaction* is another familiar form of emotional error. Things can go wrong in a more or less serious way and to overreact is to represent the situation as being worse than it actually is. I'm feeling unloved and undervalued and so your petty slight strikes me as a monstrous insult (whether I *believe* this or not). My outrage is an inaccurate reaction, based on an illusion produced by oversensitivity. Similarly, if I experience bottomless contempt for my rival when they don't give their all in a practice session (perhaps because I've had one too many inept rivals) I am overreacting: I am misrepresenting a minor slip as a major shortfall. By contrast, someone who is outraged when their rival fails to put up a fight at the main event need not be misrepresenting the nature of what has occurred. Their reaction is inapt without being inaccurate.[9]

I'll return to inaptness in a moment. First let's distinguish an emotion's accuracy from its desirability. Anger that is inaccurate may have extremely desirable consequences, it may have great instrumental value. If I am a politician who needs to make an impassioned speech, transference or overreaction may be the only way I can do it. Perhaps the fate of my country hangs on my ability to rant and so I must work up a rage on the matter. None of this shows that my anger is at all accurate, rather it means that I ought to manufacture an anger that is quite inaccurate. Conversely, there are forms of anger that are perfectly accurate but highly undesirable, as when our politician has to keep a cool head in delicate negotiations with a ruthless adversary. Here anger at the adversary's attitude would be accurate but the politician should do all he can to avoid it.

Now let's return to the aptness of emotions like anger. I'll examine three forms of anger whose inaptness is a reflection neither of their failure to represent reality correctly nor of their undesirability.[10] In all three cases, there is a genuine wrong (indeed a wronging), the sort of thing to which blame *could* be an apt reaction. (Thus these cases differ from that in which I blame my rival.) But some feature of each case renders the reaction inapt. In the first, it is a feature of the blamer.

Consider a friend who has violated your confidence several times before. You have just done the same to him in a matter of some importance and he is furious with you. Most would think his reaction misplaced but I doubt this inaptness is down to his misrepresenting some aspect of the situation. Ignoring the beam in one's own eye is quite unlike transference or overreaction. After all you have wronged him in a significant way and he is registering this fact correctly. Nor, in his fury, does he portray himself as a reliable character. His anger does not involve thoughts of himself at all, except in so far as he is the victim of a wrong by you. And that he is. It would be even more implausible to maintain that his fury is inapt in virtue of its undesirability. His fury could have any consequences you like (including none at all) and it would still be inapt. Given the history, we might well think it unfair for him to punish you or to express his fury in ways that disturbed or upset you but the inaptness of his fury does not depend on his doing any of these things. The fury itself is inapt.

---

[9] Rawls differentiates what he calls 'moral' emotions like blame, indignation, and resentment, emotions which characterize their object in 'moral' terms from emotions like anger (Rawls 1999: 427) and envy (Rawls 1999: 467) which do not. For Rawls, blaming your dilatory rival would be inaccurate, at least where the rival has done you no wrong in violating the norms of rivalry.

[10] It may still be that accuracy is a *necessary* condition for aptness.

Turn now from the blamer to the blamed. Suppose my friend John forgets that I have recently changed jobs, a move about which I was very nervous, and he makes no inquiries about how things are going. I am resentful and bring the matter to his attention whereupon I discover that he is extremely distracted by various troubles of his own. Here John has wronged me in forgetting about the new job and, to that extent, my anger is well founded. But he has a good excuse. Were John to offer me this excuse, he shouldn't pretend that he has been a good friend to me. Nevertheless his excuse does affect whether anger is apt. How?

I should not concede that my initial burst of anger was inaccurate. John's excuse does not show that I made a mistake or an error in blaming him. (That would be so if I were misinformed about whether he knew of my new job or of how nervous I was about it.) Is continued blame instead inapt in virtue of its undesirability? Again, ignoring John's excuse could have any consequences or none and yet still be inapt. Perhaps it would improve his memory and thus make him a better friend if I remained angry. So the inaptness of continued blame is a product neither of its inaccuracy nor of its undesirability.

Perhaps my blame represents John as being without excuse and so is after all inaccurate? That would be to write the aptness conditions of blame into the representational content of blame (Hieronymi 2004: 132–3). But one can't really suppose that every blame-feeling represents the absence of each of the conditions which would constitute an excuse. The complexity and open-endedness of these excusing conditions should deter us from incorporating them into blame's content. It is more plausible to suppose that blame represents its object as being simply without an excuse. But what exactly is an excuse? Surely an excuse is just a condition that renders blame inappropriate. So this suggestion incorporates claims about the aptness of blame into the content of blame itself and to do that is to concede the point at issue. The aptness of blame must be a different matter from its accuracy if the aptness of blame is needed to *explain* the conditions under which blame is accurate.

My third case of an inapt reaction focuses on the relation between the blamer and the thing blamed. Suppose you commit some significant but not heinous offence against me, and are without excuse. After ten years it still rankles. Perhaps I don't display my continued annoyance but I still feel it. Most would agree that this anger is inapt. I shouldn't bear grudges like this; I should get over it. Even if my grudge is on the whole desirable (as the only thing that keeps me going) it remains inapt. Forgiveness might remain inappropriate (perhaps because it has never been requested) but one can get over a past offence without actually forgiving it and, in many cases, the sheer passage of time renders this appropriate.

Our complaint against those who bear grudges is not that they are making a mistake about what happened or even about its significance. We may acknowledge that the wrong was serious and that it is correct to recall it as such. Though resentment always troubles a friendship, it is frequently apt. What is inapt is to resent the wrong at such a distance in time. At what distance may depend in part on the gravity of the offence without it being the case that blame's duration somehow represents (or misrepresents) that gravity. (Blame of short duration can accurately represent a serious offence and so forth.)[11]

We have examined several forms of blame or anger and I have urged that their inaptness is due neither to their inaccuracy nor to their undesirability. The difficulty in explaining appropriate blame as blame which accurately represents wrongness should make us equally wary of reversing the direction of explanation. For example, Gibbard suggests that 'wrongful' means 'blameworthy', that to be a wrong is to render blame apt (Gibbard 1990: 44–8). I have not attempted to explain what it is for an act like disloyalty to be wrong. One of the lessons of our discussion is that it is rather hard to say exactly when blame is an apt reaction to a wrong and no analysis of deontic notions like 'wrong' and 'wronging' is required for my theoretical purposes. I am exploring the idea (a) that it can be valuable for certain acts of disloyalty to count as wrongs and (b) that this is valuable where it is valuable for certain reactions to disloyalty to count as either apt or inapt. That may be the correct account of the value of such wrongfulness even if it does not tell us what it is for disloyalty to be a wrong.

What conclusions can we draw from our discussion about the value-tracking hypothesis? On this hypothesis, the value of habits of blame derives from blame's tendency to track the blame-independent value of various relationships. Were aptness and accuracy the same thing, this hypothesis would be confirmed. Valuable blame would be blame that tracks (by accurately representing) how the blame-independent value of an involvement like friendship is affected by various forms of wrongdoing. Since accuracy and aptness are distinct, the value-tracking hypothesis cannot take that form. But there are other possibilities. Blame might track the value of a relationship like friendship other than by representing that value (whether accurately or inaccurately). I'll explore this possibility by discussing Scanlon's recent theory of blame.

7. Blame without anger?

According to the value-tracking hypothesis, blame is an appropriate reaction within friendship because it is a reaction to a friend's misbehaviour that tracks the value of the friendship. How might blame track the value of a relationship? One possibility is this: to blame someone is to have a belief about them, say the belief that what they

---

[11] How do the three grounds for the inaptness of blame just reviewed apply to guilt? As I'll argue in Sec. 8, the mere fact that you have an excuse does not render guilt inapt. Nor does the fact that your victim has wronged you in much the same way. You should feel bad about breaching the confidence even of an inveterate gossip. But the passage of time might well lessen the aptness of guilt, if not remove it altogether.

have done reduces or undermines the value of your friendship with them. That would certainly be an attitude that tracked the value of your relationship. But whether or not blame involves this belief, it isn't exhausted by it.

Recall our charming rascal. Here I do believe that what he has done tarnishes our friendship but I can't bring myself to blame him for it. I think he is to blame without actually blaming him. What is missing? Recall that I also regret his behaviour and regret it because it undermines the value of our friendship. Here my regret tracks the value of the relationship. Like anger (and unlike belief) regret or sorrow can be deep, appalling, searing, etc. Still I'm not blaming the rascal, however sorry I am. Indeed I may feel sorry in part because I can't. Rivalry is a different case that makes the same point. My belief that the failings of my rival tarnish the value of our rivalry may be accompanied by regret without my blaming him for his failings. We can't get to blame simply by adding the colour or violence of an emotion to the representational capacities of belief. Regret may be an all-consuming, life-destroying experience without being anything like blame. I shall spend the rest of this section discussing Scanlon's attempt to fill this gap without treating blame as a form of anger.

For Scanlon, the case of the charming rascal shows that we can judge someone to be blameworthy without actually blaming them. Scanlon then asks what more is required for blame. Considering betrayal of friendship, he says this:

> The judgement that you were betrayed by your friend—a judgement that what he did was an instance of a certain kind of wrong—is one that either you or a third party can be in a position to make. But taking seriously the fact that one has been betrayed involves more than making this judgement, and more than making this judgement plus feeling a certain emotion (a special kind of resentment perhaps). It involves seeing one's relationship with the person as changed, and one's interactions with the person as having a different meaning, seeing oneself as having different reasons governing these interactions and having the intention to be guided by these reasons.   (Scanlon 2008: 137)

Scanlon maintains that emotions like anger and resentment are inessential to blame. Betrayed by his friend Joe, Scanlon decides

> Not to rely on or confide in Joe as one would in the case of a friend, and not to seek his company, to find it reassuring, or to have the special concern for his feelings and well-being that one has for a friend's. To revise my intentions and expectations with regard to Joe in this way, or in some less extreme way, is to blame him. I might also resent his behaviour, or feel some other moral emotion. But this is not required for blame, in my view—I might just feel sad.   (Scanlon 2008: 136)[12]

---

[12] I agree that sorrow is normally appropriate in such a situation: after all a valuable relationship has been damaged or destroyed. Furthermore, such sadness may compete with anger for our limited emotional energies and, on some occasions, it may be appropriate to confine oneself entirely to sorrow. But, I would argue, to react 'more in sorrow than in anger' is not to blame.

Here Scanlon proposes to capture the non-cognitive force of blame by saying that blame involves certain emotional and practical elements, in addition to the belief about blameworthiness. Where my friend behaves badly towards me, it is no longer appropriate for me to hope that he gets the job he wants over some well-qualified competitor, nor to help him prepare for the interview, nor to be pleased when he gets it. And to blame him is to actually change my attitudes and intentions towards him in these and other ways.

We can now see what may be missing when I judge my friend to be blameworthy without actually blaming him. I appreciate that the normative situation between us has changed in respect of what we should feel about one another and how we should behave towards one another. And it has changed because 'meaning' of our interactions has now changed. But I can't react appropriately. My hopes, policies, and intentions remain unchanged. Where the wrong I suffer constitutes a betrayal of the friendship, the friendship should end whilst in other cases it may be appropriate to continue the relationship whilst putting a certain distance between us. In the case of the charming rascal, I can't bring myself to do either of these things.

Scanlon's account of what it is to blame a friend involves elements which do not represent the value of the friendship, e.g. the hopes and intentions I have with regard to my friend's job application. Nevertheless, these elements are sensitive to the meaning and importance of our relationship and thus can track its value. Scanlon's initial statement of his view goes as follows:

To claim that a person is *blameworthy* for an action is to claim that the action shows something about the agent's attitude towards others that impairs the relations that others can have with him or her. To *blame* a person is to judge him or her to be blameworthy and to take your relationship with him or her to be modified in a way that this judgement of impaired relations holds to be appropriate.   (Scanlon 2008: 128–9)

This makes it clear that the elements in blame that do not represent value—the revised attitudes and intentions—are expressions of the judgement of impairment. The appropriateness of the former depends on the accuracy of the latter. For our purposes, we can treat Scanlon's judgement of impairment as a judgement about the value of the relationship. An impaired relationship is a relationship that has lost at least some of its value, a loss which changes how it is appropriate for the friends to behave towards one another. The norms of friendship are grounded in the value of friendship and blame is appropriate when the impairment, the loss of value, is a consequence of a violation of these norms.[13]

---

[13] Scanlon thinks that facts about reasons are prior to facts about value and so what it is for friendship to be valuable is for it to give us certain reasons (Scanlon 1998: 95–8). Scanlon might agree that impairment was tied to disvalue without thinking that it is grounded in disvalue.

Scanlon explains that not all forms of impairment provide even *prima facie* grounds for blame. For example, two people may simply grow apart. In that case it is no longer appropriate for them to treat each other as friends, though neither is at fault. By contrast, the kind of impairment involved in Scanlon's account of blame 'occurs when one party, while standing in the relevant relation to another person, holds attitudes toward that person that are ruled out by the standards of that relationship, thus making it appropriate for the other party to have attitudes other than those that the relationship normally involves' (Scanlon 2008: 135). The examples of blame that is accurate but inapt considered in the last section show that things are a little more complicated but Scanlon has the resources to accommodate these complexities. Scanlon can maintain that though in each of these examples there is a violation of the norms of friendship, a withdrawal from the friendship would not be an appropriate response to that wrong.[14] Because I did it myself, because of the excuse, because of the length of time that has passed, your wrongdoing, though a violation of the norms of friendship and correctly represented by me as such, does not de-value the friendship as it otherwise would. So withdrawal from the friendship would not be an appropriate response to that wrong. Thus the appropriateness of blame is grounded in the blame-independent value of friendship.[15]

Should Scanlon's account of blame be accepted? In marginalizing 'reactive attitudes' like anger and resentment, Scanlon departs from familiar treatments of blame.[16] One might target this aspect of Scanlon's view directly. Suppose that I overcome the rascal's charm long enough to become infuriated with him, a fury I regard as perfectly justified. Nevertheless, I still can't prevent myself helping out when he needs it, hoping for the best for him, etc. After all, I still love him. Relationships like this are a staple of imaginative literature. Here Scanlon must maintain that the rascal's charm blocks real blame. But isn't my anger a form of blame? It would be a little odd to say 'I'm right to be furious with you but I don't blame you for what you did since you are still my best friend.' Can't I blame you though I'm sticking with the relationship as is?[17] Now suppose that I do succeed in walking away from the rascal but without rancour, 'perhaps because I regard him as not worth being angry at' (Scanlon 2008: 160). Here Scanlon says that 'I am blaming him, even if this is accompanied by no hostile feelings' (ibid.). But isn't

---

[14] He discusses the case of wrongs you have committed yourself (Scanlon 2008: 175–7).

[15] Scanlon also says that 'a complete rejection of blame would rule out important relations with others' (Scanlon 2008: 168) but I take it Scanlon does not think these relations are important because they involve blame but rather that these relations should involve blame because they are important for other reasons.

[16] The phrase 'reactive attitudes' comes from (Strawson 1974: 6). For accounts of blame that give these attitudes a central role, see (Gibbard 1990: 44–5) and (Wallace 1993: 74–83).

[17] Note this is not a case in which I am reaffirming an earlier revision of my attitudes (Scanlon 2008: 131). The rascal may have wronged me already without provoking anything more than impotent rage.

a person who is not worth being angry at *ipso facto* a person who it is not worth blaming?

I share the critic's misgivings here but to stop at this would be to miss a deeper motivation for adopting Scanlon's view. Suppose we think that blame targets something that tarnishes the value of a significant interpersonal relationship. Given this premise, it is clear why blame should comprise just the elements Scanlon mentions. You wouldn't count as valuing a relationship unless you felt sadness or regret at its decline. Furthermore, it wouldn't be an inter-personal relationship you valued unless changes in its value brought about changes in your attitudes (emotional and practical) to the other party. And, given the widespread assumption that relations like friendship involve a particular concern with the interests or well-being of the other party, one's emotional and practical attitudes to their well being must be in play. Why add anger to the mix?

Some think that without the reactive attitudes, blame becomes a rather bloodless, anaemic thing but Scanlon maintains the opposite. In the first of the above quoted passages, he implies that someone who merely resented the rascal's behaviour would not be taking it seriously. Scanlon later returns to this theme, claiming that anger can't be what gives substance to blame. Suppose you are out to preserve your dignity in the face of a betrayal and to avoid demeaning yourself. Is impotent rage (however appropriate) the best response? Surely the crucial thing is to distance yourself from the person who has wronged you? (Scanlon 2008: 130, 144, 169.)

Yet anger does seem essential to blame-involving relationships like friendship. Having identified 'the range of feelings and reactive attitudes which belong to involvement or participation with others in inter-personal human relations' as being 'resentment, gratitude, forgiveness, anger or the sort of love which two adults can sometime be said to feel reciprocally, for each other' (Strawson 1974: 9), Strawson tells us that a world in which these feelings had decayed would be a world 'in which there were no longer any such things as inter-personal relationships as we normally understand them' (Strawson 1974: 11). Indeed 'the human commitment to participation in ordinary interpersonal relationships is, I think, too thoroughgoing and deeply rooted for us to take seriously the thought' of abandoning these reactions.

Strawson may be right that we can't 'take seriously the thought' of living with others without the reactive attitudes. To cause trouble for Scanlon, we don't need anything so strong. The fact that there are important human relationships whose impairment renders the reactive attitudes appropriate and whose value would be undermined by the total absence of such reactions will suffice (Wolf 2011: 336–7).

Scanlon's account of blame fits relationships like rivalry rather nicely. Rivalry presupposes a capacity for all sorts of feelings, among them joy, disappointment, respect, and contempt but it requires no anger. The norms distinctive of rivalry are not buttressed by such personal antagonism. Where the feeble efforts of your rival undermine the value of the rivalry, you should change your hopes and expectations and also your policies and intentions to reflect the fact. But, whilst it would be strange not to regret what has occurred, annoyance is at best superfluous.

In a world without anger, relationships like rivalry would persist. Furthermore, people would still do each other favours and reciprocate benefits received and so forth. All sorts of co-operative interactions based on well-founded mutual expectations might flourish. But, as I'll urge in more detail in Chapter 4, the specific sorts of relations we now have with our friends, acquaintances, and even with our partners in conversation could no longer exist. Scanlon is right that angry feelings alone are often insufficient. You may also have to express that anger in various ways, perhaps by terminating the relationship. But these reactions are apt precisely as expressions of anger. On the other hand you might end a friendship because you realize that you are incapable of anger towards your friend and where you do, walking away from the friendship is not a form of blame, rather it is product of the realization that you can't blame.

I don't doubt that blame is usually accompanied by the emotional and practical elements Scanlon describes. Avoiding someone and no longer hoping they do well are natural expressions of anger and, in many contexts, anger loses much of its point unless it finds a suitable expression.[18] But it is as expressions of anger that avoidance, etc. are best understood and not just as manifestations of a 'judgement of blameworthiness'. The best response to a dilatory rival is to walk away. You may also feel angry but nothing need be lost if you don't. By contrast, a form of friendship in which people were never hurt by disloyalty, etc. might have a value of its own but not the one familiar to us.[19]

I conclude that blame is indeed a form of anger and that our interest in the appropriateness of blame as anger is part of what makes relationships such as friendship valuable to us. On this value-constituting account, the value of our tendency to feel guilt and blame does not lie in their ability to track the blame-independent value of certain relationships, rather these tendencies are valuable for their own sake and help to explain why friendship is valuable for its own sake.

---

[18] Note it may often make sense to *let someone know* that you are angry with them, even if it wouldn't be appropriate to *express* your anger to them (Owens 2006: 110–11).

[19] Could Scanlon repair his proposal by saying that blame is a response to a specific sort of impairment of a (valuable) relationship, namely an impairment that involves one's being wronged? Such a move is suggested in the first quoted passage where Scanlon's says that judgements of blameworthiness concern 'a certain kind of wrong' and it would enable us to distinguish the rival from the rascal since only the latter wrongs us. I'm unsure whether invoking an independent notion of a wronging at this point would serve Scanlon's wider purposes. In so far as he offers an explanation of the sort of wrong he has in mind, it is as an act that impairs another (valuable) relationship that he calls the moral relationship. See (Morris 1976: 96–7), (Scanlon 1998: 161–4), and also (Scanlon 2008: 139–52). This suggests that he may regard the idea of impairing a relationship as analytically more fundamental than that of a wronging. If so, the problem of differentiating the rival's impairing from the rascal's remains.

8. The scope of blame and the nature of guilt

In this final section, I shall do two things. First, I'll draw out some implications of the account of blame I have been defending. In particular, I'll argue that blame has a much broader scope than is commonly supposed. Second, I'll relate blame to its counterpart guilt and argue that the scope of guilt is even wider than that of blame.

Many writers place rather tight restrictions on suitable objects of blame; they hold that the blamed object must be a responsible agent, acting voluntarily and without excuse for the blame to be apt or even accurate. Are these restrictions well motivated? Let's begin with the restriction to agents. Can I sensibly blame my car for breaking down? The most honest answer would be an expression of ambivalence. On the one hand, we are frequently enraged by our cars, kettles, and computers and we don't hesitate to describe such anger as a form of blame. On the other hand, we freely admit that it is rather silly to blame inanimate objects for their malfunctions. It is a sign of maturity, in both the individual and the human race, that we are less inclined than we once were to allow the inanimate world to anger us. One might distinguish different senses of blame—for instance, one might differentiate 'moral' from 'non-moral' blame—but I doubt our ambivalence here is a result of some ambiguity in the word 'blame'.

I can certainly be angry at my car because it has malfunctioned. There are standards governing the behaviour of cars, computers, and kettles. The car has gone wrong by breaking down and the going wrong is significant: traffic is backed up and I am miles from work. There need be no inaccuracy here unless anger must represent its object as a wrong or a wronging. What is odd about such anger might just be that it could not possibly be an apt reaction. There is no valuable relationship I could have with my car or kettle which depends on such irascibility.[20] If I never felt such anger, nothing of that sort would be lost.

Consider now the other 'reactive attitudes' like indignation, resentment, feeling aggrieved, bearing a grudge or holding it against someone. I suspect that these other attitudes do represent their objects as wrongs. For example, it seems to one who feels resentment that they (or someone with whom they identify) have been *wronged* by the object of their resentment. Hence the peculiar directedness of resentment, the fact that it casts its possessor in the role of somebody's victim. Someone who resents their car for breaking down or their dog for chewing the

---

[20] Of course there is a manufacturer but usually I'm not thinking of him when I blame the kettle, only of flaws in the kettle that may or may not be attributable to the manufacturer. One might think it equally silly to get enraged with the dog for chewing the furniture (though the anger accurately reflects the dog's failure to conform to the rules instilled by training). On the other hand, one might think that a dog can support the sort of relationship in which anger is apt.

furniture is indeed under some sort of illusion. But it does not follow that blame must regard its object in the same light. Accurate blame might have a wider scope than accurate resentment.

The scope of even *apt* blame may be wider than many philosophers suppose. For example, people regularly blame both themselves (and others) for their foolishness. They don't just judge themselves *to* blame for it, they feel self-directed blame, they kick themselves. Here you correctly represent yourself as having gone wrong, as having violated a significant practical norm, though you have neither wronged yourself, nor committed a wrong. I don't know whether it is apt to blame oneself for one's foolishness—perhaps there is no general answer to this question. In any case, those who blame themselves (or others) for their foolishness, as we all regularly do, might well be under no illusion.

Are we aptly blamed only for what we voluntarily do?[21] Does blame extend altogether beyond the sphere of agency? As Hume reminds us, 'sentiments are everyday experienced of praise or blame, which have their objects beyond the dominion of the will or choice' (Hume 1975: 322). We freely blame (and indeed *resent*) people for their desires, thoughts, emotions, and so forth with little regard for the degree of control they have over these mental phenomena (Owens 2000: 115–21). In the case of forgetfulness discussed earlier, my friend John required an excuse to avoid blame though he might have had little control, either direct or indirect, over his memory. Part of what we value in a friend is that they remember, think, feel all sorts of things about you and these memories, thoughts, and feelings have the precise significance they do because they are non-voluntary.[22] So the absence of such thoughts and feelings will be an occasion for appropriate anger. I conclude that we should refrain from placing a priori restrictions on the objects of blame. The scope of apt blame is best revealed by reflection on what constitutes a valuable relationship, not by the application of abstract notions of fairness or desert. Indeed, blame itself is a feeling we blame people for either having or lacking. People are held to account for their blame and their anger even though it is quite unclear how much, if any, control they have over it. And that is because blame as anger is part of the value of certain involvements.

The example of John's forgetfulness can be used to make a further point. John should be excused because he is having a hard time at work: his excuse renders blame inapt. But an excuse need not disarm *guilt* nor render otiose the expressions and

---

[21] (Gibbard 1990: 293–300) and (Rawls 1999: 389–90) share this assumption with many others.

[22] Violations of epistemic norms may also be apt objects of blame and guilt. Suppose my friend is gullible or dogmatic and as a result forms or clings to unjustified beliefs about me. At least where the topic matters to our relationship, anger may be an apt reaction. This is so even if this gullibility or dogmatism stands alone as an autonomous character flaw (so isn't e.g. a manifestation of a wider thoughtlessness or malice) and whether or not the belief does any material damage (Owens 2000: 123–6). For more detailed discussion of the issues raised in this paragraph, see (Owens 2000: ch. 8).

consequences of guilt such as apology and reparation.[23] Even though John has an excuse for forgetting my interview he ought still to feel bad about this. As a good friend he will not regard his distracted state of mind as absolving him from guilt.[24] This observation brings us to our next topic, the feeling of guilt. Guilt and blame as anger are not the same thing but nor are they unconnected. As Gibbard puts it, guilt is the 'first-person counterpart' of anger (Gibbard 1990: 139). What does that mean? There are several ways of extending our account of blame to accommodate guilt.

It has been proposed that guilt is *fear* of (or anxiety about) blame (Williams 1993: 219). Since blame is usually unpleasant to the blamed it is a suitable object of fear. Nevertheless guilt can't just be fear of blame; where you have done nothing wrong, you can still fear blame without feeling at all guilty. Guilt must be fear of a blame with certain credentials. Is guilt fear of apt blame? I doubt it. Were guilt fear of apt blame then guilt would be inapt (because inaccurate) unless blame were apt. And, as we have just seen, guilt at excusable wrongdoing may be entirely apt even though blame is inapt. Perhaps guilt is fear of accurate blame. On this view, guilt is accurate whenever some norm has been violated and guilt is apt whenever fear of blame is an apt reaction to that wrong.[25] So fear of blame might be an apt reaction even to an excusable wrong.

There is a problem. Blame is anger and anger differs from fear in that whilst anger is a response to something you know, fear requires uncertainty: you can't be angry that John stole your bike unless John did indeed steal your bike and you know it (Gordon 1987: 32–43). On the face of it this tells against a fear-based account of guilt since guilt seems to be a response to an evident fact. True, there are a range of phenomena which do not require knowledge and are at least close relatives of guilt (I'm thinking of compunction, scruples, and pangs of conscience.) So it may well be that some forms of guilt involve uncertainty. The problem with the proposal before us is rather that it puts the uncertainty in the wrong place.[26] If the object of your guilt is uncertain, that is because you are uncertain whether you have or will have done something wrong, not because you are uncertain about whether you will suffer (accurate) blame for it. The aptness of guilt (or compunction, or scruples) is not a function of the probability of blame.

---

[23] In earlier writings on this point (e.g. Owens 2008: 419), I ran together the aptness of guilt and that of blame.

[24] Given this it might be appropriate for John to seek my forgiveness and for me to grant it even though it wouldn't be appropriate for me to blame him. Once one has been forgiven, guilt is no longer apt (though it may not be inapt either).

[25] Thus guilt, like blame, may be an accurate reaction to a wide variety of wrongs (Scanlon 1998: 270–1). Those who breach their dietary regime are usually doing something wrong, i.e. breaching some norm. So guilt here would be accurate since fear of accurate blame is accurate when that blame would be accurate. The aptness of such guilt is a further question.

[26] I was helped to see this by discussion with John Tasioulas, Rosanna Keefe, and Rob Hopkins.

One could avoid this difficulty by claiming that guilt is anxiety not about the occurrence of accurate blame but rather about the probability that it would be accurate were it to occur. What makes you anxious is a certain normative situation, or the prospect of such a situation (Velleman 2006: 157). Alternatively one might abandon a fear-based account altogether and propose instead that guilt is itself a form of blame, namely self-directed blame (Morris 1976: 100). On this view, to feel guilt about something is simply to blame yourself for it and such guilt is apt just where self-directed anger is apt. Gibbard objects that this distorts the experience of guilt (Gibbard 1990: 139): when you kick yourself, you are the primary focus of your own attention whilst with guilt it is almost invariably someone else who plays that role. But when you kick yourself for wronging another can't both parties be at the front of your mind? And isn't that how it is with guilt also?

Our discussion of excused wrongings might raise a further doubt about whether guilt can be self-blame. True, we do get angry with ourselves and such anger is often apt just when other people should be angry with us also. But where the wrong we did was excusable, the aptness of guilt and blame come apart. In these cases first-person guilt is apt even though third-person blame is out of place. Why so? A plausible hypothesis here is that an excuse disarms third-person blame but not first-person blame because whilst we are able to cut others some slack, we are not permitted to do this in our own case.[27] Without attempting to resolve these issues, I hope we have said enough to suggest that my view of blame is consistent with a plausible account of guilt.

In this chapter, I have focused on wrongs, on actions and attitudes that tend to render blame and guilt apt. But I have also spoken of wrongings and of breaches of obligation. Now a wrong need be neither a wronging nor the breach of an obligation. Since wrongs, wrongings, and breaches of obligation all involve guilt and blame, I have ignored these differences but to take matters further, we must attend to them. In Chapter 2, I'll focus on wronging, or the violation of a right, and on how it differs from committing a wrong. In Chapter 3, I'll turn to obligation. Readers may find it helpful to refer back to Figure 2 as the discussion proceeds.

---

[27] David Velleman suggested this to me.

2

Wronging

In the last chapter, I traced the value of something's being a wrong to the fact that it renders blame and guilt apt. For example, I argued that friendship matters to us (in part) because it renders certain actions wrongful and that the wrongfulness of these actions matters to us (in part) because they render apt emotional reactions like guilt and blame. The aptness of guilt and blame is something that we value, at least in the context of relationships like friendship. But the account I gave was, in an important respect, incomplete. The characteristic wrongs of friendship are also wrongings. When I am disloyal, I don't just behave badly. In behaving badly I wrong my friend. There is a difference between committing a wrong on the one hand and wronging someone, doing wrong by them or (as the Lord's Prayer would have it) trespassing against them on the other. Whilst all wrongings are surely wrongs, it is an open question whether all wrongs are wrongings.

At this point, the reader might look for an account of what it is for one party to wrong another but I have already disclaimed the project of analysing or defining deontic notions like wrong and wronging (p. 17). I shan't explain what differentiates wrongs, wrongings, and breaches of obligation in terms that could be understood by someone with no comprehension of these notions. This leaves much scope for theorizing about the value of these phenomena. In this chapter, we'll investigate the distinctive value of those forms of wrongfulness which involve wronging some-one. I'll argue that it is good for us when some acts (say) constitute wrongings because it is good for us to control a certain aspect of the normative situation. When X is wronged by ϕ-ing, X has a say in determining the normative significance of ϕ-ing that they lack where ϕ-ing does not wrong *them* or isn't a wronging at all: they can forgive the wrong. That's why X may benefit from the fact that ϕ-ing constitutes a wrong to them. And that is what underlies their normative interest in having the *right* that ϕ not be done to them. Where this normative interest interacts with their other interests and the interests of others in a suitable way, it generates a right not to have ϕ done to you.

In the next section, I'll consider various accounts of why we might value the fact that certain action would wrong us. Then I'll present my own account that turns on our interest in being able to forgive. Having done that, I'll ask how our interest in being able to forgive (our remissive interest) interacts with our other interests, both normative and non-normative, to ensure that certain acts constitute wrongings. Finally, I assess some general claims about the connection between wrongs and human interests.

9. Wrongs and wrongings

Talk of right and wrong takes many forms. Here are three:

  (i) X's doing, thinking, or feeling the wrong thing.[1]
 (ii) X's committing a wrong in thinking, feeling, or acting a certain way. Its being wrongful or wrong for X to think/feel/act in that way.
(iii) X's wronging someone by thinking, feeling, or acting a certain way.

These English constructions have different connotations. For example, the noun phrase 'a wrong' in (ii) is not a good fit for much of what would satisfy (i). If X makes a poor move in chess or buys the shares of a dodgy bank, he has done the wrong thing but he need have committed no wrong nor wronged anyone (nor breached any obligation). A wrong tends to render blame apt. Perhaps such things as chess blunders or foolish investments can render blame apt but there is no presumption that they will (p. 41). I'll use the noun phrase 'a wrong' to cover (ii) and (iii).

It is widely agreed that one can do (etc.) the wrong thing without committing any wrong but can one commit a wrong without doing the wrong thing? I shall argue that committing a wrong can be the right thing to do, can be what one is justified in doing all things considered, can be the most reasonable choice in the circumstances, can be the best option available to you and so forth. By declining to assimilate (i) to either (ii) or (iii) we keep such a view on the table.

Turning now to the relationship between (ii) and (iii), I shall assume that only a wrong can be a wronging but the converse claim is far more debatable. Some would maintain that all wrongs are wrongings; others deny this and offer various examples. If I concrete over the Grand Canyon, I have committed a wrong by disregarding its aesthetic value even if I have thereby wronged nobody. And if I lie to you on a matter about which neither you nor anybody else is likely to believe me, I have done wrong by disregarding the value of truthfulness even if you suffered no injury. In the latter example, you are involved in the specification of the wrong that I do; nonetheless you are not wronged by my wrong. Those unconvinced by such examples will maintain either that somebody is wronged by these deeds or else they are not genuine wrongs.

---

[1] This differs from something's going wrong (p. 30) in that it applies only to what can be more or less reasonable or justified. This notion corresponds to the area of Figure 2 entitled 'Unjustified State or Action'.

In any case, the proposition that all wrongs are wrongings, that all blameworthy events involve someone's being wronged, is a substantive normative claim.

A natural question is this: what is it to do wrong in a way that wrongs someone? If X would wrong you by deceiving you then you have a right against X that he not deceive you; X *owes* it to you not to deceive you, he has an obligation *to you* be truthful to you (Mill 1991: 184–6). And owing *you* the truth is different from merely being obliged to be truthful. What is the difference between it being wrong for you to do something and your owing it to someone not to do that thing, someone who thus has a right that you not do it?

For Nagel the distinctive (and puzzling) feature of a right is that it provides us with an *agent-relative* reason not to violate it and not merely a reason to ensure that such violations do not occur (Nagel 1995: 87–9). Take my obligation to keep a promise I made you. Suppose the reason this obligation provides were an *agent-neutral* reason to ensure that promises are kept and suppose that by breaking faith in this instance I would somehow ensure that several other promises (perhaps promises made to you) were kept. Then the agent-neutral reason I have to keep this promise might be easily outweighed by the agent-neutral reasons I have to prevent these other breaches. But, Nagel says, I surely have a reason not to breach the promise I made you which is not just the agent-neutral reason I have to prevent breaches of promise as such. And this is so regardless of whether I should keep my promise all things considered. Furthermore, Nagel suggests, this fact is what makes it the case that you have a right to my performance.

Granting him that obligations do constitute reasons, Nagel may well be correct in what he says about the agent-relativity of obligation but his observations won't help to distinguish a wrong (or breach of obligation) from a wronging because they don't connect me with the wronged party in a way which could ground the fact that I wrong *them*. What we need here is not (just) agent-relativity but something more like patient-relativity. I don't just have a special reason to keep my own promises, I also owe it to *you* to act on this reason. To see the difference, recall our hypothetical example of a wrong that is not a wronging. One who thinks that it would be wrong to lie even when no one is wronged by our lying (because no one would be deceived) will also maintain that the reason I have to avoid lying myself is not just the reason I have to discourage lying as such. But they are not thereby implying that anyone has a right to the truth from me, that I would be wronging *them* by lying. Even if my reason not to lie (and thereby show respect for the value of truth) is something more than the reason I have to prevent lies as such (and thus promote the value of truth), it does not follow that in committing the wrong of lying, I must be wronging someone. That is a further thought.

So what more is involved in someone's owing it to me to keep their promise over and above it's being wrong for them to breach it? Various answers to this question, various accounts of the nature of wronging have been offered. As already indicated,

I shall not be addressing this constitutive question. Rather, in this section, I'll adapt certain answers to the constitutive question to address the question of value that concerns us. These answers all focus on some action or reaction directed at the wrongdoing (or the prospect thereof) and we'll ask whether having the status of being the wronged party with respect to that wrong might be a good thing because this gives the wronged party a special standing in respect of that action or reaction. This standing may be characterized in various terms: it may be *apt* or *appropriate* for the wronged party (and he alone) to react in a certain way or else such a reaction would only *make sense* coming from him or else the wronged party may possess a *right* to receive something or to behave in a certain way.

Though we can allow ourselves to draw upon such normative notions in explaining the value of deontic phenomena, some ways of so doing will render the resulting theory unilluminating. Consider an account of the value of wronging according to which it is good for you if a wrong counts as a wrong to you because then you alone will have standing to resent it or feel aggrieved by it. Only the wronged party (or those who identify with them) can sensibly resent the wrong done to them; others may feel blame and indignation but not resentment or grievance. As already noted, the notion of a wronging enters into the very content of resentment (pp. 40–1) and so for this proposal to tell us anything about the distinctive value of being a wronging, resenting an act must involve something more than blaming (or being indignant at) the perpetrator for wronging you.[2] Without a suitable story, we are being told only that it is good if blame for wrongings is apt, something which might be equally true of wrongs.

A more promising candidate reaction is compensation. Locke claims that when someone is wronged:

> Besides the Crime which consists in violating the Law, and varying from the Rule of Right Reason...there is commonly *injury* done to some Person or other, and some other Man receives damage by his Transgression, in which Case he who had received any damage, has besides the right of punishment common to him with other Men, a particular Right to seek *Reparation* from him that has done it.   (Locke 1988: 273)

For Locke the common right to punish is a right which anyone can exercise to use such force as is necessary to deter further wrongdoing, whilst the right to reparation is a right to compensation for the damage actually done on this particular occasion. Since it is up to the wronged party whether their right of reparation is invoked—they may choose to waive it, others may not—the fact that it is they who have been wronged puts them in a privileged position.

---

[2] Hampton claims that, unlike indignation, resentment must involve the fear that you don't deserve to be treated any better (Murphy and Hampton 1988: 54–60). I am doubtful about this. (Hieronymi 2001: 544–6) asserts that resentment involves an (inner) protest at the wrong but isn't this equally true of by-stander indignation?

This proposal invokes the idea of a *right* to reparation and thus implicitly assumes that a failure to compensate would wrong the victim. No problem. We are seeking an illuminating account of the value of something's being a wronging and to explain this in terms of its being good to give someone a right to compensation is to say something informative. But I doubt the right to compensation is of value to us whenever the status of being the wronged party is of value.

Often the wronged party does indeed have the right to receive compensation for the injury they have suffered (whether or not they have the further right to use force to extract it) and it is a good thing that this is so. But, just as frequently, talk of compensation seems out of place though there is no doubt that the injured party has been wronged. If I fail to show up to your wedding as promised, you might well expect me to do something to make it up to you, but that something is not valued as *compensation* for the wasted place at the wedding breakfast, nor even for your sense of disappointment. What you are looking for is an expression of remorse, not an effort to 'make you whole'. Furthermore, in certain cases the whole idea of 'making it up to someone' is questionable though we don't doubt they have been wronged. Suppose the wronged party has actually benefited from the wrongdoing and was never at risk of being harmed. Still it might well matter to them that this wrongdoing constitutes a violation of their rights even though it is quite unclear what 'compensation' would amount to here.

Several authors have suggested that someone with a right against others has a special standing to claim or demand action (or forbearance) from those others. For example Pufendorf tells us that an injustice is done when 'that be deny'd to another which in his own right he might demand' (Pufendorf 2003: 51).[3] On this view, where a certain action would not just be a wrong but would wrong *me* I have a special standing to demand the wronger's compliance, a standing which third parties lack. And it is this asymmetry between myself and a third party that gives the wronging its peculiar directedness, its second personal character: You are wronging *me* because *I* can demand that you perform as others cannot.

What does it mean to say that one can *demand* forbearance? And why is it a good thing for someone to be able to issue such demands? The idea may be that the wronged party can determine whether performing the act in question constitutes wrongdoing at all by deciding whether to demand it. Consider an example of Hart's. Suppose I've promised to take care of your aged mother should you have to go away. Here the beneficiary of the promise is your mother but by breaching the promise I would wrong you and not her (Hobbes 1994: 94). This is especially clear where she remains quite unaware of the arrangement and gets help from other quarters. Hart connects the fact that it is you who would be wronged by the breach to the fact that it

---

[3] See also (Hart 1955: 180–2), (Feinberg 1970b: 249–55), (Feinberg 1992: 189), (Gilbert 2004: 86–90), (Darwall 2007: 52–4), and (Wallace 2007: 27–30).

is you (rather than your mother) who has the power to release me from my promise, who has the power to refrain from demanding performance, to consent to non-performance (Hart 1955: 180 and Feinberg 1992: 188–9). So is the wronged party the person with the power to consent to non-performance, to *waive* the demand?[4]

Considered as an analysis of the difference between wrongs and wrongings this account will not cover all the cases. For example, I can't consent to enslavement (even in return for a huge donation to my favourite charity) nor to torture, lobotomization, and so forth (pp. 179–80). Since I can't consent to these wrongings, my ability to render them innocuous by consent can't be what ensures that they wrong me. Furthermore, a baby can be wronged in these and many other ways though the baby is quite unable to consent to anything. But we are not looking for a general account of the difference between wrongs and wrongings. We are interested specifically in those wrongings that constitute wrongings because their possession of that deontic status is of value to the wronged party. Wrongings such as torture do not fit this specification and so we can avoid this difficulty by recasting Hart's account as a theory, not of what it is for a wrong to be a wronging but rather of what value there is in being a wronging.

As we'll see in Chapter 7, having the power of consent is often a good thing. Nevertheless we can't maintain that it is good for ϕ-ing to constitute a wrong to X just where it is good for X to be able to render ϕ-ing no wrong by an act of consent. Let's set aside those wrongings that constitute wrongings regardless of whether it is in anyone's interests for them to possess this deontic status. Such are the torture of adults or the maltreatment of young children. Considered as an account of deontic value, Hart's proposal is not troubled by the fact that it does not apply to such wrongings. Our focus is on those acts whose wrongfulness depends on our interest in their being wrongings. Such are the wrongs of friendship that I introduced in the last chapter and will consider at greater length in Chapter 4. Disloyalty constitutes a wrong within friendship because we have an interest in ensuring that we can be wronged by such disloyalty. Unfortunately for Hart, disloyalty or insult wrong us regardless of whether we consent to them; we cannot render these disloyal acts or insulting attitudes innocuous by declaration (p. 173). So the value of the fact that these acts, beliefs, and feelings constitute wrongings cannot depend on our possession of such a power of consent. Hence, Hart's account also fails when taken as a theory of the value of an act's constituting a wronging.

---

[4] Hart must insist that it is consent we are talking about and not mere choice (Sec. 32). My promise to help your aged mother is a promise to do so only if she requests help, so there is a sense in which your mother can control what I am obliged to do by choosing whether to ask for help or not. Were choice equivalent to consent, Hart would be landed with the conclusion that your mother can consent to my non-performance after all and so must be the person (or a person) wronged by breach. But this is not so. She cannot release me from my conditional obligation to help her if she requests it; only you can do that. Only you have the power of consent to non-performance and so, Hart may add, it is you who are wronged by the breach. For further discussion of this point, see p. 222.

The idea of a special standing to demand performance is given a different spin by Gilbert:

If you fail to give me what I have a right to through your promise, I have the standing, as your promisee, to rebuke you on that account. Similarly, should you threaten to break your promise, I have the standing, as your promisee, to command or insist that you act as promised, and thus pressure you to perform.   (Gilbert 2004: 90)

Gilbert does not tell us precisely what 'standing' involves. However we construe it, it is hard to detect an asymmetry relevant to our current concerns. Take insistence first. Would it be a good thing if the promisee alone could insist on performance? Shouldn't a bystander sometimes be able to insist that I keep my promise to John when it looks as if I am about to break it? If so we can hardly explain why it's a good thing for such a breach to count as a wronging of X by supposing it's a good thing if X alone can insist on performance. On certain occasions, it might be either inappropriate or at least undesirable for a mere bystander to insist on John's rights but then, on other occasions, it might be either undesirable or even inappropriate for John to insist on John's rights. Gilbert could instead place the emphasis on the idea of a special standing to *rebuke* once the promise is broken, so the wronged have a special standing to rebuke the violators of their rights. But shouldn't we all be able to complain to someone about their breach of promise? Why would it be better if the wronged party alone were able to do this? Of course it be may be inappropriate to rebuke a wrongdoer for all sorts of reasons but that is so whoever you are.

What of the reactive attitudes that (sincere) rebuke expresses? Would it be good if the promisee were in a privileged position to feel blame or indignation about the breach of a promise made to him? To some authors it appears obvious that the wronged party has priority here, or even an exclusive entitlement to the reaction (Feinberg 1992: 183–7). But the behaviour of perfect strangers described in a newspaper can provoke my righteous indignation and why should the victim have any interest in this not being so? There are occasions on which blame and indignation from all sides is apt, occasions on which nobody should blame (the wrongdoer has a good excuse), occasions on which third parties should not blame (it is a private matter which is no concern of ours), and finally occasions on which *only* third parties should blame. An instance of the latter is where the promisee has himself breached faith with the promisor on many previous occasions and is getting a dose of his own medicine. Here third parties can reproach the promisor (and the promisor should reproach himself) but it would be a bit rich for the promisee to protest at the breach or even to inwardly resent it (Kant 1996: 452).[5]

---

[5] I'm not denying that the victim's record will also affect how much third-party blame is appropriate. My point is that the victim's misdeeds bear particularly on how much it is appropriate for *him* to blame the wrong he suffers. A bad record need not undermine the victim's ability to *forgive* the wrong (p. 42). Indeed

A final idea worth mentioning is that the wronged party is entitled to an apology, a right he might well value. There are several ways of understanding the notion of an apology. An apology may be an expression of regret or perhaps remorse at the wrongdoing in which case some of the objections just made carry over to the present proposal. (Where the wronged party has themselves committed the wrong in question, expressions of regret or remorse are better directed elsewhere.) However, an apology may also be understood as a request for forgiveness and so taken, the proposal is on the right track. We can see this by returning to Hart's example. I promise to help your aged mother and then breach that promise. You have been wronged but has your mother also been wronged? Not simply in virtue of the breach of promise at any rate. As Hart points out, performance is *owed to* you and not to your mother, 'though the mother may be physically injured' (Hart 1955: 180).[6] In so far as Hart explains the point, it is in terms of your possession of the power of release but we can better appreciate the force of his remarks by considering who here has standing to forgive. Suppose you decide to forgive my breach of promise but your mother remains unforgiving. Surely I have been forgiven for the breach; blaming me for it is no longer appropriate. Your mother might still blame me for not helping her were there some *other* basis for requiring this of me (e.g. an obligation of friendship, or perhaps that *I* led her to expect help by telling her about my promise).[7] She may also blame *you* for forgiving me (or for not foreseeing the breach). But so far as the promise goes, she has no standing to determine whether my non-performance has been forgiven. It is you, the wronged party, who have that standing.

10. Wrongings and forgiveness

Why should it matter to a promisee that breach of promise constitutes a wrong to them rather than merely a wrong in which they are involved? The wronged party has a right to forgive a wrong committed against them that bystanders lack and which no one has with respect to mere wrongs.[8] They have both the ability to forgive and the right to exercise that ability. Once the wrongdoer has been forgiven in the relevant sense, it is no longer apt for them to feel guilty and it is positively inapt for others to blame them; both resentment and indignation are now out of place.[9] We sensibly

---

he probably ought to forgive it in view of his own misdeeds, though he shouldn't *offer* or *pronounce* forgiveness.

[6] (Gilbert 2004: 100–2) and (Thompson 2004: 348–50) use something like Hart's point as an objection to Raz's interest theory of rights (Raz 1986: 166).

[7] I am here assuming a point to be argued in Chapter 9, namely that our obligation to keep a promise is distinct from the obligation we have to take due care of the expectations of performance we may arouse.

[8] Darwall includes forgiving on his list of things that the wronged party has a special standing to do (Darwall 2007: 62–3).

[9] Do we wrong someone by continuing to blame them once they have been forgiven? On the one hand, inapt blame does not always wrong its object. I doubt we *wrong* someone by blaming them for dishonesty

value the right to forgive and this is why it matters to us whether a wrong constitutes a wronging. There is no analogous phenomenon for mere wrongs.

To give this idea a run for its money, we must construe 'forgiveness' precisely. People often speak of forgiveness whenever blame ceases. Since there are all sorts of ways of overcoming or erasing both guilt and blame, this usage is extremely broad. For example, I cease to blame someone when I discover some excuse or justification for what they did, when I find it prudent or even necessary to condone what they did, when I simply forget what they did. The word 'forgiveness' has been applied to all such cessations of blame.[10] Should a pharmaceutical company invent a cure for blame, they might well market it as a Forgiveness Pill. Furthermore, 'forgive' is sometimes used as if people other than the wronged party could forgive the wrong. Downie offers us two examples of this: those who say 'I haven't forgiven Hitler for what he did' and those who say 'I haven't forgiven myself for what I did' where they have in mind a wrong against someone else (Downie 1965: 128–9). In raising the possibility of forgiving Hitler's crimes or their own, such people might be identifying themselves with the victims of the relevant wrongs[11] but it is more likely that they are simply noting the fact that they have not ceased to blame the perpetrator.

The phenomenon that interests me is not the cessation of blame or guilt but an activity that changes the normative situation. The wrong forgiven remains a wrong and one for which there is no adequate justification or excuse. Nevertheless forgiveness changes the normative situation by ensuring that guilt and blame for that wrong are no longer apt.[12] Indeed it is an activity undertaken in the knowledge (or the hope) that it might change the normative situation: one cannot forgive unintentionally. But how is such an activity to be understood? One possibility is to treat forgiveness as the exercise of a normative power.

There is such a thing as forgiving or pardoning a debt, that is releasing the debtor from his obligation to pay, and it is tempting to regard forgiveness more generally as releasing someone from a moral debt, one incurred when the creditor was wronged. Treating forgiveness as pardon would certainly help to distinguish forgiveness from mere cessation of blame. First, one chooses to forgive a debt by communicating the

---

when we have been less than honest with them on several previous occasions. On the other hand, we may well wrong someone by ignoring the excuses they offer for what they did. I'm unsure on which side of this divide blaming forgiven wrongs falls.

[10] It is also applied when I never had any inclination to blame the wrongdoer. Here the issue of blame's appropriateness does not arise and so I need go through no process of forgiveness, no process of rendering blame inappropriate.

[11] It is obscure to me exactly what such identification involves. A wife might feel able forgive the wrongs done to her husband without thinking of herself and her husband as numerically identical. Perhaps there is an identity of interests here, so harm to one is harm to the other but this won't cover cases of bare wronging.

[12] You remain entitled to be disappointed and regretful or else disgusted and horrified by the wrong that was done to you, even after you have forgiven it. Forgiveness is also consistent with continued wariness.

intention of so doing to the debtor (or some relevant person), whilst one may stop blaming without either having or communicating any intention of so doing. Second, such forgiveness operates on the normative (rather than the psychological) level: the debtor is no longer obliged to pay and it is no longer appropriate for you (or any one else) to blame them for not paying. Third, while blame may return, forgiveness is irrevocable: having forgiven a debt, one can't change one's mind and reimpose it any more than one can unforgive someone for what they did to you.[13] Forgiveness renders resurgent blame inapt. Perhaps one was too kind or hasty or even naïve in forgiving and perhaps one comes to realize this. Nevertheless, one's earlier forgiveness is not invalid simply because it was unwise and one can't subsequently invalidate it just because one comes to realize that it was unwise.

Forgiveness, as I understand it, involves no pardon or other performative.[14] For a start, one doesn't generally forgive someone simply by communicating the intention of forgiving them, simply by declaring that you hereby forgive them. One may sincerely intend to forgive, communicate this intention to the wrongdoer, and still fail to forgive because the requisite psychological changes have not occurred: one continues to blame just as before. *This* possibility of failure does not exist in the case of normative powers like pardon, promise, consent, and so forth whose successful exercise requires no psychological transformation on the part of the promisor, etc. Promises have their impact on the normative situation regardless of the (non-communicative) attitudes and intentions of the promisor; with them what matters are the intentions that the promisor represents himself as having (pp. 191–2). Forgiveness requires more than the communication of the intention to forgive. It also requires less. One can forgive someone without communicating one's intention of forgiving them, without declaring one's forgiveness either to them or to anybody else. The person forgiven might remain quite unaware of your forgiveness (and so of the fact that the burden of guilt has been lifted). They may even be dead. By contrast such communication is essential to the workings of pardon, promise, consent, and so forth. It is the communication of the intention to change the normative situation that does the normative work.

To use the terms I coined earlier, forgiveness has the second rather the third grade of choice-dependence. Obligations of an involvement like friendship were my paradigm of second grade obligations. You can't make a friend unintentionally, you must know what you are doing but, as we shall see (p. 102), you can make a friend without either aiming to do so or representing yourself as having this aim. Furthermore so

---

[13] Retracting forgiveness must be distinguished both from retracting the offer of forgiveness before it is accepted and from asserting the invalidity of one's earlier act of forgiveness.

[14] (Downie 1965: 131–2) makes both of the points that follow. He also observes that forgiveness should be distinguished from pardon that, he claims, requires a legal or institutional setting. I shall argue that whilst forgiveness of non-interested wrongings is perfectly intelligible, pardon of such wrongings would not be, so forgiveness cannot be pardon (pp. 184–5).

representing yourself isn't sufficient for friendship to arise. No friendships are made merely by declaration. ('Let's be friends' is an expression of a wish).[15] In both respects, forgiveness is like friendship. This all suggests that we might usefully compare the process of forgiving someone with the process of making friends with them. Forging a friendship and forgiving are both ways of shaping the normative landscape and friendship casts more light than pardon on what is going on in forgiveness. I'll highlight four salient points of convergence.

First, forgiveness, like making a friend, is usually an activity extending over a period of time, involving disparate but interlocking elements.[16] There are changes in what one is disposed to do and in the habit of doing; there are changes in one's emotions and attitudes; finally, there are normative changes both in what one is obliged (or in what it makes sense) to do and in what emotions and attitudes it is appropriate for one to have towards one's friend. Wanting to stay in touch, you acquire the habit of being in touch and thus become obliged to stay in touch, whilst being obliged to stay in touch ensures that you feel more inclined to, thereby reinforcing the habit and the obligation and so on and so forth. Similarly in forgiveness, by behaving civilly you come to feel less resentful and thus less inclined to rebuke thereby creating a situation in which (*ceteris paribus*) it is no longer appropriate to feel inclined to rebuke, giving you a further incentive to be civil, thereby ensuring that you feel even less resentment and so on and so forth. In the case of friendship, the two of us may set off on this path together without reaching our destination—we may try to become friends and fail. We can't become friends at will, even if we both will it. Forgiveness at will is equally ruled out. Your efforts to forgive may fail though when they succeed, forgiving is something you knowingly did.

Second, the value of friendship (and so the associated obligations) depends on its having been chosen *voluntarily*. There are many possible friends one could make, lots of whom would be good friends in their own way. One gets to choose which of these worthy connections one actually forms and one's choice must in some degree be voluntary. (Coercion and deception tarnish the value of friendship and so loosen its bonds.[17]) This point about voluntariness must be distinguished from the idea that friendship is *elective* in the sense that we are under no obligation to form particular

---

[15] Many children seem to believe that they can both make and unmake friends by declaration. Perhaps with respect to childhood friendship they are right but to become capable of adult friendship they must lose this idea.

[16] I say the act of forgiving 'usually' extends over a period of time because a sudden change of heart can sometimes be attributed to the forgiver. An example: 'a young boy, tortured by the police and knowing that he will be shot gives the name of his friend because he is afraid to die alone. They meet before the firing squad and the betrayed forgives his betrayer' (Milosz 1990: 91–2). This may encourage the 'pardon' model of forgiveness but, unless the forgiver is a saint, it is crucial to the psychological plausibility of the story that he is *in extremis*. Neither saintliness nor desperation is relevant to the validity of a pardon. (Perhaps saints or those close to death can also make friends instantaneously.)

[17] I don't think that coercion and deception necessarily deprive the friendship of all value (pp. 244–5).

friendships (or indeed any friendships at all). Perhaps friendship is usually elective but it isn't always and, where it isn't, that fact need not tarnish the value or loosen the bonds of friendship. I may be obliged to become someone's friend, even a good friend.[18] Sharing a prison cell with a person who is neither knave nor fool, I probably wrong them by refusing to respond to their overtures and keeping my distance. Still, if I do refuse to get involved, I don't acquire the obligations *of a friend* (e.g. to keep in touch after our release). The point is even clearer when the issue is whether to sustain a friendship. There are ways of ending a friendship without wronging one's friend as when you lose touch or your interests diverge but it is notoriously difficult to pull this off without causing (and meriting) resentment. Still, if I'm determined to end the friendship regardless, I can do so (though not by declaration) and thereby annul the associated obligations at the price of wronging my friend.

Again there are striking parallels with forgiveness. The value of forgiveness (and so its normative significance) depends on whether it has been chosen and chosen voluntarily: coercion and deception throw the normative significance of forgiveness into doubt. It would very often be a good thing to forgive but among those it would be good for us to forgive, we can choose whom to forgive and whom not to. Forgiveness based on coercion or deception tends to lose its value and thus its normative significance. But forgiveness need not be elective. For example, it may be an obligation of friendship to forgive a repentant friend for some wrong they have done me. I may even be obliged to forgive a repentant stranger whose life would be blighted by my resentment. Still, if I decline to forgive, resurgent blame is not rendered inappropriate in the way it would be had I forgiven.

Third, in the case of both friendship and forgiveness, there is a rather blurred boundary between value and validity. Friendships are more or less worthwhile and some 'friendships' may be so worthless that one really doesn't owe the other party anything *as a friend*. Still there is a difference between a friendship's being flawed or unhealthy and its being simply null and void. Similarly, it may a bad thing in any number of ways for me to forgive John but this need not settle the question of whether I am able (and have the right) to forgive him. For example, it is possible for me to forgive someone who is unrepentant even if such forgiveness is on the whole unwise, provided their obstinacy does not entirely deprive my forgiveness of its value. I'm unsure whether forgiveness is ever invalid (i.e. normatively inefficacious) simply because its object is so unworthy of it. We'll return to this point.

Fourth, the formation of friendship displays the same asymmetry of standing which got us interested in forgiveness. Only you can make your friends, others

---

[18] One can't be obliged to feel a certain way towards someone but one can be obliged to cultivate certain feelings and that is part of what is involved in the activity of becoming someone's friend (or in forgiving them). One is obliged to become someone's friend (or forgive them) only where something one could do might bring this about (pp. 71–2).

can't do this for you but once you have made friends with someone, the normative situation changes for us all. Blame from bystanders is now apt for certain forms of disloyalty and inapt for certain forms of intimacy (those which would otherwise be violations of privacy). Similarly, only I can forgive wrongs done to me but once they are forgiven, it is no longer appropriate for others to blame the wrongdoer for the offence he committed against *me*.[19] Suppose I have forgiven John for breaching the promise he made me but despite this you continue to blame him. I say: 'I'm sorry but I've forgiven John and the matter is now closed.' My forgiveness changes the normative situation not just for me but for you also. John is still *to* blame for what he did and though your doubts about his character may ensure that you neither trust him nor associate with him, indignant anger at what happened is now out of place.

Once again, it is important to distinguish my forgiving John from my merely ceasing to blame him.[20] I could cease to blame John because I run out of emotional energy, because I decide that I need to get along with him and so set the whole matter aside, or by simply forgetting. If I cease to blame him in these ways, it remains an open question whether a resumption of blame might be in order once my energy levels recover, or things go wrong again, or I recall what happened. And a cessation of blame for these reasons need not affect how it is appropriate for others to feel about what John did. But, we have been assuming, there is a way of ceasing to blame that renders resurgent blame inapt and when blame ceases in that way, third-party blame is also out of place.

Consider forgiveness that is valid but perhaps inappropriate. Must the rest of us cease to blame a rapist for what he did just because his victim has forgiven him, even where this forgiveness may be due to misplaced sympathy or lack of self-esteem? Care is needed in formulating the example. The victim's lack of self-esteem must not undermine their conviction that they were gravely wronged since only someone convinced that they have been (inexcusably) wronged can forgive. And whilst their soft-heartedness might lead them to cease to blame out of misplaced sympathy for the rapist, pity alone won't commit them to never blame again and thus to forgive in the required sense. Once it is clear that these and other pitfalls have been avoided, we may still be left with a case in which *we* would not have forgiven the rapist because, in our view, he does not merit forgiveness. Nevertheless, we must acknowledge that the rapist *has been forgiven* and that fact has implications for us all.[21]

---

[19] If what happened constitutes a wrong against other people as well as against myself (as will often be the case where the bystanders are my friends or family) all are still entitled to blame. Moreover, if there is a wrong in addition to all these wrongings, the wrongdoer may still be blamed after all of those he wronged have forgiven him.

[20] On many occasions, it might be indeterminate which of these two things is happening. This indeterminacy may resolve itself only in retrospect, as it may become clear only in retrospect that this was the beginning of a friendship.

[21] Forgiveness ensures that guilt on the wrongdoer's part is not longer apt without thereby making guilt positively inapt. Might the same be true of third-party blame? Might others be permitted to blame a wrong

The parallel between friendship and forgiveness hopefully dispels some of the mystery surrounding the latter but we shouldn't overplay our hand. In particular we mustn't equate forgiveness with reconciliation. For example, Scanlon maintains that 'forgiveness involves the restoration of an impaired relationship, perhaps in modified form' (Scanlon 2008: 160).[22] But there are many situations in which we forgive someone without any prospect that relations with them will be restored. Perhaps they are long dead or otherwise out of touch. Or perhaps there are no relations to be restored: think of the mother who forgives her son's murderer without even knowing who they are. Such forgiveness may be laudable without doing anything to bring about a reconciliation with the murderer. The essence of forgiveness is the transformation that renders blame inapt and such a transformation may occur outside the context of a valuable relationship.

The accounts of wronging examined in this chapter, my own included, all focus on *reactions* to a wronging; they seek to explain why it matters whether a wrong constitutes a wronging by reference to some characteristic reaction to the wrong. There are going to be cases where the reaction in question is, for some reason, impossible but where we are still inclined to think that the victim has been wronged. This would pose a grave difficulty were we trying to explain what it is for a wrong to be a wronging but our focus is solely on the value of a wrong's being a wronging. Thus, our account is intended to apply only to wrongs that constitute wrongings because it would be a good thing if they did. Provided the wrongings to which the relevant reaction is impossible do not fall into this class, the difficulty does not arise. I'll review the situation for forgiveness.

It is widely thought that we can *wrong* animals by causing them gratuitous pain. Hart disagrees: 'the moral situation can be simply and adequately described here by saying that it is wrong or that we ought not to ill-treat them' (Hart 1955: 181). Let's suppose Hart is mistaken about this. Should I be troubled by the fact that an animal may be wronged by torture even though it has no capacity to forgive the wrongs it suffers? No, provided the fact that it is wronged by torture does not depend on the animal's having some interest in counting as the wronged party. True the status of being the wronged party can be of no value to the animal but this need not settle the question as to whether the animal is wronged.[23]

What of wrongs whose status as wrongings does depend on the value of their constituting wrongings but where forgiveness is ruled out by some contingent obstacle? Even these wrongs need not trouble us provided the factors that make

---

even after I have forgiven it? My discussion suggests that the stronger claim should be preferred but weaker one would serve my theoretical purposes by giving the wronged party a distinctive form of control over the normative situation.

[22] Scanlon's account of forgiveness dovetails with his account of blame as the loosening or abandonment of a relationship in response to its impairment (Sec. 7).

[23] Similar things should be said of human babies.

forgiveness impossible do not deprive this normative status of its value to us. Take the wrongs of friendship, wrongs created by your choice of friends. It may be impossible for you to forgive an act of disloyalty if you know nothing about it. Still you wish to have friends in part because you value the fact that disloyalty within friendship would be wrongful but wrongful in a way you could forgive. Here you might sensibly value having the capacity to forgive such disloyalty even where it so happens that you can't exercise that capacity because you don't know the wrong has been done.

What of normative obstacles to forgiveness? Can there be wrongs so terrible or wrongdoers so unrepentant that forgiveness is simply impossible, that the wronged party can do nothing to render blame inappropriate? I'm quite unsure about this. According to a long (Judaeo-Christian) tradition of thought, we have the standing to forgive *all* those who trespass against us. But again this is a question we need not settle. There would be a problem here only if there were types of wronging which exist because we have an interest in such acts constituting wrongings but which are, as a class, beyond forgiveness. Take disloyalty once more. Perhaps some forms of disloyalty in a given relationship are literally unforgivable. Nevertheless, provided disloyalty within that relationship can take other forms that are forgivable, and provided that in creating the unforgivable forms of disloyalty we also create the forgivable ones, the rationale for the choices that create the relationship (and its associated wrongings) can still reside (in part) in the value we place on the capacity to forgive.[24]

11. Remissive interests

Something's status as a wronging is valuable for its own sake where the same is true of our capacity to forgive it. If so, human beings must have an interest in being able to control whether blame is an appropriate reaction to certain wrongs, namely wrongs which constitute wrongings of themselves. They must have what I shall call *remissive interests*. But on a certain conception of what makes something a wronging, the whole idea of remission seems bizarre.

It is often said that to wrong someone is to injure them where an injury involves harming the injured or at least acting against their interests. Not all harm constitutes a wronging of the person harmed but, it may be thought, wronging them at least involves a harm or a setback to their interests. If to wrong someone is to act against their interests then a theory of wronging should be a theory of how X's interests ensure that certain ways of behaving towards X (or attitudes directed at X) wrong

---

[24] The same applies to posthumous wrongs within friendship. Being dead, I am in no position to forgive such wrongs but the creation of the friendship (which created the possibility of posthumous wrong) also created many wrongs that I was in a position to forgive.

X. In connecting wrongings with human interests in this way, we ensure that the fact that an action would wrong someone is a reason to avoid it. According to the Rationalist, an action makes sense only in so far as it appears to achieve some good or avoid some evil. If a wronging involves acting against the interests of the wronged, that looks like a count against it, something that would make sense of our abstaining from it.

This account of the matter renders forgiveness problematic. Suppose I am wronged by a deed in virtue of the fact that it constitutes an action against my interests. And suppose that only facts about my interests can explain the normative significance of wrongs done to me. It is hard to see how forgiveness can affect the normative significance of a wronging so understood. For example, if a harm is both sufficiently serious to be blameworthy and bears on my interests in such a way as to constitute a wrong against me, how can I alter these facts simply by forgiving the wrongdoer? Am I any better placed than you to condone this wrong just because it was done to me? (Kolnai 1978: 215–17).

Might we dispense altogether with this talk of wronging, of obligations *owed to* someone, of rights *against* someone and instead make do with the notions of right and wrong, of the obligatory (or the required) and the permissible? Suppose facts about right, wrong, and obligation ultimately depend on facts about human interests and how they are affected by our actions. Then wouldn't it be enough to know who has done wrong and whose interests have been (foreseeably) affected by their wrongdoing? Why worry over whom, if anyone, has been wronged? Forgiveness can't affect who has done wrong, nor repair the harm wrought by that wrongdoing. How then can it be normatively significant?

To answer this question, we must expand the usual inventory of human interests. We must recognize that human beings have normative interests, interests in being able to shape the normative landscape they inhabit. In particular they have an interest in being able to determine when (certain) actions are blameworthy. Thus the interests affected by a given act of ϕ-ing are not the only interests that go to determine ϕ-ing's normative significance. Other interests are relevant, interests in the normative situation, interests that are relevant even though ϕ-ing does not constitute an action against them.

Forgiveness is here to serve such normative interests. We can make it inappropriate for people to blame a wrong done to ourselves by forgiving the perpetrator. Forgiveness does not render blame inaccurate, it does not change the fact that the act forgiven constituted a significant wronging. Rather forgiveness renders blame inapt. Why so? Not for any of the reasons mentioned in Section 6 (excuse, passage of time, etc.).[25] What renders blame inapt is the value of the victim's being able to control the

---

[25] To think it appropriate to forgive an offence is not to think that blame for that offence is inapt already. Rather it is to think that you ought to render blame for that offence inapt. By contrast, to recognize

normative significance of the wrong done to them by initiating the psychological process described in the last section. That interest combines with other interests (both normative and non-normative) to determine the aptness of blame. To *suffer* from a wrong is to have some non-normative interest that is adversely affected by it. But these are not the only interests relevant to determining the pattern of apt blame. If the victim of the wrong also has an interest in controlling whether blame is an apt reaction to this wrong, then this remissive interest must be taken into consideration even though it has not (we may assume) been harmed by the wrongdoing. And once the remissive interest is factored in, it makes sense that the wronged party should have the power to control whether blame is an apt response to action against their interests.[26]

I reckon that the function of forgiveness is to serve an interest of the forgiver. This might seem strange. Isn't forgiveness primarily of benefit to the forgiven? Very often it is the perpetrator who requests forgiveness and the victim who is reluctant to provide it. This makes the wronged party's interest in being able to forgive look like a by-product of the wrongdoer's interest in being forgiven. On the other hand, the fact that (unlike a promise (pp. 223–6)) forgiveness need not be accepted to be valid suggests that the forgiver's interest is indeed primary. The wrongdoer might remain quite unaware that they have been forgiven, that guilt and blame are no longer apt responses to what they did. They may even be dead. And a wrongdoer who is aware of being forgiven can't invalidate forgiveness simply by rejecting it (e.g. because they regard it as insulting). The forgiver may see a point in forgiving regardless of whether such forgiveness serves the actual or perceived interests of the forgiven.

The idea of a remissive interest makes perfect sense provided we distinguish the aptness of blame from its accuracy (Sec. 6). Someone who adopts a purely representational account of the aptness of blame will have a hard time seeing how either the choices of the wronged party or the psychological processes described in the last section could render blame inapt. After all, neither does anything to change the nature of the wrong done so why should they affect how it is appropriate for anyone to represent the wrong? But if the aptness of blame is not solely a matter of accuracy but is in part down to its non-representational properties, and the value of an emotion with such properties is conditional on the psychological context in which

---

that someone has an excuse (or that time has passed or that they have already been forgiven, etc.) *is* to recognize that blame is inapt already.

[26] Note that the remissive interest explains how it is possible to forgive an act even when it constitutes a wronging purely in virtue of our non-normative interests. To use the jargon I shall introduce in the next section, our remissive interests can ensure that non-interested as well as interested wrongings are forgivable. This is so because the forgiveness changes the psychological context in which blame occurs. An act of pardon could not effect the same transformation because it need involve no psychological change (pp. 184–5).

it occurs (and on whether that context has been chosen) the air of mystery dissipates.[27]

I have explained why there is value in a wrong's constituting a wronging by ascribing a normative interest to human beings. As already observed normative facts in which we have an interest must be social realities (p. 10). For example, we can have an interest in whether a wrong is a wronging, only if its being a wronging would make a difference to our lives of a sort that might affect someone's interests. There may well be wrongings that go unrecognized but there is value in a wrong's being a wronging only once its status as a wronging is socially recognized. Any unrecognized wrongings will have a deontic status that is not worthy of choice and so the existence of such wrongings cannot depend on our interest in their constituting wrongings. The same applies to forgiveness. One has an interest in being able to forgive (to render blame inapt) only where the appropriateness (or otherwise) of blame is a social reality. So I am assuming that where wrongs can be forgiven, their status as wrongs must have been recognized in various ways. Absent such recognition, forgiveness is pointless and so the status of being a wronging is without the relevant value.

12. Wrongings and interests

We are operating on the assumption that the normative significance of deontic notions is to be explained by connecting them to human interests. In this section, I want to return to the general issue of how this connection should be understood. Let's consider in rather more detail the idea from which I distanced myself in the last section that all wronging involves an injury to the interests of the wronged party:

Injury Hypothesis: An act wrongs X in virtue of being an action against some interest of X's (or else the adoption of an attitude wrongs X in virtue of the fact that its adoption is against X's interests).[28]

Two observations. First, acting against someone's interests is not meant to be sufficient to ensure that you wrong them. I act against your interests by outbidding

---

[27] The relevance of the *value* of blame can be brought out by asking why there is no negative counterpart of forgiveness. Should someone do me a series of good turns beyond the call of duty, I can't ensure that praise is an inappropriate response to these acts by 'discounting' them, as I can ensure that blame is an inappropriate response to their wrongings by forgiving them. Why not? One answer relies on the idea that blame is a bad thing in a way that praise is not. The aptness of actual blame may be a matter for regret as the aptness of actual praise is not. Hence we all have a normative interest in being able to render blame inapt that we don't have in being able to render praise inapt. This normative interest in controlling the aptness of blame is distinct from but dependent on our non-normative interest in controlling the probability of blame's occurrence.

[28] The *Injury Hypothesis* as I shall construe it is widely accepted. It is implicit in Raz's interest theory of rights (Raz 1986: 166) and in Scanlon's notion of reasonable rejection (Scanlon 1998: 213–18). See also (Thomson 1990: 222–23), (Mill 1991: 188–90), and many others.

you in the auction for your dream house, or by painting the interior of my house in a colour you find it unpleasant even to imagine but in neither case do I wrong you or anyone else. We are not seeking a sufficient condition for wronging. Rather, the *Injury Hypothesis* proposes a necessary condition for an act (or attitude) to constitute a wronging. Second, the *Injury Hypothesis* is an explanatory hypothesis. It does not claim merely that every wronging of X involves action against some interest of X's. It claims that the latter fact explains the former. And the latter won't explain the fact that ϕ-ing constitutes a wronging unless it also helps to explain the nature and gravity of the wronging it constitutes. In what follows, I shall call interests that might do the job 'significant' interests.

What exactly is it for something to be an action against one's interests? Since I mean to reject the *Injury Hypothesis*, we should construe 'acting against someone's interests' broadly and thereby present the hypothesis in its weakest and most plausible form. For now, we won't allow the notion of a wronging (nor that of appropriate blame) to be used in specifying the interests that a wronging is an action against; we will, for the moment, abjure normative interests. Beyond that, we can be extremely liberal. Action against someone's interests need not amount to inflicting harm on them. Nor should we assume that action against someone's interests makes them worse off. For example, one way of wronging someone is to act against their interests by distributing the products of a co-operative enterprise unfairly. Here the products of the enterprise are benefits, things that my associates have an interest in possessing but their failure to receive these benefits neither harms them nor makes them worse off than they currently are. Rather I am wronging them by failing to give them something they deserve.

It is legitimate to employ the notion of desert here because to say that someone deserves to get something is not yet to say that they would be wronged by not getting it, though it may provide grounds for that conclusion (Feinberg 1970a: 245–6; Scanlon 1998: 196 and 216–18). Sometimes people are entitled to what they don't deserve and they may also deserve things to which they are not entitled (think of inheritance rights). But desert can also serve as the basis for entitlement (awarding the prize at a dog show) and where it does, desert helps to explain why certain deeds constitute wrongings.[29]

Undeserved attitudes can also wrong. Suppose I come to believe, without any great evidence, that my brother drove my father to an early grave. When my brother learns of this belief, he will feel traduced. Perhaps I never express the belief to anyone and he discovers it quite inadvertently by reading my diary. Outrage, indignation, etc. are in order here quite apart from fear of further harm or damage: my brother may feel this way even if we are already estranged. Nor does he think that his being wronged

---

[29] (Rawls 1999: 276) characterizes this as a 'non-moral' sense of desert by which I assume he means that one can fail to give someone what they deserve without wronging them.

depends on his having found out what I think of him (i.e. on the distress that discovery causes). Rather he simply values being regarded as a decent person and the fact that my belief is both ungrounded and against this interest ensures that it wrongs him.

Consistently with the *Injury Hypothesis*, we may even employ the notion of a wronging itself in our account of why certain deeds constitute wrongings provided the wronging mentioned in our *explanandum* is of a different sort from the wronging mentioned in our *explanans* (Scanlon 1998: 214). So, for example, one might maintain that a promisor wrongs a promisee by breaking their promise because the breach harms the promisee's interest in having correct information about what the promisor is going to do *but only given that the promise was not extracted in a way that wronged the promisee* (Scanlon 2003a: 267). This statement remains illuminating even when the italicized phrase is added because the wronging involved in say duress or deception is different from the wronging whose status we are trying to explain (i.e. breach of promise).

According to our liberal interpretation of the *Injury Hypothesis*, all wrongings are against the victim's interests but the way in which they bear on those interests varies from case to case; some involve harm to the wronged, others make the wronged worse off without harming them. And each wronging is a wronging only against assumed background of other wrongs and wrongings. For the sake of giving the *Injury Hypothesis* the weakest possible interpretation, I'll add one further category of wrongs to the list, namely *symbolic wrongs*.[30]

We all have an interest in how others regard us and so can wronged by a bad attitude. At least we have such an interest when the other is a friend, an acquaintance, a colleague, when they are part of our 'social space'. Our life goes worse if such people think badly of us. Perhaps we have a further interest in whether or not this bad attitude is *expressed*. Expression here must be distinguished from communication (Owens 2006). Obviously it may be worse for me if a bad attitude is communicated to me or to others. It might also be worse when a bad attitude gains expression in my antagonist's behaviour even where that expression does not communicate their attitude to me or anyone else. It is my misfortune that my former partner feels such unwarranted hostility towards me. Suppose they go further and cut the eyes out of my photograph (Hursthouse 1991: 59–60). Though no one ever learns of it, their gesture compounds the wrong involved in having the hostile attitude because it constitutes action against an interest of mine. My life goes worse when such antagonism is manifested in this way, whether or not it does any further damage.

---

[30] There is a vast literature on symbolic value (anthropological, psychoanalytic, and so forth) but analytical ethicists have tended to ignore it. One exception is (Nozick 1993: 26–35).

The existence of symbolic wrongs is consistent with the *Injury Hypothesis* since they constitute action against our interest in such bad attitudes remaining unexpressed. These wrongs are real and can be grave. Should an acquaintance respond to news of your fatal illness with laughter, this is a significant matter whether or not you learn of it. On the other hand, if someone responds to the news that I am trapped in a mine shaft with a rescue attempt which they know to be futile, they thereby serve an interest of mine even if I die in ignorance of their gesture. Some will think such concerns rather fetishistic. No matter. I aim to refute the *Injury Hypothesis* and acknowledging interests in expression only makes my task more difficult.

The *Injury Hypothesis* is undermined by the existence of what I call *bare wrongings*, actions that are not wrongings in virtue of their constituting actions against anyone's interests (pp. 15–16). Bare wrongings will appear at regular intervals throughout this book. We'll consider in detail promises from whose breach everyone benefits but the list should also include, for example, a trespass on your property that leaves no trace and forms of disobedience that do nothing but good and even, I'll argue, certain instances of rape. Such wrongings can be grave but none constitute action against the (significant) interests of the wronged.

One might regard these as symbolic wrongs because they express a lack of respect for certain values (e.g. fidelity to promises, the sanctity of property and bodily integrity). But when breach of promise (and so forth) involves bare wronging, it is unclear what interest constitutes the object of one's contempt. To sneer at someone's death or, on the positive side, to engage in an obviously futile attempt to rescue them is to express an attitude to something whose importance is obvious, namely continued survival. To express contempt for someone's interest in survival is to wrong them. But why should breach of promise be expressive of a bad attitude unless there is something bad about failing to do the thing one has promised to do? And why should rape be expressive of a bad attitude unless there is something bad about what you intend to do to the victim?

In Part II, I'll conclude that the existence of bare wrongings is inconsistent with the *Injury Hypothesis* however broadly we construe the notion of 'acting against someone's interest'. I'll also suggest that we are wronged by bare wrongings because we have an interest in being able to ensure that certain deeds constitute wrongings should we so declare. What grounds these bare wrongings is a normative interest, an interest in being able to control the normative situation by declaration. It underlies our need to be able to accept promises, consent to sex, and likely many other things. Once such an interest is acknowledged as a possible ground of a wronging, we must further broaden our conception of how interests ground wrongings. On the *Injury Hypothesis*, one wrongs someone in virtue of acting against their interests but a bare wronging need involve no action against the victim's interests (whether normative or non-normative). The victim can mould their deontic environment by accepting a promise from me whether or not I keep this promise, or by refusing to consent to sex whether or not I go ahead. These wrongings are grounded in an interest which need not be affected by the wronging, namely an interest in its counting as a wronging, a normative interest. Sometimes no significant interest (whether normative or non-normative) is affected by these wrongings in which case the wrong in question is a bare wronging.[31]

There are *interested* and *non-interested* wrongings. In the case of a non-interested wronging, the wronging involves action against a non-normative interest. Such disregard is a wronging regardless of whether there is any habit of recognizing it as blameworthy. What makes it a wrong is the underlying interest it adversely affects and what makes it a wronging of X is the connection (left unspecified) between that disregard and X's interests. To explain why it is a wronging, there is no need to make sense of our choosing to make it a wronging and so no need to suppose that its being a wronging has any value for us (that we have a normative interest in the matter). A wronging can be a wronging whether or not its being a wronging has value. Second, there are interested wrongings. I call both bare wrongings and non-bare wrongings whose existence depends, in part, on our interest in their constituting wrongings *interested wrongings*. Both bare wrongings and the other interested wrongings require that we are in the habit of recognizing them as such. There is no convention-independent wrong of breach of promise nor of disloyalty in friendship. Until suitable habits of recognition are in place, wrongs of this sort do not exist.

For future reference, I'll coin some terminology to describe the various ways in which our interests, both normative and non-normative, might be related to one another. I'll distinguish five possible relationships. First, one interest might be *reducible* to another. For example, normative phenomena might matter to us only as a means to some non-normative end (e.g. social co-ordination). Could every normative interest be reduced to our non-normative interests in this way, we would lack any distinctively normative interests and the notion of a normative interest would be of little theoretical importance.

Second, our interest in ϕ-ing might be distinct from but dependent upon another interest we have in ϕ-ing. For example, an interest in the normative status of ϕ-ing might be distinct from but dependent upon a non-normative interest in whether ϕ-ing will occur. Such a relationship of *direct dependence* very often obtains in regard to our deontic interests.[32] Normally there is value in one's being obliged by friendship to perform a certain act only if this act would do our friend some good. The

---

[31] One might argue that breach of promise and so forth constitutes an expression of contempt for the underlying normative interest and thereby constitutes action against that interest. Perhaps but this isn't why breach of promise wrongs you (p. 148).

[32] Similarly the non-normative interests in expression that ground symbolic value are both distinct from and directly dependent on other non-normative interests, e.g. on our interest in staying alive.

dependence relation here is asymmetrical: it only matters whether one is obliged to perform because it matters whether one performs but one's performance might have value whether or not there was further value in one's being obliged to perform. Even so, our interest in the act's being obligatory here is distinct from (i.e. irreducible to) our interest in whether the act actually occurs. The obligation of friendship is not valuable simply a way of making the friendly act more likely. And it is only in the presence of the normative interest that action against the non-normative interest constitutes a wronging.[33]

Third, our normative interest in ϕ-ing might be distinct from but dependent upon our non-normative interest in φ-ing, an act somehow related to ϕ-ing but not in such a way as to ensure that the occurrence of ϕ-ing was of interest to us. Call this *indirect dependence*. For example, our normative interest in being able to determine whether X's failing to ϕ as promised constitutes a wronging of ourselves might depend not on any interest we have in the occurrence of ϕ but rather on our (non-normative) interest in the occurrence of other acts somehow related to ϕ. Indirect dependence, like direct dependence, is an asymmetrical relation. We arrive at the fourth possibility by removing this asymmetry. Our interests in ϕ and φ are *embedded* when we couldn't have one without the other, when our interest in ϕ depends (directly or indirectly) upon our interest in φ and vice versa.

Our normative interests might be indirectly dependent upon or else embedded in our non-normative interests. Both possibilities make room for the existence of bare wrongings. Both should be contrasted with the final option, that the normative interest which ensures that a given act constitutes a bare wronging is simply *independent* of all our other interests and in particular of our non-normative interests. I shall take up the question of whether the normative interests underlying bare wrongings are dependent on, or embedded in, or else independent of our non-normative interests in Part II (Secs. 28 and 34). For now I want to ask how we should conceive of the relationship between our remissive interests and those interests that ensure that the act in question constitutes a wronging.

As already noted, there is considerable disagreement about the proper scope of forgiveness and the course of these controversies reveals the interests underlying our practice of forgiveness. Arguments about either the aptness or the very possibility of forgiveness tend to focus on the nature and significance of the interests which make the act of ϕ-ing a wronging, on the extent of the perpetrator's responsibility for it, and on the value or disvalue of the feelings of blame and guilt. This indicates that our remissive interest in respect of a certain wrongful act of ϕ-ing is dependent on our interest in ϕ-ing and/or in the reactive attitudes directed at its agent. Were ϕ-ing an object of no interest to us, or were we indifferent to whether people felt guilt or blame

---

[33] Deontic value here is a form of conditional value (p. 19).

about ϕ-ing, we could have no remissive interest in ϕ-ing. But it doesn't follow that our remissive interest here is just an interest in the probability of ϕ's occurrence, or in the probability of our reacting to it with blame and guilt once it does occur. Rather, we have an interest in the aptness of blame and guilt that is irreducible to but dependent on these other concerns.

Our remissive interest in respect of ϕ-ing seems to depend on the other interests we have in ϕ-ing and in reactions to ϕ-ing. So the relationship here is what I just called direct dependence. Note that the interest in ϕ-ing on which our remissive interest depends might be an interest not in ϕ-ing's occurrence but in its normative status. We can forgive wrongings whether they are bare, interested, or non-interested. So the interests in ϕ-ing on which our remissive interest in ϕ-ing depends can be both normative and non-normative. How forgivable a breach of promise is, for instance, may depend on the strength of the underlying authority interest that, together with the character of the promissory practice, determines the gravity of the breach.

In Chapters 1 and 2, we've examined wrongs (and wrongings) and how they render blame apt. In Chapter 3, I shall turn to another deontic phenomenon: obligation. Not all wrongs (or wrongings) involve breach of an obligation because not all wrongs (or wrongings) involve action. In shifting our attention away from blame and onto practical deliberation, consideration of obligation reveals a further source of deontic value.

3

Obligation

Until now, I have identified breaches of obligation as actions that tend to render blame or guilt apt but obligations also help to make sense of what we do. For instance, the fact that I am obliged to meet John at the bus stop ensures that it makes sense for me to be there. A conscientious person, one who takes their obligations seriously, will not just feel guilty if they don't show up; they will be motivated to discharge their obligations.

For the Rationalist my obligation makes sense of my being there by furnishing me with a reason to show up. This reason presents my appearance as desirable in some respect and thereby recommends it. If I'm aware of the reason, that reason will be a factor in my deliberations about whether to show up. Thus, at least in the conscientious person, obligation motivates ϕ-ing by serving as a consideration that recommends ϕ-ing in the subject's deliberations, which counts in favour of the proposition that they ought to ϕ.

Many Rationalists go further. According to what I'll call *Simple Rationalism*, any reason for ϕ-ing counts in favour of ϕ-ing with a certain weight or strength. That having a glass of wine with dinner would be pleasant and make me sociable recommends the wine. That it will disturb my sleep and inhibit this evening's work counts against it. I determine what I ought to do by weighing these considerations and deciding what would be best all things considered. Deliberation about whether to ϕ is a matter of weighing the considerations that count for or against ϕ-ing and thereby determining what would be best all things considered.[1] According to Simple Rationalism, an obligation is just one more reason to be weighed in deliberation.

I have promised you that I'll remain clearheaded this evening. Given this I am obliged not to drink. How should this consideration affect my deliberations? For Davidson, the fact that an action would breach a promise 'is a count against the action, to be weighed along with other reasons for the action' (Davidson 2004: 177). This suggests that obligations are just one more input into the process of determining

---

[1] The model can be elaborated in various ways. For example, one might also reason about whether to deliberate at all, about whether it might not be best in this instance to curtail deliberation but such higher-order reasoning is supposed to share the weighing structure of the lower order deliberation it supplants.

what action would be reasonable or justified all things considered; duties and obligations have no special normative force attached to them and so we can accommodate them within the model of practical deliberation suggested by Simple Rationalism. One can see why Davidson might say this. After all, having carefully considered the matter, I may decide not to keep my promise. Furthermore this may be the right thing to do, the most reasonable course of action available to me in the light of all the relevant factors. Nevertheless Davidson's description seems to miss something important about a promise. The fact that I promised you that I would abstain does not merely recommend not drinking like the prospect of a restless night; it means that this is *demanded* of me.[2]

At this point, we could invoke blame. Perhaps I am obliged not to have a drink with dinner because not drinking would be blameworthy. On what I'll call the *Sanction Theory*, it is the prospect of blame that constitutes the element of demand in obligation. The Sanction Theory purports to explain the phenomenology of demand within the framework of Simple Rationalism but, as we shall see in the next section, it seriously distorts the motivational psychology of the conscientious agent. We can't turn reasons into obligations simply by tacking on blame.

Other Rationalists have proposed that we abandon Simple Rationalism. For them an obligation shapes practical deliberation not by constituting a point in favour of fulfilling it; rather it constrains or limits deliberation. Once you are obliged to do something it is no longer entirely up to you to judge whether doing the required thing would be best all things considered. Hence the phenomenology of demand. I agree that obligation constrains deliberation but I doubt that this fact can be reconciled with Rationalism about Obligation in any of its guises. At least I shall argue this for the case of interested obligations, those forms of obligation that exist because they are good for us, because they are worthy of choice. Interested obligation does not motivate compliance in the conscientious by identifying some good in compliance. Nor does it motivate compliance by constituting a consideration that counts in favour of the proposition that one ought to comply. Obligations are not factors in the practical deliberations of the conscientious agent, they are not reasons for action.

In Chapters 1 and 4, I take my examples of wrongings and obligations mainly from the domain of personal relationships. In the present chapter, I'll focus more on obligations that are the products of promises (and commands) rather than of personal relationships. The latter obligations remain personal in that they are owed to some specific person, a person who would be wronged by breach, but we should bear in mind that there may well be things we are obliged to do even though failing to do them would wrong nobody (pp. 45–6).

---

[2] Many have thought that obligation comes with an imperatival force. When Kant introduced the notion of obligation by distinguishing the *counsels* of reason from the *commands* of reason, he was associating himself with a long philosophical tradition (Kant 1996: 69, 71, and 169).

13. The sanction theory

Those who fail to fulfil their obligations are vulnerable to the reactive attitudes I discussed in Chapter 1. Suppose I breach my promise, then

   (i) blame, indignation, rebuke, or reproach are *prima facie* apt reactions in those who learn of it and resentment in the wronged party (the promisee);

  (ii) guilt or remorse are *prima facie* apt in the wrongdoer.

Can the aptness of such blame reactions account for the special force of demand that attaches to an obligation?

    One way of understanding a demand is as a form of pressure. We speak of people being 'obliged' to do things under various forms of pressure, as when the highwayman obliges me to hand over my money. Suppose blame reactions are construed as penalties, as painful episodes whose undesirability provides their object with an incentive to avoid them. Then we could trace the obligatoriness of certain behaviour to the fact that we sanction it by blaming it. Such an account of obligation requires us to adopt a certain view of blame. For example, if blame reactions were simply negative assessments of those who breach their obligations, blame wouldn't pose much of a threat. Demanding something of someone involves more than simply making it clear that you will think the worse of them if you don't get it. But if, as I argued in Chapter 1, blame is a form of anger, it becomes more plausible to regard blame as a sanction.

    Several authors have adopted the *sanction theory* according to which being under an obligation is a matter of being subject to these forms of social and psychological pressure.[3]

> Morals do not look like obligations to us, that is, do not seem like morals to us—and therefore we can have no sense of duty—unless there exists about us and above us a power which gives them sanction.   (Durkheim 1957: 73)

The sanction theorist need not imagine that the prospect of a sanction is ever the sole reason for discharging a genuine obligation. There is a difference between being 'obliged' to do something by the highwayman and being under a genuine obligation to do it. The sanction theorist can capture this difference by stipulating that we are under an obligation to do something only if there is good reason for us to perform that action independently of the fact that non-performance would be sanctioned (Pufendorf 2003: 44–5) (So, threats and sanctions aside, I have good reason to keep my promise not to drink but no good reason to give the highwayman money.)

---

[3] See (Feinberg 1970a: 6–7), (Mill 1991: 183–4), (Adams 1999: ch. 10), and perhaps Freud (Velleman 2006: 132–42). I leave it open whether motivating compliance is the only function of a sanction. And I express no view about whether the sanction theory constitutes an adequate account of *legal* obligation.

One under an obligation to ϕ can no longer simply settle the case on its merits; rather he must take account of the pressure he is under to decide in favour of ϕ-ing. That pressure influences his decision precisely by providing him with a further reason to fulfil his obligation, a reason independent of the intrinsic desirability of the act he is under an obligation to perform. Though obligations play a distinctive role in our practical deliberation in that obligations are reasons with sanctions attached, on the sanction theory this role can be captured within the model of practical deliberation which I called Simple Rationalism: blame adds weight to reasons of obligation.

The sanction theory enjoys a number of theoretical advantages. First, and most obviously, it differentiates the obligatory from the merely advisable or justifiable (from what we have most reason to do): the latter need not have a sanction attached to it. Second, it allows for genuine obligations to be overridden; even if there is good reason to keep one's promise, the best (the right) thing to do may be to breach the promise and incur the sanction. The sanction theory thereby accommodates an essential feature of the ordinary concept of obligation, namely that obligations can be more or less stringent, i.e. more or less easily overridden.[4] For a sanction theorist, an obligation's stringency reflects the strength of the sanction attached to their breach. Breach of a minor promise should provoke only a mild rebuke and so forth.

Thirdly, the sanction theory can offer to explain the scope of obligation, why obligation falls only on our actions. We can wrong someone in forgetting their birthday or by feeling an anger they don't merit, and in many other ways that don't involve us performing any action. Such errors are apt objects of guilt and blame (p. 41). But neither forgetting nor feeling anger are forms of agency and so, at least in one familiar sense of the word, we cannot be under an *obligation* to recall someone's birthday or to calm down.[5] This is something the Simple Rationalist will struggle to explain. Deliberation about what to believe, desire, and feel involves the weighing of reasons no less than deliberation about what to do. Yet deliberation about what to believe, desire, or feel isn't governed by a sense of being under an obligation to believe or desire certain things or to feel a certain way. Though we can act simply because we are obliged to act, we can't believe, desire, or feel a certain way simply because we are so obliged.

One natural thought here is that action is subject to the will—we can do what we do 'at will'—whilst belief, desire, and emotion are not. Perhaps we can do something simply because we are obliged to do it only when it is the kind of thing we can do 'at

---

[4] I shall distinguish the stringency of a promise from its solemnity. See pp. 161–3 and Sec. 44.

[5] You might be obliged to *do* certain things with a view to ensuring that you recall something or induce certain feelings in yourself (e.g. in the context of friendship or forgiveness) and if you are obliged to succeed here and not just to try then you must actually produce the feelings in question. Such an obligation will shape your *practical* deliberations about how to influence your feelings towards someone but it will not influence how you feel about them directly.

will'. Elsewhere, I have argued that we can do something at will when we can bring it about simply because it strikes us as desirable (Owens 2000: ch. 5). Perhaps only what can be brought about simply because it strikes us as desirable can (also) be brought about simply because we are obliged to bring it about. The sanction theorist can make use of this idea to place a limit on the scope of obligation. Deliberation about what to believe, desire, or feel is in one crucial respect unlike deliberation about what to do. Deliberation about whether to do something is focused on the desirability of that action and the desirability of an action is directly affected by the prospect of sanctions. By contrast, to deliberate about what to believe, desire, or feel is not to deliberate about the desirability of acquiring various beliefs, desires, or feelings, rather it is to deliberate about whether they are accurate (or apt or justified . . .), something not directly affected by any sanctions that might be attached to them. For example, the believer forms a view about what is so by considering evidence for the truth of the belief, not by assessing the costs and benefits of holding that view. So, though it is possible to sanction belief and possible to influence belief by means of such sanctions, sanctions can't be expected to influence us via deliberation about what to believe in the way that sanctions on action can and do. Hence obligations lie on action but not on beliefs, desires, and feelings.

The sanction theory's virtues notwithstanding I doubt we can explain what it is for someone to be obliged to do something by supposing that breach of obligation is *sanctioned* by blame. Any theory of obligation must provide an adequate account of how the recognition of an obligation should motivate compliance with it and the sanction theory fails this test.

What role does an obligation play in the deliberations of a conscientious agent? Recognition of the obligation should suffice, other things being equal, to move the conscientious person into action. A conscientious person is one who fulfils their obligations because they recognize that this is rightly demanded of them.[6] On the sanction theory, to recognize an obligation to keep a promise (say) is to link the non-fulfilment of that promise to certain forms of pressure. This link can be understood in several different ways, all of which misrepresent the motivational psychology of a conscientious agent.

One possibility is that, in recognizing his obligation, the agent comes to think that there is a significant likelihood of suffering an unpleasant reaction should they breach and they give this prospect a suitable weight in their deliberations. It can hardly be denied that this correctly describes the motivational psychology of many. Yet those of us who fit this description are not being moved by the recognition of their obligations as a conscientious agent would. Could we be sure of avoiding the blame (or the guilt)

----

[6] As we shall see, this recognition is usually habitual.

by careful concealment (or psychopharmacology) we would have no special reason to fulfil our obligations.

The sanction theorist may reply by reminding us that there must be reason to discharge a genuine obligation that is independent of the sanction attached to it. This suggests a second possibility. Perhaps the reason that recommends performance of the obligatory act must also be such as to justify the imposition of a sanction on those who don't comply. (After all, unjustified sanctions are often as likely to provoke defiance as compliance.) It follows that if our agent feels that he is under a genuine obligation, he must think of the imposition of a sanction as not just likely but also as justified. But this further stipulation won't solve the problem. A truly conscientious agent should not need the prospect of an actual sanction to move him into action, whether he thinks it would be justified or not.

A third possibility is that, in recognizing an obligation, the conscientious agent considers it right that breach of the obligation be sanctioned, without having any views about how likely that sanction might be. But it remains unclear why thoughts about even hypothetical sanctions should play any role in moving the conscientious person into action.[7] The conscientious agent is not designing a system of incentives for getting either themselves or others to do what they ought to do anyway: they are deciding what to do. In the course of their deliberations about what to do, a Rationalist might expect them to consider at least some of the factors which would also be relevant to working out which behaviour ought to be sanctioned (the seriousness of the interests at stake, etc.) but, if so, they will think of these factors as grounds for compliance, not as grounds for sanctioning non-compliance. Yet a fully conscientious agent can (and on some views must) keep his promise simply because he recognizes that it is *actually* demanded of him and the motivational force of this actual demand cannot be captured by reference to the fittingness of hypothetical sanctions.

Despite its failure, the sanction theory does offer to explain our three features of obligation. Can any other form of Rationalism about Obligation account for these features whilst avoiding the above objection?

14. Scanlon on wrong

How should facts about obligation shape deliberation? In particular, how should a promise shape our thinking about whether to fulfil it? For a Simple Rationalist these are the alternatives: either a promise provides us with a good reason to fulfil it, a

---

[7] In the case of some obligations (e.g. to pay a fair tax), one might feel obliged to fulfil them only where there is a system of sanctions in place to ensure that (enough of) the less conscientious fulfil them also. Still, once the system is up and running, the conscientious citizen would feel obliged to pay even if he alone could evade the sanctions.

reason we ought to weigh in our deliberations, or it provides us with a decisive reason to fulfil it, a reason which ought to conclude our deliberations. Neither option is attractive. People are sometimes justified in breaking their promises so even the conscientious promisor need not regard his commitment as decisive. But nor will he treat his commitment as a mere point in favour of the promised action, on a level with the pain of disappointed expectations or the damage to his reputation for reliability. That would be permissible only if he had expressed an intention without actually committing himself to action. Indeed, people often avoid committing themselves to act precisely so as to remain free to decide the case on its merits.

Some writers sympathetic to Rationalism about Obligation nevertheless reject the Simple Rationalist model of practical deliberation. Scanlon, for instance, draws our attention to the complex structure of theoretical deliberation and suggests that practical deliberation may display a similar complexity. Theoretical deliberation isn't just a matter of weighing the evidence for and against a given proposition p; it also involves working out what counts as good evidence for p and what does not. Similarly, in thinking about whether to take that drink, I must be sensitive not just to how much I would enjoy the drink say but also to whether I should be indulging myself at all on the day of my father's funeral. The fact that the drink would give me pleasure, a consideration which constitutes a good reason to drink in many contexts, may count against drinking it in this one (Scanlon 1998: 50–5).

Scanlon's objection to Simple Rationalism is not meant to tell against Rationalism more generally. Both those considerations that get weighed in practical deliberation and those that determine which considerations ought to be weighed in practical deliberation are tied to facts about what is good or desirable. Scanlon differs from the Simple Rationalist in that he denies that we can determine which considerations should count by weighing anything. I shan't inquire whether the Simple Rationalist could elaborate his model to accommodate all of Scanlon's examples. Instead, I shall ask how this is meant to help with obligation.

While discussing how the notion of wrongness might be accommodated within a Rationalist framework, Scanlon makes the following suggestion:

'being moral' involves seeing certain considerations as providing no justification for action in some situations even though they involve elements which, in other contexts, would be relevant. The fact that it would be slightly inconvenient for me to keep a promise should be excluded as a reason for [not] doing so. Even if I am in great need of money to complete my life project, this gives me no reason to hasten the death of my rich uncle or even to hope that, flourishing and happy at the age of seventy-three, he will soon be felled by a heart attack. Against this, it might be claimed that I do have such reasons and that what happens in these cases is that I conclude that an action (breaking the promise or hiding my uncle's medicine) would be wrong and that the normative consequences of this conclusion then outweigh the very real reasons I have to do it. But this does not seem to me, intuitively, to be correct. It does not seem to be true even of most of us, let alone of a person who was fully moved by moral reasons, that the moral motivation not to act wrongly has to hold in check, by outweighing, all these opposing considerations. It is, phenomenologically, much more plausible to suppose that, certainly for the fully moral person and even for most of us much of the time, these considerations are excluded from consideration well before the stage at which we decide what to do. Being moral involves seeing reason to exclude some considerations from the realm of relevant reasons (under certain conditions) just as it involves reasons for including others. (Scanlon 1998: 156–7)

This line of thought offers us a way out of our difficulties about promising.[8] The fact that a certain action would breach a promise is not just one consideration amongst others to be weighed against the inconvenience of keeping the promise; rather (at least) minor inconveniences altogether lose their justificatory force in the face of a promise. Scanlon thereby gives facts about what we are obliged to do a special role in shaping our deliberations. And he does so without implying that a promise is always a decisive consideration in favour of fulfilment, for the interests of others and even major inconvenience to oneself might still justify breach of the promise. On this view, the special force of demand attaches to a consideration where, and to the extent to which, it excludes other potentially relevant considerations.

For present purposes, I shall take what Scanlon says about his uncle to be correct but when applied to promises, his remarks are rather less convincing. Scanlon tells us that his own need of money is neither a reason for him to kill his uncle *nor* a reason for him to hope that his uncle will die without his intervention. Scanlon says that 'this factor is excluded from consideration well before the stage at which we decide what to do' and 'being moral involves seeing reason to exclude [such] considerations from the realm of relevant reasons'. So it is not just that one should not *act on* this consideration, it is rather that this consideration loses its ability to justify anything at all, including various attitudes to what one must do and to what might happen. Presumably reluctance to refrain from hiding vital medicine and regret that one couldn't are also insupportable.[9]

Promises are different.[10] Suppose that I am running late and to make a midday meeting with you, I must fight my way onto the first train that comes into the station rather than await the pleasantly empty one some way behind it. This is, by most standards, a minor inconvenience and not something that should get me to break a serious promise. Nevertheless, it would be strange if I forced my way onto a packed train without reluctance. Furthermore, as I stand pressed against my fellow passengers, I rue the day I made this promise and I might even wish that the train would break down at the next station, allowing us all to get off, even at the cost of making it

---

[8] (Scanlon 2006) develops this line of thought in more detail. For some related ideas, see (Williams 1985: 185).

[9] We need not read Scanlon as saying that the nephew is *obliged* to avoid these feelings and attitudes, but only that he would be wronging his uncle in having them.

[10] The points that follow apply to other interested obligations, e.g. obligations of friendship (pp. 98–100).

impossible for me to keep my appointment. Here the reasons furnished by the inconvenience are shaping my attitude to what I must do even as I do it. Am I failing to take my promise seriously?

So long as what obliges me to take the train is simply my promise, rather than the further fact that the person I am meeting will suffer serious injury if I don't show up or some such thing, it seems entirely apt for me to regret my incarceration on the train and, if it breaks down at the next station, to feel a certain relief. These attitudes are apt however solemnly I promised to be there. One might doubt this because one thought that a breach of promise is serious only when the breach involves some further injury over and above the breach of a promise. Indeed this is Scanlon's view and perhaps leads him to assimilate the case of a promise to that of the uncle. In Parts II and III, I subject this aspect of Scanlon's view to detailed criticism. Here I'll just observe that many people will (however reluctantly) force themselves to board a crowded train simply because they have made a firm promise and without having any clear idea as to what, if any, further injury might be suffered by the promisee were they 30 minutes late. They'll also feel perfectly entitled to their reluctance, regret, wishes, and so forth.

It seems we can't avoid our dilemma and explain the special normative force that attaches to the promise by supposing that a promise altogether deprives certain considerations favouring the breach of that promise of their normative significance. These considerations live on to justify various attitudes to what one must do. Still the promise might prevent us from treating these considerations as having justificatory force *in our practical deliberations*. A conscientious promisor does not decide what to do by weighing the pain of travelling on the crowded train against the inconvenience that their lateness would cause the promisee. (Were this how you decided to keep your promise, you'd be well advised to keep this to yourself.) I shall argue that this narrower exclusion is just what we need.[11] But before investigating the psychology of conscientious agency any further, let's examine some other forms of constraint on practical deliberation.

15. Policies and habits

Very frequently we decide what to do and intentionally do what we have decided to do without deliberating about whether to do it, and without judging that we ought to do it. For example I might decide to run this morning because I have a policy of running each morning. Or else I might decide to run this morning because I am in

---

[11] Scanlon himself makes a related suggestion in a different context. Discussing a case in which one decides one ought to 'play to win', he says that one's opponent's feelings should be irrelevant to which shot one plays (i.e. to practical deliberation within the game) but are highly relevant to one's hopes and to what one takes pleasure in (Scanlon 1998: 51–2).

the habit of taking a morning run. In neither instance do I run this morning because, having considered the pros and cons, I judge I ought to run this morning. Can the case of running because you are *obliged* to run (perhaps because you have promised) be compared to running out of either policy or habit? In this section, I'll describe the workings of policy and habit whilst in the next, I'll ask whether either of them constitutes a plausible model for conscientious action.

Let's start with policy. A policy of running every lunchtime is adopted when I choose to engage in that pattern of behaviour for reasons that make the whole pattern look good. I might adopt this policy because of the health benefits of regular exercise, or because I generally need a break in the middle of the day. Having adopted the policy of running, the mere fact that I have resolved to run can make sense of my implementing the policy; I need not even raise the question of whether I ought to apply the policy in this particular instance. If one's running as a matter of policy depended on one's continued awareness of the reasons that led one to adopt the policy, policies would be an idle wheel in the motivational economy of the rational agent.

By adopting a policy of running, I can avoid the costs of deliberating each morning about whether to run, of weighing up the pros and cons of running in order to arrive at a judgement about whether to run on that particular day. These costs include the time and energy consumed by any deliberation but also the costs of any errors I'm likely to commit when forced to deliberate in unfavourable circumstances. If I can decide in advance then I can deliberate when I'm calmer, more focused, less tired than perhaps I would be at the time of action. Furthermore, my policy of running may ward off the temptation not to run. When I resolve to do something, I frequently anticipate that I'll be less inclined to do it when the time comes. Lunch looks more and the run rather less inviting as midday approaches. Knowing this, I've resolved to run rather than eat and such resolutions frequently enable people to resist the temptations they are directed against.[12]

Bratman and Holton suggest that a policy performs these psychological functions by preventing reconsideration of the policy and its implementation (Bratman 1987: ch. 5; Holton 2009: 121–5). Were I to reconsider my decision to run each lunchtime I would incur the costs of deliberation and if I reconsider this decision anytime near lunch, my appetite for food will be significantly greater than my appetite for exercise. And here's the thing: *were* I to consider whether to run on this particular morning, I might quite sensibly decide not to run (it's now raining, I've already incurred the costs of deliberation and since I've being running so religiously, whether I go today will make little difference to anything). Nevertheless, I am right not to reconsider. Running today may be rational because non-reconsideration of my decision

---

[12] (Bratman 1987: 2–3) emphasizes the deliberation-saving, (Raz 1999: 71–2) and (Holton 2009: 9–12) the temptation-avoiding functions of policy.

to run is rational even though, were I to reconsider, I would rationally decide not to run.

Bratman (1987: 66) and Holton (2009: 141) both speak of rational 'habits' of non-reconsideration.[13] Neither thinks that the mere fact that I have resolved to run every lunchtime makes my running this particular morning at all desirable. Should the rain cause me to hesitate, I can decide to stick to my policy without considering whether I *ought* to stick to my policy, without considering its merits. Of course I *could* make such a judgement and act on the basis of it. I could contemplate the very considerations outlined above, considerations that count in favour of sticking to one's resolutions: the costs involved and so forth. Against the background of these considerations, the fact that I have resolved to run would be a count in favour of running. But such a procedure is self-defeating since it incurs the costs of deliberation and makes one vulnerable to temptation by reopening the issue of what one ought to do. The special benefits of resolute action are won only if one is not motivated by the prospect of those benefits. To use the jargon I introduced earlier, conforming to these reasons requires that one not comply with them (p. 15).

Of course, it would be foolish to maintain that one should never revise one's policies, or ask oneself whether they should be applied in this instance (Holton 2009: 75). When a tropical storm is in progress, one must reconsider whether to run. But (living in a rainy climate as you do) a summer shower shouldn't lead you to contemplate abandoning your daily run even though the prospect of getting wet is a genuine inconvenience. This is not the kind of reason you should even consider acting on, though regret at the rain and hope that it will stop are perfectly in order. Your policy has an exclusion zone around it, one that rules out consideration of discomfort but not of threats to your safety. Policies exclude a certain range of reasons from our deliberations and should block deliberation altogether in those many instances in which the only reasons recommending breach of policy fall within the excluded range.

Does this model of policy implementation pose a threat to Rationalism? It rules out Simple Rationalism but not its more sophisticated cousins. On the contrary, it seems nicely to integrate the insights of Objective and Subjective Rationalism. The subjective (compliance) aspect is present in that the original choice of policy must be intelligible in virtue of the policy's apparent benefits. (The benefits need not be real for the adoption and maintenance of the policy to be intelligible, provided your belief in them is intelligible). The objective (conformity) aspect is present in that one can intelligibly stick to a policy without being guided either by a continued awareness of

---

[13] I agree that policy implementation involves habits of exclusion. I may nevertheless *choose* to exclude the rain from my deliberations and choose to do so from habit. True, if I need to *deliberate* about whether to exclude the rain from my considerations, I'll lose much of the benefit of so doing. But that shows only that my choice of exclusion need not be a product of deliberation about whether to exclude. Exclusion may be something that I intentionally do, perhaps by reminding myself of my policy.

the reasons which led one to adopt the policy (or by any other reasons) provided that by sticking to one's policy under these conditions one conforms with certain reasons. Those reasons are the very ones I outlined when describing the psychological function of policies. They determine what constitute good 'habits of non-reconsideration'.

But more constraints are needed to arrive at an adequate model of policy implementation. It must be the case that *you would not implement the policy if you judged that the reasons for which you adopted the policy no longer applied*. One need not recall these reasons to intelligibly implement the policy but where one does recall them and where it is clear that they no longer apply, one must reconsider the policy.[14] Should one refuse to reconsider it, carrying on simply as a matter of policy is no longer intelligible. I clearly recall that my policy of going for a run every lunchtime is based on the notion that this will add five years to my life span. Then I learn that running is more likely to cause a seizure. I have now lost my original reason to run and thereby acquired a decisive reason to re-open the issue of whether I should run. My running resolution no longer makes sense of my running. Where I don't realize that the original reasons for the policy no longer apply, it may still be rational to implement it without deliberation; to that extent, policies are a source of rational intelligibility. But where I know that the original reasons have gone, sticking with the policy makes no sense.

The need for this constraint suggests a further point: in characterizing the way policies make sense of action, it isn't enough to allude to the merely instrumental benefits of being disposed to adhere to one's policies (saving on the costs of deliberation and so forth). For example, by adopting the intention of drinking a mild toxin when someone offers you a large reward for adopting such an intention, you acquire a disposition possession of which is highly beneficial, namely the disposition to drink the toxin when the time comes (Kavka 1983). But since the reward is for forming the intention, not for executing it, the benefits of that disposition will make little sense of your manifesting it by drinking the toxin, precisely because you judge that there is no good in actually drinking.

Let us now turn to habitual action, to ϕ-ing from habit (when this includes mental actions like refraining from deliberation). Here are three features of such action:

(1) A habit of ϕ-ing is acquired by choosing to ϕ on a number of occasions.[15]
(2) To ϕ from habit on a given occasion, I must not ϕ because I have on this occasion deliberated about the merits of ϕ-ing.
(3) To ϕ from habit is, normally, to ϕ intentionally.

---

[14] (Bratman 1987: 65) and (Holton 2009: 160) both endorse this principle though Raz appears to reject it (Raz 1999: 197).
[15] To vote Republican out of habit, one must have voted for the Republicans at least once before. Beyond that it is open how much repetition is required for habit formation.

I don't deny that things lacking one or more of these features are standardly called habits but I do wish to distinguish habits as I understand them from other psychological phenomena and, in particular, from automatic movements.

William James suggests that a habit of ϕ-ing is something like a tendency to ϕ which is acquired by ϕ-ing (James 1950: 122) (and this *may* be what Bratman and Holton mean when they speak of 'habits of non-reconsideration'). Jamesian habits need satisfy neither (1) nor (3). To modify an example from O'Shaughnessy, many times a day I move my tongue into a gap in my teeth (O'Shaughnessy 1980: 60–2). This is something I find myself doing. Furthermore, I may be doing this because I did it in the past. In that sense my action is habitual. Nevertheless tongue movements are normally unintentional; usually I'm no more aware of the motion of my tongue than I am of the beating of my heart. And my habit of tongue movement is unlikely to be a product of my previously choosing to move my tongue.

Though the idea that habitual action is automatic has become entrenched amongst philosophers of action,[16] I doubt this reflects the scope of everyday usage even among philosophers. When my department is proposing to appoint one of its own graduates to a permanent position, some might worry that we'll get into the habit of appointing our own students. Their fear is not that the department will appoint insiders without choosing to but rather that we'll cease to consider the merits of outsiders. I don't deny that some non-intentional activity may be called habitual but I do deny that all habits are routines excluding choice and intentionality. Suppose I am in the habit of running every lunchtime yet when I open the front door this morning it is raining steadily. Here, if I run this is because I *chose* to run, the rain notwithstanding. And I decided this not because I decided that the costs of getting wet were outweighed by the benefits of running but rather because I decided (out of habit) to ignore the rain and run without deliberation. Here I chose *what to do* without forming any judgement about what I ought to do (not even the judgement that running is rationally permissible[17]).

True my habit of ϕ-ing *could* be a factor in deliberation about whether to ϕ. I might judge that I have reason to do what I am in the habit of doing because following habit saves time and other scare cognitive resources, etc. But in so far as one thinks in this way one is not acting *out of habit*. One who acts out of habit does not consider the pros and cons of acting out of habit; their habit of ϕ-ing is not treated by them as a

---

[16] For example, 'sometimes, as in the case of habitual action, we act without choice at all' (Holton 2009: 69). Mill furnishes a precedent for my own usage: 'Many indifferent things, which men originally did from a motive of some sort, they continue to do from habit. Sometimes this is done unconsciously, the consciousness coming only after the action: at other times with conscious volition, but volition that has become habitual' (Mill 1991: 173). An older precedent is the Aristotelian notion that virtue is a habit of choice.

[17] I add this to cover cases of ties and incommensurability that the Rationalist should not find problematic (p. 14).

consideration in favour of ϕ-ing which feeds into deliberation about whether to ϕ. To ϕ out of habit may involve choosing to ϕ but it involves no judgement that one ought in this instance to ϕ out of habit.

On the other hand, the fact that one is in the habit of ϕ-ing does not imply that one always ϕs out of habit, i.e. without deliberating about the merits of ϕ-ing. Nor does it imply that it would always be intelligible for one to ϕ out of habit. Habits, like policies, exclude only a certain range of reasons from deliberation. It would be no less strange for you to run through a tropical storm out of habit than to do so as a matter of policy.[18]

To sum up, the similarities between those habits that generate intentional action and policies are striking. Both have generality: I may be either in the habit of going for a daily run or else have a policy of going for a run.[19] Both may involve choice: you can choose to run out of habit or as a matter of policy. Both stem from choice: I adopt the policy of going for a run every morning by choosing to go for a run every morning and I get into the habit of going for a daily run by choosing to go for a run on a certain number of days. Both limit deliberation by excluding certain reasons. Still both the thing chosen and the way reasons support the choice differ markedly in the case of habit.

A policy of running every lunchtime is adopted when I choose to engage in that pattern of behaviour for reasons that make the whole pattern look good. By contrast, the choices that generate my habit of running are decisions to run on particular days and there need be no constant factor here. I choose to run on Monday because the sun is shining and I need some exercise, on Tuesday to distract me from work and because I need some exercise, on Wednesday to get away from a family row and because the sun is shining, etc. And by Friday week I am in the habit of taking a daily run. There is no reason or set of reasons for which I adopted the habit of a daily run: I acquired the habit of running each lunchtime by running for a different reason on each of a sufficiently long series of days.[20] Suppose I now judge that none of these reasons still apply. Mightn't it still make sense for me to run out of habit?

A sophisticated Rationalist may agree that policy differs from habit on this point. One must reconsider a policy if one knows the original reasons for adopting it no longer hold. One might be able think of new reasons for it (e.g. the fact that people

---

[18] Note what we have here is a habit of choice, namely choice of exclusion. When I intentionally run out of habit the rain notwithstanding, I *choose* to exclude the rain from my deliberations and so run in the rain without deliberating about the merits of running in the rain. This exclusionary choice is itself made out of habit and without deliberation.

[19] For some doubts about the parallel on this point, see (Thompson 2008: 158–9).

[20] These reasons might be mutually inconsistent: I might have gone for a walk on Day One to please my parents, on Day Two to defy them.

now expect you to carry out the policy and will suffer if you don't) but adopting the policy on those grounds would involve a new decision, a decision to adopt a different policy with the same content, rather than persistence of the old policy. With habit (the Rationalist may allow) provided one would stop if one judged there was no reason of any sort to go on, one intelligibly acts out of habit. The reasons that led one to acquire the habit in the first place have no special significance.[21] But what if one (rightly) judges that there is nothing desirable about manifesting the habit, about running on this particular day? I shall suggest that ϕ-ing out of habit can still make sense, can still constitute intentional activity, even when ϕ-ing involves neither actual nor apparent conformity with reason.

Some habits are virtues.[22] A *virtue* of ϕ-ing is a habit of ϕ-ing that is valuable for its own sake. Intelligible policy implementation involved the absence of a certain judgement, namely the judgement that the reasons for which one settled on the policy no longer apply. This can't be a condition for the intelligible manifestation of a habit of ϕ-ing but we can require the absence of an analogous judgement, namely the judgement that ϕ-ing is no virtue. I propose that there are at least two ways in which an action can be intentional. First, in virtue of being sensitive to your views about whether there is anything desirable about performing the action. Second, in virtue of being sensitive to your views about whether there is anything desirable about the habit that the action manifests.[23] If a habit of ϕ-ing can be valuable for its own sake then one can judge that there is nothing desirable about ϕ-ing (on this occasion) without judging that ϕ-ing is no virtue, without judging that ϕ-ing (on this occasion) would not manifest an intrinsically desirable habit.[24]

---

[21] The line between policy and habit is frequently blurred by the fact that if I've implemented my policy of running on a sufficient number of occasions, I've probably acquired the habit of running and so, if I carry on running, that action may now be intelligible as a matter of habit. But this will not be so where having had little chance to implement my policy, I have acquired no habit that might make sense of my run. And the underlying contrast remains even where both policy and habit are getting me to run.

[22] Here are two models of virtue. On the *resolution* model, one acquires the virtue of fidelity to promises (for instance) by adopting a policy of keeping promises for the right reasons, whatever they might be (Kant 1996: 258). On the habit model, one can acquire the virtue of fidelity by keeping promises for all sorts of reasons, e.g. love of praise or fear of punishment (Aquinas 1988: 32–3). Still once one has the habit/virtue and acts from virtue then one keeps promises 'for their own sake', provided one is sensitive to whether fidelity is a virtue. It might be that each model of virtue has its place but the habit model suggests a more plausible picture of moral education, of how one inculcates the virtue of fidelity in children for instance.

[23] The man who eats sawdust behaves unintelligibly because he sees no good *either* in the sawdust *or* in being in the habit of eating sawdust (p. 13).

[24] Must a habit be a product of choice in order to make sense of choice? Isn't it sufficient for intelligible agency that you behave in a way you are disposed to behave only so long as you fail to believe the said disposition is a bad thing? True it is too much to require that you positively judge the habit you manifest to be a virtue. Virtue need not involve the thought of itself. But virtuous motivation does require more than the mere absence of such a judgement. Virtue must be a habit of choice. Suppose my face twitches and I could stop if I became convinced that the twitch was unsightly but I never consider the matter. I doubt

My proposal raises at least two questions. First, how can a habit be good except in virtue of the desirability of the actions to which it gives rise? Second, granted that a habit can be good for its own sake, how can your attitude to the value of the habit make sense of an action that manifests the habit when the value of the habit is no guide to the value of the action to be decided upon?

As to the second question, the Rationalist must insist that a habit's being valuable for its own sake isn't directly relevant to the intelligibility of the actions that manifest that habit. No rational agent could get themselves to ϕ simply by reflecting that it is a good thing they are in the habit of ϕ-ing. To make that move, they'd need the further idea that there is something desirable about manifesting the habit of ϕ-ing on this occasion.[25] This would be so if, for instance, one foresaw weakening one's valuable habit of ϕ-ing should one fail to ϕ on this occasion. But where there is nothing desirable about ϕ-ing then, in the eyes of the Rationalist, ϕ-ing will make no sense. The Rationalist is right that no course of practical reasoning could get you to ϕ. If to get yourself to ϕ you must reflect on the merits of ϕ-ing and make a judgement about whether you ought to ϕ, reflection on the value of the habit of ϕ-ing will not help you. But it does not follow that the value of the habit of ϕ-ing cannot make sense of your ϕ-ing. All that follows is that it cannot do so via deliberation about whether you ought to ϕ, via the contemplation of considerations that recommend ϕ-ing.

Why must the intelligibility of habitual agency turn on our attitude to the proposition that the habit we manifest is valuable *for its own sake*? Why won't instrumental value do the job? Why isn't it enough to make sense of my ϕ-ing that I believe (or at least fail to disbelieve) that my habit of ϕ-ing causes some good effects? There is no valid inference from the proposition that there is some good in my habit of ϕ-ing to the proposition that there is any good in my now ϕ-ing but that is equally true whether the value of the habit is instrumental or non-instrumental.

Recall that we are out to make sense of one's ϕ-ing even where one judges that there is nothing desirable about ϕ-ing. Suppose the value of the habit of ϕ-ing is purely instrumental: it derives from the value of its effects, behavioural and otherwise. It is hard to see how that sort of value could render intelligible the manifestation of the disposition where it is known that there are no such desirable effects. Our discussion of policy implementation pointed to the same conclusion. By adopting the intention of drinking a mild toxin when someone offers you a large reward for adopting such an intention, you acquire a highly beneficial disposition, the disposition to drink when the time comes. But the benefits of that disposition make little

---

that means that I am twitching intentionally, for I never intentionally twitched, never saw any point in so doing.

[25] In this connection, see Thompson's discussion of 'transfer principles' (Thompson 2008: 163–74).

sense of your manifesting it by drinking the toxin, precisely because you judge that there is no point in actually drinking it.

Let's turn now to our first question: are any habits valuable for their own sake? No one will deny that a habit can be desirable because it is a cause of actions (or omissions) desirable for their own sake. The habits of exclusion that underwrite the operation of policy possess this sort of instrumental value. But we do think of many habits as having a different kind of value, a value not derived from the value of the actions they motivate.

Suppose that a friend and I are in the habit of going for a run together. This habit may be a valuable aspect of our friendship, part of what makes our friendship good for its own sake. Of course, going for a run is often a good thing and doing good things with your friends is itself a good thing but our shared habit may be good for another reason, namely because it ensures that we are *obliged* to run together. It has become a point of loyalty to turn out for our daily run. Now, as I'll argue in Chapter 4, such bonds of loyalty are not just by-products of the activities that make friendship a good thing; rather they help to make friendship the good that it is. Part of what people are characteristically looking for in a friend is someone who is bound to them and to whom they are bound in various ways. If so, our shared running habit can be good for its own sake because it is a constitutive element of something else that is good for its own sake, namely a shared obligation.

Suppose I'm right about this. At least suppose that some people think about friendship in the way I just described and that their thoughts are not manifestly incoherent. Then we can entertain the following possibility: our running habit ensures that it makes sense for us to run even though there seems to us to be no good in running today, even though it is clear that everyone would benefit from staying home. My present interest is in cases in which the force of habit is the force of obligation but it could appear instead as a personal ideal or as a worthwhile custom whose violation would be regrettable rather than blameworthy. In any case, habit can make sense of behaviour even where you judge that there is nothing desirable about manifesting the habit, provided the habit might be valuable for its own sake. The value of a genuine virtue is not just a reflection of the value of its effects and so its ability to make sense of action is not confined to cases where the action constitutes a valuable effect. The habit need not actually be valuable for its own sake. Provided it is the sort of thing that might be valuable for its own sake and I don't believe otherwise, my habit of running can make sense of my run. And it can make sense of my running even though there is no way of reasoning from the value of the habit to the value of the run.

In the next section, I'll examine in more detail how the value of a habit can render its manifestation intelligible by ensuring that it would be a wrong (i.e. be a breach of an obligation) to behave otherwise. Since obligation involves exclusion, our discussion of the policy and habit should cast light on obligation. Since some such wrongs can be bare, we should look to habit rather than to policy as our model of conscientious agency.[26]

16. The conscientious agent

I offer no account of obligation as such. I am concerned with interested obligation, with obligations that exist because they have been chosen and so with those aspects of obligation that can render it choice-worthy. For brevity's sake I shall omit this qualification from now on. One choice-worthy aspect of obligation, examined in Chapter 1, is that breach would render blame and guilt appropriate. In this chapter, I'm concerned with another choice-worthy aspect of obligation, with how obligation shapes or rather blocks deliberation in the conscientious agent. For us to be under a demand, both aspects must be present: exclusion must make sense *and* blame or guilt must be apt but my focus here is on the deliberative aspect of a demand. The claim that it is actually a good thing for exclusion to make sense will be argued in the next chapter. Here I prepare the ground by asking what it would be for duty to have value.

Unlike me, Raz does offer an account of the nature of obligation and it will help to contrast what he says with my less ambitious treatment. For Raz, an obligation to ϕ furnishes us with a *protected reason* to ϕ (Raz 1999: 178–82). A protected reason to ϕ combines two different sorts of reason: a first-order reason which recommends ϕ-ing and exclusionary reasons which recommend not acting on various reasons which count against ϕ-ing. An exclusionary reason is a second-order reason: a reason not to act on other reasons. Such exclusionary reasons may prevent one's first-order reason to ϕ from being overridden in deliberation by the set of reasons that count against ϕ-ing because it disables some members of that set. Hence they protect this reason. The reason provided by an obligation to ϕ is just such a protected reason. So Raz offers us a two-dimensional theory of obligation: an obligation is a combination of a first-order reason to fulfil the obligation and second-order reasons not to act on various other reasons which recommend not fulfilling it.[27]

Raz illustrates his account of obligation by contrasting *orders* that impose obligations with *requests* that do not. To request is to communicate the intention of hereby giving the recipient a reason to perform the requested action (Raz 1986: 35–6 and Raz 1999: 100–1).[28] Whether or not requests furnish us with reasons Raz is surely right that, if someone asks you to do something, it very often makes sense to comply with

---

[26] I am unsure whether disloyalty in friendship can be a bare wronging but breach of promise (etc.) certainly can.

[27] For a more detailed and more sympathetic examination of Raz's account of obligation, see (Owens 2008).

[28] Raz notes that a request need involve no expression of a desire for the requested action (and one may express a desire for something that one is not prepared to *ask* for).

their request. For example, when a passerby asks me to help them lift a sofa, I might help them simply because they asked me to. Still I am not obliged to help in this way, I am not wronging them if I refuse (Feinberg 1970a: 4–5). Commands are intended to put their recipients under an *obligation* to comply.

What does it mean to say that an order is intended to place the recipient under an obligation? Raz maintains that whilst a request leaves it up to the recipient to decide whether to comply, an order takes that decision out of their hands. The right response to a request is to weigh the reason provided by the request against the other reasons that bear on the case. There is no wrong in giving the request its proper weight and then deciding to refuse it. As Raz says of the petitioner 'if his request is turned down and he is shown that there were sufficiently strong reasons to refuse his request he may be disappointed but he has nothing to complain about' (Raz 1999: 83). Orders are quite different: 'the fundamental point about authority [is that] it removes the decision from one person to another' (Raz 1999: 193). The recipient of a valid order is not meant to judge the case on its merits. In particular he is not meant to treat the order as one factor in his deliberations, to be weighed against other considerations (like the inconvenience to himself of obeying it). Rather the order is there to pre-empt deliberation, to take the decision out of his hands. This is because the order should exclude at least some of the considerations that recommend disobedience from your practical deliberations (without prohibiting you from either hoping that your attempts to obey will be frustrated or groaning under the yoke).

Though greatly indebted to his theory of obligation, I reject Raz's account of the difference between requests and orders. So far as their role in shaping deliberation goes, requests and obligations are on a par. If I am requested to do something, then it makes sense for me to do it without my deliberating about whether to do it, without my weighing the pros and cons. The point of someone's *asking* me to give them a light is precisely to by-pass the issue of the desirability of my giving them a light, is precisely to take the matter our of my hands. And the more urgent the request, the wider the range of countervailing reasons that it makes sense for me to exclude from my deliberations (pp. 228–9). The difference between a request and an order is that you *wrong* the authority by disobeying a valid order but need not wrong the petitioner by refusing a valid request. One often requires no excuse to deflect blame for refusing a request and guilt is as frequently out of place. A power of request exists where it is good thing that the petitioner is able to ensure by declaration alone that it makes sense for someone to fulfil their request without regard to various excluded considerations.[29] And

---

[29] There are many circumstances in which an exercise of the power of request is not a good thing. Here the request may be inappropriate, or blameworthy, or even altogether invalid.

this may be so whether or not it would also be a good thing for blame and guilt to be apt if the request is refused.[30]

I also reject Raz's two-dimensional theory of obligation. Why should we suppose that either requests or obligations make sense of compliance by generating first-order reasons for compliance? How could one create a reason for someone to ϕ simply by communicating the intention of hereby creating such a reason, of hereby making it the case that there is something desirable about ϕ-ing? Obligations make sense of compliance but they do so by blocking deliberation about whether to comply, not by contributing to it. *Obligation is not a factor in deliberation.*[31]

In Raz's view obligation (and policy) shapes deliberation from the inside by contributing both first- and second-order reasons (Raz 1999: 65–73). For one under an obligation to ϕ, there is already a (first-order) count in favour of ϕ-ing. The effect of the (second-order) exclusionary reasons associated with the obligation is not to block deliberation but rather to give this first-order reason for ϕ-ing a more untrammelled influence within deliberation. Our discussion of both policy and habit suggests otherwise. The mere fact that you have a policy or a habit of ϕ-ing constitutes no reason in favour of ϕ-ing. Rather the effect of the habit or the policy is simply to block (or at least constrain) deliberation about whether to ϕ. Should that block be lifted, the agent must consider the matter on its merits. The same is true of obligation.

Obligation clearly differs from policy, habit, and request in that those who violate their obligations are wrongdoers and so vulnerable to guilt and blame. But, as we saw earlier, the aptness of guilt and blame is not a factor in the deliberations of the conscientious agent. Indeed, if we are specifically concerned with what it is to act out of a sense of obligation, habit in particular provides rather a good model of what is going on. Like an obligation to ϕ, a habit of ϕ-ing makes sense of your ϕ-ing without deliberating about the merits of ϕ-ing. And it makes sense of your ϕ-ing without deliberation by making sense of your failing to consider a wide range of reasons that recommend not ϕ-ing. Furthermore, it can make sense of your ϕ-ing in that way whether or not there is anything desirable about your ϕ-ing. For example, where your being in the habit of telling the truth or keeping your promises is a good thing because this habit is part of a social practice of telling the truth or keeping your promises which is itself a good thing, then it makes sense for you to keep this promise or tell this truth out of habit even when only evil will come from so doing, even when to do otherwise would be a bare wronging.

---

[30] True, acceding to a friend's request is often an obligation of friendship. Here it *is* good that blame and guilt be apt, yet the difference between orders and requests remains (p. 100).

[31] Calling an obligation to mind can be a good way of getting yourself to do something it is hard to do (just like rehearsing a long-standing policy). But we shouldn't think that this involves treating either the obligation or the policy as a factor in one's deliberations. Rather in all these cases (obligation included) a potentially valuable block on deliberation momentarily comes your attention, often with the result that the block is reinforced.

In Chapter 1, we saw that it might be good for blame to be an apt reaction to something even if the actual occurrence of that reaction would not be a good thing. Similarly, what is valuable for its own sake need not be individual instances of exclusion but rather a certain normative situation, one in which (a) it makes sense for people to exclude certain reasons from their deliberations and (b) guilt (and perhaps blame) are apt where they fail to do so. Once there is a practice of exclusion, it does make sense for people to exclude certain reasons from their deliberations in that they thereby subscribe to a good practice. And this is so regardless of whether the act of exclusion has any value. A normative interest is an interest in whether the norms are valid (are in force) and not in their observance or non-observance in any particular case.

A final qualification. In Part II, I'll argue that I am bound to keep my promises only if there is practice of taking promises seriously but it can't be that I am bound to keep my promises only if I am personally in the habit of taking promises seriously. So it must make sense for me to conscientiously keep my promises, exclude various factors from my deliberations, and so forth even when I am not personally in the habit of so doing. Here a new source of motivation comes into play: I imitate the behaviour and attitudes of those who are in the habit of being conscientious, people who do possess that virtue. And just as habitual agency counts as intentional only if I don't believe that the habit I manifest has nothing to be said for it, so imitation is intentional on the same condition. More of custom, habit, and imitation in Part II. In the next chapter, I shall consider obligations that do depend, in large part, on the peculiar habits of the individuals to whom they apply, namely the obligations constitutive of involvements like friendship.

I'll conclude this section by drawing out some implications of our account of conscientious agency. Our discussion of the sanction theory highlighted three features of obligation. The first was the difference between the obligatory and the merely reasonable. We have surely succeeded in making that distinction. Second, we have also made room for the possibility that a perfectly genuine obligation might be overridden. Indeed we can see how an obligation can be quite trivial and yet still make a demand on us. It excludes some relevant considerations and thereby shapes deliberation but the zone of exclusion may be tiny (Raz 1977: 223).

The third point to be explained was the fact that obligations lie only on actions and not on belief, desire, and emotion. The sanction theorist accounted for this by observing that obligation could not play the role in deliberation leading to belief, desire, and emotion that it plays in practical deliberation. That's the right sort of answer but our analysis of obligation in terms of exclusion suggests that the answer should take a different form.[32] Every agent must have the capacity to determine

---

[32] My answer gives obligation a wider scope than does the account I earlier attributed to the sanction theorist. On the former, one can be obliged to form a certain intention, whilst on the latter one cannot. See (Owens 2000: chs. 5–7).

which reasons have weight in his practical deliberations and which do not. An agent who lacks this capacity is not fully in control of their practical reasoning. In particular, agents can choose to discount genuine reasons for action when under an obligation. But can we discount genuine reasons when thinking about what to believe or how to feel about things?

I doubt that believers, for example, have a capacity to discount evidence of which they are currently aware in their theoretical deliberations; at least I doubt that they have such a capacity simply in virtue of being rational believers. (Thus it is hard to see how doxastic habits of exclusion could originate in acts of exclusion.) To 'discount' evidence here is not just to decide that it is misleading or unreliable in the light of other, better evidence; it is to put no weight on it regardless of its probative force. Can one choose to discount suspicious entries on one's partner's credit card bill in order to preserve one's belief in their fidelity? Of course people do sometimes discount such evidence because of the obvious benefits of so doing. But such wishful thinking generally is and perhaps must be subterranean. You can't get yourself to discount evidence which you recognize to be perfectly good evidence against your partner simply by reflecting on the benefits of so doing. (At least you can't do this simply in virtue of being a rational believer.) Nor could you get yourself to do this by reflecting on some obligation that you felt not to entertain doubts about your partner's fidelity. You can't decide to give genuine reasons for belief no weight in your theoretical deliberations. Thus there is no such thing as conscientious believing (though one may be conscientious in performing the actions which lead to belief, i.e. in gathering evidence and thinking about it).[33]

17. Blame, exclusion, and conflicts of obligation

Obligation has two aspects: deliberative and reactive. These aspects are distinct but they do interact. In particular, facts about exclusion help to determine how we should react to breach of obligation. I'll illustrate the point with promissory obligation but I'm assuming that the same applies to other forms of interested obligation.

The distinction between excluded and non-excluded reasons is clearly present in everyday thinking about promises. Take a firm but informal promise to accept an academic job in another city. Consideration of subsequent offers is excluded by this however good they are.[34] The Chair would be annoyed if she learnt that you seriously entertained a better offer even though you eventually decided it wasn't quite good enough to justify inconveniencing her department. On the other hand, if in the

---

[33] This asymmetry between belief and action is connected to the asymmetries described in (Owens 2000: ch. 2).

[34] You can ask to be released from the promise or at least deliberate about whether to ask for release but that is a quite different matter.

meantime the promisor's marriage breaks up, it is generally understood that they are entitled to weigh their interest in staying close to their children against those of the new employer and perhaps come down against the move. Similarly, accepting a lunch invitation excludes consideration of subsequent invitations (even from a potential lover whom you have been pursuing for some time) but not of significant domestic crises.[35] You have reason to care for a sick child yourself rather than attend a lunch even if you could ask a neighbour to take care of them instead. This reason may or may not outweigh the lunch but you can at least consider whether it does without being accused of a lack of conscientiousness.

So what determines whether a reason for not fulfilling a promise is excluded by that promise? Is it, for instance, that the non-excluded reasons themselves impose obligations? In fact many non-excluded reasons impose no obligation. You are neither obliged to live five miles away from your children rather than 150 miles nor forbidden to leave your sick child in the neighbour's hands for a few hours. Another attractive but inadequate hypothesis is that non-excluded reasons are more important or weighty than excluded reasons. The prospect of a wonderful job or a lasting romance is pretty important by most standards, yet this sort of reason is excluded whilst many less pressing domestic needs are not. I'll take up the issue of how the zone of exclusion around a promise is to be determined later (Sec. 44). For now, relying on an intuitive sense of its dimensions, let's see what work it can do for us.

The distinction between excluded and non-excluded reasons marks an important difference in how we should react to breach of promise. Suppose there are reasons recommending breach of a promise that are not excluded by that promise. One hackneyed example involves failing to show up to a lunch because you must help a seriously injured agent (Raz 1977: 227). But, as already noted, a perfectly conscientious agent may breach their promise in less dramatic situations. You have reason to care for your sick child yourself and this sort of reason may be weighed in the balance against whatever considerations recommend keeping the lunch date. Suppose the latter are overridden. Your failure to conform to these reasons for lunching should lead you to try to make it up to the host or at least offer him an explanation for your non-attendance (Raz 1999: 188; Raz 2004: 189–93). Yet you don't wrong the promisee simply by breaching your promise. It is inapt to feel guilt about skipping lunch in order to rescue an injured person or care for a sick child; blame would be equally out of place. Here you have *respected* the promise by giving it the right role in your deliberations even though you did not *fulfil* it. The

---

[35] I am overlooking various complexities. What if you could have anticipated the domestic crisis or the end of your marriage when you made the promise? Does that mean you ought to have considered these issues already and are not entitled to do so again? This probably depends on how inevitable it really was.

conscientious person respects their obligations and that need not involve fulfilling them.

A rather different case of non-fulfilment is one in which the considerations which count in favour of keeping a promise are outweighed but only once reasons excluded by the promise are taken into consideration. That person I have been pursuing for some time invites me to lunch on the day I am meant to be seeing you. Both of you are about to leave town for a while. Such a serious romantic prospect means a whole lot more to me than lunch with me means to you. Isn't it reasonable for me to seize what may be my only chance? Aren't I striking a fair balance between your disappointment at not seeing me before you leave town and the possibility of a life-transforming relationship? Yet consideration of such a subsequent invitation is just the sort of thing a promise to have lunch is meant to exclude. Similarly, the benefits which accrue to me from taking a job at a much more prestigious or attractively located department may greatly outweigh the passing disappointment and temporary inconvenience which my backing out causes the less well appointed department. Yet, once more, respect for my promise to take the job is incompatible with even considering a better offer.

Where I fail to respect my promise, I have thereby wronged the promisee. Earlier I argued that expressions of remorse, the seeking and granting of forgiveness, etc. are all in place even where the wrong should be excused (pp. 41–2). The same is true where the wrong is justified. Should I decide to stand you up in favour of my romantic prospect, I will feel guilty, whether or not I think I did the right thing. Similarly if I renege on my acceptance of a much less attractive job. Indeed such feelings are in place whenever one seriously considers breaching a promise for excluded reasons, even if one decides to fulfil it. This is not something a fully conscientious person would have done.

Since my breach of promise is justified, it *would* be inapt for others to blame me purely for breaching promise (setting secondary effects to one side),[36] though it would also make sense for them to do so. Furthermore, it would be reasonable for the promisee to release me from my promise. You are a worse friend if you refuse to let me have lunch with the romantic prospect and then blame me when I go ahead anyway. And it would be obtuse for the Chair to hold me to my acceptance of her offer now I have a much better offer in hand. Still guilt remains apt should release be withheld (or be otherwise unavailable). Like explanation and compensation, guilt has its own significance. It constitutes an *acknowledgement* of the promise. One who takes their promises at all seriously will sometimes fulfil, sometimes respect, and sometimes acknowledge them. Conscientiousness is a matter of degree and only someone who neither respects nor acknowledges promises and fulfils them by

---

[36] This does not apply to cases where I am responsible for getting myself into a situation in which the promise must be breached (pp. 248–9).

accident alone is totally devoid of it. A decent person will at least acknowledge those promises he feels he can't respect.[37]

Can we avoid these various distinctions and complications by refining the content of the promise in question? Most promises, it may be thought, are hedged with tacit qualifications. Perhaps my promise to meet you for lunch, for instance, is really a promise to meet you for lunch provided my child is not sick, a romantic prospect does not appear, and so forth. And perhaps you understand this perfectly well. I agree that the content of a promise may be tacitly qualified in this way and there are lunch promises that should be so understood. Where the promise is so qualified the promise simply does not apply in the envisaged circumstances: blame, guilt, even compensation or explanation would all be out of place. But very often that is not how things are with lunch promises and it isn't how things stand in the above examples in all of which the reactions just mentioned are appropriate. To understand what is going on here, we must do more than refine the content of the promise.

In the examples discussed so far the promise excludes reasons suggesting non-performance. Promises also exclude (inconsistent) obligations in that they forbid us to act on these obligations or to allow them to shape practical deliberation. Our discussion of how excluded reasons can justify breach of promise casts light on clashes of obligation and in particular on conflicting promises. You are invited to sing at two different weddings and accept both invitations: no need to check the dates as one couple need to marry before the summer while the other can't marry until later in the year. Nevertheless, as you could not have anticipated, the weddings are fixed for the same day. An agonizing dilemma results. Sometimes the prior promise takes priority but not always and its mere existence does not invalidate all subsequent promises that turn out to be inconsistent with it (pp. 247–8).[38]

Where the dilemma is real (i.e. where it can't be resolved by reference to non-excluded reasons) a good person must fail to respect *both* promises. You'll decide what to do by weighing various relevant considerations (how well each wedding will go without your singing, how much you'll enjoy the event, etc.). Yet such weighing is exactly what a promise is meant to forestall. As to the lucky couple, if you were to claim that you showed up simply because the promise you made to them was more solemn than that you made to the other couple, they would be content and even sympathetic. If you instead report that you came because, having set both promises aside, you judged that they needed you more, their relief that you've come will be tinged by annoyance that you didn't allow them to make that call. As to the couple

---

[37] It is less clear that becoming a more conscientious person always makes you a better person (Feinberg 1970a: 24).

[38] Here the two obligations are mutually excluding. Other obligations exclude without being themselves excluded. The need to save the child's life means that I shouldn't act on my promise to meet you for lunch but the lunch promise does not exclude the requirement to rescue.

you leave in the lurch, guilt will soon replace the agony of decision even though you have no doubt you made the right choice. One who felt only regret here would not be taking their commitment seriously. Of course, you will try to make it up to the offended party, perhaps by buying them an especially fine wedding gift but such a gift will be well received only if it is taken as an expression of some remorse.

Rationalism about obligation has moved some to deny that obligations can conflict in the way I describe.[39] There are no 'rational dilemmas': you can't find yourself in a situation where whatever you do will be an unreasonable thing to do (unless this alludes to a prior piece of foolishness which got you into the mess). One can deal as reasonably with the most unpalatable alternatives as with the most attractive. In particular one can make a reasonable choice in the case of conflicting promises. Now suppose that being conscientious were a way of being reasonable, that it amounted to dealing reasonably with one's obligations. Then there could be no 'moral dilemmas', i.e. situations in which whatever you do you'll be wronging someone.

If I am correct, one can indeed be subject to conflicting demands. The singer can't avoid wronging at least one of the couples. He acted on a mistaken belief and, we may suppose, the mistake is one that any reasonable person would have made. Some regard reasonable mistakes as excusing the commission of a wrong, others as providing a justification for the wrong.[40] I will remain neutral on the point. Both excuse and justification render blame inapt but neither renders guilt inapt.[41] So either way, we would expect one who finds themselves in the situation just described to feel guilty about doing what they must do (Marcus 1996: 31–3) and perhaps to seek the antidote: forgiveness.

My opponents may allow that feelings (and expressions) of profound regret are apt (and even required) where one promise must be sacrificed to another. Such regret is apt whenever one finds oneself unable to follow the recommendations of a weighty reason. But they deny that these feelings of regret should amount to anything like guilt or remorse. I'll briefly indicate why I think the invocation of regret will not capture the phenomenology of conflicting demands.

Suppose you have a limited quantity of a life-saving drug to distribute amongst a group of sick people with whom you have no prior connection. All are equally deserving but not all can be saved. Here you may bitterly regret having to decide who lives and who dies. You may wish that this task had fallen to someone else or, more charitably, that nature would take the matter out of your hands. Once the

[39] For example, (Thomson 1990: chapter 3), and (Foot 2002: 186). (Kant 1996: 378–9) also denies the possibility of conflicting obligations, though his Rationalism takes a rather different form from that considered here.
[40] For the former view, see (Gardner and Shute 2007: 86); for the latter, see (Baron 2005).
[41] The point is made for excuse on pp. 41–2.

choice is made you will (quite reasonably) feel awful about the resulting deaths, not just *qua* compassionate observer but as someone who brought those deaths about. And these feelings of agent regret will not be assuaged by your confidence that you made the right choice. Still in so far as you are convinced that you did the right thing, you won't think of yourself as having *wronged* those who died: in the circumstances, you were under no obligation to save them. You might well ask them for their understanding but not for their forgiveness.

Now suppose that you actually promised the drug to one group of people. You then discover to your horror that more lives may be saved by giving it to another previously unknown group. Even if you remain convinced that you should save the greater number, doesn't your promise alter how you would think and feel about what you must now do? (After all, using the drug to save other lives is exactly what this promise was meant to exclude.) Wouldn't you vastly prefer that you had not made this promise at all? True, you would still feel awful about having to deny the drug to anybody. But if reallocating the drug involves a breach of promise, there is a further element of distress, one that registers the fact that you are now (albeit justifiably) wronging those people.[42] The distress here is not just a deeper regret, as if you'd discovered that the group who must be sacrificed is larger than you thought. It is, I suggest, of the same sort as that which one feels when one commits an excusable wrong, namely guilt. You might well ask their forgiveness for what you must do.[43]

The suggestion that guilt is an apt reaction to both excusable and justified wronging may make one wonder why most of us would prefer to have a justification for what we are doing rather than a mere excuse. If we are wronging someone and so vulnerable to guilt either way, why should this matter? To see why, note that guilt is not the only aversive reaction to our own wrongdoing. A wrongdoer often feels ashamed of themselves. Rawls contrasts guilt with what he calls 'moral shame':

In one we focus on the infringement of the just claims of others and the injury we have done to them, and on their probable resentment or indignation should they discover our deed. Whereas in the other we are struck by the loss to our self-esteem and our inability to carry out our aims: we sense the diminishment of self from our anxiety about the lesser respect that

---

[42] 'There is no contradiction or other impropriety in saying "I have an obligation to do X, someone has a right to ask me to but I now see that I ought not to do it". It will in painful situations sometimes be the lesser of two moral evils to disregard what really are people's rights and not perform our obligations to them' (Hart 1955: 186).

[43] Foot argues that certain guilt feelings are 'irrational without being discreditable' (Foot 2002: 41). She gives the example of feeling guilty at giving away the possessions of someone lately dead. This strikes me as a rather different sort of case: we would think no worse of someone who felt no *guilt* here whilst a decent person couldn't breach their promise to provide the drug without compunction. For a more convincing description of moral conflict, see (Raz 1986: 405–6).

others may have for us and from our disappointment with ourselves for failing to live up to our ideals.   (Rawls 1999: 391)[44]

Now Rawls may have thought that 'moral shame' is apt whenever guilt is apt, which emotion you happen to feel being determined more by the direction of your attention than the facts of the situation. But, in certain circumstances, guilt is more apt than 'moral shame'.[45] One who has a justification for what they did should be invulnerable to the shame that rightly afflicts those with a mere excuse. An excuse is an allowance made for some form of weakness or malfunction that distorts one's agency. For example, having given the drug to the wrong party because my resolve failed in the face of their heart-rending pleas, I won't just feel guilty, I'll also hold myself in contempt. One who distributes the drug with justification suffers no such irresolution and their self-esteem should remain intact. This contrast is perfectly consistent with the fact that both the justified and the excused should feel guilt for what they have done or had to do.

This chapter considered the deliberative significance of obligation but it did so without seeking to answer the question: when should I discharge my obligations? One needing advice about (for example) which promises they should keep and which they should break will come away disappointed. In what follows I describe in some detail the conditions under which a promise binds but I doubt there is anything general or systematic to be said about the conditions under which one is justified in breaking a valid promise. I claim only this: where a promise binds (a) it makes sense to exclude certain reasons from your deliberations about whether to keep it and (b) blame and guilt are appropriate should you fail to do so.

Our discussion of 'wrong', 'wronging', 'obligation', and 'justification' in the last three chapters fills out the logical geography diagrammed in Figure 2 (p. 20). I'll now use these analytical tools to explain the workings of one kind of social institution, namely valuable relationships like friendship. In Chapter 1, I suggested that part of the value of friendship lies in the fact that it renders blame reactions appropriate. In the next chapter, I'll argue that another aspect of the value of such relationships is that they make sense of certain constraints on our practical deliberations. Obligation, in both its deliberative and sentimental aspects, enriches human life at least in the context of involvements like friendship. Thus, by the end of Part I, it will be clear how such obligations of involvement are rooted in our normative interests, in the fact that such obligations are good for us.

---

[44] (Velleman 2006: 58–61) argues that 'feeling ashamed' so understood must be distinguished from feelings of shame since shame can be felt whether or not there is any prospect of a negative evaluation, e.g. shame at nakedness. See also (Williams 1993: 82).

[45] Compare this: 'When we think ourselves justified in breaking, and indeed morally obliged to break, a promise in order to relieve someone's distress... this leads us to feel, not indeed shame or repentance, but certainly compunction, for behaving as we do' (Ross 1930: 28).

4

Obligation and Involvement

We have obligations to our friends; our friends can make demands on us that strangers cannot. In refusing these demands and breaching those obligations, we wrong our friends and, at the limit, betray the friendship. My friend Tim is moving house. He calls up and asks for my help. By asking this of me, he obliges me to help him and if I decline without good cause he will rightly hold this against me. It would be quite different were Tim a mere colleague or a casual acquaintance. Then I could simply consult my convenience and decline without wronging him.

Many relationships entail obligations, e.g. family, social or political relationships, but one chooses one's friends in a way one need not choose one's parents, lord, or country. I don't deny that there have been, and perhaps still are, forms of friendship which are not chosen. I maintain only that those forms most familiar to us are chosen and that this fact both contributes to the value of and cements the bonds of such friendships. Other chosen relationships also entail obligation: being an acquaintance, being a neighbour, being a guest or a host or even being someone's partner in conversation. I shall call friendship and these other relationships *involvements*. Involvements vary greatly in the behaviour required from those so involved but they have this in common: all are valuable forms of human relationship, all are in some sense chosen and all entail obligation.

Those who write about friendship often emphasize the special concern friends feel for one another and the rich emotional bonds underlying this concern. By classifying friendship with acquaintanceship and so forth, I might be taken to imply that the loving character of friendship has nothing to do with the fact that it entails obligation but this would be a misunderstanding. I shall argue that what underlies the obligation-entailing character of all such involvements is the fact that they serve our deontic interests, our interests in being bound to one another. But the features of a given relationship which create a context in which obligation is good for us will vary from relationship to relationship and it may be that the loving character of at least some forms of friendship is part of what makes it good for us to be bound to such friends.[1]

---

[1] For an expression of skepticism about this, see (Frankfurt 1999: 170–1).

On this point I have an open mind. What I do maintain is that other forms of involvement, though not loving relationships, are nevertheless good for us partly in virtue of their obligation-entailing character.[2] Since I am concerned with how deontic interests generate obligations of involvement, I classify friendship with those other relationships.

18. Friendship and other forms of involvement

In this section, I introduce the notion of an involvement, explaining and defending the idea that involvement entails obligation. Among involvements, friendship has received most of the attention in the philosophical literature but various thinner forms of involvement are hardly less important to human social life.[3] We'll begin by considering acquaintanceship.

Goffman distinguishes two elements in acquaintanceship, mutual cognitive recognition and mutual social recognition (Goffman 1963: ch. 7). To be cognitively acquainted with someone is at least to *know* them—i.e. to be able to recognize them in a range of salient contexts—not just to *know about* them. In that sense I know Tony Blair but he does not know me. Furthermore, neither of us would show any *social* recognition of the other if we passed in the street. I would not greet him and he would not acknowledge my greeting. Nor would he be likely to respond to my conversational overtures. And these behavioural dispositions reflect the normative situation between us. It is inappropriate for us to greet each other and TB need not accede to requests for face time.

Let's suppose we meet at a party and have a long conversation. TB now knows who I am, or at least he ought to know who I am when we bump into each other in the street the very next day. Mutual cognitive recognition is called for and a certain amount of social recognition is now in order. Being well mannered, TB will return my greeting and he won't feel able to refuse me a brief word. This new willingness to engage reflects a change in the normative situation. Today each of us must do various things that only yesterday we need not have done and shouldn't now do what only yesterday we could have done.

Even in this caricature of acquaintanceship, we have the essential elements of a developing involvement. An involvement is a dynamic syndrome of attitudes, of behaviour that expresses (or purports to express) those attitudes and of norms that govern both attitudes and behaviour. In acquaintanceship the crucial (though not the

---

[2] A curve is graceful in the context of a certain portrait and the portrait is beautiful (partly) in virtue of the graceful curve of the lip. Similarly, obligation is valuable in the context of this relationship and the relationship is valuable (partly) in virtue of the obligation.

[3] As Goffman says of conversation, 'It is this spark, not the more obvious kinds of love, that lights up the world' (1963: 113).

only) attitude is mutual recognition. One need have no particular affection for one's acquaintances but one should have some grasp of and willingness to acknowledge their unique position in the social world. Greeting and conversational interaction are expressions of the appropriate recognition.

The same dynamic syndrome of attitude, expressive action, and norm is at work in other involvements. Certain behaviour is valued as an expression of the appropriate attitude, one sensibly valued by the person so recognized. Guests, hosts, neighbours, and conversational partners want to be seen and treated as such. Friendship is perhaps the most difficult case due to its rich emotional underlay and the consequent complexity of the relevant norms. No adequate treatment can be given here but a brief glance reveals similar elements at work. First, a friend should have certain attitudes. For example, where someone is your friend you should hope they get the job they are applying for and wish to have. Second, a friend should express these friendly attitudes in appropriate ways. Attitude, behavioural disposition, and applicable norm all evolve in tandem: people who start to keep in touch, begin to want to keep in touch and come to feel they ought to keep in touch, all of a piece.

I've spoken of the norms constitutive of our involvements as telling us what we *should* do or feel. There are several different ways in which a friendship shapes the normative situation. Where feelings and attitudes are in question, the friendship determines what is appropriate and certain inappropriate attitudes are positively blameworthy. For example, I should hope that my friend will get the job he has applied for. If I feel indifferent then I am, in that respect, not a good friend and I may well be blamed for my indifference, should it be discovered, or feel guilty if not.

Where action is at issue, we also have *obligations* to our friends as when Tim asks me to help him to move. One might doubt that talk of obligation is in place either here or in the case of other involvements. Is TB really *obliged* to return my greeting, is he *wronging* me if he responds with a blank look? As we saw in the last chapter, obligation has two elements. First, Tim and others can blame me if I don't help out: Tim will resent my refusal and others may feel indignant on his behalf. Second, in the context of our friendship, Tim's request for help in moving house constrains my deliberations. Both elements of obligation seem clearly present in acquaintanceship also. TB may regard my approach as placing an unwelcome constraint on him and if he decides to snub me, he should anticipate resentment.

Earlier I claimed that friendly actions are valued as expressions of friendly attitudes. Is this plausible claim really consistent with the idea that we are *obliged* to perform certain actions out of friendship?[4] Stocker asks us to imagine receiving a hospital visit from a friend. Overjoyed to see him 'you are now convinced more

---

[4] Rousseau is suspicious of the whole idea that friendship binds, that friends can make demands on one another (Rousseau 2004: 103–4). For Rousseau, the value of friendly action depends on it being the sincere expression of friendly feeling, feeling which cannot be demanded of us.

than ever that he is a fine fellow and a real friend—taking so much time to cheer you up, traveling all the way across town and so forth'. But the atmosphere sours once he remarks that he came only 'because he thought it was his duty' (Stocker 1976: 462). Stocker infers that Smith's visit is deprived of its value as an expression of friendship by the simple fact that it is made for duty's sake. To Stocker's mind, for Smith's visit to have real value as an expression of friendship it must be that what Smith wants most, what will give Smith most pleasure, is cheering you up (Stocker 1976: 464–5).

Stocker is right that it would be nicer for everyone if Smith had looked forward to his visit with keen anticipation. Nevertheless, can't one value a hospital visit made without great enthusiasm but out of simple loyalty to the friendship? There are any number of reasons why even the best of friends might not derive much pleasure from such a trip. Perhaps it is a huge hassle to get to the hospital and who likes hospitals anyway? Perhaps I am suffering from a disfiguring illness. Of course, Smith shouldn't draw attention to any of this (e.g. by mentioning duty) but he hardly needs to. It will be obvious to all that he is unlikely to enjoy his visit. Couldn't I still derive satisfaction from Smith's coming because he felt he *had* to come, given our friendship? Couldn't I sincerely thank him for taking the *trouble*? Loyalty is one of the attitudes I value in a friend and his visit is an expression of that attitude. The same goes for phone calls on birthdays, etc. Frequently something is lost if these things are done without enthusiasm but such reluctance need not render them worthless as expressions of friendship.

There is an important difference between being under an obligation to do something for a friend and merely having a reason to do it. I may have good reason to buy Tim a very nice birthday present. This would be an appropriate expression of our friendship. But I'm unlikely to feel *obliged* to do this whilst I do feel obliged to accede to his request for help in moving house. One difference here is that I won't be blamed for failing to buy him a nice present but, as we have seen, one can be blamed for feelings that cannot be the subject of obligations or demands (p. 71). So what else is involved in my being subject to the demand that I help Tim move house?

I could invest time and money in securing a magnificent birthday present and, we suppose, this would be a good thing to do (it is Tim's 40th). But unless I feel positively *obliged* to commemorate his 40th with some dramatic gesture, it would make little sense for me to ignore my personal convenience (or that of my family) in deciding what to buy him. I should weigh the various other calls on my time and money against the importance of obtaining this particular present. Tim's request for help in moving house puts me in a rather different position. Tim would be offended if I treated this particular request of his as one consideration to be weighed against *all* the other relevant considerations, even as a weighty consideration. For example, he'd resent it if I took the fact that each member of my family would have to eat dinner later than usual into account when deciding whether to honour his request:

I shouldn't sum up such inconveniences and weigh them against Tim's needs for help.

Two qualifications. First, Tim wouldn't expect that all considerations counting against the fulfilment of his request be excluded from my deliberations. Only some requests impose obligations and those that do exclude only some relevant considerations. The scope of this exclusion will vary from request to request, a function of its urgency, who is making it and so forth. For example, my need to study for an important examination is likely not excluded by Tim's request and should be weighed in the balance. Second, the reasons that are excluded by Tim's request remain genuine reasons and should be treated as such except for the purposes of practical deliberation. I may aptly regret the disruption to the family routine we must endure in order to help Tim move and hope that his move will be called off. The friendly attitude on which Tim relies in making his request is not one of perfect benevolence or heedless self-sacrifice. Rather it is a willingness to discount my convenience in my thinking about whether to comply.

Am I making it sound as if Tim is in a position to *order* me to help him? Wouldn't that be rather presumptuous of him? Let's distinguish commands from demands. Tim is in a position to demand help from me: 'You've *got* to show up' he might say. Here he is demanding my compliance with an obligation created by his request. But the way a request creates an obligation is rather different from the way in which a command creates an obligation. A command imposes an obligation on me by communicating the intention of hereby imposing that obligation. For Tim to do that would indeed be an affront. That is not what he is doing. Rather he is communicating the intention of ensuring that it makes sense for me to exclude various considerations from my deliberations (pp. 86–7) and thereby implying that that is what he wishes me to do. In making his request, Tim may intend to impose an obligation but communicating *this* intention to me would be mere impudence and would do nothing to bind me. It is the nature of our friendship that turns his request into a demand (which makes it the case that I would be wronging him if I declined) not Tim's will.[5]

We've established that friendship and other involvements entail obligations but how exactly do these obligations depend on our choices?

19. Custom, choice, and involvement

People choose their friends. They also choose their guests, their acquaintances, their neighbours, and their conversational partners. Such social roles come with a raft of obligations and the fact that these roles are chosen is crucial to an understanding of

---

[5] While Raz is right to observe that one can't say 'I am asking you to do A and this is binding' he is wrong to infer that requests cannot bind (Raz 1999: 101).

the associated obligations. Equally crucial is the fact that these roles are typically socially defined, that people enter into them by selecting from a menu. I'll comment on the conventional character of obligations of involvement and then turn to their choice-dependence.

Obligations of involvement exist where individuals acquire habits of recognizing those obligations. Such habits might arise between isolated individuals but, in the usual case, these individuals are tapping into established patterns of feeling and behaviour.

The social character of the norms gives them a special significance. For example, the norms of contemporary friendship are dense and subtle. There are rules determining whether someone would be a suitable friend, when a friendship with them has begun or ended, what gifts are appropriate, how much social contact is expected, and many other things. Most of us would find it hard to articulate these rules, though we know well enough when they are violated. I suggest that the density and subtlety of the norms of friendship is part of what makes friendship valuable (and so part of what gives its norms their authority). An idiosyncratic relationship concocted *ex nihilo* by two people even over decades would be thin and unsatisfying by comparison. It would lack the distinctive value of the forms of involvement familiar to us (Raz 1979: 254–5; 1986: 311–13).

Nevertheless, to become someone's friend, it is not enough for me to adhere to a set of social customs. Individual friends select from a menu of friendships—close or distant, work or recreational, long-term or short-term, etc.—and in adopting a particular form of friendship we must specify it further. For example, we must determine how frequently it is appropriate for us to see one another. This is not usually done by explicit or even implicit agreement, by the adoption of a collective policy, but rather by our falling into the habit of interacting in certain ways. For various reasons we find ourselves seeing each other at regular intervals. Some of these reasons may be extraneous to the friendship but once we have gotten into the habit of meeting regularly, this becomes part of what we do as friends. We invent variations on a social theme.

Contrast the way social customs fix the character of obligations of involvement with the rather different role they play in determining the content of our promissory obligations. If I promise to deliver a TV set to your house tomorrow and then leave the set disassembled at the bottom of your drive at midnight, I have not fulfilled my promise though neither of us discussed at exactly what place or time or in exactly what state the TV would be delivered. Here the social context in which we both operate fills out the content of my promise by providing a set of shared understandings as to what would be involved in my doing what I say I am going to do. And it does so even though neither of us invoked it. Nevertheless, should I want the option of delivering the TV set disassembled at midnight and so forth, I can give myself that option by explicit stipulation when I make the promise and you can agree. By promising people can bind themselves to behave in almost any manner towards one another (Sec. 48). Such promissory bonds would not constitute an involvement as I understand it. They would most likely lack the density and subtlety of the bonds of friendship. More importantly, the force of these obligations would derive from the communicated intentions of the parties and not from the supposed value of the relationship they helped to constitute (see below). The ambient social background elucidates the promissory obligations constitutive of this invented relationship by helping us to interpret the relevant promises. By contrast the social context directly constrains the norms constitutive of our particular friendship: it provides a framework we must work within.

Let's now turn to the role of choice in friendship. As I'll argue in more detail below, one does not establish a friendship (as one makes a promise) by communicating the intention of undertaking the obligations of friendship. So in what sense are those obligations chosen? Obligations of involvement possess the second grade of choice-dependence, that is to say these obligations are a foreseen and thus avoidable consequence of what one chooses to do. One need not intend to become someone's friend but if one does become their friend, one does so intentionally. For example, I find myself taking the bus home from work with a certain colleague. Perhaps this colleague isn't someone I would have singled out from the others for special intimacy; friendship with him is not something I'm aiming for. Still in the course of our conversations and exchanges of small favours, a friendship grows up between us. We're not soul mates but we get along well enough and the mere fact of having spent this time together changes things between us. With more or less enthusiasm, I become his friend, i.e. acquire the feelings, attitudes, and vulnerabilities of a friend. This result could have been avoided; I could have taken a less convenient bus or contrived not to meet him at the bus stop and so forth. In deciding not to do these things, I allowed a relationship to develop which imposes various obligations on us both. We are not close but we do now matter to one another and I now owe him various forms of aid and concern that I don't owe the bulk of my colleagues.

I said earlier that involvements such as friendship are dynamic syndromes of norm, attitude, and behaviour. These syndromes are socially defined packages whose elements can't be prised apart at will. To behave in a certain way (e.g. have a series of relaxed chats with someone) is to buy into the package, is to make it the case that further attitudes are apt or inapt and new forms of behaviour permissible or obligatory. The elements of the package are tied together not by contractual commitments but because, as a whole, they constitute a valuable and socially recognized form of human involvement.[6]

---

[6] Take neighbourliness. Perhaps I want to be neighbourly in order to establish a babysitting relationship but the conventions of neighbourliness mean that an exchange of babysitting favours brings with it the obligation to listen patiently to your neighbour's troubles over the garden fence (Raz 1982: 929).

Involvements like friendship are chosen in that one can avoid getting into them. One can also choose whether to end a friendship. Again termination is not (like divorce) an exercise of a normative power. One does not end a friendship by communicating the intention of hereby releasing either oneself or the other party from the obligations of friendship. Rather where a friendship is ended this is because one does what one knows will loosen the bonds of friendship. One decides to take a different bus home. Or, having changed jobs, one simply fails to keep in touch.

The choice-dependence of friendship is a matter of degree. You might be only dimly aware that in riding the bus home with a colleague you are creating various bonds. And even when fully aware of this, the cost of avoiding this result, of getting another bus or of ignoring your colleague's conversational overtures may be rather substantial. The same applies to ending a friendship. Furthermore, a friendship may lapse without either party having decided to end it though they can't both be completely unaware of the fact that their actions and omissions will have this result. The bonds of friendship depend on its being chosen to at least some extent and the closeness of those bonds is a function of how willingly the friendship is created and sustained, amongst other things.

I am not denying that, in certain circumstances, people can be obliged to become friends and, not infrequently, one finds oneself having to continue a friendship because one can't break it off without wronging one's friend (pp. 54–5).[7] Nevertheless, friendship is choice-dependent in that one *can* always decide not to be someone's friend or to break off a friendship and thereby avoid or extinguish the obligations of a friend. Indeed, one can be *obliged* to create or sustain a friendship only because one has a choice about whether to do so. This is consistent with the fact that in declining to be someone's friend one may be wronging the other party and wronging them by violating one of the norms surrounding friendship.

There is more to be said about the choice-dependence of obligations of involvement. In particular, we should ask whether the involvement must be *freely* or *voluntarily* chosen in order to generate obligation. It is a commonplace that a promise extracted by coercion or deception does not bind. Would coercion or deception also sap the bonds of friendship? I shall address this point later (pp. 244–5). Now I want to ask whether we should assimilate obligations of involvement to other forms of choice-dependent obligation or whether the special value of such involvements grounds obligations of involvement in a distinctive fashion.

---

[7] One can also be obliged to make someone a promise even though promissory obligation has an even higher grade of choice-dependence than do obligations of involvement.

20. Friendship and benefaction

Why do we value friendship? A very common thought is that friends have a special concern for each other's well-being, for how well our lives are going. On this view, such benevolent concern plays the role in friendship that recognition plays in acquaintanceship: it is the attitude around which the relationship is constructed. Meeting a request for assistance, showing support and approval of the friend's endeavours, keeping in touch, all further our friend's interests in obvious ways. And there is no mystery about why mutual benefaction should be valued. But if we view friendship in this light, we need a story about how the obligations of friendship arise from the activity of benefaction.

The *benefactor-plus model* sets out to provide it. There are two elements in the story. First, the special concern you have for your friend is assumed to be a concern for things whose value is independent of the value of the friendship. On this view, what makes friendship valuable is one friend's concern for the other friend's friendship-independent interests. It does not follow that our interest in friendship is purely instrumental. We might well value being in a relationship of mutual concern for its own sake. The point is rather that the *content* of the concern we have for one another is independent of the friendship between us.[8]

Rousseau tells us 'benevolence and even friendship are, properly understood, the products of a constant pity fixed on a particular object' (1987: 54). Anyone sympathetic to Rousseau will be inclined to endorse our first assumption. The benevolent person's attention is focused on meeting the needs of the object of their benevolence. Whether or not benevolence is valuable for its own sake, the idea that a given deed would be benevolent is not required to move the benevolent person to perform it (Hume 1978: 478). So if friendship is a form of benevolence, the friend's attention should also be fixed on the needs of their friend. The idea that this deed would be an expression of friendship should not be necessary to move the friend to perform it.

Where does obligation come in here? A second element of the benefactor-plus model explains how the obligations of friendship are grafted onto the activity of benefaction.[9] The bonds of friendship are explained by invoking mechanisms of obligation generation that can be understood quite independently of friendship (or other forms of involvement). We are thereby led to treat obligations of involvement as promissory obligations or as obligations of reciprocation or as obligations of due

---

[8] The benefactor-plus model is a member of a class of views 'which treat friendship as a higher-level intrinsic good, one which involves appropriate attitudes to other previously given goods and evils, or more generally to other previously given normative considerations' (Hurka 2006: 233–4). Hurka gives the example of Moore who thought that the good of friendship consists in admiration of the fine qualities of one's friend (Moore 1959: 203).

[9] Sidgwick treats duties of politeness, neighbourliness, and friendship as modifications of a general duty of benevolence (Sidgwick 1981: Bk III, ch. 4).

care for expectations (i.e. as obligations with either the third or the first grade of choice-dependence). Such obligations are held to be a normal by-product of the creation and development of a friendship and are, to that extent, part of the typical friendship. In this section I shall concentrate on this second element of the benefactor-plus model, on its attempt to reduce obligations of involvement to these other forms of chosen obligation. I'll return to the issue of whether the concerns of a friend are friendship-independent in the next.

Any plausible model of how obligations of friendship arise must acknowledge the crucial importance of what people have already done in generating obligations of friendship. As we have seen, history and practice operate at two levels: the social and the individual. Social practice determines the available forms of friendship, the menu from which individual friends must choose. Particular friendships evolve out of the choices people make and the habits they fall into. Can the benefactor-plus model explain how this happens?

On the benefactor-plus model, the essence of friendship is a special concern for the well-being of one's friend. Acts of friendship are valued as expressions of that concern. That concern may be rooted in further attitudes like shared tastes and values, mutual admiration, or even love but, on the benefactor-plus model, these are relevant to the value of friendship only in so far as they generate this special concern. Normally this concern does not arise at once, nor are we born with it. Tim and I must get to know one another and it is in the process of getting to know one another that the attitudes and feelings characteristic of friendship arise between us. Though this is the usual case, the benefactor-plus model seems to allow for the possibility of friendship without history, of people who possess the required attitudes without having got to know one another. Are such people really subject to the obligations of friendship?

Suppose Tim and I, after consulting the database of 'Make Friends Inc.', take a 'friendship pill' which engenders the required benevolence. When we meet for the first time Tim immediately asks me to help him move house next weekend. Given the efficacy of the pill, I might well be inclined to agree out of concern for Tim. Furthermore, I might well think it appropriate for me to agree. Because Tim and I know that, from now on, we can rely on one another for help and support it may be appropriate for me to offer and for him to accept forms of help that are otherwise inappropriate. If so, the friendship pill has changed the normative situation between us. But why would I think of myself as *obliged* to help Tim? Given that I have never met Tim before I could feel no obligation of *loyalty* to help him out. That requires a certain history.

To my mind obligations of friendship arise once people have *formed the habit* of recognizing such obligations.[10] I am obliged to call Tim on his birthday because we

---

[10] It is worth noting that the habits of recognition constitutive of friendship need not be of long standing to generate obligations. Beyond that I'm very uncertain about the role of time in friendship. Does time

are both in the habit of recognizing such an obligation, that is we have on a sufficient number of occasions manifested a disposition to call one another, or at least to think about whether to call one another in a certain way and to feel a certain way if we don't. Or else we have acquired other habits of recognition that imply this obligation given the social context in which we are both operating. A pill might facilitate our friendship by disposing us to do what is necessary to create the obligations of friendship but no pill can make Tim and I friends. We need time to become friends. The same is true of obligations of involvement quite generally: Tony Blair must already have acknowledged me before he becomes obliged to acknowledge me. Obligations of involvement involve habits of recognition.

An advocate of the benefactor-plus model must agree that obligations of friendship cannot arise from benevolent attitudes alone; history matters. Nevertheless he will maintain that such obligations can arise from the activity of benefaction by means of obligation-generating mechanisms which are not specific to friendship and whose existence does not depend on the relevant individual's habits of recognizing those obligations but which are nevertheless sensitive to the history of the interactions between those they bind. For example, one might hope to reduce obligations of involvement to either (a) promissory obligations or (b) obligations of reciprocation or (c) obligations of due care for expectations. I shall spend the rest of the section exploring and rejecting these lines of thought.

Might the obligations entailed in friendship be promissory obligations, obligations that the friends took on by communicating the intention to undertake these obligations? This suggestion gains purchase from the fact that friends, neighbours, hosts, and guests do make each other promises, some of which are appropriately offered and accepted only within the context of the relevant relationship. Promises between friends can both express the friendship and also deepen it by binding the friends more closely together. So, it might seem, at least some and perhaps all of the obligations constitutive of a particular friendship could be promissory obligations.

To retain its plausibility, this suggestion must be modified to take account of the fact that one cannot take on obligations of *friendship* simply by communicating the intention so to do (Raz 1979: 257): 'Let's be friends' signals the start, not the end of a process (pp. 53–4). We may suppose that promissory obligations count as obligations of friendship only when the promise was given as an expression of a friendly concern, a concern that has evolved over time. Imagine that I am obliged to phone Tim on his birthday because Tim and I have promised to make such calls and since this promise was an expression of our friendly feelings, it is now a part of our particular friendship. Here we have one way in which obligations of friendship might be grafted onto

---

alone deepen the obligations of friendship? We often mention the fact that someone is an 'old friend' to explain why we go out of our way for them but it might not be the sheer passage of time that we have in mind here.

benevolent activity. We see also how obligations of friendship might be extinguished as well as created, how a betrayal of friendship can destroy the relationship it betrays. A friendship might involve an exchange of conditional promises to behave a certain way provided the other party does so too. If so, the effect of any breach of obligation is not just to wrong my friend but also to release them from their obligations. Given that our friendship is, in part, constituted by such obligations, my wrongdoing tends to destroy the very relationship which makes what I am doing wrong.

There is some truth to the promissory model of obligations of friendship. A promise can be an important way of expressing friendship and at least some obligations of friendship do start life as promissory obligations. Nevertheless I doubt that any obligation constitutive of a friendship *is* a promissory obligation. Take my obligation to call Tim on his birthday. If this is something I owe him as a friend then it is not something I owe him in virtue of the fact that I once undertook to call him on his birthday. Perhaps I did, perhaps I didn't but if this obligation is now part of our friendship then it no longer depends on whether such an event occurred, rather it depends on the particular character and value of our friendship. I should be calling Tim out of loyalty to our friendship and not because of some past undertaking. Were the past undertaking completely forgotten, I would still feel obliged to call for just this reason.

It is the same with the related phenomenon of consent, at least where consent is understood as involving the communication of an intention hereby to permit someone to do something. The existence of a close friendship between A and B may consist partly in the following fact, that A can ask B personal questions that a mere stranger could not. It might also be true that, at some less intimate stage in the relationship, B consented to A's asking him personal questions, though this is unusual. In any case what now entitles A to ask such questions is the value of their having the intimate relationship that they do, not the fact of any past consent (Raz 1986: 87–8). Contrast the relationship between B and his divorce lawyer. If B objects to the lawyer asking him personal questions, the lawyer can simply point out that B agreed to have him play a certain role that includes being permitted to ask such questions. The crucial fact here is that B did something—signed a contract or just walked into his office—and thereby communicated the intention of giving the lawyer that role.

Let's turn now to the second proposal. Anyone who thinks of friendship as a form of benevolence might hope to graft the obligations of friendship onto the activity of benefaction by treating them as obligations of reciprocation.[11] Clearly such

---

[11] Rawls suggests that friendship arises when we come across people who manifest a concern for our 'well-being'. Such good will tends to generate 'fellow feeling' and a 'desire to reciprocate' (Rawls 1999: 433). In Rawls's view, these feelings and desires are 'natural' sentiments but once we begin to trust others to act upon such feelings, this gives rise to what Rawls calls a 'morality of association'. We start to feel obliged to

obligations exist and exist between friends. The giving and receiving of gifts and other forms of aid are standard ways of expressing friendship. Since many gifts are appropriate only in the context of friendship, there are obligations of reciprocation that can properly arise only in this context. This is also true of neighbourliness and even acquaintanceship. Nevertheless, I think we should distinguish obligations of reciprocation arising within an involvement from obligations constitutive of the involvement itself. One worry might be that the value of many of the gifts that oil the wheels of friendship is largely or even entirely relationship-dependent (memorabilia, confidences, etc.) but I'll focus on a different point.

I now feel obliged to call Tim on his birthday because Tim calls me on my birthday. Is this an obligation of reciprocation like the obligation I owe to a stranger who finds my wallet and goes to some trouble to return it? When I send the stranger a nice present, I might well think of myself as discharging a debt, a debt of gratitude. Whether or not my gift suffices, there is such a thing as discharging a debt of gratitude and once this is done, this particular connection is at an end. Indeed, the gift may be given on the understanding that there will be no further contact. By contrast, when I ask myself whether I should call Tim on his birthday, I probably won't be thinking of myself as having incurred a debt when I took Tim's call on my birthday, a debt which I can now discharge by calling him. Rather I ought to call Tim because Tim and I have cultivated a friendship that involves calling each other on our birthdays and I should call him out of loyalty to that friendship.[12]

I don't deny that requirements of friendship can begin as obligations of reciprocation. If Tim buys me an especially nice birthday present, one above and beyond the call of duty (but not so much so that I can't accept) I may feel obliged to reciprocate. But, at least on the first occasion, I am likely to think of this reciprocation as having re-established the *status quo*. Neither of us is obliged to persist. However, if Tim goes on doing things above and beyond the call of duty I shall begin to think of reciprocation less as a matter of discharging debts and more as a matter of accepting a deepening of our involvement. The demands of this relationship get their normative force from the value of the relationship they constitute, not from the friendship-independent value of the benefits received within it. Similar points can be made about the decay of friendship. If I don't call Tim on his birthday, Tim may think that he no longer needs to call me on mine but he will think this only if he thinks of my failure (perhaps together with other lapses) as having changed the nature of our relationship. Several missed birthday calls on my part might have precisely this effect but, on the first occasion, it is more likely Tim will think we are still obliged to call each other

further the interests of others as they further our own and at this point our sentiments acquire a 'moral' character (Rawls 1999: 425).

[12] A related point is made by (Kolodny 2010: 183).

out of loyalty to our friendship just as we were before, my failure to call notwithstanding.[13]

The idea that obligations of involvement are obligations of reciprocation owes its plausibility to the fact that these obligations share a reciprocal structure. In each case, I should behave in a certain way towards you because you are behaving in a certain way towards me. But this similarity conceals an important difference. Underlying obligations of reciprocation is the idea of fair play: they have done you a good turn and so you must do the same when the opportunity arises. In explaining why you feel obliged to respond, you'll allude not to the value of some relationship that has grown up between you but rather to that of the benefits received. With obligations of involvement, these exchanges have a further significance: they help to constitute a valuable relationship, a relationship valuable (in part) precisely because it entails such obligations.

What makes it the case that I should scratch your back when you have scratched mine is that (a) back scratching is good for us both, (b) you have scratched my back, and (c) you need your back scratching and I can easily reciprocate. The basis for this obligation of reciprocation lies in a proper regard for our interest in back scratching. We need suppose no further interest in being bound to scratch each other's backs. It *might* be that people have an interest in treating each other fairly, that their own lives go better if they reciprocate and so forth (Scanlon 1998: 161–4). But if so, what makes people's lives go better is the fact that once such interactions must take place for reasons other than fairness, they do so fairly. We don't seek the chance to interact with strangers in order to incur the obligation to treat them in a reasonable fashion. By contrast, I shall argue that we do look for opportunities to forge the bonds of friendship and our lives go better when we succeed.[14]

Finally, let's examine the idea that obligations of involvement are rooted in our obligation to take due care when we cause others to form expectations about how we are going to behave in the future (Sidgwick 1981: 258; Mill 1991: 197). Where obligations of friendship exist, so do expectations of performance. Once Tim and I have made a few birthday calls, or honoured several requests for help we tend to expect each other to do this sort of thing. And if either of us ceases to call or to help out,

---

[13] Appeal to the idea of *loyalty* would be out of place with many involvements other than friendship. Where e.g. acquaintanceship and conversation are in question, breach of their constituent obligations might instead involve a lack of regard for the other parties' status as an acquaintance, conversational partner.

[14] Pursuing the analogy with friendship, Scanlon suggests we might regard the general principles of morality as requirements of a certain 'moral relationship', of a relationship that requires us to treat people fairly or reasonably (Scanlon 2008: 139–41). But even if immoral relationships with perfect strangers make our lives go worse, it does not follow that moral relationships with perfect strangers make our lives go better; we might wish rather that we didn't have to deal with them at all. I doubt that one can *ground* impartial morality in the positive value of some moral relationship in the way obligations of loyalty, etc., are grounded in the positive value of friendship, citizenship, and so forth.

these expectations decay and so do the obligations associated with them. But this does not establish that when one has an obligation of friendship to do these things, this obligation has its source in expectations of performance. Rather, I suggest, obligations of friendship are generated by certain patterns of past behaviour, behaviour that may *also* induce expectations which one must take due care not to disappoint.

Suppose that an obligation arises within friendship because friendly behaviour has altered expectations rather than because it has created bonds of loyalty. Our past behaviour affects what people expect us to do in the future and we can wrong them by carelessly inducing false expectations on which they come to rely. But where this is so, I can often exercise due care for another's expectations simply by giving them a timely warning before their expectations are disappointed whilst I can never discharge an obligation of friendship simply by warning my friend that things are not going to be as he has come to expect. For example, were my obligation to call Tim based solely on expectations induced by my past behaviour, I could often discharge this obligation just by letting Tim know that I won't call. But if I am obliged to call out of friendship, merely informing Tim that I'm not going to will hardly get me off the hook. Thus my obligation to call is clearly distinct from my obligation to take due care of Tim's expectation that I will call.

I have allowed that obligations are very often accompanied by expectations of performance but 'often' is not 'always' and where the connection fails, we have obligations of friendship without any expectation of performance. Suppose Tim has little faith that I will remember his birthday this year since I am currently so distracted. Still, he may rightly resent my not calling even though he had no expectation that I would. What he resents here is my failure to be a good friend, not my failure to attend to his need for correct information about how I shall behave in the future.[15]

In this section, I've argued that obligations of friendship (and of involvement more generally) derive their binding force from the distinctive value of the underlying relationship. What grounds an obligation of involvement is the choice-dependent value of that involvement. The choice in question is obligation-entailing not in virtue of some relationship-independent principle (like that requiring us to keep faith or reciprocate) but because it creates a relationship with a distinctive sort of value.[16]

---

[15] This is a further point of contrast between both obligations of reciprocation and due care for expectations on the one hand and obligations of involvement on the other. Whilst you can unintentionally incur a debt of gratitude or induce an expectation in someone else that you must now fulfil, you can't unintentionally become someone's friend (Sec. 1).

[16] Though no genuine obligations are entailed in relationships devoid of value (like henchmanship) these relationships may still give rise to obligations via the mechanisms discussed in this section. (For example, I doubt that 'immorality' alone invalidates a promise (Sec. 48).) So it may it difficult to extricate yourself from them without wronging the other party.

Now we face the question—what sort of value must a relationship have for it to entail obligations of involvement? I'll first consider another answer and then present my own.

21. Involvements and deontic interests

Scheffler joins me in rejecting the second assumption of the benefactor-plus model. He suggests that valuable interpersonal relationships can entail obligation without need of any further obligation-generating mechanism. For this to happen, he says, the relationship must (like friendship) be valuable for its own sake and must (unlike being someone's fan) be reciprocal (Scheffler 1997: 197–9).[17] But does a relationship entail obligation just in virtue of the fact that it is interpersonal, reciprocal, and has non-instrumental value?

Assuming for a moment (with Scheffler) that obligation is a special type of reason for action, there is the difficulty that only some of the reasons involved in friendship, etc., constitute obligations. I have reason to buy Tim an extra nice birthday present— I would be a better friend if I did—but I am not obliged to buy him such a present. How are we to explain why some of these relationship-dependent reasons constitute obligations while others do not? This reflection should open our eyes to the possibility that two people might be in a relationship whose value made it appropriate for them to behave in certain ways towards the other without entailing obligations. Why couldn't it be good for them to behave in various ways in virtue of their relationship without the other party being able to *demand* this of them and *blame* them if they don't get it?

Rivalry is a reciprocal, non-instrumentally valuable, and indeed chosen interpersonal relationship (p. 29). If I am X's rival, they are my rival. You can't have a rival who doesn't know of or care about your doings. Furthermore, rivalry has non-instrumental value. Having a good rival is often a great thing, e.g. in competitive sport, and not just because it makes you try harder. Healthy rivalry enriches the sport; it would be more boring and so less worthwhile without the rivalry even if people ended up running just as fast or jumping just as high. It makes life for you and the spectators more colourful and enjoyable. Rivalry is the kind of thing one *ought* to enjoy.[18] Finally, you choose your rivals in just the way you choose your friends: you can fall unwillingly into rivalry as you fall unwillingly into friendship but someone can't be your rival against your will any more than they can be your friend against your will.

---

[17] For some related thoughts, see (Scanlon 1998: 88–90) and (Scheffler 2004).

[18] Moralists like Rousseau doubt the value of rivalry (Rousseau 1987: 68, 78) but, as we have seen, Rousseau's reformation of our mores goes well beyond the devaluation of rivalry.

Rivals have reasons that others lack: the fact that X is your rival is a special reason to defeat him. Nevertheless, the practical reasons that are central to and distinctive of rivalry do not amount to obligations. Rivals disappoint when they don't train hard, when they lack daring, when they make stupid, unworthy mistakes, etc. Rivals who do this may well manifest attitudes (sloth, cowardice) that impair the relationship of rivalry. (It is different where rivalry ends because one of the parties ceases to value the sport, like friends drifting apart.) But to do this is not to wrong your rival by breaching some obligation of rivalry (though it may be to breach other obligations). And the apt reaction here (from both you and the spectators) is something like contempt on your part or humiliation on theirs—the counterpart to the respect you have for the good rival.[19] You are expected to feel exasperation at, rather than resentment of, an unworthy rival.[20]

Turning now to my own account of obligations of involvement, I reject not just the second but also the first assumption of the benefactor-plus model, namely the idea that friends are focused on each other's friendship-independent interests. In fact, the concerns of a friend are as much to do with the friendship itself and in particular with the deontic elements of the friendship. Rivals might cultivate their rivalry but not in order to embroil themselves in a network of rights and obligations. I shall suggest that friendship entails rights and obligation because those rights and obligations contribute to the value of friendship. Given that friendship is valuable in this way, it is no surprise that friendship shapes the deontic landscape without the operation of generic obligation-generating mechanisms.

Friends think about their friends, about how to help, advise, or amuse them. Friends also think about their friendship, about how to become someone's friend, about how to cultivate, express, and deepen a friendship they already have and about how to preserve it from various threats. As I noted earlier, friends are often moved to help (or visit or call) by the thought of duty. But friends don't just think about how to fulfil their obligations, they also think about how to create, maintain, and preserve the reciprocal bonds of friendship. Our lives are enriched by the existence of such bonds and impoverished when they disappear. We aim to keep such bonds in existence, to have people whom we are obliged to help (etc.) just as they are obliged to help (etc.) us.

---

[19] The requests of friends can impose obligations. In rivalry there is the challenge. A challenge is a speech act meant to ensure that it makes sense for the rival to take up the challenge simply by communicating the intention to do so. In this respect a challenge is like a request (pp. 85–7). When questions of honour are at stake, challenges can be felt to impose obligations (duelling, etc.) but in an ordinary relationship of rivalry, you are not wronging your rival if you fail to take up their challenge, though you may well incur their contempt or else show your own lack of regard for them as a rival.

[20] Perhaps a good rival has a special obligation to honour his rival, not to run him down, etc. I'm unsure. But these bonds, should they exist, are secondary and peripheral to rivalry. The distinctive value and point of rivalry lies elsewhere.

It is true that obligation tends to be recessive within friendship. When attention shifts to the *demands* of friendship, this is often a sign that something threatens to go wrong. But we shouldn't infer that true friendship is unclouded by thoughts about obligation, that being bound to one's friend is no part of the point of friendship, only an inevitable concomitant. Obligations become salient when there is a chance that they will be breached and breach is sometimes a real possibility even in the best of friendships, for the best of friends have other demands upon them. Should they resolve these conflicts, resist the temptations, and remain loyal we'll think what a good friend they are and not that our relationship falls short of some obligation-free ideal. Obligations are also salient when the bonds become closer or more distant and reflection on such normative change is a part of any living friendship.

This all suggests that human beings have deontic interests, interests in being able to bind themselves and others if they so choose. Among the things that are good for human beings are obligations. We like to be bound to one another and we aim to create and maintain such bonds. Raz agrees that human goods like friendship involve obligations essentially and furthermore he regards this fact as justifying the imposition of the relevant duty:

Friendships ought to be cultivated for their own sake. They are intrinsically valuable. At the same time the relations between friends, the relationship which constitutes friendship, cannot be specified except by reference to the duties of friendship. When this is the case the justifying good is internally related to the duty. The duty is (an element of) a good in itself.   (Raz 1994: 41)

So we now have two claims in play: *first* that, at least in the context of friendship, obligation is good for its own sake and *second* that it is the value of such obligations, the fact that they are good for us, which grounds or justifies them. I'll discuss these two claims in order.

Though he endorses the idea that obligations of friendship are good for us, Raz appears to deny that friends normally aim to create and maintain these bonds:

While promises and other voluntary obligations are undertaken by acts performed in order to undertake an obligation, friendships are not. Their practical consequences, the obligations they give rise to, are by-products of the relationship rather than its point and purpose. People may create a friendship in order to have someone to care for, but not, normally, in order to have an obligation to care for someone.   (Raz 1979: 257–8)

Were friendship a relationship of mutual benefaction Raz's last point would stand. The obligations incurred by those involved in such a relationship—obligations of reciprocation—are a by-product of their interactions; the parties to an exchange of favours are not usually out to create such bonds. They might even regret them. There is nothing amiss in regretting the fact that the only decent way you can get me to babysit for you is to accept the obligation to babysit for me in return. By contrast, to regret the fact that one is obliged to do things for one's friends out of friendship, that one is, for instance, obliged to help them if they need it, would be to fail to value the friendship appropriately.

It is quite usual to want to have a friend partly in order to ensure that there is at least one person in the world whom we *must* stay in touch with, take an interest in, etc., and who *must* stay in touch with us. Raz is right that (unlike promissory obligations) obligations of friendship can be created whether or not we act with the intention of creating them but there is nothing abnormal about acting with the intention of creating such bonds. Indeed, it would be odd to regard the bonds of friendship as undesirable by-products of one's relationship (and equally odd to be indifferent to them).[21] I allowed that people could become friends without choosing the friendship for its own sake but however prevalent such ulterior motives, friendship is intrinsically choice-worthy: it can be, and often is chosen for its own sake. And part of what makes it intrinsically choice-worthy are the bonds of friendship.[22]

To grasp the point, we must note that what is of value here is the purely normative fact that I would be obliged (or permitted) to do certain things out of friendship and not the fact that such an obligation or permission has now been activated (pp. 17–18). Though a good friend, I may well regret that I must neglect my own convenience in order to help Tim out. And I surely will regret it when blame and guilt become appropriate because I don't help him out (however justifiably). What a good friend won't regret is that, in virtue of our friendship, these attitudes and actions would be appropriate under these conditions.[23]

Our discussion has concentrated on the idea that duty is of value within friendship but friendships are constituted by permissions as much as by prohibitions. Only my friends are permitted to ask me personal questions or to call on me outside of working hours. I use the phrase 'deontic interest' to cover our interest in these permissions also. Following Raz again, I maintain that these permissions are also grounded in, or justified by the fact that they are good for us (Raz 1986: 87–8). There is much less inclination to think that permissions are inconsistent with the spirit of

---

[21] It is worth emphasizing the role of forgiveness within friendship. The deontic interest here is not merely an interest in its being the case that if we don't help our friends, we will have done wrong, etc. Rather it is an interest in its being the case that if we don't help our friends we will have wronged *them*. Earlier I suggested that it matters whether one is the wronged party because it matters whether one is in a position to forgive the wrong (Sec. 11). The point is particularly evident when it comes to the wrongs of friendship.

[22] A utilitarian may allow that obligation can be a source of pleasure or else that we can have a non-derivative preference for obligation. On such a view obligation has a value which it derives from the value of certain non-normative phenomena, namely that of pleasure or of preference satisfaction. My thought is that (in certain contexts) obligation as such is good for us and that this fact explains why we want it and/or derive pleasure from it (if we do).

[23] At one point Scanlon tells us that the benefits and the demands of friendships are but 'aspects of a single value' (Scanlon 1998: 162). Perhaps he refrains from drawing the conclusion that the demands of friendships are themselves beneficial because he equates it with the much less plausible claim that the action demanded by friendship is of benefit to the party on whom the demand falls.

friendship: aren't they a sign of the intimacy we prize? Yet they too tend to be recessive. Like the bonds of friendship, we notice them only once some change or threat renders them salient.

Not all aspects of friendship engage our deontic interests. It would not be good for us for our friends to be *obliged* to give us magnificent birthday presents since the special value of this gift would thereby be lost. And both obligation and permission play only a peripheral role in those relationships that fail to engage our deontic interests. We don't form rivalries in order to bind ourselves to rivalry and a relationship of mutual benefaction involves a direct concern with each other's non-normative interests alone. Rousseau's benefactor who gives out of pity aims to serve neither his own nor anyone else's deontic interests. Though (*pace* Rousseau) such a relationship might generate obligations of reciprocation, these obligations stem from the value of the goods and services exchanged. As we have seen, those connected in this way don't value their relationship because it generates these obligations, rather such obligations are a by-product of what is valued. That is why friendship is something other than mutual benefaction.

Relationships involving much less (if any) concern for the non-normative interests of the other party than does friendship also serve our deontic interests. Your partners in conversation are permitted to address you. They are obliged not to terminate the conversation or change the subject abruptly, not to interrupt or hog the limelight and so on. If what I wanted from a conversation was simply to be informed and amused, I could often get that more easily by reading a newspaper or listening to the guy on his cell phone. But there is something I can't get in that way, namely the status, the rights and obligations of a conversational partner. If I never valued that status for its own sake and regretted it whenever in order to be informed or amused I had to give and receive that form of recognition, I would be failing to appreciate a good part of the point of conversation. And if I made that failure obvious, my attitude might well be resented.

I hope we've now established that involvements are good for us in part because they serve our deontic interests. I further claim that the obligations of friendship (and of other involvements) are grounded in their being good for us, in their serving our deontic interests. True, the content of obligations of involvement most often (and perhaps always) reflects the content of our non-normative concerns. One should have a special concern with the non-normative interests of one's friends and, it might be thought, this is enough to explain why one is obliged to help them and so forth. But there is gap here. Even if friendship renders appropriate various forms of help and support, why should it render them obligatory? As we have just seen, there are things it would be good to do for a friend that it would not be good for one to be obliged to do. And the difference between those things and the things one is obliged to do out of friendship is precisely that the latter are things it would be good to be obliged to do out of friendship.

No obligation binds *simply* because it is would be good for us were it to bind us. The mere fact that it would be good for us to be bound to exchange birthday presents does not imply that we are so bound. For that to happen, we must have established a custom of exchanging birthday presents. But custom by itself is equally insufficient (Raz 1986: 310). I may be in the habit of expressing agreement with all the opinions expressed by my hero. That does not mean that I am obliged to endorse his every word, whatever the two of us may think. The relationship of hero worship and its constitutive customs and practices are not valuable for their own sake. Only practices that make our lives go better by satisfying a genuine normative interest can ground obligation (p. 10).

It might be thought that the normative significance of obligations of involvement cannot turn on whether they are good for us. A father fails to keep in touch with his adult children; he liked the children when they were young but has since lost interest in them. Here the father may not be failing in the duties he owes to his children considered simply as persons he brought into the world (they don't especially *need* his help and support) but he probably is failing in the duties of parenthood as generally understood. Wouldn't our dad be better off without this ongoing obligation? Nevertheless, it surely applies to him (the children are rightly resentful of his neglect) and does so regardless of his own inclinations.[24]

This example raises tricky questions about how our attitudes influence what is good for us, questions that have nothing specifically to do with obligation. Perhaps both fatherhood and its constituent obligations are good for this man, his bad attitudes notwithstanding; he just doesn't appreciate what he has got. But I need not insist on this for, even if it is conceded that such obligations are not good for him personally, it may still be the case that they apply to him because in his society there is a practice of keeping in touch with one's adult children, a practice which is good for the normal human being. Our deontic interests are satisfied only given the existence of such customs and practices, and once they do exist, they create obligations that apply to all the members of the relevant social group.

I have not attempted a general account of what one might call *relationship obligations*, of obligations that exist because they are constitutive of valuable relationships. Rather I focused on certain relationships—involvements—whose value depends on their having been chosen and I asked how they entail obligation. My answer has been that obligation is entailed in relationships with choice-dependent value where they serve our deontic interests. But the same explanatory framework may indeed apply to relationships whose value is independent of choice, relationships whose constitutive obligations lack the choice-dependence of obligations of involvement. Some familial or political obligations might exist because it is good for people

---

[24] I'm grateful to Sam Scheffler for raising this sort of example.

to be so obliged regardless of their choices. In the context of certain relationships, obligation is good for us and those relationships might include biological relations like that of child to parent or political relationships, neither of which are chosen. For present purposes, I leave this possibility open.

22. Conclusion to Part I

In Part II, I turn to obligations with the third grade of choice-dependence, those we create by declaration, by communicating the intention of hereby imposing them on ourselves or on others. We have already encountered at least one way in which the normative situation is transformed by declaration, namely when a request is made. To make a request is to exercise a normative power, a power to change the normative situation by declaration. Requests do not impose obligations or create rights *qua* requests but they do change how it makes sense to deliberate. In Parts II and III, we are concerned specifically with the power to affect people's rights and obligations by declaration, by promising, commanding, giving, taking, consenting, refusing, etc.

To understand normative power, we shall need some of the tools already employed. In particular, the idea of a non-rational form of practical intelligibility embodied in habitual and customary activity will be crucial. By invoking this idea can we explain the significance of bare wrongings, of acts that are wrong (and thus worthy of avoidance) even though no human interest is acted against? I shall argue that *all* of the wrongs created by normative power are, at bottom, forms of bare wronging. Thus the intelligibility of all obligations with the third grade of choice-dependence is tied to the intelligibility of this notion. The normative power of request is a power to ensure that it makes some sense for the person addressed to deliberate in a certain way whether or not their so deliberating has any merit. Promise, command, etc. extend this power.

This mention of bare wrongings raises a final issue about involvements: can they entail bare wrongings? Our question is not whether friends can commit bare wrongings, for friends can make each other promises as easily as anyone and they may commit a bare wronging should they breach. Our question is whether the wrongs constitutive of their friendship could be bare wrongings (for as we have seen, wrongs of breach of promise are not constitutive of friendship). On the one hand, the role of social custom in generating the rights and obligations of friendship seems to make room for this possibility. In the last chapter, we saw how the avoidance of bare wronging might be intelligible as a form of habitual action, at least when the relevant habit helps to constitute a valuable social practice (p. 84). Where the obligations of friendship are constituted by habits of feeling and action, the way is open to bare wronging within friendship and other involvements. On the other hand, the close connections between the deontic interests and the non-normative interests served by involvements suggest that this possibility may not be realized.

In the jargon introduced earlier, most of our deontic interests seem directly dependent on non-normative interests (pp. 65–6). You wouldn't wish that someone were obliged to help you unless such help were of some value to you, nor want the standing of a partner in conversation unless the information or amusement the conversation provides were worth having. We should not infer that these obligations are of purely instrumental value, that we value their imposition only in so far as they facilitate the exchange of aid, information, entertainment, etc. On the contrary, they are valuable for their own sake, though we would not value them for their own sake unless we also valued aid, information, etc.[25] For example, where my partner suffers from Alzheimer's, I may feel an obligation of loyalty to care for them myself even if, no longer able to recognize me or anyone else, they'd be better off in a home. Were the provision of medical and personal care the only issue here, I'd feel no compunction about putting them into the home but since it is good that caring for them myself be a point of loyalty between us, my feelings make perfect sense.

Could there be cases where loyalty requires me to do something for my friend, something which will do nobody any good? I'll review some potential instances of bare wrongings within friendship. One sort of example relies on the point that the use of normative power within friendship often has a special significance. We've seen how requests coming from a friend may bind as a similar request coming from a stranger would not. And perhaps this could be so even where failure to comply would be a bare wronging. Tim's request obliged me to help him move house. Could it still bind me even when my 'help' would simply get in Tim's way and even though I can fail to respond because (in his distraction) Tim has forgotten that he asked me? Doesn't his having *asked* me mean that it would be disloyal of me not to agree?

One might respond that, if I am still bound to agree, that is not simply because Tim requested this, rather it is because he made the request with the intention of thereby ensuring that I showed up, because his request expressed his *choice*. By respecting Tim's choice in this matter I might be serving his (non-normative) interest in controlling what happens in a matter of importance to him, whether or not my showing up would actually help (Sec. 32). And since in staying away I would be acting against this interest, it would no longer be a bare wronging. On the other hand, were Tim requesting my help out of politeness and not because he intended me to comply, I would not be wronging him should I fail to do so.

The request example involves the deployment of normative power within friendship. There are other examples of wrongs of disloyalty lacking this feature. For example, one should not confirm an unflattering rumour about one's friend to a third party even where the rumour is perfectly correct and one's confirming it will make no difference to whether he (or anyone else) believes it (Raz 1979: 255). But

---

[25] This is an instance of a phenomenon I identified earlier (p. 19): one thing's value can be conditional on the value of another without being valuable merely as a means to the other.

again there are ways of furnishing this wrong with a base in our non-normative interests. By gratuitously confirming the rumour, you express a lack of regard for your friend's (non-normative) interest in having a good reputation. My life goes worse if people express bad attitudes to my interests, whether or not those attitudes are communicated to me or anyone else (p. 63), and I am especially likely to be wronged by such expression where the person in question is a friend of mine, is someone who should have a special care for my interests. As a result, to confirm an unflattering rumour may be to act against my interests in a way that wrongs me because I am a friend.

I have been unable to arrive at a settled view about whether our deontic interests can generate bare wrongings. But whatever the truth about this, bare wrongings do not play the central role in involvement that they play in the exercise of normative power. Normative powers are machines for manufacturing bare wrongings. Friendship and other involvements are not.

Part II
Powers

5

The Problem with Promising

Hume regarded a part of ordinary morality as deeply problematic in that it is hard to see how it would make any sense for people to conform to its rules, except when extraneous considerations were in play. I'll focus particularly on what Hume says about promising and consent but he sees property rights and political authority as raising essentially the same issues. What makes Hume's discussion so compelling is that it is driven by two widely held assumptions—one about human action, the other about obligation—assumptions which appear to conflict.

The widely held assumption about action (which we encountered in Sec. 3) is that people can do something intentionally only if they can see some point in doing it and that they can see some point in doing it only if doing it strikes them as good or desirable in some respect (whether or not it is either good or desirable on the whole). In Hume's hands this becomes the claim that 'the Will exerts itself when either the good or the absence of the evil may be attained by any action of the mind or body' (Hume 1978: 439). In one form or another this assumption is shared by philosophers who differ dramatically about both what makes it the case that something is good and precisely how facts about what is good enter into our thinking about what to do.

The widely held assumption about obligation comes out in a question Hume puts to himself 'may not the sense of morality or duty produce an action, without any other motive?' (Hume 1978: 479). We often keep a promise or respect someone's property rights out of a sense of obligation and without regard to any good this might do. Nor do we think this unintelligible. Breach of an obligation is something it makes sense to avoid even when it appears to constitute what I call a *bare wronging*. The tension between our two assumptions generates the problem of bare wronging.

23. The problem of bare wronging

Let's begin with property:

Here are two persons who dispute for an estate; of whom one is rich, a fool and a bachelor; the other poor, a man of sense and has a numerous family. The first is my enemy; the second my friend. Whether I be actuated in this affair by a view to public or private interest, by friendship or enmity, I must be induced to do my utmost to procure the estate to the latter. Nor would any consideration of the right and property of the persons be able to restrain me, were I actuated only by natural motives.   (Hume 1978: 532)

Once we eliminate all the extraneous reasons for respecting someone's right to inherit, the admitted fact that it is still *theirs* seems a negligible consideration, one that shouldn't weigh with us *at all* (Foot 1978: 155). Now promise:

I suppose a person to have lent me a sum of money, on condition that it be restored in a few days; and also suppose that, after the expiration of the term agreed on, he demands the sum: I ask, *what reason or motive have I to restore the money?*   (Hume 1978: 479)

For what if he be my enemy, and has given me just cause to hate him? What if he be a vicious man, and deserves the hatred of all mankind? What if he be a miser, and can make no use of what I would deprive him of? What if he be a profligate debauchee, and would rather receive harm than benefit from large possessions? What if I be in necessity, and have urgent motives to acquire something to my family? In all these cases, the original motive to justice would fail; and consequently the justice itself, and along with it all property, right and obligation. (Hume 1978: 482)

Hume concludes:

From all this it follows, that we have naturally no real or universal motive for observing the laws of equity, but the very equity and merit of that observance; and as no action can be equitable or meritorious where it cannot arise from some separate motive, there is here an evident sophistry and reasoning in a circle.   (Hume 1978: 483)

Now Hume finds neither obligation nor the idea of acting on an obligation intrinsically problematic.[1] For example, Hume says that 'A rich man lies under a moral obligation to communicate to those in necessity a share of his superfluities' (Hume 1978: 482). Here it would make perfect sense for the rich man to discharge this obligation for he would thereby serve an obvious human interest. So why do the obligations generated by promising, property, etc., and the wrongings associated with them seem any more problematic to him?

Hume's first assumption is a form of Rationalism about Obligation (Secs. 3 and 16):

Rationalism about Obligation: It makes sense to do something because you are obliged to do it only in so far as (you think that?) the discharge of this obligation would serve some interest.[2]

---

[1] Though he does have his own ideas about what an obligation is. For Hume, one is obliged to do something when (a) the desire not to perform it would displease us and (b) this sentiment is one we would endorse on reflection (Hume 1978: 517).

[2] Hume holds that the value of an action depends on the value of the motives, traits of character, etc., that it manifests (Hume 1978: 477–8). Rationalism might appear inconsistent with such a view since it suggests that whether we should fulfil an obligation is a matter not of whether we should be motivated or disposed to fulfil it but rather of whether we should perform a specific action: the action of discharging it. But Rationalism is in fact consistent with the view that we ought to assess actions by first assessing the

A human interest in something makes sense of our wanting or at least valuing it by ensuring that it is good for someone in some respect. So stated, Hume's first assumption is a close relative of what I called the *Injury Hypothesis*, namely the thought that one wrongs a person only in so far as one acts against some interest of theirs (p. 61). In our discussion of the *Injury Hypothesis*, I emphasized the variety of human interests and so of forms of injury. One may wonder if Hume finds promising, etc. problematic only because he ignores that variety.

Things are worth wanting or valuing for many different reasons. Hume implies that these considerations all, in the end, concern human welfare.[3] The 'natural' obligations he recognizes (to care for one's children, or help the needy, or even return favours rendered (Hume 1978: 478–9)) involve a desire to benefit people, or to avoid harming them. Exactly whom one desires to benefit will depend on other factors—who are your children, who will benefit the most, who has been good to you—but the promotion or protection of someone's welfare is the aim in all cases. Now in the examples Hume describes, nobody will be harmed should he violate his obligations, not Hume, nor the beneficiary, nor the public and some will be much better off; hence the problem of bare wronging.[4]

Is Hume taking too narrow a view of what constitutes a harm or a benefit? Perhaps human beings have an interest in knowing what is going to happen, even if no further interest would be served by this knowledge. One important method of securing such knowledge is by making wills and accepting promises. And if this epistemic interest is what moves people to extract promises and make wills and if it is always damaged whenever a promise is broken or the terms of a will are ignored, perhaps Hume's characters are harmed after all.

It is doubtful whether being given a false belief, even a false belief about a matter of interest to you, is in itself a harm. The Russian anthropologist Maklay promised not to photograph a Malayan servant who feared the loss of his soul and so refrained from doing so even whilst the servant was asleep (Foot 2001: 47–50). Can Maklay have supposed that he would be harming the servant by taking the photograph

---

motives, etc., that give rise to them. What Rationalism does is to place a certain restriction on motives for action, namely that an agent must see some good in what he is doing: motives on which he acts must be to that extent directed at the good. This is a constraint that Hume, for one, clearly accepts.

[3] This welfarist assumption should not be confused with utilitarianism or consequentialism. A strict deontologist might object to coercion or deception on the grounds that they involve unjustified harm.

[4] Raz argues that some rights, e.g. the right to free expression, have great normative significance even though their observance (in any particular case) is of no great importance to most of the individuals who possess them. This is because a society in which freedom of expression prevails is an important common good. Raz suggests that promising may be a similar case (Raz 1986: 247–9 and Raz 1994: 52–5). Let us concede for the sake of argument that there are rights such that (a) X has a right to ϕ because X has an interest in ϕ-ing but where (b) this interest generates a right only because of the wider public interest in their right's being observed. This will not solve our problem, for breach of an individual promise may leave both the normatively significant interests of the promisee and the public's interest in a healthy institution of promising unaffected.

simply because he would be falsifying one of the servant's beliefs about what would happen to him? Even if there is a harm here, this proposal fastens on something inessential to a breach of promise. Hume's debauchee might be so debauched that he neither knows nor cares whether his affairs are being managed honestly or whether promises made to him are being kept. Still he can be wronged in either fashion. A more sober character might forget the promise or have little faith that the promisor will perform without thereby invalidating the promise.[5]

Earlier I suggested that some acts may be right or wrong in virtue of their symbolic value (pp. 63–4). Perhaps I can wrong someone by insulting them and this may be so even though the insult is communicated neither to them nor to anyone else. The insult wrongs them because it expresses an attitude that wrongs them and thereby compounds that very wrong. Might the same be true of a harmless breach of promise? By photographing the Malay, Maklay might be expressing a bad attitude towards him and thereby wrong him even though no damage is done. If so his breach of promise would not be a bare wronging, for it would have a *wrong-base* in one of the Malay's interests, in the fact that his life goes worse when the people around him express bad attitudes towards him.

But why should Maklay's breach of promise express a bad attitude towards the Malay unless there is something bad about his taking the photograph? Suppose A lets B down and C gloats at the harm that A causes B. Here C may be wronging B even if C's gloating does no harm to B because C is expressing a bad attitude to the harm that A has done B. C is expressing contempt for B's interest in this matter. But it is hard to see how Maklay's breach can be wrong in the way that C's gloating is wrong unless we suppose that the Malay has an interest in Maklay's promise being kept. Only then can Maklay be expressing contempt for that interest by breaching.[6]

Can we avoid Hume's problem by instead abandoning the assumption that human beings are concerned only with the promotion of human welfare? As already noted, human beings naturally take an interest in people's getting a fair share, in issues of distributive justice (p. 62). Suppose someone's fair share can be determined without knowing either what they own or the promises that have been made to them. Then our concern with fairness could motivate compliance with an obligation without presupposing a prior concern with what we are obliged to do.

---

[5] There may be cases in which I am not bound by a promise because I am entitled to presume that the promisee would release me from the promise given the chance (e.g. a promise given to someone who is now dead and where, as it turns out, no good would be done by keeping it). The above examples are not of this sort since I am not entitled to presume that either the Malay or the creditor would release me. For further discussion of such presumptions, see pp. 170–1.

[6] Might Makay's breach conventionally signify contempt for the interests that are harmed in other cases in which breach of promise is not a bare wronging (as flag burning signifies hostility to the nation)? I doubt that Maklay's breach has this conventional significance, at least where Maklay is scrupulous about avoiding any harm to the native. And even if it does, Maklay's breach would be wrong regardless.

We do distinguish between whether someone *deserves* to have something (given their talents, efforts, what they have already got, what use they will make of it, and so forth) and whether they are actually entitled to it (Feinberg 1970a: 85–7; Grotius 2005: 88–9). We are able to consider whether it is appropriate or fitting for them to have it apart from whether they have a right to it (e.g. because they own it). It is a moot point whether satisfaction of this interest in fairness makes our lives go better. Perhaps our interactions with others tend to lose their savour unless they are informed by fair principles of co-operation (Scanlon 1998: 161–4). On the other hand, fairness may simply be something in which we reasonably *take* an interest even though its frustration would make our lives no worse. I shall leave these questions open since I doubt that an interest in a fair or reasonable distribution can explain why we take bare wrongings seriously, however that interest is to be understood.

In the cases Hume considers neither of the characters entitled to the money deserve to have it: they have too much already. Other people deserve it more and things would be fairer if they got it. Still these others are not entitled to it and many (Hume included) would think that the money ought to go to those who are entitled to have it. So the problem remains even once we allow that human beings are moved by their fellows' deserts as well as by a desire not to harm them. A bare wronging does no one any significant harm. Nor is it a wronging because it deprives someone of an item they deserve or gives someone an item they don't deserve. A bare wronging has no *wrong-base*, no basis in facts about human interest which might explain why it constitutes a wronging. How, Hume asks, can we take such bare wrongness seriously as a guide to action?

24. The problem of normative power

Certain obligations exist because someone has communicated the intention of hereby imposing that obligation (on themselves or on someone else), because they have exercised a *normative power*.[7] For example, the promisor is obliged to perform because he has communicated the intention of putting himself under an obligation to perform by communicating this very intention. Of course, the promisor will need to do things in order to communicate this intention and, where he succeeds, his obligation will be a product of this (intended) activity (speech or whatever). But unlike, for example, the decision to accept a gift, what makes this activity generate an obligation is the fact that it communicates the choice of this obligation. This is an obligation you *undertake* rather than *incur*.

It is not just promissory obligations that have what I called the third grade of choice-dependence. When I order you to do something I impose an obligation on

---

[7] They may communicate this complex intention without actually having it, so whilst the communication must be intentional, the imposition of the consequent obligation need not be (p. 194).

you by communicating the intention to do exactly that. When I give you my car, I impose on myself and on others an obligation not to use it (without your consent) precisely by communicating the intention of hereby creating such obligations. These examples all involve the exercise of a normative power, of a power to change what people are obliged to do by communicating the intention of so doing. People often exercise such normative powers by employing a conventional form of words: 'I promise' (give, consent, marry, order, etc.) and philosophers have coined the term *'performative'* to pick out this class of verbs. But one can communicate the intention to undertake an obligation without using a dedicated form of speech.

Hume expresses doubts about the intelligibility of this sort of speech act: how can the mere fact that someone has promised, given, ordered, etc. make sense of our behaving differently from the way we would have behaved before? Speaking of promising in the *Treatise*, he says: "'tis one of the most mysterious and incomprehensible operations that can possibly be imagined, and may even be compared to *transubstantiation*, or *holy orders*, where a certain form of words, along with a certain intention, changes entirely the nature of an external object, and even of a human creature' (Hume 1978: 524).[8]

How does Hume's puzzlement about normative power relate to the problem of bare wronging? I suggest that the former derives from the latter. What makes breach of promise a wronging is that someone has communicated the intention that it constitute a wronging. Now something can be declared to be wrongful whether or not it is harmful or constitutes unjust enrichment, or bears on human interests in any other way. So such wrongfulness raises the problem of bare wronging: What sense is there in refraining from doing something simply because it has been *declared* to be wrongful?

Does the problem of normative power have a life of its own? This question is of interest for the following reason. The problem of bare wronging arises only if we impose substantive constraints on what kinds of consideration can make sense of an action along the lines suggested by *Rationalism*. And, as we shall see, constraints that are at all restrictive are also likely to be controversial. Now suppose that there were an independent problem with the idea that promising and other performatives can make something a wronging. That further problem might be one we can't get around simply by expanding our list of the sorts of considerations that can motivate sensible action. But what could this further problem amount to?

It can't be maintained that the communication of an obligation-creating intention makes literally no difference to the situation. After all, this communication is a real event and why shouldn't its occurrence be enough to make sense of our tendency to behave differently in the light of it? Perhaps the point is that the utterance of

---

[8] (Durkheim 1957: 175–95) expounds the problem of normative power in terms very similar to Hume (though without referring to Hume himself), placing great emphasis on the ritual element.

something like 'I promise' can make the right sort of difference only if 'I promise' means something that it can't possibly mean. For example, Anscombe asks rhetorically: 'how on earth can it be the meaning of a sign that by giving it one purports to create a necessity of doing something—a necessity whose source is the sign itself, and whose nature depends on the sign?' (Anscombe 1981: 100). But precisely what prevents one creating a motive, a motive that can make sense of an action, by communicating one's intention so to do to another human being? Any answer must invoke a substantive doctrine about the range of motives capable of making sense of human action. And such a doctrine will render promising problematic only in so far as it makes breach of promise look like a bare wronging.

It may be objected that the wrong of breach of promise is never created *simply* by declaration. All sorts of conditions need to be satisfied for a promise to bind: the declaration must have been made by a competent party, not acting under duress nor the victim of a trick; the action promised must be feasible and, some reckon, morally permissible also. None of this resolves Hume's difficulty for each of these conditions may be satisfied without ensuring that breach of promise is anything other than a bare wronging and this is so because mere declaration plays a crucial role in creating that wronging. True a promise must be intelligibly offered and/or accepted but the motives of the parties here might either be independent of the content of the promise (you accept a promise out of politeness) or else have no connection with the real situation (the Malay).

Most breaches of promise are not bare wrongings because most promises encourage some sort of reliance on (or at least expectation of) their fulfilment. Nevertheless, if my discussion is along the right lines, the atypical promise whose breach does no harm is in fact the central case of promising. Most frequently the wrong of breach of promise, the wronging created by declaration, involves various other wrongings. Because promisors generally think that it is wrong to breach a promise, their promises tend to generate expectations of performance and this fact tends to make breach of promise wrong in other ways. To appreciate what worried Hume about promising we must pare off these secondary wrongings. We must focus our attention on the primary wrong, on *pure* cases of breach of promise, where breach of the promissory obligation is the only wrong done.

I'll assume that Hume's puzzlement about promise derives from his commitment to something like *Rationalism*. That is what generates the problem of bare wronging and so the problem of normative power. Can these problems be solved without abandoning *Rationalism*?

25. Practice theories: Hume and Rawls

Hume thinks he can identify a human interest which makes sense of our inclination to keep our promises, respect property rights, and so forth, namely our interest in social co-ordination, in our knowing what each of us is going to do so that we can co-ordinate our activities. Few would deny that we have such an interest and that it makes sense to act on it. How is this interest threatened in Hume's examples?

The problem of bare wronging is posed by cases in which nobody will benefit from an individual promise's being kept, e.g. from a debt's being paid. The people who need the money lose it, and those who acquire it don't benefit from having it, etc. But, Hume will say, we are in danger of focusing too closely on the individual case. We all have an interest in being able to rely on the promises others make to us and in being able to make promises to them on which they can rely. This interest is served by everyone's firm adherence to a policy of keeping promises. It is not well served if we all retain the option of breaking our promises should we judge that the interests of the individuals involved would be furthered by breach of a particular promise. To give others the assurance they need if we are to co-operate, our promise must be more than an expression of our present view of what future action would be best.

If Hume is correct, the wrongings he considers are not so bare after all. When I refuse to repay my debt as promised on the grounds that everyone is better off if I keep the money, I undermine a valuable social practice and thereby harm everyone who has an interest in the maintenance of that practice. How exactly is the practice undermined? Considering a case in which there is no apparent good in adhering to a rule of justice, Hume comments: 'Taking any single act, my justice may be pernicious in every respect; and 'tis only upon the supposition, that others are to imitate my example, that I can be induced to embrace that virtue' (Hume 1978: 498). By breaching my promise, I cause others not to keep promises where they judge it would be best not to keep these promises and so we are all led not to rely on promises. This supposition can get me to keep my promise even where there is no further good in it.

Hume's is often called a *practice* theory of promissory obligation in that he thinks that the wrong involved in breach of promise can be understood only by reference to the existence of a social practice of making and keeping promises. I agree with Hume that promises don't bind unless people actually treat them as binding but I reject his other claims. I contend that the function of a promise can't be to serve our interest in social co-ordination and I suspect that to identify the true function of a promise, we must relax the constraint Rationalism places on compliance with an obligation. But before broaching those more general concerns I want to examine the two leading practice theories of promissory obligation—those of Hume and Rawls—in detail and note some of the problems which they encounter and which a better version of the theory must avoid.

The practice theory in all its guises faces *Prichard's Problem* (Prichard 1968: 173–9). Let us allow that, once the practice of making and adhering to promises somehow gets going, we all have an interest in maintaining and preserving it. That does not explain how the practice could possibly arise amongst normal human agents, how it could ever make sense for us to keep our promises. The practice of promising is a practice of giving point to an act of promise keeping by communicating the intention of giving it a point. If such a procedure makes no sense, the fact that it would be greatly to everyone's advantage if it did make sense is of little consequence.

In addressing this problem, Hume and Rawls distinguish two stages in the evolution of the practice. At the first stage, people are motivated to keep their promises by something other than a sense of obligation. Once this practice is firmly established, we reflect on its role in our lives and, realizing how we all benefit from this arrangement, we feel obliged to maintain it. At this second stage, we may keep our promises out of a sense of duty. In the next chapter, I shall myself offer a two-stage genealogy of promising, though one that takes a rather different form. Let's see how this idea is implemented first in Hume and then by Rawls.[9]

Hume

According to Hume: 'interest is the *first* obligation to the performance of promises. Afterwards, a sentiment of morals concurs with interest, and becomes a new obligation upon mankind' (Hume 1978: 523). 'Interest' here is our interest in having a reputation for reliability: 'When a man says *he promises any thing*, he in effect expresses a *resolution* of performing it; and along with that, by making use of this *form of words*, subjects himself to the penalty of never being trusted again in case of failure' (Hume 1978: 522). Should it become known that my promises are not to be trusted, I will no longer be able to get people to do things for me by promising to do things for them. To use Hume's own example, I won't be able to get my neighbour to help me take in my harvest by promising to help him take in his (Hume 1978: 520–1). And this incapacity would be a serious blow to my interests.[10]

Once the practice of promising is up and running powered by the motivational fuel of self-interest, what role remains for the 'sentiment of morals', the sentiment that concurs with or endorses the motive of self-interest when we reflect on the social benefits of everyone keeping their promises? Hume notes that while 'a present interest' may blind us to the deleterious but remote consequences of our own actions 'it takes not place with regard to those of others; nor hinders them from appearing in their true colours, as highly prejudicial to the public interest, and to our own in particular' (Hume 1978: 545). The sentiment of morals leads us to condemn other people's breaches of promise, decrying the promisor's failure to recognize that his breach of promise harms everybody's interest, including his own. And that reinforces the motive of self-interest by putting potential violators in fear of being condemned by third parties in addition to being excluded from their mutually beneficial

---

[9] For a helpful discussion of both theories, see (Kolodny and Wallace 2003: 120–5).
[10] Hobbes takes a similar line in his reply to The Fool (Hobbes 1994: 90–2).

arrangements. This is how the sentiment of morals backs up self-interest and ensures that we keep our word.

But aren't we inclined to fidelity by our own sense of what is right and not just by fear of other people's? The practice of promising, as we usually think of it, covers many cases in which it is pretty clearly not in the promisor's interests to keep their promise. If keeping the promise would be costly and I'm reasonably sure that I will never have to deal with the promisee (or anyone who knows of the breach) again, the canny thing to do might well be to breach. Perhaps I won't even be subject to condemnation by third parties. True I'm rarely completely sure that my reputation won't suffer. Nevertheless it is often unlikely that it will and yet abundantly clear that I am bound to perform. The motive of obligation must outrun that of self-interest, so how can our sense of obligation be no more than our endorsement of a practice based on the motive of self-interest?

Thus far I have been giving Hume's text the orthodox reading, a reading that fits much of his discussion. There is another interpretation. Towards the end of his treatment of promising and *after* having described how the practice serves both private and public interest, Hume says: 'We cannot readily conceive how the making use of a certain form of words should be able to cause any material difference. Here, therefore, we *feign* a new act of mind, which we call the *willing* an obligation; and on this we suppose the morality to depend' (Hume 1978: 523).[11] Apparently, all of the above notwithstanding, Hume takes himself to have made nothing of the idea that we can give ourselves an intelligible motive for doing something simply by communicating the intention so to do. In the course of his discussion, we have gone from the superstition that we can do it to the disillusioned pretence that we actually are doing it but the act of promising itself remains unintelligible.

One can reconstruct Hume's two-stage genealogy of promises around this passage as follows. At the first stage we are all mired in confusion. We imagine that it is possible to give an action a point by communicating the intention to give that action a point. And provided you don't reflect on what you are doing, you can act on that confused thought. Given how generally beneficial this confusion is, it would be no surprise if it occurred to us naturally and, with regular reinforcement, became a custom or a habit in the Jamesian sense of these terms (i.e. an acquired disposition (p. 80)). The psychological mechanisms that generate and entrench this confusion— instinct, imagination, custom, or habit—appear regularly in Hume's philosophy. Furthermore, reflection will not undo the work of imagination for, as well as the nonsensical character of promising, reflection reveals its great social usefulness. Reflection actually reinforces our confused motive for participating in the practice.

---

[11] (Mackie 1980: 100–4) gives us the orthodox reading and dismisses this passage as a mistake on Hume's part.

This reading of Hume will not please those uncomfortable with Hume's irrationalism but it does enable Hume to avoid the problem raised earlier, for at no stage does the practice run on the fuel of self-interest alone. Perhaps we *make* promises only when we expect to gain by so doing. But where keeping the promise turns out not to be in our interests after all, we may still *imagine* ourselves (in our confusion) as bound to keep the promise even before we reflect on the social benefits of the practice. And, once we do come to reflect how beneficial this confusion is, we will continue to honour a wider range of promises than those recommended by mere prudence.

By allowing Hume to bite Prichard's bullet, we secure him the first stage of his genealogy of promising but the second stage remains problematic for we are still unable to endorse our tendency to keep all of the promises usually thought binding. Where a breach of promise will remain completely undetected, there is no fear that the practice of promising will be damaged:

if we suppose, that the loan was secret, and that it is necessary for the interest of the person, that the money be restored in the same manner (as when the lender would conceal his riches) in that case the example ceases, and the public is no longer interested in the actions of the borrower; though I suppose there is no moralist, who will affirm, that the duty and obligation ceases. (Hume 1978: 480–1; see also Ross 1930: 39)

Potential promisors won't be any the less likely to keep their promises because of a breach they know nothing about and so, provided the promisee's interests are not damaged in any other way, even the most altruistic promisor would have no intelligible motive for keeping the promise. Confusion of thought might get him to keep the promise anyway but a moment's reflection will reveal that (in this case at least) the confusion serves no purpose, that his sense of obligation, though real enough, is absurd.[12]

Rawls

Like Hume, Rawls responds to Prichard's Problem with a two-stage account (Rawls 1999: 301–8). At the first stage, we have a practice of keeping promises, a practice which serves both public and private interest by facilitating social co-ordination without invoking the notion of obligation. At the second, those who already conform to the rules of this practice come both to appreciate its benefits and to realize that they are obliged to conform to its rules.

Rawls does not tell us how people begin to make and keep promises, what gets them to participate in the practice to start off with. Rawls just assumes that the practice has certain constitutive rules that people tend to obey. Now it is widely held

---

[12] Hume does not take the line that we can rarely if ever know, in any particular instance, what the consequences of a breach of promise will be (e.g. Hayek 1960: 67).

that conscientious obedience to a rule involves complying with it because one thinks that one *ought* to comply. On this Rationalistic view, those who participate in the promising practice treat its rules as guides to what they ought to do. Yet this 'ought' cannot be the 'ought' of obligation, otherwise Prichard's problem will return. Nor can it be the 'ought' of prudence otherwise the scope of the practice will be curtailed. Rawls might avoid this difficulty by maintaining that conformity to the constitutive rules of a practice is a mere custom or habit in the Jamesian sense. Whether he would wish to break with Rationalism to this extent I don't know.[13] In any case, Rawls says that his account of why we are obliged to uphold the promising practice once it exists is meant to apply to the practice 'however it may have come to be established' (Rawls 1999: 307).

Rawls's real advance over Hume comes at the second stage when we assess the practice. Here Hume relies on the thought that the practice will be damaged should we breach and thus the public interest in social co-ordination will be harmed. Rawls agrees that we are obliged not to undermine a just and socially useful practice but he thinks that those who have 'voluntarily accepted the benefits of the scheme' have a further obligation. According to Rawls's *Principle of Fairness* they 'are under an obligation to do their part as specified by the rules of the institution' (Rawls 1999: 301).[14]

For example, it is unfair to exploit the practice by promising your neighbour that you will help him with his harvest if he first helps you with yours unless you mean to perform. This is exploitation because you would be trying to secure the benefits of the practice (i.e. present aid) without being willing to bear the costs of it (i.e. future performance).[15] Note the problem here is not that you would be damaging the practice by failing to perform. Should your breach go undiscovered (you are one of many helpers) there may be no damage. Rather the point is that, whether found out or not, you would be getting something which you did not deserve in view of your unwillingness to reciprocate.

Here Rawls expands the wrong-base, the list of considerations which give breach of promise its wrongful character. No longer is it just harm. The violator may do no harm either to the promisee or the practice of promising. Still he is taking something that he does not deserve. Anyone tempted to behave like this might intelligibly refrain for this very reason even where their breach would go undiscovered. The idea that this benefit would be undeserved does not depend on some prior obligation

---

[13] See, for example, Rawls's remark that 'the doctrine of the purely conscientious act is irrational' in (Rawls 1999: 418).

[14] The Principle derives from Hart, though Hart did not apply it to the institution of promising (Hart 1955: 185). (Finnis 1980: 303) and (Fried 1981: 14–16) offer a structurally similar theory of promise, appealing to the wrong of abusing a socially useful practice.

[15] Rawls speaks of accepting the benefits of a practice here but perhaps the more neutral notion of accepting its products will serve just as well.

not to take it. Rather (we are supposing) desert can provide a ground for a judgement of wrongness.

Rawls may now respond to our earlier worries about how stage one of his account is meant to work by biting Prichard's bullet. Suppose the practice of promising did indeed originate in a widespread confusion of thought. Nonetheless once the practice has got going even the clear-headed amongst us may feel obliged to keep our promises since the practice is a socially useful one. *A fortiori* should we voluntarily accept the benefits of the practice.[16]

Imagine that, by expanding the wrong-base in the way Rawls suggests, we could bring all wrongful breaches of promise, including the seemingly bare wrongings, within the scope of the practice theory. Still, extensional adequacy is not the only test such a theory must pass. The wrong the practice theorist detects in a breach of a promise must be a wrong of the right sort (Scanlon 1998: 316). A breach of promise is primarily a wrong against the promisee since the promisee is the person to whom the performance is owed. Third parties (including potential beneficiaries) may also be wronged by the breach and perhaps these other wrongings are, in the end, more serious. Nevertheless, they usually presuppose that the promisee has himself been wronged. Can Rawls accommodate this structural fact?

Consider a case in which the promisee is not harmed by the breach. Rawls argues that the promisor has not played fair and so his breach is still a wrong. But who is wronged by this breach? Rawls would reply that the promisor is dealing unfairly with all of those who uphold and maintain the practice; we are *all* wronged whenever the practice of promising is exploited in this way, regardless of whether the promisee (or anyone else) is actually harmed. Even so, there is surely a distinct wrong of breach of promise, a wrong directed specifically at the promisee. And where is *this* wrong to be found when the promisee is unharmed by (and perhaps even ignorant of) the breach?

Rawls might respond that though the violator is being unfair to all of us who uphold the promising practice, he is being especially unfair to the promisee whose individual propensity to rely on promises he is exploiting. Even when the promisee is not harmed, he is exploited in a way that others are not and it is *via* the exploitation of him that the practice as a whole is exploited. This sounds plausible enough when we are dealing with a promisee who conscientiously keeps his own promises. But suppose Hume's debauchee is happy to accept my promises even though he doesn't take his own promises very seriously. I would still wrong him by failing to pay my debt as promised (whether or not he is harmed).[17] Yet it could hardly be said that *he*

---

[16] Thanks to Daniel Markovits for discussion of this point.

[17] It would be a bit rich of him to complain of (or even resent) the breach but it would be equally rich of a kidnapper to complain were his own children held to ransom. Both are still wronged, whether or not they are entitled to object (p. 32).

deserves better, that I would be exploiting the practice of promising by exploiting *his* devotion to it in particular. He is no more willing to play fair than I.

In this section, I have raised doubts about the two most detailed and influential practice theories of promissory obligation. Implicit in both is a certain view about the function of a promise, namely that promises are here to facilitate social co-ordination. In the next section, I shall ignore the detail of these theories and focus on that shared assumption.

26. Social co-ordination

Promises bind because people actually treat them as binding. That is the truth in the practice theory. The leading practice theorists have also maintained that promising's function is to enable us to co-ordinate our activities with other human beings. In their view, that is why it makes sense to make, accept, and keep promises. Call this the *social co-ordination hypothesis*. In this section, I shall argue that the latter hypothesis cannot sustain the former insight. First, we could have social co-ordination without a *practice* of promising and, second, we could have social co-ordination without a practice of *promising*.

As to the first point, it might seem obvious that if a promise is to be of any use as a tool of social co-ordination, people must be in the habit of fulfilling their promises. Given that we take promises seriously because they enable social co-ordination, it follows that promises would lose their binding force unless people were in the habit of keeping them. Yet at least one of Hume's near contemporaries maintained that there need be no such practice for promises to serve our interest in social co-ordination. Writing in response to Hume's *Treatise*, Thomas Reid wondered why the obligation of a promise should depend on the existence of a prior practice of promise keeping. Reid did not doubt that promises would be 'useless' unless people were (a) disposed to trust them and (b) disposed to keep them (Reid 1969: 443). But why, he asked, can't these dispositions be 'an effect of their constitution' (Reid 1969: 444)? Perhaps people are innately disposed to both trust and respect promises and have innate common knowledge of this fact about one another.[18] Call this the *innateness hypothesis*.

Reid argues at some length that the innateness hypothesis is true but our concern is not with its truth. Rather I am interested in Reid's further claim that were his hypothesis true, that alone would ensure that promises were binding. The practice

---

[18] Reid also argues that human beings can communicate the intentions involved in exercising various normative powers without employing conventional languages by instead using the natural language of voice and gesture (Reid 1969: 439–42). The practice theorist need not disagree with this but will maintain that the normative significance of these communications depends on whether there is a practice of taking them seriously.

theorist can't agree so long as he maintains that promises do not bind unless human beings are in the habit of making and keeping promises. You can't be in the habit of doing something that you have never done. There is no such thing as an innate habit. Yet, given the innate dispositions and common knowledge Reid outlines, surely promises would serve the function of co-coordinating our activities regardless of whether there was any custom of so using them. Human history might, in principle, contain only a single promise, a promise which was entered into because it served at least one party's interest in co-ordination and which was binding because breach of it would harm that interest. By adopting the social co-ordination hypothesis, the practice theorist breaks the connection between the existence of a practice and the normative force of a promise.

I take it Hume would regard the innateness hypothesis as psychologically implausible. He makes fun of the idea that our respect for property might be the product of an 'original instinct'. The rules governing the acquisition and transfer of property are too complex and variable for this to be at all plausible (Hume 1975: Section 3, Part Two). Doubtless he would say the same of the rules governing promissory obligation. We need not assess Hume's argumentation here since latter-day practice theorists are unlikely to take the same tack. Their claim is the normative one that taking promises seriously makes sense only when there is a practice of promising. Reid's hypothesis constitutes a conclusive objection to this claim, at least so long as it is underwritten by the social co-ordination hypothesis. Let's now assess the merits of this hypothesis.

All of the most considerable practice theorists maintain not just that promising serves our interest in coordinating our activities with other human beings over time but that this key interest can be served only by something like a promise.[19] They appear to endorse Hume's view that the 'invention' of promising is 'absolutely necessary' (Hume 1978: 484) because, at least when dealing with strangers, we can't generate the sort of co-operation required to get the harvest in unless human beings are in the habit of making and keeping promises.[20]

For Hume, promising is made necessary by the 'confined generosity' (Hume 1978: 495) of human beings. Hume is no egoist. He allows that human beings care for family and friends as well as for themselves. Indeed he maintains that they have a greater affection for those close to them, taken together, than for themselves alone (Hume 1978: 487). What he denies is that we have any considerable interest in the welfare of strangers (at least so long as the brute instinct which leads us to empathize

---

[19] For example, (Prichard 1968: 174–5), (Anscombe 1981: 18), (Hart 1994: 193–200), (Rawls 1999: 304–6), (Foot 2001: 45).

[20] Hume is echoing the natural lawyers: 'were not an exact observance of one's promise absolutely necessary, no man could propose to himself any certainty in whatever he designed, where he must depend upon the assistances of others' (Pufendorf 2003: 109). Hume also says that the rules of property are 'not only useful but even absolutely necessary to human society' (Hume 1978: 501).

with the physical suffering of another creature, human or animal, is not in play (Hume 1978: 481)). Given this, human beings cannot rely on the altruism of strangers to facilitate co-operative relations with them. As Hume says when discussing respect for property rights 'benevolence to strangers is too weak for this purpose' (Hume 1978: 492).

Hume's doubts about generalized benevolence seem well grounded but there is another potential source of motivational support for co-operative activity. Amongst the virtues that are 'common in human nature' Hume mentions gratitude (Hume 1978: 479).[21] If someone does me a favour, I'll be inclined to do him a favour. Conversely, if someone harms me, I'll be much less inclined to help him out in the future. Since this fact is widely known, why can't it be exploited to set up the very co-operative arrangements amongst strangers that supposedly require a promise?[22]

Co-operation could arise as follows. I offer to help my neighbour bring in his harvest while making it clear that I am doing so because I expect my neighbour to be moved to reciprocate and specifically to help me bring in my harvest next week. Since help next week is my expectation, other help given at other times would not constitute adequate reciprocation. Furthermore, since I am relying on this help, any failure to follow through would likely harm and thus wrong me. I might also make it clear that if he allows me to help without reciprocating, there will be a price to pay in that I will not depend on his gratitude again.[23]

The mechanism is formally similar to a promise, as Hume presents it. There too I indicate that I expect reciprocation because I expect a certain motive to come into play, namely conscientious adherence to the promise. And I also indicate that if there is no performance there will be a price to pay in that I will no longer depend on his conscientiousness. But the motive of gratitude lacks the feature of promising that so mystified Hume. What activates that motive is not just the communicated intention of bringing it into play but the actual bestowal of a benefit (Durkheim 1957: 181–2).[24] And a failure to reciprocate constitutes a harm where reliance is involved or unfair

---

[21] To bring the issue into focus here we must ignore some distracting connotations of the word 'gratitude'. There are *feelings* of gratitude and gifts are often valued more as an expression of such feelings than anything else. Now such feelings cannot be *demanded* and so, one might think, the whole idea of an obligation of gratitude is rather odd (Rousseau 1987: 73). What is needed to facilitate co-ordination between Hume's farmers is not gratitude so understood but rather *reciprocation* in the form of hard labour, reciprocation that can be demanded. I owe thanks to Daniel Markovits for discussion here.

[22] We could put the same question to Hobbes as follows: Why doesn't your fourth law of nature (recommending reciprocation) facilitate defensive arrangements just as well as your third law of nature (recommending the keeping of covenants made)? See (Hobbes 1994: 95).

[23] It has been suggested that empathy and reciprocal altruism are the twin foundations of social organization amongst animals (DeWaal 2006: 42–9). Only animals like ourselves who know about obligation can make any use of promising.

[24] As with Rawls's Principle of Fairness, we should perhaps leave it open whether a benefit must be involved here. Perhaps the thing bestowed only needs to be accepted for a return to be required.

dealing where it isn't. Such harm or unfairness could form part of a wrong-base that satisfied *Rationalism*.

Considering this very possibility in his discussion of the two farmers, Hume says the following:

> Men being naturally selfish, or endow'd only with a confin'd generosity, they are not easily induc'd to perform any action for the interest of strangers, except with a view to some reciprocal advantage, which they had no hope of obtaining but by such a performance. Now as it frequently happens, that these mutual performances cannot be finish'd at the same instant, 'tis necessary, that one party be contented to remain in uncertainty, and depend upon the gratitude of the other for a return of kindness. But so much corruption is there among men, that, generally speaking, this becomes but a slender security; and as the benefactor is here suppos'd to bestow his favours with a view to self-interest, this both takes off from the obligation, and sets an example of selfishness, which is the true mother of ingratitude. (Hume 1978: 519–20)

Let's allow that pure self-interest would provide a surer foundation for the sort of co-operative activity underwritten by a promise than the motive of gratitude.[25] Since Hume has failed to show that self-interest can be harnessed to that end, the comparison is irrelevant. What we should be asking is whether the procedure of invoking gratitude described above could provide a non-promissory foundation for co-operative activity. For this purpose, the motive of gratitude need only be as strong and ubiquitous as the motive (whatever it is) that actually underwrites the keeping of promises. Hume gives us no reason to doubt this. If human 'corruption' really were sufficient to render gratitude useless for purposes of social co-ordination, the chances of co-ordination by any other means look slim.

Is the distinction between promissory obligations and obligations of reciprocity as clear-cut as I have been supposing? In a particular case, it may be impossible to tell whether two people are bound by an obligation of reciprocation or by a promissory obligation. Say that my neighbour and I babysit for one another. No *explicit* agreement was ever reached but I generally babysit on Friday night in the expectation of having a child-free Saturday night. One weekend the arrangement breaks down for no good reason and I find myself having to cancel Saturday night's entertainment. Here my expectations are disappointed and I feel wronged but what was the basis of my expectation? Did my neighbour tacitly promise to babysit for me this Saturday? Or is it rather that my neighbour is just not playing fair in helping me enjoy my night out as I helped them enjoy theirs? Such questions may have no clear answer but that does not mean an obligation of reciprocation is no different from a promissory obligation. Rather what we have here are obligations of two quite different kinds that

---

[25] In fact, the motive of gratitude may have a wider scope than that of self-interest. It might lead you to reciprocate with the expected benefit even if no one would know whether you had reciprocated.

may serve the same purpose. Where social co-ordination is what matters, neither party will worry too much about exactly how it is being achieved. They will tolerate unclarity about precisely which social tool they are employing and what the basis for their obligation is.

I have been assuming that obligations of reciprocation differ fundamentally from promissory obligations but this may be doubted. When Rawls states his *Principle of Fairness*, he requires that the benefits of a social practice be 'voluntarily' accepted, with the implication that one who has had the benefits imposed upon him, or who cannot easily avoid receiving them, is not obliged to play his part. Some obligations of reciprocity may not require acceptance but setting that aside, what exactly does acceptance involve when it is required?

On one construal, someone who 'voluntarily accepts' a gift *consents* to the imposition of an obligation of reciprocation. The consent here looks very like a promise to reciprocate and seems to raise all the theoretical issues generated by such exercises of normative power. But this construal reads too much into the notion of acceptance. Someone can voluntarily accept a benefit simply by going out of their way to take advantage of it without agreeing to take on an obligation to reciprocate and indeed without even being aware that there is such an obligation (cf. pp. 3–4 and (Simmons 2001: 16–88)). If I bring my children out each day at just the right moment for them to join the supervised crocodile that takes the children to school I should expect to have to contribute to this arrangement at some point, if asked to do so. But the fact that I should expect this does not mean that I do expect it, let alone that I expressed such an expectation to anyone. The whole neighbourhood may know how obtuse I am.

In this section, I have argued that our interest in social co-ordination can be adequately served without either a *practice* of promising or a practice of *promising*. Hume and his many followers are wrong to maintain that a practice of promising is indispensable, at least for that reason, to the social life of human beings. Hume makes a number of assumptions about human psychology whose truth might render such a practice indispensable. But later practice theorists show no inclination to adopt these assumptions, nor should they.

I'll conclude by raising a final worry that prompts us to reconsider the overall direction of the argument. Hume and his fellow practice theorists are wrong to maintain that without promissory obligation social co-operation would become difficult or even impossible and that society could not exist in its present form. But can't an advocate of the social co-ordination hypothesis make do with the much weaker claim that promising is *one* perfectly good way of securing the needed co-operation and that promises exist and are taken seriously for just this reason? True, we have other tools of social co-ordination at our disposal and so there may be some overlap in function but the redundancy here is hardly complete. There are situations in which the motive of conscientiousness is available but the motive of gratitude is not. Perhaps you have lost confidence in your neighbour's gratitude but not in their fidelity. Perhaps you have nothing to offer in return but still hope that pity will lead them to promise without return. Why isn't this enough to explain why we have evolved more than one way of getting it together?

Were promissory obligation as firmly rooted in human interests as obligations of reciprocation, the practice theorist could be satisfied by this weaker claim. But our starting point was that (unlike the mechanism of reciprocation) promising appeared to generate bare wrongings whose connection to familiar human interests was obscure. Therefore the very intelligibility of promissory obligation is in question. Since the attempts of Hume and others to allay these misgivings failed, a picture of human life which minimized the role of promissory obligation or even dispensed with it altogether would be much more satisfying than one which had promissory obligation operating in tandem with other methods of co-ordination.

Recall Hume's farmers once more. We observe them conversing. The first farmer helps harvest the second's field today and the second farmer helps harvest the first's soon after. We then ask the second farmer why he helped the first farmer out and he replies by citing an obligation. What is the most plausible account of why he thought himself obliged to do this? Were Hume right to maintain that the *only* available answer here involves a promise, we might have to swallow it, even if this involved placing a deeply confused thought at the foundation of our social life. But where there is an alternative form of co-operative motivation, both intelligible and widely available, the case is quite different. Since human beings wish to make sense to themselves, dispensable confusion will be dispensed with and intelligible motives will be adopted. The anthropologist should conclude that the mechanism of reciprocation does the work of social co-ordination anywhere it can.

Far from giving promising pride of place in our social lives, the social co-ordination hypothesis renders it peripheral or even dispensable. This is exactly the conclusion that several critics of the practice theory have drawn. These writers contend that behind the façade of the exercise of normative power lies the reality of principles of reciprocity, adverse reliance, and due care for induced expectations. For them, bare wrongings are an illusion. I'll consider how well this proposal explains the character of promissory obligation in Part III.[26] In the meantime, let us try rejecting the social co-ordination hypothesis.

---

[26] See (Price 1948: 155–7), (Atiyah 1981: 184–215), and (Scanlon 1998: ch. 7). Atiyah openly admits that significant parts of our promissory practice make little sense on his model. Scanlon is more hopeful of accommodating and explaining our practices without resort to normative powers.

6

The Promissory Interest

Any account of promissory obligation must address a pair of questions:

(A) Why does it make any sense to offer or accept a promise?
(B) Why does it make any sense to keep the promises you make?

In what order should these questions be taken? There are three possibilities: (i) (A) may be prior to (B), (ii) (B) may be prior to (A), or (iii) (A) and (B) must be answered together. To my mind question (A) has priority but I'll first review the other options.

Reid maintained that we have an 'immediate perception' that breach of promise is a wrong, prior to any appreciation of the social utility of fidelity to promises (Reid 1969: 444). Reid's answer to (B) appeals solely to the intrinsic wrongfulness of breach of promise. It does not presuppose any particular answer to (A) nor even that there is an answer. However, it does suggest one form such an answer might take. Given that breach of promise is wrong, those who are not corrupt will be disposed to keep their promises simply because they know it would be wrong to breach (Reid 1969: 443–4). And if people are disposed to keep promises, it will often be possible to control their behaviour by extracting promises from them. Hence it is no surprise that people make and accept promises. On this view, far from the social usefulness of promising explaining its binding force, as it does for Hume, such utility is a by-product of this binding force.

Reid's view raises the problem of bare wronging. If breach of promise is simply wrong then there need be nothing about a breach of promise that makes it wrong other than the fact that it is a breach of promise. In particular, no human interest need be threatened by this breach. Anyone worried by the problem of bare wronging will baulk at this. They will doubt that question (B) can be answered prior to question (A) and they will look for a human interest which might move people both to make and accept promises and to keep the promises they make.

According to most writers, people make and accept promises in order to further their co-operative endeavours and people keep the promises they make out of a proper regard for the very same interest. So questions (A) and (B) are answered together. Such a view suggests that wrongful breach of promise is never a bare wronging; it has a wrong base in harm to our interest in social co-ordination, the very interest that leads us to make a promise in the first place. Where no interest is at stake, it makes no sense to keep the promise.

In this chapter, I chart a middle course between these two views. On the one hand, the problem of bare wronging needs to be addressed by relating the wrongfulness of breach of promise to genuine human interests, for it makes no sense to care about the supposed wrongfulness of breach of promise unless it is somehow linked to things that matter to us. On the other hand, I doubt that human interests ground promissory obligation in the way implied by *Rationalism*. Breach of promise need not damage the underlying promissory interest and fulfilment need not serve it. That interest is a *normative* interest, an interest in being able to impose obligations on people and thereby make certain actions into wrongings. The wrongness of these actions then explains why we should avoid these actions, why we should keep our promises. So we answer question (B) by first answering question (A).

27. The function of a promise

I am assuming that there is a promissory interest, an interest that explains why promises are taken seriously. I'm looking for a *functional explanation* of promissory obligation, an explanation that derives the binding force of a promise from its function, from the interest which explains why people go in for promising. In this section, I shall say more about what a functional explanation of promissory obligation involves but let's ask why we should be looking for such an explanation in the first place.

Does promising have a function? Don't people, make, accept, and keep promises for all sorts of reasons? For example, I can accept a promise in whose fulfilment I have no interest out of simple politeness and the promisor can fulfil their promise to me solely to please a third party. Still certain reasons for making, accepting, and keeping promises may stand out in that they explain why we have the practice of promising that we do. This is the view of those who accept the social co-ordination hypothesis. They should allow that people make, accept, and indeed keep promises for reasons that have nothing to do with the value of social co-ordination whilst regarding these other reasons as parasitic in the following sense: unless promises were made and accepted to facilitate social co-ordination, promising would not exist. A promise is a social co-ordination device because (a) it can serve our interest in social co-ordination and (b) the fact that it can serve this interest explains why promises exist and are taken seriously.[1]

---

[1] Unless rival theories of promissory obligation (e.g. the *expectation theory* discussed in Chapter 9) are read as accounts of the function of a promise, they are vulnerable to fairly obvious counterexamples (i.e. valid promises where there is no expectation of performance).

A homely analogy may help. A hammer can be used for all sorts of purposes: to prop open doors, to decorate a wall, etc., but if we wish to explain why hammers exist, why we have a tool with the features distinctive of a hammer, we should ignore these uses of a hammer and focus on one in particular. It is that use which constitutes the function of a hammer. Hammers are designed by people with this use in mind but the notion of function can be applied to social tools without designers like a promise. These social tools can also be used for various purposes but if we are looking to explain why a tool with the features distinctive of a promise exists, only one use may be relevant.

So what are the features distinctive of a promise that we might hope to explain by appeal to its function? First, normative features, e.g. the fact that promise binds to performance, that promises extracted under duress or by deception frequently do not bind, that promises must be accepted to be binding. Second, linguistic features, e.g. the fact that promises communicate the intention to hereby undertake an obligation and are sincere only if the promisor has that intention. Third, social features, e.g. the fact (if it is so) that promises do not bind unless people are in the habit of taking promises seriously. In Part III, I shall attempt a functional explanation of several such features. The purpose of this chapter is to introduce my favoured hypothesis about the function of a promise by considering how best to explain the fact that promising generates bare wrongings and the fact that promissory obligation is practice-dependent.

I maintain that promise wears its function on its sleeve. The effect of a valid promise is to give the promisee the right to require performance from the promisor. If you promise to meet me at the bus stop tomorrow, you are obliged to show up unless I release you from your promise. Your promise puts me in authority over you in the matter of whether you appear at the bus stop. We need look no further to discover the function of a promise. In saying that promising is here to serve our interest in authority over others, I am not asserting that people always or even mostly seek promises to serve their *authority interest*. Frequently, what people want out of a promise is a simple assurance that the promised action will occur. The fact that they get this assurance by assuming authority over the promisor rather than in some other way may be immaterial to them (Pink 2009: 405). Nevertheless, as already observed, the most common use of a promise need not be the use that explains the distinctive features of a promise. Hammers might be more frequently used as doorstops than as hammers.

Must promise have a single function? Perhaps promises are here to serve more than one human interest and wouldn't exist or be taken seriously unless they did. These multiple interests may be served in tandem, sometimes one, sometimes the other, sometimes both at once. Or else the one interest might have usurped the other: having been introduced to serve the first, promising came to serve the second and it is the latter that explains promising's persistence. I shall not attempt to consider all the possibilities. In the end, I would be content if it turned out that the authority interest plays a large and indispensable role in a multi-functional account of promissory obligation. But let's see how far the authority interest alone can take us and in particular, how much better it is at accounting for the distinctive features of a promise than our undoubted interest in information about what other people are going to do. Indeed, I think it better explains the undeniable fact that promising is used to serve this *information interest*.

Does my hypothesis imply that promises might *never* be used as a source of information about the promisor's future behaviour? And is this a real possibility? Hammers might never be used as doorstops. All hammers might be too small to serve or else we might have no need for doorstops at all. Surely promising is a different case? True. A device whose function is to serve our authority interests will inevitably be used to serve information interests also. But once we understand what is involved in having the relevant authority, we can see why this might be so even if *the* function of a promise were to serve our authority interest.

It is hard to imagine a world in which our *only* concern is to have authority over one another. If people have any social interests at all, surely these concerns must extend to non-normative matters. And how could we cater to our non-normative interests without collecting information about how others are going to behave? Though a world in which people need hammers but not doorstops is perfectly conceivable, a world in which people need authority over one another but not information about one another is not. Could promises provide such information, people would use them as sources of information.

I shall argue that promises are valid only in a social context in which people are in the habit of recognizing the obligations they generate. To recognize these obligations is, amongst other things, to be in the habit of giving the promise a certain role in your practical deliberations. This implies that promises as such tend to carry information about what the promisor is likely to do and so we have the desired result that promises *must* serve our information interest. Of course, an individual promise may not tell us anything much about what the promisor is likely to do. But it couldn't be that all promises were like that. All hammers might be too small to serve as doorstops but some promises must carry information about how the promisor is likely to behave.

By putting these facts together, we can explain why a speech act which grants authority will inevitably be used to garner information also, will inevitably serve *both* as an information gathering device and as a device for exercising control over the normative situation. That does not give promising a dual function. Rather promising may be a device with a single function but one which, given the general conditions of human life, will inevitably be used to serve a further purpose.

28. The authority interest

I maintain that promising exists because it serves our *authority interest*, our interest in having the right to oblige others to do certain things.[2] My claim will be that human beings have an interest in the possession of authority for its own sake, regardless of any further purpose this authority might serve, and that this fact accounts for the distinctive features of a promise.

The authority interest is a normative interest: it is an interest in the possession of a certain right, the right to impose an obligation. There are two layers of normative power here. First, there is the power to create a promissory obligation by declaration. Since the promise must be offered and accepted to be valid, this power is shared between the promisor and the promisee. Second, there is a power that resides only in the promisee: only the promisee has the power to dissolve the promissory bond by releasing the promisor. It is this second power that secures the promisee authority over the promisor.[3] The authority interest is an interest in having power to both create and abolish these obligations by declaration. Of course, we wouldn't value the ability to exercise such a power under any conditions. Sometimes human beings are better off not having the choice, even when their interests are deeply engaged and we'd expect this fact to be registered both in the conditions for the validity of a promise and in the conditions for the validity of a release. Chapter 10 confirms this hypothesis: we control obligation by declaration only when we have an interest in so controlling it.

If I am right, the fundamental promissory interest is an interest of the promisee rather than the promisor, namely the promisee's interest in gaining authority over the promisor. And indeed we think of a promise as primarily[4] a benefit to the promisee rather than to the promisor—it is the promisee who should be grateful for the promise, not the promisor—but since it is the promisor who makes the promise, this raises the question as to what interest the promisor has in the matter. The answer is reasonably obvious: we all have an interest in being able to satisfy the needs of others should we so wish. Where the promisee has an interest in acquiring authority over the promisor, the promisor often has an interest in being able to grant this authority, an interest in having the power to make promises. Furthermore, the promisor has an interest in being able to grant this authority by declaration, by simply communicating the intention of so doing. Why so? Because the promisee has

---

[2] The possibility of something like an authority interest is noted in passing by both (Raz 1986: 191–2) and (Scanlon 1998: 313) but neither puts any weight on it nor gives it any role in their theories of promissory obligation.

[3] For detailed discussion of the powers of offer, acceptance and release, see Sec. 43.

[4] Of course the ability to bind yourself to another by declaration may be of great instrumental value but I doubt that it is to be valued for its own sake. It is the value of the power to accept promises to the promisee that renders the power to promise intelligible.

an interest in being able to acquire authority simply by communicating the intention of so doing, simply by accepting the promisor's declarations.

Many will suspect that a normative interest cannot be a fundamental human interest, that one can have an interest in possessing a right only in so far as one's possession of that right serves some further interest whose object can be described in non-normative terms. In particular, one might think that our concern with authority is a reflection of a more fundamental *control* interest. But at least where breach of promise would constitute a bare wronging, this can't be so. Recall Maklay's Malay (pp. 125–6). Though he takes an interest in whether he is photographed, this does not bear on his interests in any way. So we must have an interest in authority over others that is irreducible to any interest in control over others.

Let's see how the postulation of such an interest helps resolve the problem of bare wronging and its close relative the problem of normative power. We began with two questions:

(A) Why does it make any sense to offer or accept a promise?

(B) Why does it make any sense to keep the promises you make?

I have proposed that people can always make and accept promises in the service of an authority interest. But can promisors keep their promises out of regard for the same interest? How exactly does the promisee's authority interest move the promisor to keep their promise?

The authority interest is an interest in the possession of authority and *that* interest is usually undamaged by a breach of promise. After all, a valid promise gives Hume's creditor and Maklay's Malay the relevant authority (i.e. the authority to require performance) regardless of whether either Hume or Maklay actually keep their promises. The promisee's authority interest would be harmed by this breach only if the breach somehow undermined the validity of the relevant promise, or at least threatened the promisee's ability to accept binding promises in the future. But it is hard to believe that many breaches of promise have this effect, let alone those that pose the problem of bare wronging. So if it is indeed a wrong for Hume and Maklay to breach their promises, how can *that* wrongness be explained by reference to the promisee's authority interest?

Reviving the *Injury Hypothesis*, the questioner is assuming that S's interest in X can explain why we should ϕ only if by failing to ϕ we *act against* S's interest in X (p. 61). When some control interest or interest in social co-ordination is at stake in a promise, it is often true that we act against these interests when we fail to perform. For example, to fail to show up at the bus stop when I promised that I would is often to harm you by failing to serve your interest in co-ordinating our commute, the very interest that led you to accept my promise in the first place (we may suppose). But with an interest in the possession of a normative power, things are different. An authority interest is an interest in something's being a wronging should I say so. That interest is not harmed provided it *is* a wronging if I say so and it's being a wronging does not usually depend on whether it actually happens. Now, according to *Rationalism*, it makes sense to fulfil an obligation only when such fulfilment will promote some good or avoid some evil (i.e. serve some interest). It is this assumption which drives the thought that an interest in X can explain why we should ϕ only if by failing ϕ we act against someone's interest in X. But the rationalism behind the *Injury Hypothesis* is untenable. It does make sense to discharge an obligation even where there is no reason independent of the promise to do so because there is non-instrumental value in another's having the power to ensure that it makes sense for your deliberations to be shaped by promises and other obligations.

This *normative* interest in our having the power to ensure that certain acts constitute wrongings (that it makes sense for people to avoid doing those things) explains why these acts should be avoided but it does so rather differently from non-normative interests. Suppose I make a promise to someone in the service of their interest in authority over me. Their authority interest is an interest in its being the case that I would wrong them by failing to perform (unless they release me). So my promise serves their authority interest when it makes it the case that I would wrong them in failing to perform. Furthermore where my promise makes it a wrong for me not to perform, it also ensures that it makes sense for me to perform and it does so even though the authority interest my promise serves would not be harmed by non-performance. Here the value lies in your ability to make my act a wrong, not in my forbearance. There may be no good in my keeping my promise but to do otherwise would be to wrong the promisee and so it makes sense for me to keep my promise. Thus our answer to question (A) delivers an answer to question (B).[5]

The issue under consideration is a close relative of the problem of normative power or Prichard's problem (pp. 130–1) and it might clarify matters if I respond to that problem directly. The practice of promising is a practice of ensuring that it makes sense to keep a promise by communicating the intention of hereby making sense of it. If we accept the Rationalist's view of intentional agency this puts the intelligibility of such a procedure in doubt, for one can't make it the case that there is some good in doing something simply by communicating the intention of making it the case that there is some good in doing that thing. Certain adherents of the social co-ordination hypothesis respond to this difficulty by pointing out that it would be

---

[5] It might be argued that breach of promise as such wrongs the promisee because it expresses a disregard for their authority interest even when it does no harm to that interest, just as laughing at someone's misfortune expresses a disregard for their non-normative interests even where it does no harm to those interests (p. 64). I doubt we can bring breach of promise within the scope of the *Injury Hypothesis* in this way. Our non-normative interests suffice to explain why both our misfortune and the dismissive attitudes of others to that misfortune are bad for us. Unless our normative interests can explain why breach of promise *as such* is bad for us, why should breach *as such* express a wrongful lack of regard for these normative interests?

greatly to everyone's advantage if one could do this since it would hand us an important social tool. But, Prichard replies, the fact that we are all better off if everyone believes that this procedure is intelligible, or acts as if it is intelligible, does not make it intelligible. We have done nothing to rule out the possibility that the whole practice is fundamentally confused and keeps going only because the confusion is so useful to us.

Consider an analogy. Suppose I am confronted with a ruthless and powerful aggressor. It may be sensible to take a 'berserk' pill, a pill which ensures that were I attacked I would go berserk and defend myself heedless of the cost. If the aggressor is himself rational and knows of the pill then by consuming the pill I would deter him from attacking me. Here it makes perfect sense for me to take the pill but it would not make perfect sense for me to go berserk if the aggressor nevertheless chose to attack. A berserk is someone whose behaviour makes no sense. Prichard may compare the promise to a berserk pill: its motivational effect is to get us to honour resolutions regardless of whether it makes any sense for us to honour those resolutions. Prichard need not deny the usefulness of such a 'resolve pill', nor the fact that, in certain circumstances, it might make perfect sense for us to take it. But, he will add, that does nothing to show that it would make sense to carry out the resolution in question.

Can we solve Prichard's Problem by appealing to our interest in authority rather than to our interest in social co-ordination? Such an appeal might seem vulnerable to the same objection: the fact that we have an interest in the intelligibility of a certain procedure cannot guarantee the intelligibility of that procedure. How can the admitted fact that others have an authority interest in our being able to bind ourselves to them ensure that it possible for us to do so? I agree that we can't establish the intelligibility of a normative procedure simply by showing that its possession would have great instrumental value. That might be true of all manner of delusions. But I am supposing that the ability to influence the normative situation in that fashion is valuable for its own sake. Because we can intelligibly act out of habit where the norm-constituting habit in question could be valuable for its own sake, it makes sense to act on the bonds of fidelity created by the exercise of such powers (pp. 83–4).

By postulating an authority interest we have resolved the problem of bare wronging and with it the problem of normative power. The prevalence of the practice of promising throughout human history speaks in favour of such a move but it would be good to understand how the authority interest relates to other human concerns. We cannot expect a reduction of this normative to other normative interests, let alone to our non-normative interests, but it would be surprising if the authority interest were entirely *sui generis*. Since promises generate bare wrongings, our authority interests can't be directly dependent on our non-normative interests. But we shouldn't conclude that our authority interests are completely independent of our non-normative concerns; the dependence may be indirect (p. 66). For example, it may be that a promisor must at least imagine that the making of the promise would serve some non-normative interest (unless he is promising out of habit or policy in which case he must have imagined this at some point in the past). You can promise to do only what you could intelligibly be asked to do and you could intelligibly be asked to do only what someone could intelligibly want you to do.[6] I'll consider how the authority interest might relate to our other normative interests in the final section.

29. Promises and practices

I have explained why promises bind given that people have an interest in authority over others. Our answer to question (A) delivers an answer to (B) also. I'm supposing that it is *good* for people to have authority, that the simple possession of authority over certain matters makes their lives go better (*ceteris paribus*). The normative force of a promise derives from this fact about human well-being. What must authority be like for it to be possible for you to have an interest in the possession of it? What must obligation be like for it to be good for you if others have obligations to you? At least two things must be true: (i) authority is something you can lack whilst still retaining an interest in it and (ii) *ceteris paribus* it is good for you to have it rather than lack it. To satisfy these conditions, authority must be a social reality.

We can't explain why certain norms actually are in force by hypothesizing that it would be good if they were in force unless our *explanans* is distinct from our *explanandum*, unless facts about the goodness of these norms are distinct from facts about their validity. So there must be more to the validity of the norms in which we have an interest than the fact that we have an interest in them. I maintain that such norms are valid only when people are in the habit of recognizing their authority, e.g. promises bind in a given social context only where people are in the habit of recognizing promissory obligations. That is the fact in which we have an interest. In this section I shall explain the notion of *recognition* and in the next say what a *habit* or *practice* of recognition involves.

A promisee's right to require performance from the promisor may be recognized in one of three different ways. The first and most obvious way is when the promisor *fulfils* his promise because he feels required to do so. But this is not in fact the most fundamental way of recognizing a promissory obligation. It is possible for a promisor to breach a promise without thereby wronging the promisee, without infringing their right to performance, provided the promise has played a certain role in the promisor's practical deliberations. A promise should exclude a certain range of considerations that count in favour of non-fulfilment from the promisor's deliberations when he comes to decide whether to fulfil his promise. If non-fulfilment is justified by considerations not excluded by the promise then the promisor can *respect* his

---

[6] Whether they actually want you to do it is another matter.

promise without fulfilling it. So respect for a promise is consistent with a failure to perform (pp. 90–1).

Furthermore, where a promissory obligation is neither fulfilled nor respected it may still be *acknowledged*. Such acknowledgement can take various forms. The promisor might offer compensation. The promisor might express remorse. The promisor might express regret or sorrow at breach. And third parties may react with indignation, regret, or even offer compensation themselves. But what I called the blame reactions (guilt, remorse, resentment, indignation, etc.,) are the crucial way of acknowledging the existence of an obligation. Promissory obligation exists only where the promisor is vulnerable to blame.

A promise need not raise the probability of its own fulfilment in order for it to be of value to the promisee. For example there are cases in which the promisee happens to know that performance will turn out to be impossible. He might still be glad to receive the promise because he values the promisor's willingness to ensure that it makes sense for the promisor defer to the promisee in his deliberations and to render himself vulnerable to blame should he not so defer. The promisee might be glad that the promisor was willing to put himself in this position. True there are promisors who care nothing for their promise and if everyone took that attitude there would be little or no point in accepting a promise. But even if the promisor couldn't care less, recognition of one's promise may come from third parties who react with indignation to the breach and thus affirm the reality and the value of one's promissory rights.

I shall say that a promise is *recognized* when it is either fulfilled, respected, or acknowledged. How much recognition is needed before someone's right has been recognized, before it becomes a real benefit to them? There is no clear answer to this question. So far as a given individual goes, having a particular right is compatible with one's seldom getting the performance. I would say it is also compatible with one's right to the performance being often disrespected. It may even be compatible with its rarely being either respected or acknowledged. True, authority must be recognized to some extent but that recognition might be more a function of what goes on in the right-holder's social context than of anything which happens to the right-holder himself. The benefit of a right to a given individual may lie largely in its social significance (unless the individual is specifically excluded from the relevant practice). And to what extent must a right be either fulfilled, respected, or acknowledged for it to possess that social significance? The only general answer to that question is: to the extent that is required to make your right a reality. We can't dispense with notions of right (and obligation) when specifying the authority interest.

I'll now address two objections to the account as so far presented. First, there is the worry that promises may be binding regardless of whether there is a practice of recognizing promises in the social context in which they are made. Locke claims that

The Promises and Bargains for Truck etc., between the two Men in the Desert Island, mentioned by Garcilasso de La Vega, in his History of Peru, or between a Swiss and an Indian, in the Woods of America, are binding to them, though they are perfectly in a state of nature, in reference to one another. For truth and keeping of faith belong to Men, as Men, and not as members of society.   (Locke 1988: 277)

In considering such thought experiments we must first be sure that it is promissory obligation that is in question and not, say, the obligation to take due care of the expectations one has knowingly aroused. The latter obligation may well be practice independent (Scanlon 1998: 296–7) but it is not a promissory obligation (Secs. 41–2). Second, we must be equally sure that the parties are not tacitly relying on the fact that they were both brought up in social contexts in which promises were recognized (as the Swiss and the Indian surely were).[7] Taking great care, we may be able to imagine a case in which two total strangers meet and one succeeds in communicating the intention to hereby undertake an obligation to the other even though neither has had any contact with a social world in which such declarations were taken seriously. Such people may still possess both the concept of an obligation and the other concepts necessary to formulate and understand the communicated intention.[8] Would such a declaration bind?

To the question baldy posed, I find myself at a loss for an answer. Without some notion of what function a promise is supposed to have, of why we should ever take such obligations seriously, the conjecture is impossible to assess. If the point of a promise were to convey information then these declarations would bind in so far as they convey information (and perhaps without the aid of a practice of recognition). On the other hand, if the point of a promise is, as I urge, to transmit a certain form of social authority, a form of social authority which is, in part, *de facto*, we must conclude that Locke's declaration cannot bind unless we suppose that the two parties are part of a wider social world in which promises are taken seriously. This issue here cannot be settled by appeal to a theoretically neutral thought experiment.

---

[7] Thompson suggests that Locke's characters must be members of the very same practice for their declarations to bind (Thompson 2004: 371–3). The Swiss and the Indian may imagine that they can conclude a contract but, Thompson implies, they would be wrong. True, it may be doubted whether these people really understand one another when they say 'I promise', etc., since it may be doubted that they share a language (Thompson 2004: 362–3). But if *these* doubts are set to one side and we allow that they do manage to communicate the intention of hereby undertaking an obligation etc, then it seems to me that they can promise simply because they are all in the habit of recognizing the significance of such communications. Given this background, it makes sense for them to value the normative situation purportedly created by these declarations and so it is intelligible to suppose that these declarations succeed.

[8] A real case in which one person succeeds in communicating the intention to hereby undertake an obligation to another person but where the promise is not taken seriously involves our relations with our children (Shiffrin 2008: 509–10). Promises made to and by fairly young children are not taken very seriously, yet at least some of those treated as children have as good a grasp as many adults of what it is to communicate the intention of hereby undertaking an obligation. Are such promises less binding because we take them less seriously? It seems so to me but such reactions should not decide the issue.

Now to the second objection. I have argued that a society without a practice of promising would leave an important human need unsatisfied. Does it not follow that we are *obliged* to establish and maintain such a practice? And isn't this practice-independent obligation the true source of promising's normativity?[9]

Perhaps we are obliged to facilitate the making of promises but if so this does not follow from the simple fact that there is a general human need for promises. There is deep and pervasive human need for friendship and for the social forms that make rich and satisfying forms of friendship a possibility. Yet, Rousseau might argue, individual people can live decent lives without making either friends or promises, confining themselves to co-operative relations that require only sincere expressions of intention and an impersonal benevolence. Could one lead a blameless life without promising once the practice of promising had been established, presumably one could do so beforehand. If a Rousseau does no wrong, then it is no wrong to maintain a social world devoid of promising or friendship and promising's normativity can't derive from a prior obligation to establish a practice of promising. Second, even if we are all under an obligation to facilitate the making of either promises or friends, it remains the case that until the relevant practice comes into existence, there is no wrong of breach of promise or disloyalty in friendship. Without such a practice one can't wrong someone in *that* way, even if one does somehow wrong others by refusing to get involved.[10]

So what is it for people's habits of recognition to constitute a practice of recognition, to ensure that there is a convention of promise-keeping for instance? And how do such practice-constituting habits come into existence?

30. Obligation and convention

Much human action is intelligible in virtue of its conventional character, because it involves enacting a ritual or subscribing to a practice or a social custom. In this section, I want to develop the idea introduced earlier that where the existence of a convention is (or seems to be) a good thing, that fact ensures that it makes sense to

---

[9] (Shiffrin 2008: 522–3) presses this question against Humean conventionalism about promising.

[10] In his discussion of property rights, Kant joins Hume, Hobbes, and Rousseau in denying that we wrong one another by interfering with each other's possessions in the state of nature (Kant 1996: 410–21 and 450–2). On the other hand, Kant thinks that, even in the state of nature, we can acquire a 'provisional right' to something by taking possession of it. The significance of this 'provisional right' is twofold. First, we are entitled to exercise and retain control of the thing, i.e. we do no wrong in fending others off. Second, we are all under an *obligation* to leave the state of nature and establish a civil society in which such provisionally rightful possession will be recognized and thereby be rendered conclusively rightful. Kant also implies that, in the state of nature, one does not wrong anyone in making them an insincere promise (Kant 1996: 394 and 452).

act in a conventional manner, and does so whether or not there is anything desirable about those particular actions (p. 84). Conventional action has attracted the attention of moral philosophers in part because many of them think that various obligations are grounded in social convention, e.g. the obligation to keep one's promises, respect property, obey social authority, and be truthful. Let's first ask what it is for there to be a convention and then inquire how the existence of such a convention might render the individual actions falling under it intelligible or even obligatory.

I'll distinguish two different models of social convention: the *collective policy* model and the *social practice* model. On the collective policy model a social convention is engendered by our shared intention or resolve to behave in a certain way. On the social practice model a social convention is present where certain habits become established in our community. Both habit and policy lend themselves to generating conventional agency since both liberate agents from the need to comply with a reason. Neither customary behaviour nor action on policy involves any judgement that one ought to be so acting. Indeed, to go along with convention because one judges that one ought to comply with the convention is not to behave conventionally. Conventional activity excludes such practical deliberation.[11]

Both habit and policy can be found in the writings of Hume on convention. The collective policy model emerges most clearly in his discussion of how property rights become established:

I observe, that it will be for my interest to leave another in the possession of his goods, *provided* he will act in the same manner with regard to me. He is sensible of a like interest in the regulation of his conduct. When this common sense of interest is mutually express'd, and is known to both, it produces a suitable resolution and behaviour. And this may properly enough be call'd a convention or agreement betwixt us, tho' without the interposition of a promise; since the actions of each of us have a reference to those of the other, and are perform'd upon the supposition, that something is to be perform'd on the other part. Two men, who pull the oars of a boat, do it by an agreement or convention, tho' they have never given promises to each other. Nor is the rule concerning the stability of possession the less deriv'd from human conventions, that it arises gradually, and acquires force by a slow progression, and by our repeated experience of the inconveniences of transgressing it. On the contrary, this experience assures us still more, that the sense of interest has become common to all our fellows, and gives us a confidence of the future regularity of their conduct: And 'tis only on the expectation of this, that our moderation and abstinence are founded.   (Hume 1978: 490)

Hume avoids the mistake of thinking that an obligation-generating collective policy must be embodied in a contract or a set of interdependent promises. That would require some form of collective decision-making or at least individual acts of adhesion to the social contract, a most implausible supposition in the case of the

---

[11] Thus I agree with Thompson that the social practice 'cannot enter into an agent's thoughts as a datum to which she responds' (Thompson 2008: 197).

(pre-legal) institution of property.[12] Rather, as in the case of the two rowers, the existence of the collective policy requires only that each rower have a policy of pulling his oar when his turn comes, a policy which depends on each (a) assuming that the other rower has a similar policy and (b) expecting that they will benefit if they row together. This situation may have arisen gradually over a period (when there are many rowers making a long journey), consequent upon each party's 'experience of the inconveniences of transgression'. The interlocking policies of individual rowers share the features of any policy: they block deliberation about whether to take the next stroke and they are meant to be sensitive to the disappearance of the reasons which led one to adopt the policy in the first place (p. 79). Once I realize that others are not rowing and that the boat is going nowhere, I cease to row myself. Similarly, Hume thinks, once others are pillaging at random, I need no longer respect the sanctity of property (Hume 1975: 186–8).

Hume's collective policy model fits many social conventions but perhaps not the ones which particularly interest him, namely those underlying 'artificial virtue'. Though Hume postulates no act of collective agreement, he does assume that each honest individual has (tacitly?) formulated a suitable policy, that all have resolved to keep their promises, to respect property, to be truthful, and so forth. This is plausible enough in the case of the rowers but how many people have resolved to tell the truth or keep their promises (as opposed to a particular promise they feel inclined to break)?[13] Are such doubtful resolutions really required for the virtues of honesty to have place?

There is another respect in which the rowing example misleads. Although Hume does not suppose any actual collective deliberation, the rowers' interdependent resolutions (as Hume represents them) *could* have been the result of collective deliberation. Hume's rowers are moved by a specific shared interest in getting where they need to go and they adopt a policy, both individual and collective, to be abandoned should this reason fail. That policy could have been adopted for that reason at a meeting of the Rower's Union. Are property rights, promising, etc., really in the same case?

As we have seen, Hume's genealogy of artificial virtue is a bit more complex. He acknowledges that while self-interest 'is the *first* obligation to the performance of promises, afterwards a sentiment of morals concurs with interest and becomes new obligation upon mankind' (Hume 1978: 523). The 'self-interest' pertains to our ability to get others to trust us by cultivating a reputation for reliability. The 'sentiment of morals' is our approving reaction to the existence of a social institution that enables us to predict each other's behaviour, an institution initially founded on the motive of

---

[12] It would also make it impossible for Hume to treat the institution of promising as itself the product of a collective policy.

[13] (Holton 2009: 129, 135) seems to think so.

self-interest. Once the institution is up and running, the sentiment of morals provides us with a motive for maintaining it which supplements and even, in some cases, replaces the motive of self-interest.

Hume is allowing that the reasons why people are resolved to keep their promises at t_1 need not be the reasons why they are resolved to keep their promises at t_2. Nevertheless, there is a clear connection between the reasons applying at t_1 and those applying at t_2 and we can, if we wish, imagine people making that connection in a collective act of practical deliberation. Even without collective deliberation, people who see how securing the trust of others serves their own interests will naturally come to appreciate that a device of social co-ordination serves the common good in much the same way. Since Hume supposes that we all have some concern for the common good, that will reinforce the institution. Let's call this a *Humean Genealogy* of promising. It is an extension rather than an abandonment of the collective policy model since the policy's ability to make sense of its own implementation still depends on there being a course of deliberation which could get us first to adopt it and then to readopt it.

I think Hume realized that even this form of genealogy could not fully explain the phenomena since, as he acknowledged, there are cases where it makes sense to keep a promise (or respect someone's property) though there is absolutely no 'reason' for so doing (p. 133). In fact, we should not take it for granted either that human beings began to keep their promises for some common reason or that they carried on keeping them for related reasons. Such strong empirical assumptions are not needed to render promise-keeping intelligible. Different people might have different reasons for keeping promises on different occasions. Provided there are reasons enough to ensure that a sufficient proportion of promises are kept, habits of promise-keeping will become established. And once established, habits have a momentum of their own.

We must be clear what sort of habit we have in mind. William James founds property rights on habit:

Habit is thus the enormous fly-wheel of society, its most precious conservative agent. It alone is what keeps us all within the bounds of ordinance, and saves the children of fortune from the envious uprisings of the poor.   (James 1950: 121)

But our habit of keeping promises or abstaining from the property of others can't be a Jamesian habit, an automatic routine. Perhaps our honesty is heedless much of the time but we are too often subject to temptation for honesty to be completely automatic. The habit of conscientiousness is a habit of choice. Furthermore the manifestation of the habit constitutes intentional agency only because it is sensitive to our view of the intrinsic value of the habit, of whether it is a virtue rather than a vice (p. 82).

Habits of conscientiousness are not purely personal habits like my daily walk. A conventional obligation is generated by the customs prevalent in a particular social environment, not by the habits of isolated individuals. Nor are these habits a collection of personal customs like the English practice of going outdoors whenever the sun shines, a habit which each may acquire independently. The habits which ground the institution of property are transmitted from one person to another, they spread through society and once widely established constitute a collective habit. I'm calling such collective habits *practices*. The existence of a suitable practice explains why it might make sense for me to respect someone's property even though (a) there is in this case no reason to respect it and (b) I have not myself acquired the habit of respecting it. To feel obliged to leave the goods of others alone, I need not be in the habit of so doing: the habits of others can make sense of what I do.

In Chapter 3, I argued that it often makes sense to choose to do something because you yourself have repeatedly chosen to do it, because you have a personal habit of doing it. But it also makes sense to do something because *others* have chosen to do it, because there is a practice of doing it. For example, when I find myself surrounded by people who walk along the street with their underwear exposed, it makes sense for me to expose my underwear also. And this makes sense on the very first occasion I do it. The repeated choice need not be my choice. Nor (as the example makes clear) need it provide any reason for my choice (though such fashions do originate in choices based on reasons).[14] The mode of transmission here is a form of imitation (Oakeshott 1991: 468–9): I choose as others choose. To imitate another is not to accept their judgement about what you (or one) ought to do; it is not to take their advice. (After all, they themselves may be exposing their underwear against their own better judgement.) Nor is it to obey some order, an order they are in no position to issue. Nor is it to prudently adjust your behaviour to theirs or to think, in the manner of Hume's rowers, that you ought to maintain a mutually beneficial social practice. You just intentionally imitate what they intentionally do.

Weber and Durkheim are each at pains to distinguish imitation from various subliminal forms of social influence, such as those involved in crowd psychology and emotional contagion (Weber 1947: 113–14; Durkheim 1970: 124–30). They rightly conclude that to imitate is to reproduce the actions of others, not to be infected by them. But Durkheim goes on to classify imitation as a manifestation of mere 'instinct' or 'reflex', remarking that:

our way of conforming to the morals or manners of our country has nothing in common, therefore, with the mechanical, ape-like repetition, causing us to reproduce motions which we witness. Between the two ways of acting is all the difference between reasonable, deliberate behaviour and automatic reflex.   (Durkheim 1970: 127–8)

Durkheim has failed to consider all the options. When I decide to expose my underwear because others are exposing theirs, this is something I do intentionally,

---

[14] What was once an expression of solidarity with prisoners has become fashionable behaviour.

provided I wouldn't do it if I believed that the habit of displaying one's under-wear was worthless (p. 82). In this way fashionable clothes may be worn simply because they are *à la mode* and rituals may be enacted simply because they are established.[15]

Custom and practice play a crucial role in Hume's story about obligations of allegiance.[16] Speaking of our rulers, he says

> Nothing causes any sentiment to have a greater influence upon us than custom, or turns our imagination more strongly to any object. When we have been long accustomed to obey any set of men, that general instinct or tendency, which we have to *suppose* [my italics] a moral obligation attending loyalty, takes easily in this direction and chooses that set of men for its objects.   (Hume 1978: 556)

Nevertheless I doubt Hume sees practice as a source of intelligible agency. The 'suppose' in this passage registers a tension between the phenomenon noted here and Hume's endorsement of the Rationalist doctrine that 'the Will exerts itself when either the good or the absence of the evil may be attained by any action of the mind or body' (Hume 1978: 439). Indeed, Hume says that when a ruler no longer serves the interest in social stability that led us to install him, the obligation of allegiance ceases:

> If the sense of interest were not our original motive to obedience, I wou'd fain ask, what other principle is there in human nature capable of subduing the natural ambition of men, and forcing them to such a submission? Imitation and custom are not sufficient. For the question still recurs, what motive first produces those instances of submission, which we imitate, and that train of actions, which produces the custom? There evidently is no other principle than interest; and if interest first produces obedience to government, the obligation to obedience must cease, whenever the interest ceases, in any great degree, and in a considerable number of instances.   (Hume 1978: 553)

This last inference makes our practice of obedience look like a policy we must abandon once the original reasons for adopting it are gone. Ultimately Hume cannot allow that obedience remains intelligible once it becomes clear that the original reasons for it have lapsed and none have appeared to replace them. He admits that 'men are mightily addicted to *general rules* and that we often carry those maxims

---

[15]   Scheffler argues that both personal habits and social practices do provide reasons for action because by giving us a sense of stability in time they 'help to compensate for our lack of control over our mobility in time, they provide a way of domesticating portions of time, and they provide assurance of our own reality as temporally extended creatures' (Scheffler 2010: 300). The case of fashion suggests that what matters is the replication of choice rather than the passage of time (Weber 1947: 121). In fashion you choose as others choose but the idea of regular and dramatic social change is essential to fashion. I also doubt that the passage of time gives other obligation-generating practices their significance. Someone *might* keep pro-mises or respect property because they thought they were subscribing to a long-standing tradition but this would be an unusual and indeed questionable attitude.

[16]   See also (Wittgenstein 1953: Sec. 199), (Bentham 1988: 40), and (Austin 1995: Lecture 6).

beyond the reasons, which first induced us to establish them' (Hume 1978: 551) but in Hume's eyes this is an *addiction*, not a source of intelligible agency.

Promising requires a non-Humean genealogy. To make sense of our fulfilment of a promissory obligation where there is no reason to fulfil it other than the validity of the promise, we must see it as grounded in social practice rather than in collective policy. Unlike policies, habits may render our behaviour intelligible even once we realize that the reasons that led us to perform the actions through which we acquired the habit no longer apply and provided we don't also take the view that there is nothing to be said for it, that our habit is pure vice. Those without the habit can tap into this source of practical intelligibility by imitating those who already possess it.

31. The genealogy of promise

This section is an exercise in speculative genealogy. To trace the true origin of the practice of promising we must amass historical evidence but when the intelligibility of a practice is in question, there is a point in demonstrating how it could have evolved by series of steps that each make sense, whether or not it actually came about in that fashion. There is no guarantee that promise has an intelligible genealogy:

> The entire history of a thing, an organ, a custom can in this way be a continuous sign-chain of ever new interpretations and adaptations whose causes do not even have to be related to one another but, on the contrary, in some cases succeed and alternate with one another in a purely chance fashion.   (Nietzsche 1968: 513)

Our past may indeed be a series of meaningless ruptures but since human beings wish to make sense to themselves, a *Nietzschean* genealogy will not be our first resort. We should try for an account of human history that construes it as an intelligible progression, though not as one which recapitulates a course of collective deliberation.

Having shown how his two farmers could get out of their bind by way of a promise, Hume says this:

> But though this self-interested commerce of men begins to take place, and to predominate in society, it does not entirely abolish the more generous and noble intercourse of friendship and good offices. I may still do services to such persons as I love, and am more particularly acquainted with, without any prospect of advantage; and they may make me a return in the same manner, without any view but that of recompensing my past services. (Hume 1978: 521)

The suggestion is that promissory obligation arises from a background of obligations to friends and intimates. The reference to 'recompensing past services' indicates that Hume thinks of promissory obligation as rooted in obligations of reciprocation. As we have seen, reciprocation is not a good model for obligations of friendship (pp. 107–9). Still there may be a grain of truth in Hume's thought that the origins of promissory obligation lie in obligations of involvement.[17]

The bonds of kinship, primitive friendship, etc., probably supplied our first experience of obligation. I have argued that these obligations exist because at least in the context of those relationships, they are good for us. So how did the delights of these more intimate bonds generate the wish to bind strangers with whom we have no such connection, and furthermore bind them by declaration? Why should a felt need to connect with more particular acquaintances in this way render the idea of normative power over strangers attractive to us? The idea of changing people's obligations by declaration is already present in the phenomenon of request. Requests as such do not impose obligations, they merely ensure that it makes sense for the audience to do as you have asked them to do (by changing how it makes sense for them to deliberate). But in the context of relationships like friendship, requests can easily be binding. When a friend asks you to help them move house, you may be obliged to show up and be so obliged simply because the friend asked you for help and regardless of whether they actually need it (pp. 99–100). Since we have already tasted normative power within friendship, our more intimate involvements supply the materials required to construct the practice of binding strangers to perform by declaration.[18] But why should we wish to do so?

Whilst obligation possesses a special value in the context of friendship, it is also (like many other such goods) valuable outside the context of friendship (etc.,). Consider a non-normative good like emotional support and advice. This has a special value when offered in the context of friendship and someone who only ever got it in the context of friendship need not be missing out. But such a person *would* be rather fortunate. Most of us find we require the emotional support and advice of strangers from time to time. We value this good for its own sake and thus we also value the ability to obtain this good from strangers (by asking or even paying for it) where we cannot get it from friends. Now much the same applies to an *obligation* to provide support and advice. Even in the context of friendship, such an obligation is not valued simply as means to obtaining support and advice; it is valued for its own sake (pp. 112–14). Perhaps someone who only ever gave or received this normative good in the context of friendship would not be missing out. But friends are not always around to satisfy our normative any more than our non-normative needs. Hence the value

---

[17] Durkheim identifies the 'real contract' (in which items of value are physically exchanged) and the 'blood contract' (in which a symbolical kinship is established between the contracting parties) as the precursors of what he calls 'consensual contract' (Durkheim 1957: 175–207).

[18] 'The mere fact that an institution is required does not mean it will appear at a given moment out of the void. There must be something to make it of, that is, current ideas must allow it to come about and existing institutions must not oppose it but rather supply the material needed to shape it' (Durkheim 1957: 191).

we place on promises, on being able to obtain this good by declaration, by way of a mechanism whose efficacy does not depend on our being involved with one another.

Suppose A and B are strangers to each other. A feels the need to bind B and, given that they are strangers, may be unable to do so by request. B, for reasons of his own (perhaps self-interested, perhaps altruistic) is inclined to satisfy this need of A's and so plays along. He communicates the intention of hereby binding himself to perform. There is nothing unintelligible about such a declaration—each party possesses the conceptual materials necessary to both make it and comprehend it when made. Nor is there anything unintelligible about the idea that such a declaration binds—each party is familiar with requests that bind. The only issue is whether it actually binds. A and B are free to treat it as if it does. Now suppose that some contemporaries of A and B also wish to bind one another. And there are yet more people (e.g. the children of A and B) who imitate what A and B do. Furthermore all of these people develop or acquire the habit of blaming those who fail to take their promises seriously and of feeling guilty when they fail to do so themselves. Once enough of us are in the habit of recognizing promises in these ways, we are all obliged to take promises seriously whether or not we have personally employed them. Once a practice of promising has become established, a practice that serves our authority interest, imitation becomes obligatory.

Some writers wonder how we could travel from a starting point where 'promises' are made but have no more significance than say a declaration of intention, to an end point at which they bind us all in the normal way.[19] There must be an answer since a whole range of familiar social institutions such as money could not otherwise exist. A medium of exchange is a substance which people are obliged to accept (regardless of its intrinsic value) in return for valuable items because of the great social utility of having an obligatory medium of exchange. This obligation developes without the aid of banks, exchequers, and so forth (Hume 1978: 490). Some start to treat the medium as possessing a certain value and once enough people of the relevant social group behave in this way, all are obliged to accept it on first contact. No doubt there is a transitional period when it is unclear whether this obligation exists but this can't put the end result beyond reach.

In the case of social authority, the establishment of suitable habits of recognition resolves certain indeterminacies. In particular, they fix the authority's (a) identity, (b) jurisdiction, and (c) the stringency of their commands. As to identity, they select from amongst those with the minimal qualifications for being a suitable authority the people who are actually in authority. As to jurisdiction, they determine who is ruled by which authority. As to stringency, they determine how grave a wrong it is to flout

---

[19] (Thomson 1990: 304) implies that if promises bound only after a period in which they were treated as binding, a binding promise could never eventuate.

the orders of this authority or at least they limit the range of acceptable views on this matter. Should Germans take their laws more seriously than Italians, i.e. should their habits of fulfilling, respecting, and acknowledging their laws be stronger, then it is appropriate to feel worse about violating the law of Germany than the law of Italy.

Do these indeterminacies have analogues in the case of promising? I'm assuming all humans have some interest both in the possession of certain normative powers and in having the chance to exercise them. Though the weight of this interest might vary from individual to individual, I'm assuming there are no systematic differences between adults that ought to be registered in the practice of promising. If so, a practice is not needed to resolve the indeterminacies of identity and jurisdiction that inevitably arise in the case of political authority. But in the matter of stringency, to a significant extent the issue is left open by the underlying authority interest and it remains open unless and until the practice resolves it.

Let's focus on the pure case of breach of promise, the case in which breach of promise would be a bare wronging. How serious a wrong is it? I have said that there is a consensus on the following point: a decent person should feel some compunction about breaking such promises. If Maklay or Hume took their commitments lightly, that would be a mark against them. So we agree that, say, breaching such a promise even in order to further human knowledge or culture in a significant way (Maklay) or to help the indigent (Hume) would wrong the promisee, though it might well be justified. After all, these are just the sorts of consideration the promise was meant to rule out. That is why a decent person would feel bad about doing it. But how bad should they feel?

Different cultures will offer different answers or even no answer at all. Think of deathbed promises. Some would feel awful about breaking such a promise, would regard it as a terrible thing to have to do to someone, quite on a level with inflicting serious physical harm. Others will regard such scruples as overblown. In their view, there is no comparison between breach of even a solemn commitment that passes unnoticed and does no harm on the one hand and a physical assault on the other. Where the latter attitude prevails, the right thing to say is that the obligations imposed by deathbed promises are not particularly stringent. Where neither group predominates, there is no right thing to say. We can only remark that some people get more worked up about this sort of thing than others and that a wide range of such reactions is apt.

Note it would be a mistake to suppose that the stringency of a promise is fixed on a case by case basis by the communicated intentions of the parties. The communicated intentions of the parties do indeed fix the *solemnity* of a promise, that is (to put it crudely) how much the promisor must sacrifice to keep his promise (Sec. 44). And the seriousness of his breach will, of course, be determined by how far short of that standard he falls. So *ceteris paribus* breach of a very solemn deathbed promise will merit more blame than breach of its casual cousin. But that is not because the parties have between them determined the significance of the wrong of breach. Rather what the parties have determined is what would constitute keeping the promise and thus how close the promisor came to keeping it. The normative significance of his coming as close as he did—the aptness of blame and so forth—is determined by the practice, not by them.

In Part III, I shall argue that the interest in authority we share with other human beings and which underlies promissory obligation does fix various aspects of the normative structure of promissory obligation. For example, it ensures that promises extracted under duress do not bind the promisor. But I suspect that this shared interest in authority does not settle exactly how serious breach of promise is as such. We all have an interest in being able to create bare wrongings by declaration but different societies will give this interest a different weight in their practices of recognition. If that is correct then our authority interest cannot settle the stringency of those promises; only our shared habits of recognition will do that, or not as the case may be.

A final observation. Nothing in this chapter (or in this book) is meant as an aid to answering the deliberative question: should I keep this promise? (p. 95). I have said something and shall say a great deal more about the validity conditions of a promise, about the conditions under which a promise binds. But I have said little about when breach of promise is justified, about just when one ought to keep one's promises, and I doubt there is anything general or systematic to be said on that matter. In particular, my talk about the weight of our authority interest, or about how seriously promises are taken within a given community should not be interpreted as an attempt to answer such questions. In the above passages, I am not discussing whether a promise should outweigh the considerations that recommend breach of it in our deliberations. This chapter seeks to explain why it often makes sense to act on a promise and why it is often appropriate to react to breach of promise in certain ways, without laying down when one ought to keep one's promises. As I urged in Part I, obligation is not a factor in deliberation; its only engagement with deliberation is to block it (p. 87).

7

The Possibility of Consent

By consenting to sexual contact, medical treatment, or a visit from the repairman, I ensure that people can have sex with me, treat me, or enter my house without wronging me. Both promise and consent determine who is wronged by a certain act but whilst promising creates obligations, consent abolishes them. A promise ensures that the promisee is wronged by a breach that might otherwise be innocuous; consent ensures that the consentor is not wronged by some deed that would otherwise be far from innocuous.

For Hume, the problem of normative power was raised as much by the phenomenon of consent as by the practice of promising and a similar solution was required:

Were the interests of society nowise concerned, it is as unintelligible, why another's articulating certain sounds, implying consent, should change the nature of my actions with regard to a particular object, as why the reciting of a liturgy by a priest, in a certain habit and posture, should dedicate a heap of brick and timber, and render it, thenceforth and forever, sacred. (Hume 1975: 199)

It is clear enough what Hume has in mind. If I invite you into my home, at least part of what I am doing is to *permit* you to enter, is to declare that you would not wrong me by entering. And such a declaration can make all the difference between an innocuous entry and a trespass. But how? How can I make it the case that you wouldn't wrong me simply by communicating the intention of hereby ensuring that you would not wrong me? If there is a serious reason for you not to enter my house, how can I abolish that reason by declaration?

In the case of promising, I traced Hume's doubts about the possibility of normative power to his doubts about the existence of bare wrongings. The example of trespass fits that diagnosis nicely. It is not hard to imagine cases of trespass which constitute bare wrongings and even with trespasses that cause harm of some sort, we may well be able to argue, as we did in the case of promising, that such harms are by-products of the bare wrong of trespass (Gardner and Shute 2007: 11–12). It is much less obvious that our diagnosis can cope with consent to sex or to a medical procedure. Are the wrongs, the violations of bodily integrity that would occur in the absence of consent really bare wrongings? I shall argue that the wrongs rendered innocuous by consent are all bare wrongings, are all wrongings that affect no human interest. And once their status as bare wrongings is acknowledged, there is no mystery about how mere declaration could affect their status as wrongings. It is perfectly intelligible to suppose that bare wrongings are created and abolished by declaration.

To see how all that might be so, we must first differentiate the power of consent from others ways in which our choices influence the normative situation. In the Introduction, I identified three grades of choice-dependence amongst obligations and our discussion in this chapter will move through the grades. In the next section, I'll examine obligations with the first degree of choice-dependence, outlining various ways in which the fact that we have chosen a certain action or outcome can ensure that it no longer wrongs us. In all these cases, choice is normatively significant because we have a non-normative control interest in the matter, an interest in controlling the action or outcome in question. In the sections that follow, after recalling the rather different role choice plays in creating and extinguishing obligations with the second grade of choice-dependence, I'll argue that we need the sort of direct control over the normative situation which the power of consent provides. This is because we have a specifically normative interest in being able to render certain acts permissible, a permissive interest.

32. Consent and choice

The English word 'consent' and its cousins 'permit', 'authorize', 'allow' can refer to a form of promise. To consent to your driving my car tomorrow may involve agreeing to this, i.e. promising you the use of my car. (Perhaps that is how Hume is employing the term.) But I shall use 'consent' to mark a phenomenon that shares in the mystery of promising without itself being a form of promise.

On my usage, consent involves not the granting of a right but just the waiving of it. To consent to S's dentistry is to intentionally communicate the intention of hereby making it the case that S does not wrong you by whitening your teeth, etc.[1] This intention can be communicated in any number of ways (silence *can* mean consent). On this usage, having consented to dentistry tomorrow, you may rescind or revoke your consent. (There is no such thing as revoking a promise.) Or else, without actually revoking your consent, you may do things that make it impossible for S to take advantage of it: like travelling to another city. And you may do these things without yourself wronging S *simply* because you previously consented (rather than

---

[1] This formulation will require revision (p. 181). Also there may be consent-like powers that work on aspects of the normative situation other than wronging. Suppose a friend learns that I am meeting a group of mutual acquaintances in a bar. Since relations between us have been a bit strained recently, he may think it appropriate to ask whether he could join us even though no one thinks he would otherwise be wronging me. Thanks to Yeo Chuan Tat for pressing me on this point.

because you have aroused expectations and so forth). In consenting you undertake no obligation to ensure that others can take advantage of your consent. I don't deny that an act of consent to dental treatment often implies some sort of agreement to co-operate with the dentist. Frequently there would be little point consenting to some-thing unless you meant to facilitate its occurrence. But, as we shall see, this is not invariably true and even when it is true, in consenting to ϕ-ing you might just be communicating a present intention of allowing ϕ-ing to happen whilst retaining the option of calling things off: 'OK go ahead but once I discover how painful the procedure actually is I might not be able to go through with it' or else 'OK you can do it provided I'm around to have it done'. Here you consent to a procedure without committing to it (Raz 1986: 82–3).

Consent, like promise, raises the problem of normative power. If it is hard to understand how you can oblige yourself to visit the dentist just by declaring that you are so obliged, it is equally hard to understand how you ensure that the dentist does not wrong you by operating on you just by declaring that this will be so. Yet the magic of consent receives much less attention than the magic of promising.[2] I suspect that we are less troubled by consent because we tend to confuse the power of consent with a rather different phenomenon that I shall call the significance of choice. In ordinary talk, 'consent' is freely used where choice is what really does the work but we must differentiate and, I propose, the best way of so doing is to reserve 'consent to ϕ-ing' for cases where you (intentionally) communicate the intention of hereby making it the case that someone would not wrong you by ϕ-ing.

Before focusing on the power of consent, let's first consider the significance of choice. How might whether S wrongs you by ϕ-ing depend on your choices? Suppose S sticks a knife into me. If the knifing is part of a medical procedure that I have chosen rather than a mugging that I have not, it is unlikely to wrong me. But why? An obvious suggestion is this: choice bears on the normative status of an action where we have an interest in having the occurrence of such actions depend on our choices. On this hypothesis, the significance of choice reflects our interest in controlling what is done to us.[3]

We may have such a control interest for quite a number of reasons. For one thing, the fact that someone has chosen to be subjected to a medical procedure may itself be a good indication that it is in their interests to be subjected to the procedure. Provided they are free to choose and well-informed, the patient may be the best

---

[2] The parallel between promise and consent is emphasized by (Thomson 1990: 350–1), (Shiffrin 2008: 500–1), and (Watson 2009: sec. 4) with a view to making promising seem less problematic. See also (Hart 1955: 184).

[3] Of course, I do think we also have interests in controlling the normative situation, interests that cannot be reduced to our interests in controlling the non-normative situation. But I use the phrase 'significance of choice' to mark those forms of normative control which even writers who do not agree with me about this would acknowledge.

judge of whether it is worth their while to suffer the pain and expense of surgery given the benefits that may be forthcoming (Mill 1991: 114). Similarly, the fact that someone has chosen to walk onto the football field may be the best indication that it is in their interests to participate in this contact sport with all the risks entailed. Here it is a good thing if what happens to one depends on one's choices because what happens is more likely to be in one's interests if one has chosen it. And whether ϕ-ing is likely to be in my interests is obviously relevant to the question of whether ϕ-ing wrongs me.

Furthermore, the fact that I have chosen to ϕ may actually *make* it the case that ϕ-ing is in my interests rather than merely indicate that this is so. People often enjoy things that they have chosen or actively decided upon over things that merely happen to them regardless of their choice. They enjoy choosing to enact something worthwhile like a football match. One might have enjoyed the football match even if one had been forced to take part but such enjoyment would have a lesser (or at least a different kind of) value. Additionally (or alternatively), my voluntary participation in the match may be a good both for me and for others because it expresses my adherence to a certain valuable sporting tradition and my participation has this expressive significance only because it depends on my choice. In both of these ways, the fact that I have chosen to walk onto the football field may help to make it the case that others do not wrong me when they crush and tackle me (Raz 1986: 84–8; Scanlon 1998: 251–3).

Can the value of self-expression give a choice normative significance regardless of the value of the thing chosen or declined? Your choice of a good will lack expressive value unless you think you can decline it but it does not follow from this that you should value being able to choose something positively bad. And even where you should value being able to choose between the bad and the good, the significance of this choice still depends on the choice-independent significance of the options. A choice between trivial things could not have expressive value however important you thought they were. To put it another way, there need be no *pure* control interest here (p. 183).

Choice often carries a further social meaning. For example, much of human life is governed by considerations of honour. Certain deeds attract admiration and bestow prestige whilst others humiliate or embarrass. Clearly it is in our interests to be admired because of rather than to be embarrassed by what happens to us and whether our interactions with others are a source of prestige or shame is frequently a function of whether we chose them. Take bodily exposure. Often it is not embarrassing to be observed naked or to be seen dressed as a fairy provided one has chosen to be so observed. One does not incur the same disdain when one's appearance is obviously deliberate (acting, working as a model, swimming, etc.) and where this is so, it is in our interests to be able to choose whether we are exposed to public view. Other forms of social meaning are comparative. If I live in a society in which most people are allowed the choice of whether to wear a crash helmet whilst cycling, the fact that I (and people like me) are deprived of this choice will be demeaning. It carries the message that they but not I are competent to decide this matter (Scanlon 1998: 253). And this may be so whether or not choice has, in this instance, the other forms of social and psychological significance just described. Given that I have an interest in not being demeaned, I also have an interest in having the ability to control my headwear.

I conclude that choice bears on the normative status of an action where we have an interest in controlling such actions by means of our choices. It is worth noting that this control interest is in play even when there is no question of anyone's being harmed. As we have seen, though many acts are wrongs because they harm some- one's interests, some are wrongs for a rather different reason, namely because they are unfair, an unfairness which need not involve harm, e.g. where you get an unfair share of the proceeds of our co-operative enterprise. Here the rest of us might both benefit from and deserve to receive a larger share of the products of our joint enterprise, even if being 'deprived' of this share constitutes no *harm* to us. Now just as citing the victim's choice is a defence against the allegation that you wronged them by harming them, so choice can rebut the allegation that your behaviour was unfair to us. For example if we, your partners in the co-operative enterprise, freely choose to grant you such generous terms, this may well remove the unfairness. Our choice has normative significance here because our interest in the distribution of these benefits gives us an interest in controlling how they are distributed for the reasons already canvassed.

Having reviewed some of the ways in which having a choice can matter, we are now in a position to see how choice, operating independently of consent, influences the normative situation. Recall that to consent to S's ϕ-ing was to intentionally communicate the intention of hereby ensuring that S does not wrong you by ϕ-ing. Choice does its normative work rather differently. First, choice in the above examples has a non-normative object. The patient chooses to undergo surgery, the football player chooses to take the risk of being hit, etc. Their choices may ensure that certain physical assaults no longer wrong them but what they are choosing is the surgery and the risk, not the normative status of the assault. Second, it is the choice and not the communication of the choice that matters. If my choice makes it OK for the surgeon and the other players to touch me then provided they know of my choice, they are not blameworthy for so doing.[4] It does not matter whether they learnt this fact because I intentionally let them know that this was my choice.

This last point is particularly obvious where your action has its impact on me even though there is no further interaction between us. Do you wrong me by possessing

---

[4] As Andrew Simester pointed out to me, the fact that I have chosen to play football or have sex makes *some* difference even if the other parties do not know or care whether I have chosen to do so.

some offensive drawings? That might depend on whether you put them in a place where I am likely to see them without choosing to. If I see them only because I choose to see them then my objection to being shocked is undermined and this has nothing to do with whether I have communicated my choice to you or anyone else, intentionally or otherwise.[5] Nor does it depend on my views about how my choice will affect the normative situation: perhaps I will feel wronged by the sight of your drawings regardless. What gets you off the hook (with regards to my shock) is simply that you knew I would see them only if I chose to.

Despite these differences it is no surprise that the significance of choice and the power of consent are often conflated.[6] My sitting in the dentist's chair or walking onto the football field does have the effect of letting others know that I have made a certain choice. Furthermore I typically know that fact. Therefore it is usually the case that I intentionally communicate my choice by so acting. Finally, I typically know that my choice will have a certain effect on the normative situation. Therefore, it is usually the case that when I make a normatively significant choice I intentionally change the normative situation. Nonetheless the normative significance of my choice here need not depend on any of this. It might depend only on its being known that I have chosen (or am very likely to have chosen) the surgery or the game.

We have been assuming that consent must be communicated to be valid but this may be denied. Perhaps consent is an interior mental act, something like the act of changing the normative situation by performing this very act with the intention of hereby changing the normative situation.[7] One may, for all sorts of reasons, choose to communicate the fact that one has consented to the relevant party and only in rather unusual situations will you authorize someone to do something without somehow informing them of the fact. But, on this model of consent, such communication merely informs them of a change that has already taken place; it does not make that change. Neither consent nor choice need be communicated to be normatively significant.

To test this hypothesis, suppose X says to Y, 'I've inwardly authorized Z to walk across my land to work but I'd like to be the one to tell him so'. Y then pre-empts X by informing Z. Will Z feel entitled to walk across X's land on his way to work? It seems not. Most people would still feel the need to go and *ask* X for permission, even

---

[5] Must I choose to look where I know offensive drawing may be found, or merely where I know I am not meant to look? I leave this open. Either form of knowledge may be acquired without communicating with you.

[6] In Sec. 47, I'll contend that we can understand the validity conditions of promise, consent, and other exercises of normative power by thinking of them as choices about whether to exercise a normative power and asking under what conditions such choices are normatively significant. So understood the power of consent becomes a special case of the normative significance of choice, where the underlying control interest is an interest in controlling the normative situation by declaration. In this chapter, I use 'choice' and 'control interest' in the narrower, non-normative sense just introduced.

[7] This possibility was suggested to me by Pete Graham. See also (Austin 1962: 9–10).

if they had absolutely no doubt that Y was reporting X's words correctly. They wouldn't feel that they'd actually been given permission to walk across X's land until X had communicated this permission to them, or at least allowed this permission to be communicated to them. Is this because, in general, one isn't entitled to act on pieces of information that one isn't entitled to have? I doubt that is what is going on here. Suppose X tells Y in confidence that he believes that Z is in any case entitled to walk across his land (he's looked into the legal situation) but that he wishes this fact to be concealed from Z. Again Y tells Z. Here Z may still feel a little queasy about acting on this information but that's not because he doubts that he can cross X's land without trespassing, whilst if he knows that X has refused to communicate his 'permission', trespass is precisely what he will fear.

The contrast between consent and choice on this point is stark. Suppose I do everything I can to stop you knowing that I have freely chosen to play football (perhaps you'll look down on me if you think I played voluntarily). I wish you to believe that I am on the pitch only under duress. That does not change the fact that, because I have chosen to play, playing is more likely to be in my interests in all the ways discussed earlier. And your knowledge of the fact that I have freely chosen to play is what entitles you to crush and tackle me should you be on the opposing team. Whether it so entitles you is not dependent on whether I set out to conceal my choice from you.

What of 'presumed consent'? The patient is unconscious and the doctor operates in order to save their life. Is the doctor operating on the assumption that the patient would have consented if asked? The neighbours have left the bath running and, though they are strangers to me, I enter their empty apartment in order to switch it off. Do I feel entitled to do this because I presume they would have agreed? The answer is unobvious. On the one hand, I'd be much less likely to go in if I thought the neighbours wouldn't agree which perhaps indicates that counterfactual consent shares at least some of the normative significance of actual consent. On the other hand, most people would still enter their neighbour's apartment with some reluctance, a reluctance that need not derive entirely from doubts about what their neighbour would say. This suggests that they are engaged in justified wronging, a wronging that presumed consent does not abolish.

These issues can't be resolved here but, for my purposes, two points will suffice. First, counterfactual consent is no substitute for actual consent whenever actual consent is available. The doctor cannot argue that he didn't need to ask me when he had the chance because he knew I would have agreed. On this point, choice is like consent: whatever the normative significance of counterfactual choice, it is no substitute for actual choice. Second, choice and consent differ once more in respect of communication. The significance of counterfactual choice does not generally depend on whether it would have been communicated whilst the significance of consent does. If counterfactual consent can indeed abolish the bare wrong of bodily assault or trespass (at least where actual consent is impossible) the counterfactual in question concerns what would have been communicated.[8]

Consent involves communication.[9] It is noteworthy that the same is true of other exercises of normative powers such as promising and commanding. You are not wronging me by failing to show up at the bus stop unless you have communicated to me the intention of *hereby* (i.e. by means of this very communication) obliging yourself to appear. Perhaps you can inwardly vow to meet me at the bus stop but, even supposing such vows do bind, you do not owe it *to me* to appear. And this is so even if you happen to tell me about your vow (setting the effect on my expectations aside). Some might think that this is because a promise must be accepted by the promisee to be binding and nobody can accept a promise that hasn't been communicated to them. I agree that binding promises must be offered and accepted but I doubt this is what explains the need for communication. An order need not be accepted to be valid but it must be communicated. I can't put my subordinates under an obligation to do anything simply by performing an inner mental act. Even if they somehow learnt of this act, they still haven't been told to do anything and it is the telling which binds.

I'll conclude this section by noting how my usage of 'consent' differs from one familiar alternative. On this alternative usage, to consent to something is to wittingly forfeit the right not to have it done to you. For example, Nino maintains that one has consented to a change in the normative situation just when one (voluntarily) does something which one knows will have that change as a necessary consequence (Nino 1983: 296). So the criminal who knowingly violates a (just) law has 'consented' to his punishment because he knowingly deprives himself of the right not to be punished. Though Nino's notion of consent differs from my own—even when the criminal intentionally forfeits his right he exercises no normative power—it is helpful to consider how such forfeiture works.

Suppose we are put on notice that everyone who enters a certain house, club, or park must obey certain rules. By choosing to enter the relevant house, club, or park do we thereby *consent* to obey the rules? Nino would say yes. I would agree only if we acquired these obligations because by entering the park we intentionally communicated the intention of hereby undertaking an obligation to obey these rules. That seems unlikely.[10] On a more natural reading of the example, our choosing to enter

---

[8]   As Brad Hooker observed, when thinking about how to administer a relative's estate, imagining what they would have chosen is different from imagining what they would have agreed to. Each has its own significance.

[9]   Jenny Saul and Peter Goldie pointed out that it might be enough for the consentor to have tried to communicate their consent and for the consentee to reasonably believe that they have received the relevant communication. (My medical consent form is lost in the post but, due to a mix up, the hospital thinks they have received it.) In any case, the asymmetry between choice and consent remains.

[10]   The park example comes from (Raz 1986: 83–4). In other cases, it is more plausible that a normative power is being exercised by means of a communicative act. For example, if you put a coin in a slot in order

the park has a rather different normative significance. By entering the park we choose to accept the benefits of having access to a public park and therefore it is only fair that we should carry the burden of conforming to the relevant restrictions.[11] It matters that we know of these restrictions (if it does) because this removes an objection to our being subject to any sanctions attached to their violation, namely that we might (reasonably) have been unaware that our entry had this cost. On this more natural reading, the example involves no exercise of a power of consent, though it remains a case of 'consent' as Nino defines it since by entering the park one intentionally forfeits the right to ignore the rules of the park.

The normative significance of choice in the park example derives from our control interests. If someone freely chooses to enter the club in the knowledge that certain rules will be applied to them, that may indicate that it is in their (non-normative) interests that these rules be applied to them, or else it may be the case that giving effect to their choice here enables them to express their adherence to an important institution and so forth. (This why we don't wrong them by sanctioning a rule-violation.) A similar rationale can be given for the significance of choice in the generation of obligations of reciprocation and of due care for expectations discussed in earlier chapters. The role of choice in all these cases is to justify the imposition of a certain burden and for choice to play that role, we need suppose only that people's non-normative control interests are at stake. We need not assume that people have any normative interest in the matter, any further interest in what does or does not constitute a wronging.

33. Consent and normative interests

So what is the function of consent? What does this social tool do for us that can't be done by making choices? Consent enables us to determine by declaration whether something constitutes a wronging. Who would benefit from having such a power? Creatures with only non-normative control interests could get by without. Human beings are not such creatures. We need to mould our normative niche. But it does not follow that we need to control such matters by declaration. I have already urged that the value of friendship and of other forms of involvement depends on our being interested in the normative situation for its own sake, on our having deontic interests. But the wrongs and obligations of friendship are not abolished by declaration and so

to purchase a parking ticket, you thereby communicate your consent to the conditions of purchase (whatever they may be). There is a record of your communication in the fact that the ticket was issued, should the owner of the car park wish to consult it. For a different view of such examples, see (Raz 1999: 103).

[11] (Hart 1955: 184–6) contrasts this obligation-generating mechanism with both promise and consent. See also (Simmons 1976: 287).

the interest that generates a power of consent is of a different sort. I'll make the point by means of an example.

You are giving a lecture at a conference with parallel sessions. In the way of these things, it is likely that a significant proportion of your audience are sitting in the room under a misapprehension as to whose lecture this is. They'll discover their error once you start to speak and will likely wish to leave. But, at least in many social contexts, it is rude to leave a lecture once the speaker has begun. Without the ability to remove this element of rudeness, you are faced with the prospect of having to endure either the insult of a mass exodus or the restlessness of a captive audience. There is a way out. You can begin your talk by announcing your name and topic and inviting those who are here by mistake to take the opportunity to leave the room. Then (in many social contexts) they can leave without wronging you.

How should we understand this announcement of yours? One might construe it as the expression of a choice: you intend that those in the room under a misapprehension should leave. But this may not be what you intend at all. Haven't we all found ourselves in talks unwillingly and then been unexpectedly entranced by the speaker and their subject? Mightn't you imagine that the same will happen once you begin to speak? Entertaining such hopes, you do not intend that people leave just because they are there by mistake, nor are you trying to communicate such an intention. Rather your announcement is directed at the normative situation. You mean to alter the normative significance of their leaving the room should they (against your wishes) choose to do so. You mean to ensure that their departure would not be an insult by consenting to it.

So far so good: we have a power of consenting to ϕ-ing whose exercise involves no choice of ϕ-ing, no intention that ϕ-ing occur. Now imagine that some of the people in the audience are your friends. They too have made a mistake but, unlike the rest, they should stay out of loyalty. Can you ensure that they would not be wronging you in leaving simply by declaring that this is so? Surely not. If it were clear that you wished them to go or that you'd otherwise benefit from their going, perhaps they'd be happy to go. But a mere declaration would not make that sort of difference. They couldn't leave without compunction so long as you have an interest their staying, or at least in controlling whether they do stay. Here the bonds of loyalty can be waived by your choices but not by your declarations.[12]

---

[12] I agree that friends (no less than strangers) can employ the power of consent to change what would count as a wronging between them. What I deny is that they can abolish *those wrongs grounded in the value of their friendship* in this way. Someone who thinks that insulting one's friend behind their back is not a form of disloyalty provided they consent has misunderstood the nature of friendship. The same is true of permissions. If my right to ask my friend personal questions is grounded in the value of our relationship, my friend can't deprive me of this right by withdrawing his 'consent' (p. 107). Rather he must transform the nature of our friendship, something that can't be done by declaration.

Still our lecturer example indicates that we do have an interest in controlling the normative situation of strangers by declaration. This interest comes apart from our interest in controlling what they actually do in two ways. There are cases in which we grant a privilege without either having or communicating the intention that it be exercised. For example one can invite people to a party whom one neither wants nor expects to show up, a fact they may be well aware of. Here you give them the right to show up without communicating any intention that they show up. Perhaps you invite them for form's sake and just don't care whether they show up. Perhaps you invite them in order to ensure that they won't show up (they won't come when invited by *you*, though they would have come had your partner invited them first). Either way, you have granted them the right to attend.

Conversely, we sometimes communicate the intention that someone be at our party without thereby consenting to their being there, without thereby making it the case that their presence would not wrong us. Suppose I want Kate to attend but Kate has had a falling out with my partner. I tell Kate 'I'd love you to come but I prefer not to invite you myself. I would rather my partner invite you and they will do so only if you ask them.' Here I am telling Kate that I mean her to come, without thereby consenting to her coming, even though I have an (independent) power of consent. If Kate showed up without bothering to get permission from my partner, Kate would be wronging us both since neither of us has consented.[13]

Given the many different ways in which our choices can affect the normative situation, why do we need a power of consent? Why do we need to be able to control the normative situation by declaration? I shall suggest that we need consent to serve a normative interest, an interest not dissimilar from that which underlies promising. For Hobbes, all obligations—indeed all wrongings—have their source in promising and we must be able to release each other from our promises. For Hobbes, the power of consent just is this power of release (Hobbes 1994: 94). Hobbes's assimilation of these two normative powers is no more plausible than the view of obligation that motivates it but it does suggest an illuminating parallel. One who proposes to substitute choice for consent may be asked to do the same with the power of release. And the difficulties that confront the latter project reveal the flaws in the former, or so I shall urge.

Promising is here to serve the promisee's authority interest, an interest in having a certain form of control over the normative situation, in being able to choose whether others are required to fulfil a promise. This authority interest can be satisfied only if the promisee has power of release. For a promise to bind it must be both offered and accepted and so the promisor and the promisee are on a par so far as the *creation* of the obligation goes; there is no asymmetry of authority here. It is only with the power of release that the desired asymmetry emerges. The promisee can abolish the

---

[13] I'm not consenting conditional on my partner's consenting since my consent is redundant once they have consented.

obligation by declaration and this declaration is effective whether accepted by the promisor or not; the promisor has no similar power (pp. 220–2). This power of release employs the very mechanism by which the obligation is imposed, the communication of the intention to hereby change the normative situation. Merely intending to promise does not bind you even if the promisee somehow learns of your intention. You must actually communicate the intention to bind yourself by way of this very communication. Similarly what releases is the intentional communication of the decision to hereby release and not the decision itself. To act in anticipation of release is to wrong the promisee.[14] Indeed outrage at being pre-empted in this way might lead the promisee to abandon their intention to release.

Can we ground this power of release in the significance of choice?[15] That the power of release can be exercised without any corresponding choice suggests a negative answer. I can release you from a promise whilst making it quite clear that I intend you to do what you promised to do. Indeed the release might be my means of getting you to perform, if I think you are more likely to do so 'of your own free will'. Conversely, I might decline to release you from a promise, whilst making it clear that I couldn't care less whether you actually perform. Perhaps I extracted the promise at the behest of a third party who wishes you to be held to it.

Recall that promising generates bare wrongings. In particular, a promise can ensure that behaviour that the promisor has no interest in controlling is a wrong to him. Maklay's Malay has no interest in his being able to choose whether he is photographed (pp. 125–6). Having this choice would improve neither his life chances, nor his social standing (neither he nor anybody who shares his beliefs would know of the photograph), nor express his endorsement of important values (his worries are simply illusory). In so far as we ground the significance of choice in our (non-normative) control interests we must conclude that the Malay's choice lacks any normative significance, yet surely the Malay has the power to release Maklay from his promise. I argued that though controlling whether Maklay takes his photograph will do the Malay no good, the Malay does have an interest in being able to control the normative significance of Maklay's action. The Malay does have an interest in being able to control by declaration whether it makes sense for Maklay to deliberate about this issue in a certain fashion and how it is appropriate for us all to react should he fail to deliberate in this fashion. And the Malay's interest in possessing this normative power is distinct from any interest in having the power to determine what Maklay will actually do.

---

[14] I am thinking of a case in which I do something which makes it impossible for me to fulfil my promise on the assumption that you will release me from it. I doubt that I wrong you if I merely fail to *intend* to fulfill such a promise (Sec. 38).

[15] Scanlon proposes to ground the need for 'consent to agreements' in the significance of choice (Scanlon 1998: 260 and Scanlon 2003a: 263–6).

Hobbes is wrong. Despite their formal similarities consent is not release, for consent renders innocuous many actions whose wrongfulness is not the product of a promise. Nevertheless, the problems confronting any attempt to explain the power of release in terms of the normative significance of choice reappear when we try to do the same for the power of consent. This fact indicates that underlying our possession of the power of consent are normative interests similar to but not identical with the authority interest that grounds the power of release. And that should make us wonder whether the genealogical hypothesis we floated for promising might not apply to consent also.

In the last chapter, we suggested that promissory obligation might have emerged from a background of obligations of involvement. People's lives are made better by obligations which are arise in the context of an involvement and so they acquire an interest in forging similar bonds with strangers, bonds which must be created by declaration. Now involvements also entail permissions: I am permitted to ask my friend personal questions which others are not. Such permissions are part of what gives friendship its value and don't we all have an interest in spreading such permissions more widely? The ability to create permissions by declaration is just what we need.

34. Permissive interests

In this section, I'll seek to establish two points. First, that there are bare wrongings not created by a promise. Second, that we have an interest in being able to authorize these acts by declaration and that there is nothing unintelligible here. The latter *permissive interests* are what ground the power of consent.[16]

The wrong of rape is a bare wronging (Gardner and Shute 2007: 3–8). This might sound absurd. Most rapists do their victim great physical or psychological damage. But, as in the case of breach of promise, we must carefully disentangle secondary wrongs from the primary wrong that they accompany. In the case of promising, the primacy of the bare wronging comes out in two ways. First, there are cases in which the primary wrong occurs without its usual accompaniments but remains a serious matter.[17] (Breach of a solemn deathbed promise.) Second, the harms and other

---

[16] This book discusses grave wrongings in the clinical, dispassionate idiom of much contemporary moral philosophy. Those who, for instance, employ this idiom when describing the use of innocent shields in war are not thought to be failing to take war crimes seriously. Their tone does not carry that implication, at least for those who are likely to read them. By contrast, the tenor of the discussion of rape that follows might carry that implication for some readers. I do not intend to imply that rape is not a grave wronging; indeed my point is precisely that it is. Perhaps it is a mistake to treat any fraught matter in this fashion but, if the method is sound, we should not shy away from applying it to human sexuality.

[17] (Thomson 1990: 316–30) discusses cases of breach of promise and violations of bodily integrity where the victim's interests are not affected. She suggests that in both cases the victim has a genuine right or claim that this not be done to them but that their claim is of 'zero stringency'. The latter claim is plausible in the

secondary wrongs that typically accompany the bare wronging acquire much of their normative significance from the context of bare wronging in which they occur. For example, people do expect others to keep their promises and so suffer psychologically when this does not happen. People rely on promises to their detriment and so suffer material damage when the promise is breached. Both reliance and outrage at being let down are reasonable largely because breach of promise is independently wrongful. For analytical purposes, the central cases of breach of promise are the statistically peripheral ones in which no harm aggravates the primary wrong.

So it is with rape:

It is possible, though unusual, for a rapist to do no harm. A victim may be forever oblivious to the fact that [they were] raped if, say, [they were] drugged or drunk to the point of unconsciousness when the rape was committed and the rapist wore a condom... Then we have a victim of rape whose life is not changed for the worse, or at all, by the rape. [They do] not... 'feel violated'. [They have] no feelings about the incident since [they know] nothing of it. (Gardner and Shute 2007: 5)[18]

Gardner and Shute go on to stipulate that nobody else learns anything of the rape and that the rapist dies soon afterward, so neither the victim's social standing nor other people's sense of security is affected. These stipulations notwithstanding, bare rape (as I shall call it) is a grave wrong.

Where the victim discovers what has happened to them, the secondary wrongs kick in. They would be rightly outraged and probably shattered. And when the rape is experienced as it occurs, this experience is often traumatizing, even when no physical damage is done, precisely because it is the experience of a great wrong. It is crucial to grasp the order of explanation here: if what made rape wrong were the brute fact that it tended to have a shattering or traumatizing effect on those who became aware of it, a tranquilliser could render it innocuous.

Consent to sexual relations is a paradigm case of an exercise of the power of consent. Merely by intentionally communicating the intention of hereby authorizing you to have sex with me, I ensure that you do not commit the egregious wrong of rape, whatever other wrong you may do me. But if rape is a bare wronging, this power of consent cannot be based on any control interest, on any interest we may have in our choices controlling what happens to us. In a case of bare rape, I have no such interest. Since there is no physical or psychological damage, nor risk of such we may suppose, there is no role for judgement (good or bad) as to whether the risk is worth

---

case she mentions (where you pinch the nose of someone in a coma (317)) but not when applied to pure rape.

[18] The bracketed phrases render the example gender neutral. I have seen reports of doctors accused of drugging their patients and then abusing them whilst unconscious. To make Gardner and Shute's point, we need not suppose that such incidents have no collateral effects, only that their gravity is not proportional to the gravity of those effects.

it to me. Since I do nothing, no expressive value is at stake. Since I do not experience it, pleasure and pain are not an issue. Since nobody knows of the rape except for the rapist, my social standing is unchanged and fear will not spread through the land.

Of course rape and other violations of bodily integrity are usually dreaded quite independently of the damage involved. This fear is clearly a cost to those who suffer it but the normative significance of this dread is unclear. Why should bare rape be regarded as demeaning and humiliating given that the victim's other interests are quite untouched by it? Compare a bare rapist with someone who (deliberately) imagines committing bare rape on an acquaintance. The real and imaginary rapes are equally harmless we may suppose. The acquaintance would doubtless prefer that this not be imagined and may even fear its being imagined. But fear of imaginary rape lacks the normative significance of fear of bare rape and, one might suppose, this is because the wrong of imagining rape (if wrong it be) is much less grave than the wrong of committing it.

Perhaps the wrongfulness of bare rape derives from the symbolic meaning of the act, from the fact that it expresses a bad attitude to the interests of the victim. Raz suggests that:

The natural fact that coercion and manipulation reduce options or distort normal processes of decision and the formation of preferences has become the basis of a social convention loading them with meaning regardless of their actual consequences. They have acquired a symbolic meaning expressing disregard or even contempt for the coerced or manipulated people. (Raz 1986: 378)

Along these lines one might propose that such acts as bare rape are wrong because they express a bad attitude to the victim's non-normative control interests. Though bare rape is not itself an instance of coercion or manipulation since the victim's will is not engaged, bare rape might still symbolize the wrong committed when people are forced or tricked into having sex and do so in a way which merely imaginary rape does not.[19]

I agree that we might attribute this symbolic significance to bare rape. The question is whether this fact can ground its wrongfulness. Suppose the bare rapist is scrupulous about the avoidance of coercion, harm, humiliation, and so forth. Would his act still carry the relevant symbolic significance? And, if so, would it mean any more to us than his *imagining* committing the bare rape? Perhaps it would, perhaps it wouldn't but I doubt that the wrongness of bare rape depends on our answer. Suppose the resemblance between bare rape and coerced sex was much less salient to some other social group or else that this resemblance struck them as no more significant than that between coerced sex and imaginary rape. Perhaps their society has different symbols of coerced sex or none at all. Still, I would argue, it is in

---

[19] See the discussion of the special significance of penetration in (Gardner and Shute 2007: 21–5).

their interests that bare rape (rather than imagined rape) be recognized as a wronging. Bare rape ought to be recognized as a wrong. One might respond that this is so because bare rape *ought* to be treated as a symbol of coerced sex. But isn't that just to say that it ought to be treated as being wrong in the same way as coercive sex?

There is a second form of symbolic meaning bare rape might carry: it might convey contempt for our normative interests and, in particular, our interest in rape constituting a wronging unless we declare otherwise. Could this be the ground of its wrongfulness? I don't deny that some instances of rape might constitute expressions of contempt for the underlying permissive interest. But most instances of rape (including those that involve action against the victim's non-normative interests) do not harm the permissive interest. Rape tends not to deprive its victim of the power of consent.[20] So where bare rape is treated as expressing a bad attitude to the victim's permissive interests, this will be a matter of convention and, as we have just seen, convention can't be the whole story about why bare rape is wrong. There is a further difficulty. You don't usually *wrong* someone simply by expressing a bad attitude to their interests unless those interests are sufficiently serious to ground the wrongfulness of other, non-symbolic forms of wrongdoing. So unless we allow that the victim's possession of a permissive interest is already sufficient to ground the wrong of bare rape, we can't assume that it constitutes the wrongful expression of a bad attitude towards this interest.

In our social world, there is at least one bare wronging not created by a promise: the wrong of rape. Consent operates on the bare wrong of rape. Furthermore, consent operates directly *only* on the bare wrong: one can't abolish those secondary wrongs that occur in the course of most rapes merely by declaration. We've seen that many of the wrongings of friendship are unaffected by declaration and the point is even more obvious when we consider action against our non-normative interests. Earlier I claimed there were whole classes of wrong to which one cannot consent (p. 49). We can now see why: many wrongings are not bare wrongings.[21] I can't make it the case that I am not wronged by a serious physical injury, for instance, simply by declaring that this is so. The significance of the injury depends on its affecting my interests (including my control interests) and though my choices might influence how it affects my interests, my declarations alone will not.

---

[20] Certain feminist writers have argued that at least some women cannot ensure that sex with them is wrongful by refusing sex because they lack the relevant social authority or standing. They lack this standing precisely because rape is so prevalent in their social context. The word 'no' coming from their mouths cannot have the illocutionary force of refusal because it cannot be understood as a communication of the intention to hereby make sex wrongful (Langton 1993: 322–8). If these writers are correct, rape could indeed deprive victims of the power of consent. Nevertheless a given rape would be wrong even if this were not true of that particular rape and it is rather unlikely to be true of any acts of *bare* rape.

[21] Being a bare wronging is thus necessary for something to be a possible object of consent. It may or may not be sufficient.

Hume thought consent unintelligible because he made two assumptions. First, he assumed that all wronging must involve action against the interests of the wronged. Second, he assumed that if the wrongfulness of a wrong depends on how it affects our interests then one cannot remove the wrongfulness of a wrong merely by declaration. Hume's second assumption is sound but it does not apply to bare wrongings. In their case, why shouldn't one be able to affect the normative significance of the act by declaration since its normative significance does not depend on whether it involves action against any human interest?

It will seem obvious to many that consent can have an impact on the normative significance of deeds other than bare wrongings. Furthermore, it may appear equally evident that, even in the absence of consent, choice can affect the normative significance of a bare wrong like rape. I'll deal with these queries in order.

As to the first, an expression of consent is often also an expression of choice, of an intention that the act consented to should actually occur as a result of the consent. And where this is so, the normative character of a physical injury may be transformed by the choice. Think of the difference between a lover's bite and a rapist's. Purely *qua* physical injury, they are on a par but one exacerbates the wrong of rape whilst the other may enhance the good of sex. Since for many lovers being able to control whether you are bitten is a good thing, their choice turns the bite into a good thing.[22] By contrast, lobotomization or (voluntary) enslavement can't be good in the same way whether chosen or not.[23] Doubtless choice makes some difference in their case but not such as to prevent these acts from wronging us. Hence consent does not appear to transform their normative character. The case of simple killing is more complex. Lying on the battlefield mortally wounded and in great pain, perhaps I can consent to being put out of my misery by a comrade. Here consent is significant as an expression of choice and if I have enough of an interest in being able to choose death in these circumstances, it may ensure that the killing does not wrong me.

Even where consent is not an expression of choice, consent may have an indirect impact on the significance of such injuries, physical and psychological. You do not want sex with me. Given the choice, you would rather not and you let me know as much. But, for any number of reasons, you might not want it to be the case that, should I go ahead anyway, that would make me a rapist and you a rape victim.[24] So you waive your veto, that is you communicate the intention of hereby making it the case that should I go ahead despite your preferences, I would not be raping you. And, we may suppose, you do so freely (the simple fact that you don't intend me to have sex with you need not entail the presence of a consent-invalidating duress). Here,

---

[22] This is a case where pain and physical damage may be a good thing.

[23] They may have instrumental value but not value for their own sake.

[24] Consenting might even be a way of ensuring that no sex took place. A rapist aroused by the idea of rape would be discouraged by consent.

because your consent is not an expression of your choice I might still be wronging you by persisting in the face of your reluctance. But I would not be committing the egregious wrong of rape and that alters the significance of any secondary wrongs in so far as their significance depends on the context in which they occur rather than on their intrinsic character as injuries. Your fear is no longer fear of rape and your distaste or even disgust are not reactions to the experience of rape. The marks I leave are not lover's bites—they may well be a focus of embarrassment or even resent-ment—but nor are they remnants of a rape. By removing the primary wrong, your consent changes the character of these secondary wrongs.

I have said that to consent to ϕ-ing is to communicate the intention of hereby making it the case that ϕ-ing would not wrong you. This formulation must be refined in the light of my latest example. There, in consenting to sex, you don't set out to make it the case that sex with you would not wrong you. You know (and may indeed insist on the fact) that sex with you would still wrong you. Nevertheless, there is a way in which sex would wrong you in the absence of consent and you intend to make it the case that sex does not wrong you in that way.

Turning to the second query, can sex that has been chosen constitute rape? It must be so if the interest that generates the wrong of rape is an interest in being wronged by sex unless you *declare* otherwise. And it is so. Someone chooses to be raped where they intend that the rapist have sex with them after they have explicitly refused their consent. This choice is somewhat perverse but by no means impossible (virgins seeking martyrdom) and the choice may well make a difference to the character of what transpires. For one thing it may lessen or even in some cases abolish the wrongfulness of the secondary effects of the rape. But the primary wrong remains: to have sex in the teeth of an explicit refusal is to rape. There is a sense in which '"No" means No' even where the perpetrator is correct in supposing that the victim wishes them to go ahead.

I conclude that to explain the significance of bare rape and of its antidote consent, we must ground the wrong of rape not in some interest supposedly compromised by the rape itself but rather in a normative interest, in an interest in its being the case that one is wronged by the rape *unless one consents to it*. This is what I call a permissive interest. And this interest is in play even though it is not under threat. Just as breach of promise need not harm the authority interest, so rape need not harm this permissive interest. Nevertheless, a regard for the normative status of these wrongings will prevent the conscientious from committing them.

I have been writing as if consent is here to serve the consentor's interest in giving consent but doesn't the consentee have an equally fundamental interest in receiving it? If we had no interest in being permitted to have sex, why would anyone have an interest in being able to permit us to have sex? The promisor's interest in being able to grant authority depends on the promisee's interest in being able to acquire it (pp. 146–7). Why isn't it the same with the permissions granted by consent? This objection overlooks the fact that a permissive interest is not just an interest in being able to permit something by declaration. It is also an interest in that thing's constituting a wronging in the absence of such a declaration. And though others may well have an interest in having your consent to sex, it is hard to see how they could have an interest in being wrongdoers should they have sex with you without your consent.

Our objection to rape is but one aspect of our concern with bodily integrity. I am seriously wronged by medical procedures to which I do not consent, however beneficial and risk free they may be. I am mildly wronged when someone removes a hair from my head as a souvenir whilst I'm asleep. I may even be wronged by cannibals who desecrate my dead body. There are often secondary wrongs here, wrongs tied to risk of harm, or psychic distress or public humiliation but the primary wrong is clearly a violation of bodily integrity, a violation which is objectionable regardless of whether there is a loss of some form of bodily control which I might sensibly value.

The cluster of normative interests around the body encourages the thought that all such interests must be connected with non-normative interests, interests in control over what happens to our body. Imagine a world in which nobody has much interest in physical sexual activity—human beings have learned to reproduce and gain erotic pleasure in other ways—and yet vestigial sexual organs remain (rather like the appendix). In such a world, could bare rape have anything like the significance it has in our own lives? And doesn't that indicate that the weighty permissive interest we have with respect to sex is dependent on the weighty non-normative interests surrounding sexual activity as presently constituted? Indeed but as I previously noted, such dependence can take various forms (pp. 65–6). It may be no coincidence that normative interests cluster around the body, i.e. around the very thing that is also the object of numerous non-normative concerns, without it being the case that these normative interests are grounded in these non-normative concerns. Rather each may be embedded in the other. The whole set of bodily interests—normative and non-normative—may come in a package whose elements can't either be pulled apart or arranged in order of explanatory priority.

35. Conclusion to Part II

Our discussion of normative powers has been far from comprehensive. For example, rights of ownership involve both normative powers (e.g. the acquisition and transfer of property) and bare wrongings. People are frequently horrified to discover that their house has been burgled even if no damage has been done, nothing has been taken, no embarrassing information revealed and so forth. They feel their home has been violated and their privacy traduced (Gardner and Shute 2007: 11–12). Ownership raises issues of its own which cannot be dealt with here. The same may be true of other normative powers like the power to issue commands within a social hierarchy. Instead of exploring new terrain, I'll raise the worry that we could dispense with normative interests altogether by instead postulating what I'll call *pure control interests*.

Suppose human beings have an interest in controlling what happens to their bodies, in having the occurrence of various forms of bodily contact depend on whether they intend that these forms of bodily contact occur, an interest which is distinct from and perhaps independent of facts about how these forms of bodily contact bear on their other interests. Earlier, I based our control interests on our interest in such goods as pleasure, self-expression, and social standing (pp. 166–8). But we are now supposing that our control interests go beyond anything covered by these concerns. Can we ground the existence of bare wrongings in such pure control interests in accordance with the *Injury Hypothesis*? Rape for example would be an action against our interest in being in control of what happens to our body, even where we remain quite unaware of it. And the bare wrong of breach of promise might be grounded in our interest in being able to control what others do, where our interest in controlling the latter extends beyond our interest in goods like pleasure, self-expression, and so forth. Perhaps Maklay's servant does have an interest in controlling whether he is photographed, one harmed by breach of promise.

It has already been established that people have an interest in controlling the normative situation distinct from *any* interest they might have in controlling what actually happens (p. 173). If so, normative control interests must exist regardless of whether we have *pure* control interests. This point will be reinforced by my discussion in Part III, where I undertake the task of explaining in detail the character of the social practices that surround the exercise of normative power. Authority interests and permissive interests are required not just to address abstract philosophical questions about the very possibility of promise and consent but also to explain their workings. One who postulates pure control interests must show that such interests would make a non-redundant contribution to this explanatory task and our discussion in this chapter and elsewhere provides grounds for pessimism. Since normative control interests can ground the possibility of bare wronging all by themselves, pure control interests look dispensable.

Having set pure control interests aside, I'll briefly review the social phenomena we have discussed and the normative interests which ground them. Our normative interests take various forms and underwrite different norm-generating mechanisms. Recall Figure 1 (p. 11). Is this array of powers really necessary? Is there any element of redundancy here? Compare forgiveness and consent. Both serve our interest in controlling when blame is an appropriate response to an act or an attitude. Why do we need them both? If we can consent to wrongs before the fact and thereby render blame inappropriate doesn't that make forgiveness redundant?

Forgiveness is not pardon and does not work by declaration (p. 53). Consequently, forgiveness is often hard in a way consent cannot be. Forgiveness confronts the accomplished fact (or at least the prospect) of a wronging and seeks to render blame for it inappropriate. This cannot be done at will and may turn out to be a psychological impossibility. Even where possible, it may involve a tremendous struggle. By contrast, consent is at will (i.e. by normative declaration) and always before the wrong has occurred. Consent pre-empts the struggle that forgiveness frequently involves. If consent could be retrospective and could cover the whole range of wrongs that can be forgiven, forgiveness would look like a laborious form of consent. But our remissive interests extend over a much wider range of wrongs than our permissive interests. For instance, we can forgive wrongings that consist in damage to our non-normative interests alone (non-interested wrongings). By contrast we have no intelligible interest in being able to abolish such wrongings by declaration; the more laborious route must be taken. Of course it can be as hard to decide whether to consent as whether to forgive but whilst implementing the decision to forgive is often even harder, implementing the decision to consent is almost always the easy bit.

Why is it possible to forgive wrongings that involve action against our non-normative interests but not possible to consent to them? I have argued that what determines whether blame is an apt reaction to such wrongings is not just the damage to our non-normative interests but also our normative interest in being able to control whether blame is apt; hence our ability to forgive. But if this remissive interest can help to determine the significance of such a wronging, why can't our permissive interests play a similar role? Why shouldn't the power of consent operate directly on the normative significance of such wrongings in virtue of our supposed need to be able to control their normative significance by declaration? After all neither forgiveness nor consent engage with whatever non-normative interests ground the wrong.

This proposal ignores an important difference between forgiveness and consent. Though forgiveness does nothing to ameliorate the original wrong, it does change the psychological context in which blame occurs. Since the value of blame is conditional on that context, forgiveness engages with our non-normative interest in whether blame occurs. And our normative interest in controlling whether or not blame is apt is plausibly dependent on (though distinct from) our non-normative interest in controlling whether or not blame occurs (pp. 66–7). Since forgiveness is not meant to right the original wrong, it need not engage with the interests that generate that wrong but only with our interest in the occurrence of blame. By contrast, performatives like pardon and consent engage with neither set of interests. They need change neither the original wrong nor the psychological context in which subsequent blame occurs. So it is hard to see how the power to abolish wrongs by declaration can be (non-instrumentally) good for us unless the wrong has no wrong base, unless it constitutes a bare wronging.[25] Only where the base of the wrong is a permissive

---

[25] I don't deny that such a power might be very useful in many circumstances but, as we have seen, the mere fact that a normative power would be useful does not mean that it can have any influence on what it makes sense for us to do or feel (pp. 148–9).

interest (i.e. an interest in the act's constituting a wrong unless you declare otherwise) can mere declaration engage with the wrong base in the required way. Thus only bare wrongings can be subject to erasure by diktat.

Finally let's compare the deontic interest with the authority interest and the respective obligations they generate. Is there a threat of redundancy here also? At first glance, getting involved with people (making friends with them, being neigh-bourly, etc.) might look like an uncertain and indirect way of achieving what can be achieved more surely and swiftly by means of a combination of promises and consents. In making or accepting promises, I bind myself to others by declaration. If I can acquire the obligations of a friend in the same way, why bother with the tortuous business of shaping my psychology and behaviour; why not just say 'Let's be friends' and thereby create all the obligations which friendship involves?

In fact, it would be practically impossible to capture the network of normative bonds and liens that characterize a normal friendship in an explicit agreement and to update the agreement so as to mimic the evolution of a friendship. And this difficulty is indicative of the deeper fact that the emotional and behavioural context of a friendship gives these ties and openings a rationale quite different from that furn-ished by an agreement. That rationale underwrites the norms of friendship and dictates the course of their evolution and it cannot be laid down by declaration. Our normative interests are not satisfied by normative powers alone. We need to be able to shape the normative landscape in the ways described in Part I, as well as in those discussed in Part II. Neither form of intervention is redundant. Together they make the social world malleable.

Part III
Practices

8

What is a Promise?

Throughout Part II, we assumed that to make a promise was to exercise a normative power, an assumption shared by practice theorists like Hume and Rawls. Furthermore, we assumed that one could make sense of such a power only by supposing that it exists in virtue of our shared habits of recognizing the authority of promises. Where we diverged from other practice theorists was in our account of the value of these habits of recognition. For Hume and Rawls, these habits serve various non-normative interests such as our interest in information or social co-ordination. I rejected this idea and proposed that we rethink the relationship between wrongs and human interests, postulating normative interests to explain the value of normative powers and their capacity to bind us.

Not everyone accepts the assumptions on which our discussion has depended. Some deny that a promise involves an attempt to create an obligation by declaration. This is the view I gestured at earlier according to which the exercise of normative power is a façade behind which lies the reality of principles of reciprocity, adverse reliance, and due care for induced expectations (p. 141). In Part III, I shall consider a specific version of this view (call it the *expectation theory*). My purpose here is not just to eliminate a competitor. I also want to examine our promissory practice and see how much of it can be explained in terms of an authority interest that is distinct from any interest in information about what others are going to do. Normative institutions are, in part, creatures of their time and place. But, I shall argue, many aspects of our practice of promising reflect an authority interest that underlies all such practices and we should see these features replicated again and again.

The three chapters that follow tackle different aspects of our promissory practice. The present chapter asks what is communicated by a promise, what attitudes a promisor must have if his promise is to count as sincere. In Chapter 9, I turn to the promissory bond itself, explaining such things as the stringency of a promise and the promisee's power of acceptance and release in terms of the underlying authority interest. Chapter 10 examines the validity conditions of a promise. Not all promises bind the promisor to perform and a good theory of promissory obligation should tell us which promises generate obligations. I shall argue that the above mentioned aspects of the practice of promising are all informed by the function of a promise, by the underlying human interest which explains why promises exist and are taken seriously. None are accidental features of our social practice.

This new focus on the detail of our social practices will help with a natural worry about the conclusions of Part II. There I argued that breach of promise was, in essence, a bare wronging. Those who regard bare wrongings as an illusion might feel the need reconstruct that practice on the more secure foundation of an information interest. And should they do a good enough job of it, the explanatory apparatus of Part II will be rendered redundant. In Part III, I demonstrate just how much of our promissory practice would be lost were it reconstituted in this way. None of the features I shall consider can be understood on the basis of our information interests but only through our interest in authority over others. Thus the authority interest grounds not just the very possibility of normative power; it fills in much of the detail of the social practices that embody it. I'll begin by defending our assumption that promising is an exercise of normative power.

36. Promising and normative powers

Few writers maintain that a promise is a *pure* exercise of normative power. There are some, like Scanlon, who reject the whole idea that a promise communicates the intention of hereby undertaking the obligation to perform. They propose instead that a promise communicates a firm intention of performing the promised action and that this communication somehow generates an obligation to perform (Scanlon 1998: 306–7). I postpone until Chapter 9 the question of how the simple communication of an intention to ϕ might be thought to create an obligation to ϕ. More numerous are those who think that a promise to ϕ communicates *both* the intention hereby to undertake an obligation to ϕ *and* the intention to actually fulfil that obligation. For example, Hume tells us that 'the act of the mind, which enters into a promise and produces its obligation...must necessarily be the *willing* of that *obligation* which arises from the promise' (Hume 1978: 516), adding later on that 'when a man says *he promises anything*, he in effect expresses a *resolution* of performing it' (Hume 1978: 522). Call this the *hybrid* view.[1] In this chapter, I shall reject the hybrid view, arguing against both Hume and Scanlon that a promisor need not communicate the intention of performing. A promise is in fact (like giving and commanding) a pure exercise of normative power.

---

[1] See also (Searle 1969: 60–2). American law appears to support this idea. *The Restatement (Second) of Contract* says that 'a promise is a manifestation of an intention to act or refrain from acting in a specific way, so made as to justify a promisee in understanding that a commitment has been made' (Section 2). For scepticism about whether the making of a legally binding contract must involve the communication of an intention to perform, see (Ayres and Klass 2005: ch. 2).

To engage with the issues here, we must first get a little clearer about what it is for an utterance to *communicate* a given intention. I cannot offer a serious treatment of the notion of communication.[2] Rather I shall formulate two (related) tests of what is communicated by an utterance, tests which serve to indicate which notion of communication is in play. Many utterances involve the speaker's communicating that he is in a certain mental state. Suppose that utterance U communicates that S is in mental state M. It follows that if S utters U without being in mental state M, there is something wrong with S's utterance, a wrong of insincerity. To apply this first test, we need not know what kind of flaw insincerity is. Nor need we deny that people ought sometimes to be insincere, all things considered. I assume only that there is something wrong with insincerity: insincere utterances are flawed utterances.

As to the second test, when this flaw is made explicit the resulting utterance is odd in a distinctive way. Someone who proclaims the insincerity of their own utterance makes a statement which is absurd without therefore being self-contradictory. Insincere statements can be true and they can remain true even when they acknowledge their own insincerity. If so, we have a second way of discovering whether, for a given utterance U and a given mental state M, someone who utters U communicates that they are in M: take someone who utters U whilst stating that they are not in M and ask whether their utterance is incoherent in that distinctive way. I shall call such incoherence *Moorean absurdity*.[3]

Let us now apply these tests to various exercises of normative power in order to discover what, if any, mental states they communicate. I say 'I give you my car'. Here I communicate the intention of giving you my car. And since to give you my car is to ensure that you acquire certain rights and that others acquire the corresponding obligations, am I not communicating the intention of changing the normative situation in just those ways? This hypothesis certainly seems to pass our two tests. First, someone who said those words in all seriousness without having any intention of changing the normative situation would be guilty of a form of insincerity. Second, if he made this explicit by saying 'I give you my car but I do not intend that you should hereby acquire the right to use it' he would be saying something absurd.

It might be suggested that a giver does not merely *communicate* the intention of changing the normative situation; he must *actually* intend to change it. Perhaps one

---

[2] For discussion of the notion of communication, see (Owens 2006). The distinction between expression and communication may be significant here. One can communicate an intention without expressing that intention, e.g. when one deliberately lets someone know that one has an intention without actually telling them this. In promising, it is sufficient that one communicates the fact that one has the relevant normative intention; one need not express this intention. Nevertheless, I shall treat 'expression' and 'communication' as interchangeable in what follows.

[3] See (Moore 1993: 210). By using Moore's name, I don't wish to commit myself to any particular analysis of statements like 'p but I do not believe it'. In particular I am not assuming that the oddity of such statements depends on assertion's role in communication. There may be more than one variety of Moorean absurdity.

who does not mean to augment the rights of his audience is not really giving, whatever words he might say. And perhaps someone who says 'I give you my car but I do not intend that you should hereby acquire the right to use it' is uttering an outright contradiction, is uttering a sentence that could not possibly be true. Not so.

For a start, it is perfectly possible to unintentionally make a gift. Suppose that, so far as I know, I do not own any of the umbrellas in the rack but you clearly need an umbrella to get yourself home without a soaking. You are not prepared to steal but I devise a cunning ruse to get around your scruples. I point to one of them and say 'Take my umbrella' thereby communicating the intention of making you its owner. Here I am not joking; my utterance is perfectly serious because I mean to represent myself as speaking with a certain intention. But I am being insincere because this is an intention I do not have. I cannot intend to make you the umbrella's owner because I do not believe that I own it. Now suppose that I am the unwitting owner of the umbrella to which I point. Then when I say 'Take the umbrella' I succeed in giving it to you inadvertently. The first thing this shows is that one can give someone a gift unintentionally, provided one intentionally communicates the intention of so doing.[4] It is the communication of the intention to give and not the giving itself that must be intentional. The second thing this shows is that the sentence 'I hereby give you my umbrella but I do not intend you to acquire ownership of it' could be true.

It may now be wondered whether the communication of the intention to create an obligation must itself be intentional for it to bind the speaker. A speaker may inadvertently give his audience the impression that he is communicating the relevant intention. Provided a reasonable hearer would believe that he had spoken with the requisite intention, could that be sufficient for the speaker's words to bind, whatever he may actually have intended (Atiyah 1981: 146–8)? I doubt it and I shall illustrate my doubts with a case of promising.

One cannot make it true that someone has promised by misunderstanding them, however well founded one's misunderstanding. Many misunderstandings turn on the difference between merely expressing an intention to do something and promising to do it.[5] Talking to you on the phone, I take myself to be communicating a present intention to holiday with you while you take me to be promising to holiday with you. There need be no fraud or insincerity here, nor even any negligence; perhaps some subliminal noise on the line dulled your hearing at the vital moment. Neither of us is to blame for the miscommunication. When the confusion becomes apparent, I should not just brush you aside. I should do what I can to join you. Still, I did not promise to join you and if I do not you might accuse me of a lack of consideration

---

[4] It is not required that I intend to communicate this intention, merely that I do so intentionally. Communicating this intention need not be one of my aims for my communication to bind.

[5] Other such misunderstandings turn on the difference between giving and merely loaning and on that between ordering and merely requesting.

but not of a breach of faith. Suppose instead that I (alone) was aware that there had been some interference in the line but did not bother to check whether my nuanced reply got through. I am now at fault and would need to do more to make up for the misunderstanding. In some circumstances I might even have an obligation to go but, if so, the basis of this obligation would be your reasonable conviction that I promised and the reliance you placed on that impression, not the fact that I did. I am required not to honour my word but to take responsibility for the confusion I caused.

What is true of promises is equally true of gifts and commands, at least in so far as all of them are thought to affect the appropriateness of such reactions as blame and guilt. For their words to constitute exercises of the relevant normative power, givers, commanders, etc. must intend to communicate the relevant norm-creating intentions.[6] But is this all that is required of them? Mustn't a sincere giver or commander at least intend that the world be a certain way, that it conform to the new normative situation he has created (Searle 1969: 64)? I doubt it. True, these utterances do on many occasions communicate information about what further intentions the speaker has in exercising his normative powers but such communications are not required for this exercise to occur.

Often the speaker either has very little influence over whether the world will conform to the normative situation he is creating or else is unwilling to exercise whatever influence he has. I may give you my car because I am tired of fending off the car thieves in my neighbourhood. As a decent person, I may wish that your property rights in the car will be respected without having any confidence that this will occur and without having any intention of helping to fend off the thieves. I am giving you the car precisely to rid myself of this responsibility. So far as I can see, my behaviour here is impeccable. In any case, there is no wrong of insincerity. And I might be quite explicit about why I am doing what I am doing without courting absurdity: 'Please take the car off my hands, if you think you will have better luck keeping hold of it.' Were I indifferent to whether your car was stolen this would be a count against me but even here the fault would not be a wrong of insincerity. And if I made my unfortunate attitude explicit, whilst you might resent my indifference, my words would be perfectly intelligible and I would still succeed in changing the normative situation.

We have just considered cases in which I communicate the intention of changing the normative situation without communicating the intention of making the world conform. Are there cases in which I communicate the intention of ensuring that the

---

[6] The law often holds people to gifts and contracts (though not marriage contracts) even though they had no intention of entering into them provided they appeared to do so or went through the prescribed procedure. (This may be for evidentiary reasons.) The same may be true of the moves people make in games. My notion of normative power covers only those norms that determine the appropriateness of reactions like guilt and blame. Legal liability is a different matter.

world ought to be a certain way, whilst also declaring that I shall do what I can to ensure that it will not be that way? A present might be given with a view to attracting the attention of thieves and a command may be issued with a view to provoking disobedience, thus creating the opportunity for punishment. Nothing prevents such a malevolent intention being made explicit. By making it explicit, the speaker exposes his malice to public view and that may be to wrong its object even more. But the wrong exposed here is hardly a wrong of insincerity; the speaker is being blatant not cunning. Nor do his words invalidate either the gift or the order. Indeed, his audience may be happy to accept this exercise of normative power, confident that his plans will be frustrated.

I conclude that givers and others who exercise normative powers do so by intentionally communicating the intention of hereby exercising them. While so doing, they may communicate other intentions or mental states. Conversely they may communicate the intention of exercising a normative power by communicating some quite distinct mental state (e.g. I may give someone a present by saying 'I am sure you would like this'). But what is essential to the exercise of a normative power is simply the communication of the intention of hereby changing the normative situation. The speaker need not declare that he intends the world to live up to the demands that he is imposing on it.

Let's now return to promising. What intention does a promisor communicate? If promising is anything like giving and ordering, a promisor must purport to speak with the intention of hereby changing the normative situation by putting himself under an obligation to perform (Raz 1977: 211; Finnis 1980: 298). As with these other exercises of normative power, a promisor need not actually have the intention he purports to have, though he must deliberately purport to have it. A promisor need not actually intend to put himself under an obligation because he might promise assuming his promise will be void. For example, I might promise to go on holiday, only on the assumption that you'll decline my kind offer.[7] But if you unexpectedly take me up on it, I am obliged to follow through because I deliberately communicated the intention of undertaking this obligation by means of these words.[8]

Our two tests confirm that I do indeed communicate the intention of hereby undertaking this obligation. There is something wrong with promising only on the

---

[7] The idea that a promise must be accepted to bind is defended on pp. 223–6. Reid tells us that 'what makes a promise is that it be expressed to the other party with understanding, and with an intention to become bound, and that it be accepted by him' (Reid 1969: 454). If I am right a binding promise might be made intending that it be refused and so non-binding but such a promise would not be sincere. A sincere promisor is operating on the assumption that his promise will be accepted (though, as we shall see, he need not be operating on the assumption that performance will be required of him).

[8] Hume fails to distinguish the falsehood that for a promise to bind the promisor must intend hereby to undertake an obligation from the truth that for a promise to bind the promisor must intentionally communicate the intention of hereby undertaking an obligation. As a result, he imputes incoherence to our promissory practice (Hume 1978: 523–4).

assumption that your promise will be rejected (or will be void for some other reason) and this wrong is plausibly a wrong of insincerity. True, an offer may be sincere though I anticipate a refusal but I can't sincerely offer only on the assumption that I will be refused. Second, making this insincerity explicit would involve a kind of incoherence. Someone who says 'I hereby promise to accompany you but I do not mean to undertake any obligation to accompany you' may happen to be speaking the truth but their utterance has the self-undermining quality of a Moorean absurdity.

Thus far promising runs in parallel with other exercises of normative power but, on the hybrid theory, there is an important difference: a promisor also communicates the intention of fulfilling his promise, of ensuring that the world conforms to the demands he is making on it. At first sight our two tests of what is communicated seem to confirm this hypothesis. A promise that the promisor does not intend to fulfil is, in the eyes of most writers, a paradigm of an insincere promise.[9] The absence of the relevant intention makes promising suspect and saying 'I promise to do this but I have not made up my mind to do it' would be odd in many salient contexts. Why would the speaker purport to be undertaking an obligation to do something unless he is also purporting to intend to discharge that obligation? But there is a danger of over-generalization here. It may often be insincere to promise without intending to perform and odd to admit that this is what you are doing without it being the case that every promise communicates an intention to perform.

I tell you that I went into a house today (Grice 1989: 37). In most conversational contexts, you would naturally infer from my way of putting things that it was not my own house that I went into: this is not something I say but, in those contexts at least, it is a clear implication (or implicature) of what I say. And if this implication is known by me to be false, many will think me insincere. However, these observations are consistent with two further facts. First, there are conversational contexts in which this implication is absent. Say we both know that I have only just returned to civilization from a house-free part of the world. Now I can exclaim 'I went into a house today!' without implying that it was not my house. Second, even in contexts in which the implication would naturally be understood, it is possible to explicitly cancel it by adding 'but I do not mean it was not my own house'. Without further explanation this utterance remains a bit strange—one might wonder why the speaker chose to put it that way—but there is nothing Moorean about it (Grice 1989: 42). Perhaps 'I promise to come but I have not yet made up my mind to do so' is in the same case?[10]

---

[9] See (Austin 1962: 50), (Searle 1969: 60), and many others.

[10] Austin wobbles on this point. He maintains that 'I promise but do not intend' is parallel to 'It is the case but I do not believe it' (Austin 1962: 50 and 136) but also admits that ' "I promise to do X but I am under no obligation to do it" may certainly look more like a self-contradiction ... than "I promise to do X but I do not intend to do it" ' (p. 54).

I shall undermine the hypothesis that a promise communicates the intention to perform in three stages, thereby restoring the parallel between promises and other exercises of normative power. First, I argue that someone who promises to ϕ need communicate no intention to ϕ. Second, I identify some promisors who do not even communicate the intention that their promise be fulfilled. Third, I describe a promisor who communicates the intention not to fulfil their promise.

37. The purity of promising: prophylactic promises

I begin with two assumptions. The first is that there is a mental state of 'intending to ϕ', a state distinct both from merely wishing or wanting to ϕ and also from intending to make ϕ happen. The second assumption is that practical irrationality comes in at least two forms. First there are people who suffer from *irresolution*, who do not do what they judge they ought to do because, though they intend to do it, they fail to carry out this intention. Second, there are *akratics*, people who do not do what they judge they ought to do because they cannot make up their minds to do it, because they cannot even form an intention to do it.[11] I shall briefly enlarge on these two points.

There is much controversy about how exactly the notion of intending to do something should be understood. For example, some maintain that one who intends to ϕ must believe that he will ϕ whilst others maintain that one who intends to ϕ need only believe that he will try to ϕ. Be that as it may, most allow that there is a state of having set oneself to ϕ that tends to get you to ϕ but is unlike merely desiring to ϕ in that it involves having made up your mind to ϕ rather than to perform one of the many alternative actions which you have some desire to perform. One who has decided to ϕ will not deliberate about whether to ϕ and will think and act on the assumption that he will (at least try to) ϕ when the time comes. The policies described in earlier chapters may be intentions with a general content but we need not rely on the details of what was said earlier to make the present point.

Intending to ϕ, so understood, is distinct from intending to ensure that ϕ is done, that is from intending to do something which will (or might) bring it about that ϕ is done. A clear example of the latter is where ϕ is to be done by someone else. To intend to ensure that my partner kills our business rival is not to intend to kill our business rival. Nor is it merely to wish that my partner would kill her. It is to intend to do something that will (or might) bring it about that my partner does kill her. Such intentions are sometimes directed towards our own future activities. Suppose I must kill the business rival myself and I cannot set myself to do it: the very thought horrifies me. Still I know I might well do it whilst drunk so I get myself drunk in my

---

[11] I take this terminology from (Holton 2009: 72). Holton also distinguishes resolutions from mere intentions (Holton 2009: 76–7), a distinction which I ignore for ease of exposition.

rival's company with a view to getting myself to do it. Beforehand I do not intend to kill her; rather I intend to do something which will make me kill her.

This example brings our second assumption into play. There are two different reasons why I might need to get drunk in order to kill my rival. In one sort of case I have already made up my mind to do it: I am no longer deliberating about whether to do it and I have been thinking and acting on the assumption that I shall (try to) do it and so forth. But when I reach for the knife, I find I just cannot bring myself to use it. This is a case of irresolution, of failing to execute my intention. Here drink is needed to overcome an inhibition, an obstacle to executing my intention.

But my description of the example suggests a rather different possibility. I said I could not set myself to do it because I could not bear to think about the issue in any detail (and so could not even lay the necessary plans). Here the problem is that whilst I may have come to the conclusion that I ought to do it, I have not yet made up my mind to do it, I have not got into the frame of mind where I am thinking and acting on the assumption that I shall (try to) do it. This is akrasia. Note that persistent experience of irresolution can itself be a cause of akrasia. If I have found in the past that when it comes to it I cannot bring myself to kill, this knowledge may prevent me from even forming an intention to kill.

With these assumptions in place, we can now describe cases in which someone promises without communicating the intention of keeping his promise. Sometimes a promisor cannot form the intention to do the thing he is promising to do but can still intend to do something that he believes will get him to fulfil his promise. Suppose that the making of a promise to give up smoking is itself the act that will enable him to keep it; a valid promise is the very incentive the promisor needs to ensure performance.

I have judged that I ought to give up smoking—in the interests of my family perhaps—but I cannot set myself to give up. Perhaps the attractions of cigarettes are just too obvious or perhaps experience of my past failures prevents me from even deciding to give up. So in desperation I do what I have never done before, I solemnly promise to give up.[12] Being a stern man of my word, I know that this is likely to ensure that I give up smoking. Perhaps the promise works by making me resolve to give up smoking so I am subsequently thinking and acting on the assumption that I will (try to) refrain from smoking. Perhaps it works just by making me feel too ashamed to give in to the temptation of smoking once the opportunity presents itself, whether or not the very prospect of such shame enables me to adopt this policy in advance. Either way, the promise is the incentive needed to ensure performance.

---

[12] Note I am promising to give up, not promising to *try* to do so. A commitment to make a serious effort to give up would not do the trick.

Let us now apply our two tests of whether someone is communicating an intention to perform. In the case envisaged, I am not promising in order to ensure that I will carry out a prior decision to do the promised thing. I have made no such decision and I will not make it until I am already bound by the promise, and perhaps not even then. So if a promisor must communicate the intention of doing the thing he is promising to do then I am being insincere when I promise to give up smoking. But there need be no wrong of insincerity here and I can remove any suspicion of such a wrong by being quite explicit about my situation. This engages our second test. There is no incoherence in saying that you are promising to do something that you have not decided to do in order to get yourself to do it. In sum, both tests are failed: our promisor need not communicate the intention to do the thing he promises to do.

Does this example miss its target? Just as there is a difference between intending to do something and intending to make it happen, is not there also a difference between promising to do something and promising to make it happen? In these examples, perhaps I am not promising *to* give up smoking at all but rather promising to make myself give up smoking, i.e. to do something that will get me to give up smoking. One who promises to make themselves give up smoking—say by taking nicotine pills—need not communicate the intention *to* give up smoking; they need only communicate the intention of making it the case that they will give up smoking. And, of course, the latter intention is one I do have because I intend to do something (i.e. make this promise) that I believe will get me to fulfil it.

The critic is surely right that promising to get myself to do something is different from promising to do it *tout court*. Nevertheless, this observation does not solve the problem. I mean to get myself to give up smoking by making a promise. What promise is that? If it is a promise *to* give up smoking then we are back where we started. We have a promise to give up smoking that is not backed by any intention to give up smoking. On the other hand, if I intend to give up smoking by promising to do something which will make me give up, we need to know what it is that I am proposing to do. If nicotine pills are available, the problem is solved: I am proposing to take the pills. But, in our example, there are no pills and no other means available except for a binding promise to give up smoking. So once more we are left with a promise to ϕ ungrounded in any intention to ϕ.

38. The purity of promising: promises assuming release

Thus far we have focused on cases in which the promisor does not intend to perform because he is in no position to form such an intention, at least until he has made the promise. In this section I shall discuss cases in which the promisor has no intention of performing because he does not anticipate being held to his promise. Here the promisor expects to be released from his promise either by the promisee or by circumstances and he promises only on that assumption. I shall argue that someone who promises only on the assumption that he will be released may still promise sincerely.[13]

Before proceeding, we must first raise a general issue about intention: under what circumstances should one form a *conditional* intention, i.e. an intention to ϕ given that condition C obtains? All intentions are formed against a background of assumptions about the future. I decide to go to the cinema tonight assuming, for example, that the tickets will not cost $50 each and an indefinite number of other equally obvious things. However, it would be quite wrong to conclude that my intention is in fact a conditional intention, an intention to go to the cinema provided the tickets do not cost $50 and there is no transport strike and so on. Rather I simply intend to go to the cinema at a certain time to see a certain film (Davidson 1980: 94–5).

Suppose you tell me you are going to the cinema this evening and I ask you what you will do if the tickets cost $50. One likely response is a shrug of the shoulders. Why should you think about that improbable contingency? You really want to see the film and so you *might* determine that you would go regardless. On the other hand, perhaps the plan ought then to be reconsidered. But it simply is not worth the effort of deciding the point (even though it has been explicitly raised) given that the tickets will not cost that much. Here your intention to go is formed on a certain assumption but your intention is not to perform the act conditional on the truth of that assumption.

When do we form conditional intentions? We form a conditional intention when some contingency is both uncertain and crucial to how we are going to behave and we need to resolve the matter in advance. If I am intending to stay with my friend Dexter but there is some chance that he will have to leave town at the last moment, it might be a good idea to decide in advance what I shall do if he cannot accommodate me. If I wait to see what happens before making any decisions, I risk ending up with nowhere to stay.

Let us now return to promises. I am short of money and I ask my friend Janet for a loan. I know she would be perfectly willing to simply give me the money and I also know that she will not ask for it back once it is given. But I am proud and do not want to appear to be taking charity. On the other hand, I really do not know whether I shall ever be able to pay her back. I promise to repay, sure that I will never be required to do so and Janet accepts my promise of repayment in order to save my face, even though she has no intention of holding me to it. Here I have not formed the intention of repaying. Is there anything amiss with my making the promise?

---

[13] Thus promising on the assumption that you will be released is quite different from promising on the assumption that your promise will be refused (pp. 194–5). In the former case you are intending to put the promisee in authority over you, whilst in the latter you are not. If the function of a promise is to serve the promisee's interest in having authority over the promisor, we should expect this difference to be crucial to whether the promise is sincere.

Some might doubt that this is a genuine promise given what Janet and I know about each other's intentions. But suppose we later fall out and Janet demands repayment. Will I not feel both trapped and bewildered? I am bewildered because I did not foresee this contingency and have no idea what to do. I am trapped because I am in a genuine dilemma: I have an obligation I can discharge, if at all, only with great difficulty. Of course, I will draw Janet's attention to the fact that neither of us expected that she would require me to repay and this fact is relevant: breaking a promise on which others have relied is worse than breaking a promise on which no reliance was placed. But, as Janet will doubtless reply, that does not get around the fact that I still owe her the money.

At this point, one might insist that my initial promise was sincere only if I formed the *conditional* intention of repaying the loan should Janet demand repayment.[14] Does my promise communicate at least the conditional intention to repay if asked? Once again, we should apply our tests of insincerity. The first test is passed where I do something wrong in making this promise without having the conditional intention to perform. But what could my wrong be? Am I wronging Janet by putting myself under an obligation to her without intending to discharge it though both she and I are quite sure that I will never be called upon to discharge it? As we saw, it is reasonable to form a conditional intention only when it is an open question whether the condition will be satisfied and this is not an open question, at least before the unexpected falling out. Would it not be a foolish waste of time and energy to attempt to form a view on how I would balance Janet's request for repayment against the other pressing demands on my limited financial resources, given how certain I am that she will not even ask? If so, Janet could not reasonably expect me to form such an intention and could not object to my failure so to do. Since my promise is valid, I must recognize that, were Janet to require repayment, I would be under an obligation to comply. But there is quite a range of obligations I might find myself under if the future goes in unexpected directions, some of which would conflict or be hard to discharge in other ways. Must I determine what I would do if the future puts me in such awkward and unlikely situations before I take on any of these obligations?

Let us now turn to our second test of insincerity: Can I make my attitude explicit without courting absurdity? Since both Janet and I are trying to save my face, the present example is not a good test of this. Here is another case that lacks this troublesome feature. Suppose a rather well-known academic is asked by the much more junior editor of a collection of papers to promise to submit her contribution

---

[14] Considering a related example, Bratman maintains that the promisor must have the conditional intention of performing if required to do so. Bratman speaks of 'impermissibility' here suggesting that he thinks of this as a moral requirement (Bratman 1979: 253). And Pink claims that if someone promises you some money 'they do not promise honestly if they doubt or disbelieve that by then they will actually have the funds required' (Pink 2009: 410).

within six months. It is common knowledge between the editor and the contributor that the latter will not be held to her promise: should six months pass without submission, the deadline will be waived and an extension agreed. Yet the editor is requiring a promise from all the authors and he wants at least to *begin* by treating the well-known contributor as he treats the others. The contributor has no idea whether she will make the deadline nor what she will do if she does not, so she replies 'I shall commit to six months like everyone else but I am sure you will not hold me to it: we will see how things are in six months' time.' The contributor's promise strikes me as binding; why else would she be so annoyed were she unexpectedly held to it? Doubtless the contributor is not behaving well in saying what she says but she could hardly be accused of insincerity, nor is her utterance in any way unintelligible. I conclude that someone who promises to ϕ need communicate neither the intention to ϕ nor the intention that they ϕ.[15]

I have confined myself to cases in which the promisor does not expect to be held to their promise because they assume that the promisee will not require performance. The promisor may be confident that performance will not be required of them for many other reasons. Perhaps the promise is a conditional one and, unlike the promisee, the promisor happens to know that the relevant condition will never be satisfied. Perhaps the promisor knows that the promisee will soon be dead or otherwise unable to hold them to their promise. There may often be something wrong with making a promise without forming the intention of keeping it because you do not expect to be required to keep it but that depends on the details of the particular example and the wrong in question need not be a wrong of insincerity.

I trust the argument of the past two sections has established that one can make a promise while communicating neither the intention of keeping it nor the intention that it be kept. That takes us much of the way towards restoring the parallelism between promising and other exercises of normative power. But, as we saw above, there are cases in which someone may exercise a normative power whilst expressly intending that the world flout the normative demands he is creating. Is there any analogue of this for promising?

You and I are neighbours. Your unwashed wreck sits on the driveway beside my shiny new model. Each weekend I tell you that you ought to wash your car and each weekend you fail to do so. I am sick of your maintaining that you have no obligation to wash your car and you are sick of my telling you what to do. I set out to extract from you a promise that you will wash your car next week, a promise that I would

---

[15] Nishi Shah suggested that in cases of this sort it might be indeterminate whether the speaker is being sincere or insincere in what he says. If so, it is equally indeterminate whether 'I promise to ϕ' communicates an intention to perform, for someone who communicates an intention to ϕ without actually intending to ϕ is definitely being insincere. So we have a definite promise without a definite communication of the intention to perform.

prefer you did not keep since that would definitely put you in the wrong. You wish to terminate our conversation with your dignity intact. You say 'OK, I promise to wash the car since that is what you want but you'll be lucky if I do it.' I walk away pleased that you will so clearly be in the wrong, you walk away pleased at your own defiance. Perhaps you are in the wrong here even before you break your promise—to intend to wrong me may itself be a way of wronging me—but if so, the wrong you do me involves not insincerity but a rather blatant contempt.[16]

This story makes little sense unless you succeed in making me a valid promise despite communicating the intention not to perform. And you do succeed in making me a promise because you succeed in communicating the intention to place yourself under an obligation to perform. Neither your objective nor mine can be achieved unless you bind yourself to performance. Our perversity here is neither linguistic nor logical and people who feel as we do might be glad that our language affords us this satisfaction. But why does the story make any sense at all? How could either of us think that the words you utter here are of any real significance? How could we derive any pleasure from this exchange? To answer this question we must return to the function of a promise.

39. Diagnosis

I allow that a promise *usually* carries the implication, or communicates the information that the promisor intends to perform. What I have argued is that the implication is absent in some contexts and is explicitly cancelled in others. This result has the theoretical advantage of making promising line up with other exercises of normative powers like giving and commanding. By contrast, on the hybrid view, promising is a mongrel speech act, neither a simple expression of intention nor a pure exercise of a normative power. It cannot have been the wish for an elegant theory that made people overlook cases in which one promises without communicating the intention to perform.

So what is the theoretical motivation behind the hybrid account? Hume and his many followers take the view that the bindingness of a promise depends on its having some value and that the value of a promise lies in the information it carries about what the promisor is likely to do. Using these assumptions we can derive one part of the hybrid account from the other as follows. A promisor binds himself by communicating the intention of binding himself to perform. Now if the bindingness of his promise depends on its value and its value depends on its conveying

---

[16] Contrast this case with one in which one *promises* to break a promise. I doubt that such a promise is binding at least where it is understood as a promise to both ϕ and not-ϕ. Such an utterance could not be understood as an attempt to put oneself under an obligation to do anything. The promisor in my example is not promising to break his promise; he is merely communicating the intention of breaking his promise.

information about what the promisor is likely to do, then the promisor must communicate an intention to bind himself by communicating information about what he is likely to do. How can the speaker's announcement that he intends to bind himself tell us anything about what he will actually do? It does if he announces that he intends to bind himself to ϕ by announcing that he intends to ϕ. Of course, you can communicate the information that you intend to ϕ without communicating the intention of committing yourself to ϕ-ing but to promise is to do the latter by doing the former.

The argument just given has its merits. First, its starting point that a promisor binds himself by communicating the intention of hereby undertaking an obligation to perform is perfectly correct. Second, promisors do very often communicate the intention of hereby undertaking an obligation to ϕ by communicating the intention of ϕ-ing. It is a familiar fact that we can perform one speech act by performing another (e.g. make requests by asking a question like 'Would you be able to . . . '). There are some speech acts which are normally performed via other speech acts and it may well be that communicating an intention to ϕ is the normal way of promising to ϕ. My problem is with the conclusion that a promise can *only* be made by communicating the intention of performing. What supports this conclusion is the false assumption that the value of a promise depends on the information it conveys.

This diagnosis is confirmed by the fact that my earlier examples would make little sense were the value of a promise to be explained along informational lines. Take a case of assumed release. Here performance will likely never be required of the promisor and even if it were it is quite unclear whether it would be forthcoming. Such a promise carries little if any information about the promisor's future behaviour, so how can it bind? Take the case of a prophylactic promise. Why should someone who makes such a promise feel bound to perform? Since he is so upright, his promise assures us that he will form the intention of performing so his promise does indeed have informational value. But that is not why it binds. Rather it is the other way around: it is because the promisor takes his promise so seriously that it conveys the information it does about his future performance. So the bindingness of this promise can't be explained on the basis of the information it communicates about the speaker's future intentions.

In Part II, I suggested that human beings have an authority interest, an interest in having the right to require performance from other people over and above any information interest they may have in being able to foresee what those people are going to do. Promising understood as the exercise of a normative power is ideally suited to serve this interest. A promise puts the promisee in authority over the promisor in the matter of the promise, for the promisor is under an obligation to perform unless the promisee releases them. And, as we have seen, a promise may do this regardless of whether it purports to convey any information about what the promisor is likely to do. The fact that one can sincerely promise without intending to perform suggests that people have an interest in the possession of such a right which is distinct from the interest they undoubtedly have in knowing who will do what.

This theory certainly makes better sense of our examples. As to cases of assumed release, I can save my face by giving Janet a promise of repayment in return for her money because that promise grants Janet the right to require me to repay. That right is something that might sensibly be valued even though my promise carries little or no information about what I would do if required to repay.[17] Similarly the editor is, at least initially, treating the famous contributor as he treats the others by asking for the right to require the contributor to submit. If this were not a real cost to the contributor, the whole 'treating everyone equally' procedure would be pointless, since she and the editor need not be attempting to deceive either themselves or the other contributors. As to prophylactic promises, the promisee's interest in having the right to require me to perform is one I can serve by making him a promise. It is my regard for the wrong of breach of promisee, a wrong grounded in his authority interest, which provides the motivational fuel for performance and thereby gives my promise its informational value.

The characters in my example of perverse promising also, in their own twisted fashion, acknowledge that rights to require performance have a value that is independent of the information conveyed by their possession. True, you have no inclination to respect the right you grant me by your promise and neither do I wish you to respect it. Yet both of these unwholesome attitudes depend on the idea that the sheer possession of this right is significant. You show your contempt for me by disregarding it and I attain the moral high ground by getting you to wrong me by disregarding it.[18] No attitude to the value of information, however twisted, could account for our behaviour. Your promise conveys no relevant information. In particular, you are not showing your contempt for me by trying to deceive me about what you are going to do. And I am not trying to put you in the wrong by getting you to deceive me.

I agreed that a promise normally does convey information about what the promisor will do and that people very often make and accept promises for that reason and that reason alone. Indeed, I have allowed that a promise to ϕ usually carries the implication that the promisor intends to ϕ, so typically something has gone wrong if their promise is not a good indication of whether they are disposed to ϕ. Still I maintain that the distinctive features of the speech act of promising are to be

---

[17] Whether or not Janet actually values this right, possession of the right may have value, though it has little or no informational value.

[18] Pink notes that, on the normative power conception, it is coherent to discourage trust in one's own promise, a result which he implies is absurd (Pink 2009: 411–12). But if the statements of the parties in my example were literally incoherent, they couldn't be characterized or criticized in the above terms.

explained by reference to our interest in the authority rather than in the information they convey. In particular the sincerity conditions of a promise are best explained in this way. What distinguishes a promise from those other speech acts which also convey information about the speaker's future behaviour to his audience (e.g. expressions of intention or predictions) is precisely that a promise conveys this information, when it does, by purporting to transform the normative situation.

40. When have we promised?

The scepticism about promissory obligation considered in Part II was a philosophical view, motivated by theoretical concerns about the intelligibility of promising. In the course of formulating and dealing with those concerns we have arrived at a sharper conception of what promising actually is. But once this sharper conception is on the table a more modest form of scepticism about promising may begin to seem attractive. This scepticism starts from a point already noted, namely that it may be hard to know when someone has committed themselves to ϕ-ing.

I have been putting great weight on the distinction between the communication of an intention to do something on the one hand and the communication of an intention to hereby undertake an obligation to do it on the other, a distinction not well marked in ordinary conversation. We very often commit ourselves to ϕ-ing by communicating our intention of ϕ-ing. How do we tell whether someone is committing themselves to ϕ-ing or merely communicating the intention of ϕ-ing? Is there a method reliable in more than a minority of cases? It is easy enough when the speaker uses 'I promise', 'Trust me', etc., or else qualifies an expression of intention with 'but I'm not promising'. Things are rarely made so explicit and, without these conventional markers, can we be confident of understanding the force of the words we hear? If not, doesn't that throw doubt on the practical importance of the distinction?

The absence of markers and the difficultly of specifying a reliable method of discrimination is not in itself particularly worrying. For example, we can usually work out whether someone is speaking ironically even without the aid of markers and even though it is hard to specify any method for doing so which is both reliable and generally applicable (Davidson 1984: 270). Few would conclude that the distinction between literal and ironic usage is unimportant. A more searching sceptic will focus on indeterminacy rather than ignorance. Occasionally there may be no fact of the matter about whether I meant to be speaking literally but such indeterminacy is infrequent. By contrast there seems often to be no fact of the matter about whether someone has given a promise. If indeterminacy in normative force is extremely widespread, if we tolerate pervasive unclarity in these matters, doesn't that suggest that promises are inessential to social intercourse and that our lives would be little changed if we dispensed with them altogether?

The sceptic is quite right that people very often hover between a promise and a mere expression of intention (or some other less committal form of speech). For example, people rarely undertake a definite obligation to comply with our suggestions and we rarely require this of them. Indeed it is often a breach of etiquette to ask someone to bind themselves. Rather we adopt a strategy of ambiguity in our dealings with one another: we say things whose normative implications are left unclear. You propose a trip to the museum next Friday. I reply that I'd like to go and that we can be in touch to arrange a time. Have I promised to join you at the museum on Friday or have I merely expressed the present intention of going, reserving the right to change my mind (having taken your expectations into account)? Very often there is no answer to this question and neither side wishes to press the point. It would frequently be rude of you to demand a clear promise and it would as frequently be rude of me to say that I am not promising.

The same is true of other normative powers. Many social organizations are hierarchical in that those higher up are entitled to issue instructions to those underneath them, at least in respect of their work within the organization. However, except in military settings, commands are usually avoided. Offices are not parade grounds. A sensible supervisor does not get themselves into a position where they need to issue an order. Rather they make 'requests' of their subordinates, they say things whose normative force is left tactfully opaque. It is understood that the ambiguity can be resolved if necessary but usually it doesn't come to that. One can't infer from any of this that the existence of this power of command is an unimportant or dispensable feature of the life of a hierarchical organization. On the contrary, it informs almost every professional interaction between the supervisor and their staff.

Similarly, the possibility of a firm commitment informs a whole range of social interactions in which no clear promise is actually given. I didn't ask you to *promise* that you'd accompany me to the museum on Friday (even though I'm not prepared to go on my own) because that would have been an imposition. I'd have been asking for a power of veto over your activities. On the other hand you didn't explicitly decline to promise because that would have been rude in a different way: you'd have been reserving to yourself the right to decide whether my Friday should go as planned. So we leave it unclear who has the authority to decide whether you'll show up. This is typical of casual social arrangements but even in this sphere, things can develop in ways that make it appropriate to clarify matters. Once you start to equivocate about whether to show up, I can often require you to commit yourself one way or the other. Or else, if there is a long history of disagreement between us about when such social arrangements should go ahead, it might be appropriate for me to require a promise at the outset. Though we often leave it open who can decide the fate of our plan, the possibility of allocating this authority (perhaps to us both so neither can defect from the arrangement without the agreement of the other) is ever present and shapes our interactions. We fail to resolve these ambiguities, not because the difference does not matter to us but because it does.[19]

Throughout this chapter, I have been assuming that the obligations one takes on when one promises to do something are significantly different from those one acquires by expressing the intention to do it or predicting that one will do it or by raising expectations that one will do it in some other way. In promising one hands over the authority to decide whether one does it to one's audience; one does not merely incur the obligation to take their expectations into account when deciding what to do. In the next chapter, this assumption is defended.

---

[19] Even where it is clear to all that a promise has been given, we often dwell on the intrinsic merits of the proposed action in persuading the promisor to keep it. 'But you promised' tends to be a last resort.

9

The Promissory Bond

Some writers would have us abandon the whole idea that promising is an exercise of normative power. For them, to promise to do something is to incur an obligation to do it by communicating the intention of doing it. According to the *expectation theory*, an expression of intention can commit one to perform where it induces an expectation of performance. The expectation theory makes no room either for bare wrongings or for the normative powers that produce them. Nor do its advocates accept that promises bind only where there is a practice of recognizing their binding force. They simply reject the assumptions on which I have been operating until now.

In the last chapter, I argued that a promisor need not communicate the intention of performing. In this chapter, I'll raise a further issue for the expectation theory: how in any case could the mere communication of an intention generate an obligation to fulfil the intention communicated? Expectation theorists have an answer but their answer fails to capture either the nature of the demand generated by a promise or its high grade of choice-dependence. Having made these points, I'll examine the promissory bond itself. I'll argue that crucial aspects of the bond's structure and force are fixed by the underlying promissory interest. The expectation theory and my own offer very different accounts of how this interest shapes the promissory bond and I shall recommend the latter. But let's begin by considering one form of speech whose normative significance the expectation theory seems well suited to explain, namely prediction.

41. Predicting and promising

What obligations does one take on in making a prediction about one's own behaviour? Suppose there is an anti-war demonstration tomorrow and you are trying to persuade me to participate. My attitude is this: as of now, it seems to me that the war is wrong and that the matter is of sufficient importance for me to give up my Saturday morning to the demo. However, I am reluctant to make a final judgement about whether to join the demo. Each day the newspapers contain new information relevant to my assessment of the war, information that might affect my decision. You have hired a bus to take a party to the demo and want to know whether you should reserve a seat on it for me. In reply to your requests for a decision, I say this: 'Since it is already Friday, its pretty unlikely that I'll change my mind after reading tomorrow's newspapers, so I predict that I'll be there and it would be reasonable for you to rely on this prediction and allocate me a seat on the coach: however, I have not yet finally decided to go.'[1]

What obligations lie on those who make such statements? First, I ought not to deliberately mislead you. If I have no interest in the war and I'm aiming simply to get you off my back, I am in the wrong. Second, my prediction should be a reasonable one, given the evidence I have. Suppose amusing diversions are often arranged at the last minute for Saturday morning and I know that given the choice between such frivolities and a political action I always choose the frivolity. If I ignore this embarrassing fact in making the prediction then I am in the wrong, for I am getting you to rely on an obviously ill-grounded prediction. Third, should Saturday morning's newspapers convince me that the war is in fact justified, I may have a duty to warn you that I shan't be there and thereby give you the chance to fill the empty seat.[2]

This list of obligations might be incomplete and it is certainly underspecified (e.g. how much trouble must I take to warn of my impending absence?) but the general idea is clear. It is often bad for others to have false expectations about how I am going to behave and I have some obligation to ensure that this does not happen by making only well-grounded predictions about my future behaviour and warning them when these predictions are likely to be falsified. Nor is this true only of predictions about my own future behaviour. People have an interest in knowing the truth about all sorts of matters: past, present, and future. The obligations which lie on me when I make predictions about my own behaviour are just those which I am under whenever I give someone information on a matter of importance to them.

The obligations just noted are chosen in that it is up to me whether I raise expectations by making predictions. They have what I called the first grade of choice-dependence and no more. By freely making predictions and thereby raising expectations, I have taken on these obligations whether or not I anticipate these obligations. Suppose the audience I am addressing is openly incredulous and I make some fairly wild predictions, confident that they will not be believed. I should have realized that my words would be overheard by more credulous people who would rely on them. Here I did not intend to put myself in a position where my careless predictions would wrong these people but that is what I have done. (Had these people

---

[1] My prediction may communicate my belief about the future even in the absence of a decision.

[2] If I fail to discharge one or more of these obligations, I may have a duty to compensate you for carrying an empty seat, perhaps by making a suitable donation to the anti-war movement. I agree with Scanlon that the appropriate measure of compensation here is what lawyers calls 'reliance costs', i.e. the compensation should ideally restore you to as good a position as you would have been in had the false expectation never been aroused (Scanlon 2003a: 240). It is not required that you be put in as good a position as you would have been had this expectation been fulfilled.

instead overheard a promise of mine and mistakenly thought it was intended for them, that would put me under no *promissory* obligation to them, however foreseeable their misapprehension, because I did not intentionally communicate the intention of undertaking any obligation to *them*.)

Turn now to the communication of intention. I discover there is going to be a newspaper strike on Saturday so I am in a position to make up my mind on the Friday after all. I decide to attend the demo and announce this decision to you. Clearly, I am under an obligation not to mislead you either about what I intend or about the likelihood that I shall act as I intend. And I must take reasonable steps to warn you should I change my mind. So long as I am simply communicating my present intentions, the relevant principles are the very ones that govern prediction. But in communicating an intention I can go further. Sometimes, in communicating an intention to attend the demo I thereby commit myself to attending, I put myself under an obligation which cannot be discharged by a timely warning and which cannot be avoided just by pointing out that my original intention was both reasonable and sincere. Where I merely predict that I shall attend, I am not obliged to ensure that this prediction turns out to be true; should tomorrow's newspaper quite unexpectedly convince me the war is right, I have no duty to go on the march.[3] But if I communicated an intention to attend, things *may* be different.

Here is one account of why that is, an account inconsistent with the expectation theory. To promise to ϕ is to communicate the intention of hereby undertaking an obligation to ϕ. Now, as already noted, one often communicates the intention of undertaking an obligation to ϕ by communicating an intention of ϕ-ing (p. 205). It is much harder to communicate the intention of undertaking an obligation to ϕ by merely predicting that you are going to ϕ. Perhaps there are special contexts in which a prediction could be so understood but, in the above examples at least, this isn't the case.[4] Since the expectations theorist rejects the whole idea that a promise is the

---

[3] As (Sidgwick 1981: 304) remarks, 'we are not bound to make our actions correspond with our assertions generally, but only with our promises'. For (Anscombe 1981: 100) 'It's not the *prediction* by itself that it's an offence not to make come true'. (Atiyah 1981: 105 and 163–4) argues that the law also distinguishes between deception and breach of promise.

[4] There is such a thing as warranting that p (Atiyah 1981: 161–4). Suppose I am selling you my house. In the course of the negotiations, I assure you that it does not suffer from subsidence. According to English law if once the sale has been made the house then threatens to collapse, I am obliged to pay to prevent this or else to compensate you if it can't be prevented. If I want to reassure you during the negotiations without taking on this obligation, I must add 'but please make your own inquiries'. It seems right that testimony given in such a solemn context might generate more onerous obligations than mere prediction. Let's describe what I am doing here as *guaranteeing that* the house won't subside. *Guaranteeing that* is like *promising to* in several respects: first if I guarantee that p and p threatens to turn out to be false, I must intervene or compensate, etc.; second, these obligations fall only on those who communicate the intention of providing such guarantees. Does a guarantee straddle the boundary between a prediction and a promise? Guarantees are best thought of as a special kind of promise. True, in guaranteeing that p I need not

communication of an intention of hereby undertaking an obligation, how he is to explain the fact that we can usually make a promise by expressing an intention but not by making a prediction?

This fact should strike the expectations theorist as rather surprising.[5] Potential promisees have an interest in not being wrong about how promisors are going to behave and why can't this interest be served by a prediction as well as by a promise? If this interest is as much at stake in the one case as in the other, why isn't the normative situation the same? The expectations theorist might at this point appeal to the interest the speaker has in not being obliged to make his predictions true: such an onerous duty would simply discourage the provision of useful information and so be bad for everyone. This would indeed explain why we don't have it as a rule that anyone who predicts that p is obliged to do whatever they can to ensure that this prediction turns out to be true. But it hardly accounts for the fact that I can commit myself to attending by communicating an intention to attend but not usually by predicting that I will. After all, in predicting that you'll be at the demo because you are going to decide to attend the demo, you are representing the matter as being as much under your control as you are when you announce a decision to attend the demo. So why should it be any more of a burden to make this prediction true than to carry out a corresponding decision?

The expectations theorist might reply that in predicting a decision to attend, I'm leaving it open whether I shall actually attend, whilst in announcing a decision to attend, I am not leaving this possibility open. That is why I take on an obligation to attend in the latter case but not in the former. But what does 'leaving it open' mean here? It can't just mean that I have not actually made up my mind whether to attend, for the question at issue is why this fact should matter when it is already pretty certain that I will make up my mind to attend. Nor can it mean that I am not yet absolutely certain to attend: no one thinks it absolutely certain that I shall do something simply because I have decided to do it. Perhaps my decision to attend makes it a bit more likely that I shall attend but it is hard to see why this should subject me to a wholly new obligation. In the example under discussion, my prediction alone is enough to make it reasonable for you to keep a seat free; the further decision makes no significant difference.

A prediction may give *more* security than a declaration of intention. Consider a case where I make a prediction about my own behaviour without representing this behaviour as being under my control. We have both been invited to a certain party

communicate any intention to bind myself to make p true. However, I am communicating the intention to undertake certain (conditional) obligations. For example, to guarantee that there will be no subsidence is (in part) to promise to shore the house up if it threatens to fall down or else to compensate for its collapse. For a different account of these matters, see (Pink 2009: 409–10).

[5] It directly undermines the view of those who try to derive promissory obligation from a general duty of veracity, for example (Price 1948: 155–7) and (Warnock 1971: 101–11).

tomorrow. You will enjoy the party very much provided I am not there and you come to me for an assurance that I will not attend. I give you this assurance not by declaring an intention to stay away but rather by telling you that though I'd love to go to the party, unfortunately my doctor has announced that I'll be in bed for the next 48 hours with the side effects of the vaccine he has just given me. You are relieved to learn that I shall be barred from attending, not by my fickle intentions but by hard medical fact. Still, should the doctor's information turn out to be incorrect, I would not be obliged to stay away from the party (though I might be obliged to give you some kind of warning of my presence). Yet had I given you the assurance you wanted by expressing the intention to stay away, I might well be under an obligation not to attend.[6]

How is the expectation theory to explain this? Again it is quite unclear why your interest in the fulfilment of my assurance should be affected by whether it took the form of a prediction or of an expression of intention. And it is equally unclear why my interest in not being committed to staying away from the party because I voluntarily announced that I would be unable to attend should be any greater than my interest in not being so constrained because I voluntarily announced that I had decided not to attend. The expectations theorist can explain why a firmer expression of intention or a more confident prediction should increase the responsibilities of the speaker towards his audience, where this responsibility takes the form of having adequate grounds for the statement in question: the more confidence you induce in your audience, the more evidence you must have for its truth. What he can't explain is why an expression of intention should sometimes generate a specific, underived obligation to perform.[7]

In the last chapter, I argued that a promisor must *intentionally* communicate the intention of hereby undertaking an obligation. The expectations theorist will also find it hard to explain why it should matter whether the promisor is aware of incurring an obligation to perform. As already noted, one's responsibility for the

[6] In this case, I represent the matter as being beyond my control but one often makes a prediction about one's own behaviour which leaves it open whether the matter in question is under one's control. For instance, I may assure you that your friend Jones will pass his driving test on the basis of a piece of information I don't feel able to divulge (for instance that he has bribed the examiner). Here you can make any assumption you like about whether I have any influence over the matter. Suppose the information turns out to be misleading. If I discover before the exam but after speaking to you that the bribe was not paid, I am under no obligation to make it true that Jones will pass by offering him free driving lessons (or paying the bribe myself), however inconvenienced you'll be by this unexpected failure. Provided I was originally entitled to rely on this information, warning you is enough. But if I announced the intention to make him pass, the matter may be quite otherwise.

[7] The qualification 'underived' is important here. Someone who makes a prediction on shaky evidence may be obliged to make that prediction true in order to prevent his audience suffering significant loss when acting in reliance on it where making the prediction true is the only way of preventing this loss, that is if warning or compensation are impracticable. But here the obligation to perform derives from the prior obligation to exercise due care in forming expectations.

expectations aroused by one's predictions does not depend on any of this. Why should it be any different with those aroused by expressions of intention? If one can incur an obligation to perform by communicating an intention of so doing, why can't one do so unwittingly?

42. The expectation theory: Scanlon

In this section, I shall elaborate my critique of the expectation theory by examining Scanlon's recent statement of it. Scanlon's general project is to characterize ethical concepts like promising 'in a way which brings out our reasons for taking [them] seriously as a guide to action' (Scanlon 2003b: 282). In the case of promising, this involves arguing that 'the obligation to keep a promise can be explained in terms of general principles arising from the interests that others have in being able to rely on expectations about what we are going to do' (Scanlon 2003b: 283). Promissory obligations are 'one special case of a wider category of duties and obligations regarding the expectations that we lead others to form about what we intend to do. These duties and obligations in turn are a special case of more general duties not to lie or to mislead people in other ways' (Scanlon 1998: 295).

A noteworthy feature of these duties and obligations is that their binding force does not depend on whether anyone is in the habit of recognizing them (Thomson 1990: 303–4; Scanlon 1998: 296–7). Should I harm someone by deceiving them, I likely wrong them regardless of whether people tend to blame such deception, are inclined to avoid it, and so forth. But, Scanlon admits, 'the moral constraints against lying and other forms of deception ... differ in important respects from the principle governing the case of promising itself' (Scanlon 1998: 322). Nevertheless, he sets out to explain the latter in terms of the former.

I'll start by considering Scanlon's account of those general duties not to mislead people. Scanlon sees these duties as striking a balance between the audience's interest in getting correct information and the speaker's interest in not taking on substantial burdens every time they make an assertion. For present purposes I shall allow that the obligations not to deceive, to be reasonable, and to warn can be accommodated within this explanatory framework.[8] Scanlon thinks that those more onerous duties 'regarding the expectations that we lead others to form about what we intend to do' will be amenable to a similar treatment and here we begin to encounter some familiar difficulties.

---

[8] These duties may be implicit in Scanlon's Principle [D] which requires one to 'exercise due care not to lead others to form reasonable but false expectations about what one will do when one has good reason to believe that they would suffer significant loss as a result of relying on these expectations' (Scanlon 1998: 300).

Scanlon argues that human beings have an interest in being assured of the truth of certain propositions, an interest independent of anything that they may do in reliance on them. For example, I may want a well-grounded assurance that a certain awful event won't occur even though there is very little I could do either to prevent it or to prepare for it. The desire for such an assurance is usually a desire for *knowledge* about what is going to happen and such knowledge may be sensibly valued even where it is of little practical import. Your audience might simply wish to know how something that matters to them will turn out, to be relieved of the doubts and uncertainties generated by their ignorance on the point. But they don't just want peace of mind; they want the truth (Scanlon 1998: 303).[9] Where the truth depends on what you are going to do, they will wish to know what you are going to do. And if you deceive them on the point, you have wronged them regardless of whether any practice of being truthful has been established.

Now a speaker can let his audience know what he is going to do without thereby committing himself to doing it. Nevertheless Scanlon maintains that some of those who provide such assurances do place themselves under an obligation to ensure that the proposition in question is true and that they do so without communicating an intention of hereby undertaking this obligation. This is so when the conditions laid down in *Principle F* are satisfied:

If (1) X voluntarily and intentionally leads Y to expect that X will ϕ (unless Y consents to X's not doing so); (2) X knows that Y wants to be assured of this; (3) X acts with the aim of providing this assurance, and has good reason to believe that he or she has done so; (4) Y knows that X has the beliefs and intentions just described; (5) X intends for Y to know this, and knows that Y does know it; and (6) Y knows that X has this knowledge and intent; then, in the absence of special justification, X must ϕ unless Y consents to ϕ's not being done. (Scanlon 1998: 304)

As formulated, Principle F applies to any assurance about what the assuror 'will do' and not just to assurances given by communicating an intention. So construed, Principle F is vulnerable to the examples involving prediction I considered in the last section.[10] Yet Scanlon later denies that there is any analogue of Principle F governing assertion: 'Insofar as there is an obligation to make what one has said

---

[9] In a case like that of Maklay's Malay (pp. 125–6) it does them no good to know the truth about what is going to be done (as opposed to being falsely reassured on the point).

[10] It might be thought that Scanlon can fend off these examples by invoking the parenthetical clause in (1) where it is stipulated that X's performance depends on Y's consent. But it is not difficult to construct examples in which I predict that I will do something conditionally on your wanting me to do it without thereby undertaking any obligation to do it. Suppose you want me to attend a demo against the chlorination of the water supply. I am not at all convinced by your arguments against chlorination but I do know how difficult I find it to defy you and so I predict, on excellent evidence, that when the time comes, I will give in and decide to attend the demo (so long as you still wish it of course). I may make this prediction with all the knowledge and aims that Principle F requires. Still I am violating no obligation to you if I don't show up because I unexpectedly encountered an even more imposing advocate of chlorination.

be true, this is a consequence of a duty … to protect against loss, and this duty can be fulfilled by a timely warning' (Scanlon 1998: 322). I shall take this denial to cover predictions about one's own future actions as well as assertions about other matters. Thus I construe Principle F as an attempt to describe the conditions under which the communication of an intention to ϕ generates an obligation to ϕ.

If Scanlon is right, one can incur an obligation to ϕ simply by communicating an intention to ϕ with the aim of providing the assurance that one will ϕ under certain conditions of mutual knowledge. Thus one can incur an obligation to ϕ without doing what I earlier said was essential to promising, namely communicating an intention to undertake an obligation to ϕ. If so, providing assurance by communicating a bare intention to ϕ under the conditions laid down in Principle F has a quite different normative significance from doing so by predicting that one will ϕ under those conditions.

It is difficult to try Principle F by example without having a litmus test of just when one is communicating an intention hereby to undertake an obligation. Consider the following case: 'I sell you a house, retaining an adjacent vacant lot. At the time of our negotiations, I state that I intend to build a home for myself on that lot. What if several years later I sell the lot to a person who builds a gas station on it?' (Fried 1981: 9). Imagine that, when I expressed that intention, you and I had all the aims and mutual knowledge specified in Principle F. Have I wronged you? I need not have done provided no promise was made and I was sincere and reasonable in all that I intended but it may not be possible to describe cases like Fried's in a way which makes it obvious that Principle F is satisfied without my having communicated the intention to undertake an obligation.

Rather than attacking Principle F directly, we should ask whether attention to information interests alone would lead us to expect that under certain conditions an expression of intention might bind the speaker to perform whilst a prediction made under exactly the same conditions would not. Both the hearer's interest in having correct information and the speaker's interest in not being made to ensure that this information is correct are indifferent to whether the speaker conveys the information by declaring an intention or by making a prediction. No doubt there will be cases where the behaviour in question is not under the predictor's control. But there will be many other cases where it is under their control and yet their assertion generates no obligation to act. As we have seen, even where one explicitly represents the matter in question as being under one's control, one isn't required to perform when one only made a prediction. If Principle F is meant to accommodate this fact, it will be hard to ground that principle on our information interests alone.

Until now, I've been focused on the idea that promissory obligation binds to performance. As I observed in the last section, another point that distinguishes these obligations from those generated by prediction is the role of choice. Scanlon's Principle F attempts to capture the importance of choice here by requiring that

'X voluntarily and intentionally lead Y to expect that X will ϕ'. Setting aside the issue of voluntariness until Chapter 10, why should he require that the relevant expectation be aroused intentionally? On this point, Scanlon says only that when Principle F is in the offing 'there are solid generic reasons to want the additional degree of control over one's obligations that a requirement of explicit consent provides' (Scanlon 1998: 260). I assume he means that where the greater burden of an obligation to perform is in prospect, rather than the lesser burden of an obligation to warn, minimize damage, and so forth, it is appropriate to give the speaker that extra degree of protection. If this reading is correct, then Scanlon's account of why promissory obligations must be chosen here presupposes that promisors do incur larger burdens than predictors, a fact he has yet to explain.

According to Scanlon, although communication of a bare intention can bind to performance, promissory obligation is a more specific phenomenon than the obligations generated by Principle F (Scanlon 1998: 306). There are various forms of words and gestures I can use when promising to show up and what they all have in common, for Scanlon, is that they 'indicate to you that I believe and take seriously the fact that, once I have declared this intention under the circumstances, and have reason to believe that you are convinced by it, it would be wrong of me not to show up' (Scanlon 1998: 307). Scanlon's idea is that what promising adds to the communication of an intention designed to convey an assurance, etc. is an explicit acknowledgement by the promisor of the obligations he is incurring in communicating that intention. Such an acknowledgement strengthens the assurance which the promisor is conveying and thereby reinforces his obligation to perform, all in accordance with Principle F.

Scanlon describes this as 'a kind of moral multiplier effect' (Scanlon 1998: 308). Principle F, which has nothing particularly to do with promising, ensures that (in certain situations) we take on obligations to perform when we communicate an intention. By adding 'Trust me', etc., to our announcement we both acknowledge the obligation generated by this communication *and* reinforce that very obligation, for in acknowledging the duty generated by Principle F we strengthen the promisee's expectations and thereby increase our obligation to perform under Principle F (Scanlon 1998: 322).[11]

Scanlon applies this apparatus to explain how phrases like 'but I'm not committing myself' work without supposing them to affect the normative situation by declaration: 'a person who says, "I firmly intend to ϕ, but I don't *promise* to" gives the kind of warning which makes Principle F inapplicable, and expresses the judgment that, having given this warning, he or she is free to decide not to ϕ' (Scanlon 1998: 404). The moral multiplier Scanlon invoked to explain the peculiar force of a promise has

---

[11] Related moves are made by (Atiyah 1981: 192–3) and (Pink 2009: 414–15).

now gone into reverse. Someone first expresses a firm intention to ϕ, an expression that would by itself arouse an expectation that one will ϕ and thus an obligation to perform. But by adding the words 'I don't promise' they undermine this expectation and thereby extinguish the obligation. An explicit refusal to acknowledge such an obligation destroys the very obligation that it denies.

Scanlon's account of promissory obligation picks up on the fact that both parties are focused not only on what will or won't be done but also on the normative situation being created. But he goes wrong in construing the function of the promisor's expressions of commitment as being to reinforce the expectations of the promisee. There are cases in which a potential promisee seeking an assurance of performance has reason not to extract a promise (that is to be satisfied with either a prediction or a bare statement of intention) because they know that insisting on a promise would make it *less* likely that the promisor will perform. Suppose the promise would be felt as an imposition by the promisor, a fact known to the promisee. This shared knowledge won't invalidate the promise should it be extracted: what the reluctant promisor would resent is precisely the bond they had been placed under. But since this promise is known by all concerned to make the performance less likely, it can hardly create an obligation to perform by reinforcing the promisee's expectation of performance.

Suppose you are trying to get me to give you a lift home. I happily express the intention to give you a lift home but I am reluctant to promise. Why so? It is not that I am dubious about whether it would be reasonable to execute this intention; it is just that I don't want to be *bound* to do this unless you release me, I don't want to be in your power in that way. Knowing me as you do, you might decline to insist on a promise precisely in order to make yourself *more* confident that I will perform. You know how I hate to be bound. Had you extracted a promise from me rather than accepting my statement of intention with good grace, resentment might have overpowered my natural decency and led me to break the promise once some minor obstacle arose. By leaving me in charge, you make it more likely that I will surmount any unexpected difficulties and deliver a lift home. Thus, the force of 'I promise' can't be explained in the way Scanlon suggests.[12]

Scanlon is the latest in a line of thinkers who locate the normative significance of a promise in the expectation of performance it arouses. A key challenge for that approach has always been to distinguish a promise from a mere expression of intention and the most common response is that a promisor *invites* reliance on, or

---

[12] (Pufendorf 2003: 110–11) tells us that 'great men' are reluctant put their social inferiors in a position to *require* things of them by making them promises but are still happy to express benevolent intentions towards them and thereby place themselves under duties of *veracity*. Pink maintains that it would be 'really very odd' (Pink 2009: 413) to invite someone to assume that you will ϕ whilst declining to promise to do it. Here is one context in which this would be perfectly intelligible.

at least trust in his expression of intention. For example, Adam Smith makes the distinction as follows: 'Though I say I have a mind to do such a thing for you, yet on account of some occurrence do not do it, I am not guilty of breach of promise. A promise is declaration of your desire that the person for whom you promise should depend on you for the performance of it' (Smith 1978: 472). I have argued that this won't do. First there is no general obligation to make our statements true once we have invited reliance on them: to invite someone to trust your prediction is not to promise to make it true. Second, even where our statement is an expression of intention, we can invite reliance on it without making a promise. The statement 'I'm going to do this for my own reasons, and I'm happy for you to rely on my doing it, but I won't have wronged you if, for reasons I cannot presently anticipate, I decide not do it' both makes sense in context and does not constitute a promise.[13] I say things of this sort where I wish to provide useful information about what my current plans are without surrendering the right to decide whether I must stick to them. A promise communicates the intention of hereby undertaking an obligation to perform and though, in many contexts, one can do that by inviting reliance on the expression of an intention to perform, the two acts are distinct: one can do one without doing the other.[14]

To conclude, let's compare what I have said against the expectation theory with a more familiar line of objection. Prichard remarks that 'any attempt to base the obligation to keep a promise on promising's being the creating of an expectation is doomed to failure' because the expectation that someone will keep a promise is founded 'at least in part' on the belief 'that he has bound himself simply by promising' and that he will be motivated by this bond (Prichard 1968: 171). Prichard's worry is that either an expectation theory will presuppose rather than explain the promissory bond or else it will fail to capture the idea that a conscientious promisor can be motivated to fulfil his promise by the fact that he has promised alone.[15]

We can generate a version of Prichard's worry for Scanlon's account as follows. Principle F applies when X has managed to convince Y that he will ϕ. Now when X expresses the intention of ϕ-ing to Y and Y comes to believe that X will ϕ on the basis of X's statement, X must have convinced Y that X sees some point in ϕ-ing. That point cannot simply be the fact that X has created the relevant expectation in

---

[13] (Raz 1977: 216) considers statements of this sort.

[14] A speaker very often leaves it unclear whether in inviting reliance on an expression of intention he is making a promise or not. I may tell you that I'm going to the museum on Friday with a view to persuading you to go on Friday too whilst also leaving it open whether I am *promising* to be there and you may seek to resolve the ambiguity by asking whether I am committing myself to being there (p. 206). Such negotiations highlight the distinction on which I am insisting.

[15] Prichard's objection to the expectation theory complements his worry about the practice theory, which I discussed earlier (pp. 130–1).

Y by making this statement, for Y wouldn't have this expectation at all unless X had convinced Y that X saw some *further* point in ϕ-ing. But the value of promising as a social tool depends on the fact that people can bind themselves to do something even when they neither have nor appear to have any reason for doing that thing apart from their promise (Kolodny and Wallace 2003: 130–2). For example, those who regard promising as a device of social co-ordination maintain that promising earns its keep in situations in which the parties have no reason (or at any rate no sufficient reason) to do what they promised to do prior to their promise. Recall Hume's farmers who feel no love for each other but who need the other's help in order to get the harvest in. Either these farmers do have sufficient reason to help one another prior to stating that they will or they do not. If principles of reciprocation and so forth are enough to get co-operation going, then the obligation generated by Principle F does no more than reinforce the prior obligation of reciprocation (pp. 138–40). If, on the other hand, the farmers lack sufficient reason to help one another prior to their statements, then Principle F can't give them such a reason. Either way, the expectation theory fails to capture the special social value of a promise.[16]

I agree with these critics that promising, as the expectations theorist understands it, could play only a secondary role as a device of social co-ordination. But some expectations theorists might be willing to swallow that result. The critique of the expectation theory I have offered in this section and the last is more radical. I have argued that even in those cases in which the parties *do* have an independent reason to perform and so the antecedent of Principle F is satisfied, Scanlon's machinery can't explain why they should be under any obligation to perform.

43. The relational structure of a promise

A promise binds to performance because the promisor has intentionally communicated the intention of hereby so binding himself. To my mind this is a practice-invariant feature of promising. Are there any other practice-invariant features of the structure of the promissory bond, features held in place by the underlying promissory interest? In this section I shall argue that every promise has the following structure: there are two distinct persons—promisor and promisee—such that (a) the promise binds the promisor only if it is accepted by the promisee; (b) the promisee is the party who would be wronged by a breach of the promise; (c) the promisee has the power to release the promisor from their promise. We'll see that the expectation theory struggles to explain each of these structural features.

---

[16] (Kolodny and Wallace 2003: 136–44) argue that Scanlon cannot (as he hopes) evade this difficulty by appeal to information-based principles other than Principle F (cf. Scanlon 1998: 306–9).

I'll start by considering the third of these features: the promisee's power of release. How is this to be understood? Scanlon's Principle F ends with 'unless Y consents to ϕ's not being done'. Why is this clause inserted? A little earlier on, when making the point that you can't get out of a promise to drive someone to work simply by warning the promisee that you won't perform, Scanlon says that 'on most people's understanding of promising, I am not free to do this. I am obligated to drive you to work unless you "release" me' (Scanlon 1998: 301). I take it that Scanlon means the last clause of Principle F to capture this idea of 'release' but the scare quotes around this word intimate doubt about whether it will be possible to do this within his framework. His doubts are well grounded.[17]

The last clause in Principle F is simply a repetition of the parentheses in the first: 'X voluntarily and intentionally leads Y to expect that X will ϕ (unless Y consents to X's not doing so)'. The idea of 'consent' gets in via the *content* of the expectation that X arouses in Y: what Y expects is that X will ϕ unless Y consents. Furthermore, it is clear from the context that 'consent' refers to choice of action, not of obligation: X's obligation is to ϕ unless Y chooses otherwise. In Scanlon's view, Y can't choose to release X from this *conditional* obligation, an obligation based on the conditional expectation X has induced in Y. Given this expectation, all Y controls is whether the antecedent of the conditional obligation is fulfilled. So, on this model, the power of release is no normative power, no power to change the normative situation by declaration. Y need not imagine that he can abolish X's obligation to ϕ simply by declaring that X is no longer obliged to ϕ. Rather Y expects that whether X ϕ-s will depends on whether he chooses that X should ϕ and this expectation of choice-dependence is what gives Y's choice its normative significance.

Earlier I established that both consent and release do indeed involve an exercise of normative power (pp. 174–6) but here I want to raise another issue about Scanlon's proposal. On Scanlon's view, it is a mere contingency that the promisee should have any influence over what the promisor is obliged to do. Everything depends on the specific content of the expectation he induces in the promisee. Suppose I'm desperate to give up smoking and you are the only tobacconist in town. I make you swear both not to sell me any cigarettes and furthermore, to pay no heed to any future attempts of mine to release you from this promise. If my reading of Principle F is correct, in this case you have a clear obligation not to provide me with cigarettes regardless of my choices, pleas, etc. This obligation of yours is something I have no influence over. Of course, when I come begging for cigarettes, it may be hard for you to decide what to do all things considered but so far as the obligation generated by Principle F goes, your duty is plain. For Scanlon, the power of release is a dispensable aspect of the

---

[17] My critique of Scanlon's discussion of the power of release was inspired by (Gilbert 2004: 94–102).

content of the expectation induced by the promise and so the tobacconist's promise is unexceptionable.

Were this a clear case of a binding promise, the authority interest theory would be in serious trouble for here, the promisee gains no authority over the promisor.[18] A binding promise must be such that it *could* serve the promisee's interest in having authority over the promisor. This implies that the tobacconist's promise should be rather puzzling as indeed it is. When I plead for cigarettes and urge you to disregard the commitments you previously made to me, how should a conscientious person respond? Most would find it hard to say whether they would be wronging the smoker (by breaking faith with him) should they give in to his demands for cigarettes and a good theory of promissory obligation will explain our bafflement. According to the authority interest theory, promises exist because promisees have an interest in controlling the normative situation. What would constitute the smoker's having such control in the situation envisaged? Would they have it only if the tobacconist were wronging them by selling them the cigarettes (because of the tobacconist's earlier declarations) or would they have it only if they could now permit the tobacconist to sell (by present declaration)? There is no clear answer. Hence our bafflement about what the promise requires. I conclude that the promisee's power of release is essential to a fully intelligible promise, a fact the expectation theory cannot account for.

I am not claiming that the point (for the promisee) of every promissory transaction is to obtain the power of release. If I promise my friend on their deathbed that I'll look after their children, my promise gives them the power to determine whether or not I shall be obliged to perform, a power they can exercise, at least so long as they live. But my friend values the promise simply as a way of ensuring that his children are properly looked after: he cares not whether he could release me from the promise in the few hours remaining to him. All this is perfectly consistent with the idea that granting authority is the function of a promise (p. 144). What is not consistent with that idea is the existence of promises that constrain us in such a way that they couldn't possibly be used for that purpose.

Here is a further question about release: given that a promissory obligation is waivable, why must the person with the power to waive be the very person who would be wronged by breach of the promise? On the authority interest theory, the

---

[18] The theory is not similarly troubled by cases in which the promisee is obliged not to release the promisor because he is obliged to do all he can to ensure that the promise is kept (perhaps for the sake of some third party). That fact does not deprive the promisee of the power of release; rather it means he cannot exercise it without wronging someone. In some such cases he would be behaving badly towards the *promisor* by releasing him. Suppose the promisor has struggled to keep his promise in the expectation of being held to it only for you to release him on a whim just as he is about to complete performance. Resentment should be expected but (*pace* Gilbert 2006: 220–2) that doesn't show that the promisee lacks the power of release. On the contrary it is precisely because he retains this power that its exercise is resented.

answer is obvious: the function of a promise is not merely to bind the promisor to perform, it is to give the promisee control over whether the promisor would be wronging *him* by not performing. The removable bond placed on the promisor is the means whereby the promisee attains that control. So the interest that grounds the wrong of breach is the same as that which grounds the power of release, namely the promisee's authority interest. Given that, the promisee must be both the person who would be wronged by breach and the possessor of the power of release.

The expectations theorist might offer an alternative explanation of this fact along the following lines. First, the wrong of breach of promise is the wrong of disappointing the expectations of one's audience. Second, where there is a power of release, this is because the speaker has induced the expectation that he will perform conditional on his audience's wishing him to do so. Hence the party with the ability to consent to non-performance will also be someone who is wronged by non-performance. To test this explanation, consider an audience interested not in whether what happens will depend on their choice but rather in whether it will depend on the choice of some third party. Adapting an earlier example (p. 51), X can induce in Y the expectation that X will look after Y's mother unless Y's mother thinks otherwise (and regardless of the views of Y). In that case, on the expectation theory, the person with the 'power of release' will be Y's mother but it may well be that the only person who is meant to expect that help will be offered is Y himself and so (according to the expectation theory) only Y would be wronged by breach. Here the expectations theorist cannot explain why the power of release should be vested in the very person who would be wronged by a breach, as it surely is (for breach would wrong Y and not Y's mother).

Thus far I have been assuming that a promise requires two distinct parties— promisor and promisee—but if one can make promises to oneself then the parties to a promise need not be distinct persons. Our discussion of release bears on this question. I doubt one can undertake promissory obligations to oneself because I doubt that the idea of a valuable power of release would make much sense in a case of self-promising. Release is either too easy or too hard. It is too easy if we think that a person can release herself from a first-person promise at any time, simply in virtue of being the same person as the promisee. What would be the point of undertaking an obligation that provided for release at will? Whose authority interest would be served by such a promise?[19] Suppose one instead denies that the earlier self who made the promise is identical with the later self who must keep it. Nevertheless, we imagine, the psychological continuity between them (memory and so forth) means that the later self is bound by the promises of the earlier self. Now release

---

[19] Having assumed that 'covenants' can be 'forgiven' (Hobbes 1994: 86), Hobbes concludes 'Nor is it possible for any person to be bound to himself; because he that can bind can release; and therefore he that is bound to himselfe onely, is not bound' (Hobbes 1994: 174).

becomes impossible at the very moment it becomes meaningful, namely when the earlier self is replaced by its successor, for the earlier self is no longer around to exercise the power of release.[20]

In rejecting the idea that you can bind yourself by means of a promise, I am not denying that there may be another performative—call it a *vow*—which is here to do just this.[21] Perhaps you can wrong yourself by abandoning your diet. And perhaps you wrong yourself because you vowed to stick to your diet, because you performed some act of hereby imposing an obligation on yourself (Velleman 2006: 24). I have reservations about this understanding of vows but my present point is different. Since vows make no provision for release, the interest which gives vows (so understood) their normative significance must be quite distinct from the interest which gives promises their normative significance, namely the authority interest. So the binding force of a vow can't be based on the normative significance of a promise (nor vice versa).

I'll turn now to the first feature of a binding promise, that it must be accepted by the promisee, a point which I have taken for granted until now. On most accounts of promising a valid promise requires something of the promisee as well as of the promisor but they differ over what is required. For Scanlon a binding promise must give the audience an assurance of performance, where an assurance is a belief that something one wishes to happen will happen. Thus to be assured that p, an audience must both want it to happen and come to believe that it will happen. We can't give a binding assurance to someone who doesn't believe our assurance or doesn't care to have it. An assurance is accepted when the speaker gets the audience to expect performance and that is enough to engage Principle F. For this to happen, neither party is required to think about the normative situation but, where a promise is in question, there is a further stage. Now the speaker acknowledges that he is creating an obligation to perform, an obligation he takes seriously and the audience believes his assurances on this point also. A promise requires both promisor and promisee to form beliefs about the normative situation.

I maintain that a valid promise can be made to someone who neither expects performance, nor wishes it to happen. One can accept a promise in order to give a previously untrustworthy promisor a chance to redeem themselves, to create an opportunity to show them up, or out of sheer politeness, in each case without any expectation that they'll perform. Politeness or malice can equally motivate the acceptance of a promise in whose fulfilment one has no further interest.[22] But

---

[20] I'm grateful to Laura Franklin-Hall for discussion of this point.

[21] As Brad Hooker pointed out, an indissoluble marriage may be thought of as involving an exchange of vows rather than of promises. The indissolubility of marriage within many cultures rests on the idea that marriage involves a third party (God) who can dissolve the marriage.

[22] For further discussion, see (Scanlon 1998: 311–12) and (Shiffrin 2008: 486–90). The expectation theory is vulnerable to this objection only if it is taken (in the way Scanlon presents it) as an analysis of promissory obligation rather than as an account of the function of a promise (Sec. 27).

I agree with Scanlon that a valid promise requires a contribution from the promisee and where the promisee can't or won't make this contribution, the promise will not bind. So what is that contribution?

Hobbes tells us that 'to make covenants with brute beasts is impossible because, not understanding our speech, they understand not, nor accept of any translation of right' (Hobbes 1994: 85). For Hobbes, the problem with beasts is not that they don't expect us to do what we say we'll do but rather that they don't grasp the idea of granting a right and so can't 'accept' such a grant.[23] But what would it be to accept such a grant? One possibility is that it involves the belief that the grant has been made. That would give us the second stage of Scanlon's model of promising without the first, thereby protecting it against the examples which show that a valid promise can be made to someone who neither expects performance, nor wishes it to happen. But we are not yet out of the woods. A valid promise can still be made to someone who does not even believe that a valid promise is being made to them.

In the last chapter, I considered cases in which the promisor makes a promise under the impression that their promise is invalid (p. 192). That, I argued, need not prevent them from being bound by the promise. If I promise you this umbrella thinking it to be someone else's umbrella, I am bound to give it to you should it turn out to be my umbrella. A binding promise requires only that I communicate the intention of hereby giving you ownership of the umbrella. Now suppose that you suspect that I don't own the umbrella in question and therefore cannot promise it to you. Out of politeness you accept my promise anyway and it turns out that I own the umbrella after all. Wouldn't I be wronging you by failing to give it you? If so what does your 'acceptance' of my promise involve?

At this point we should give a hearing to the idea that a valid promise requires nothing at all of the promisee (Shiffrin 2008: 491–3). What a binding promise requires from the *promisor* is that they knowingly communicate the intention of hereby undertaking an obligation to the promisee to perform. One might imagine that the promisee need only be mentioned in the content of this communication to acquire the right to performance. The first President Bush made a campaign promise not to raise taxes. When he went ahead and raised them, didn't he thereby wrong the American electorate (or some part of it) by breaching his promise, though they did nothing to accept it? I would argue that if Bush did wrong the electorate, that is only because they responded to his statement by voting for him. Where there is no such response it is much less plausible to suppose that the promisor is bound to the promisee. Suppose a complete stranger wants to ensure that they have no more than two children and so sends me a postcard promising this to me. I do nothing. Here it is

---

[23] 'But that a promise may transfer a right, the acceptance of the person to whom it is made is no less required here, than in the case of transferring a property' (Grotius 2005: 719–20). See also (Pufendorf 2003: 116).

very doubtful that they would be wronging me in having a third child and this is surely because I did nothing to accept their promise (Fried 1981: 41–3).[24]

So what is involved in accepting a promise? The power of acceptance here is the counterpart of the power of promise. Each is a power to change the normative situation by declaration (in the presence of the corresponding declaration). For a promise to bind, the promisee must communicate the intention of hereby binding the promisor by accepting their promise. In some contexts, a failure to refuse might suffice to communicate acceptance, in others a positive declaration is required, in yet others something like voting or claiming the prize can communicate acceptance. Acceptance so understood is quite different from the 'acceptance' required for obligations of reciprocation to kick in (p. 140). One can accept goods and services without being aware of the normative consequences of such an acceptance; one simply needs to take advantage of them. By contrast, someone who didn't know that accepting a promise binds the promisor to perform could not accept (or refuse) a promise in the relevant sense.

Having clarified the notion of acceptance in play, we can now ask why promises must be accepted to be valid. Again the idea that a promisee acquires authority over the promisor does the work. Human beings often value authority for its own sake but that doesn't mean such authority is always a benefit. And even where it is a benefit, the potential promisee may not wish to accept (in either sense of the word) that benefit from the promisor. Given that promising is here to serve the promisee's interest in authority, it would be absurd if the promisee had no way of declining an authority it was not in his interests to acquire. And he should be able to decline it by using the very mechanism by which it is acquired, namely a declaration (where this includes declarative omission).

A potential promisee might wish to decline a promise for many reasons. An authority acquires the responsibility of deciding how to exercise their authority, of deciding whether and when they should issue commands. That is a call many of us would prefer not to have to make. There are better or worse ways of exercising authority and we can be blamed for exercising it badly. Or else we may not wish to be in a relationship of command with this person at all. (Rather *give* a friend the money they need than *loan* them it.) True, once someone offers us a position of authority, that fact alone compels us to decide whether or not to accept; we can't avoid exercising this much control over the normative situation. Still people often prefer

---

[24] (Thomson 1990: 296–8) gives a related example. There are ways of elaborating the story on which my silence might signify acceptance. Suppose I know Fried's couple well, see them frequently and after discussing their plans with them many times, receive their postcard without comment. Here, by not rejecting their promise, I might well be taken to have communicated acceptance and then it is much more plausible to suppose that they will wrong me should they breach.

to refuse in order not to have to decide subsequently whether to release or to compel performance.

Where the promise is indeed a benefit, one might still decline to accept it on the grounds that such acceptance would incur obligations of reciprocation. You might promise me the loan of your bike and I might decline this promise to avoid 'being obliged'. It is by exercising the normative power of acceptance that we 'accept' the promise in the wider sense in which acceptance of a benefit incurs obligations of reciprocation. Mightn't the offer alone oblige us to reciprocate? Maybe, but a refusal often pre-empts such debts. In any case, there is a crucial difference between declining to accept a benefit and returning the benefit once it has been accepted. If I accept the promise of the loan of your bike, and then decide that, after all, I shan't be needing it, I am in a different position from that I would have been in had I declined your offer in the first place. Different forms of reciprocation may be appropriate. In sum, for these and other reasons, having a binding promise may not be in the promisee's interests and so acceptance is required for it to bind.[25]

I'm not denying that one person can acquire authority from another without the latter's accepting this authority. For example, if you injure me, I may have acquired a right to compensation from you, i.e. a right to have some money (etc.) that you previously had a right to. Here I acquire this right without doing anything to acquire it. I might release you from your obligation to compensate but that would be an exercise of my acquired authority over you, an authority I cannot decline. I cannot decline this right to compensation because my possession of this right is not based on any authority interest of mine, on any interest in being able to bind you by declaration. Rather it is rooted in my non-normative interest in not suffering harm and in being 'made whole' should I suffer it (Kant 1996: 422). Therefore, my acquisition of this right from you depends neither on my declarations, nor on yours. But when the mechanism that grants authority is here to serve the recipient's authority interests, it must work with their consent.

44. The solemnity of a promise

According to the expectation theory, one wrongs the promisee in breaching one's promise when one fails to give due weight to the promisee's expectations of

---

[25] Does consent require acceptance to be valid? If consent is like promise then yes but if consent works more like release from a promise then no. I incline towards the latter view; the grounds for requiring acceptance in the case of promise seem not to apply. First, consent is unlikely to be a burden. If I consent to your stroking my knee, you don't acquire any normative power over me for whose exercise you might be held responsible. Of course, you must decide whether to stroke my knee but you had to make that decision anyway. Second, though the consent may well be a benefit to the consentee (and so something which calls for an expression of gratitude) it is primarily a benefit to the consentor (pp. 181–2).

performance. On my own view, one wrongs the promisee in breaching one's promise where one fails to allow the promisee to decide whether one performs. But what is it to allow the promisee to decide whether one performs? And how does this differ from giving due weight to the promisee's expectation of performance? I claimed earlier that one could be obliged to have certain kinds of evidence for one's statements about future performance, and be obliged to warn of non-performance without being under any obligation to perform. What does it mean to be under a specific obligation to perform and how does this connect to the idea that the promisee has the right to decide whether you perform?

The materials for answering these questions were provided in Chapter 3, where I observed that an obligation constrains your practical deliberations by preventing you from acting on a certain range of reasons. Where the obligation derives from a promise, the promisee is free to weigh these excluded considerations in determining whether to require you to perform. In this section, I shall use this account of obligation to elucidate a feature of promising which has yet to receive the attention it deserves, namely the fact that some promises are more firm, serious, or solemn than others. The expectation theory yields a fairly simple account of solemnity but we must work harder to describe how three different factors interact to set the strength of the promissory bond: the communicated intentions of the parties to the promise, the practice of promising of which they are part, and the underlying promissory interest.

I previously distinguished the solemnity of a promise that is my current concern from its stringency (pp. 162–3). The solemnity of a promise determines when one counts as having failed to respect one's promise. On most views of promising, one can breach a promise without failing to respect the promise and thus without wronging the promisee. All sorts of obstacles to performance may arise and in the face of at least some such obstacles, one is no longer obliged to perform. So a failure to respect one's promise is not a simple failure to do what you said you were going to do. The solemnity of a promise determines how much one has to do to respect that promise. By contrast, the stringency of a promise is a matter of how grave a wrong one commits in failing to respect it, how guilty one should feel about this, how much blame is apt and so forth. As I observed, stringency and solemnity are easy to confuse because the blameworthiness of breach is, in part, a function of the extent of your failure to respect your promise. But, the expectations theorist and I will agree, these two things must be kept apart.

On the expectation theory, a binding promise induces an expectation of performance in the promisee. Now some expectations are firmer than others. The expectations theorist settles the solemnity of a promise by asking how firm an expectation of performance the promisor induced in the promisee (in accordance with Principle F and so forth). Other things being equal, the stronger the expectation he intentionally induces, the more trouble the promisor must go to in keeping his promise if he is to count as respecting his promise. The more the promisee expects performance, the more likely his interests are to be damaged by non-performance, the more the promisor must do to bring performance about. So the solemnity of a promise is fixed by the parties.[26] By contrast, its stringency is fixed by the underlying promissory interest, namely the promisee's interest in having correct information about how the promisor will act. Of course, how grave a wrong you do someone by failing to respect the promise you gave them will depend on how much their interests were at stake in the matter. And that will depend, in part, on the solemnity of the promise. But, in the eyes of the expectations theorist, the normative significance of harm to these interests is independent both of the intentions of the parties and of the habits and dispositions of those around them.

If the criticisms already made are telling, this account of the matter cannot be correct. There are promises that bind though the promisee does not expect performance and would be unharmed by non-performance. And even where a promise does raise expectations of performance, the strength of the expectation induced cannot explain the strength of the obligation to perform. In earlier sections, I allowed that the stronger the expectation you induce, the better the evidence you must have for it and perhaps the more you must do to warn of non-fulfilment, etc. but none of this delivers an obligation to perform, however weak. The obligation to perform has a quite different rationale: it gives the promisor the right to *decide for* the promisee whether he will perform. How can we accommodate variations in the solemnity of a promise within this alternative model?

Let's treat the making of a promise as a two-stage process, initiated by a request from the promisee for a future performance. True a promise is sometimes offered without any prior request but no binding promise results unless the promisor's offer is accepted and it is illuminating to treat the required acceptance as involving a request for performance.[27]

Recall that the point of *asking* someone to ϕ is to ensure that it makes sense for them not to decide for themselves whether they ought to ϕ. If someone asks me to ϕ, it makes sense for to me exclude various considerations which recommend not ϕ-ing from my deliberations (pp. 86–7). Requests are more or less urgent and the urgency of the request determines the scope of this exclusion. The more urgent the request, the more reasons recommending non-compliance it makes sense for me to exclude from my practical deliberations and thus the more trouble it make sense for me to go to in seeking to comply.

One might suppose that the urgency of a request is a function of the perceived importance of its subject matter. Indeed, the parties' shared sense of the latter will

---

[26] Though Scanlon allows that a background practice could in principle make a contribution here (Scanlon 1998: 310–11).

[27] A request (like acceptance) may be made with any degree of reluctance or indifference.

often help the recipient understand how urgent the request is meant to be. Nevertheless, the urgency of the request is not determined by the perceived weight of the interests that would be served by complying with it. You can make an emphatic request for something known to be quite trivial (e.g. to test willingness to oblige) and you can make a tentative request for something that is known to be very important to you (because you fear a humiliating refusal). Rather the urgency of a request is determined by the communicated intentions of the supplicant, by how emphatic it is: a request is as urgent as it is meant to be taken to be.

A promise is as solemn as it is meant to be taken to be. One can make a solemn promise about a trivial matter and a much less solemn promise about something quite serious. Of course, when interpreting a promise you will have regard to various signs of how firmly a promise is intended (formality of context, tone of voice, choice of diction, etc.) and one of these signs will be the parties' shared perceptions of how important fulfilment of the promise is to the promisee.[28] Promises about matters the promisee is known to regard as important will normally be understood as firm promises but the parties can discount this presumption, they just need to make it clear what their intentions are. I propose that the communicated intentions of the parties (when they make and agree to the imputed request) fix the solemnity of a promise by determining the scope of the promissory exclusion. The more solemn the promise, the more reasons recommending non-performance it makes sense for the promisor to exclude from their deliberations, the more trouble it makes sense for them to go to in keeping their promise.

Does the importance of a promise's subject matter have more to do with its solemnity than this allows? Can one really make a more solemn promise to meet someone for lunch than to save them from death? Suppose the promisor is a famous surgeon whom the promisee asks to attend the bedside of a gravely ill relative. Even in this extremity, the promisee might regard their own request as a bit of an imposition. After all they know that the surgeon is a busy man and they do not expect him to devote his entire life to his work. Nevertheless, they give it a try. Here the surgeon might make and the relative might accept the rather off-hand promise of a house visit. Should the surgeon fail to show up, the promisee might well feel less resentful (though more devastated) than would a colleague of the surgeon who'd been left to lunch alone.

I don't deny that elements of the social background can play a role in determining the exclusionary force of a promise. For example, there is a general understanding that a social arrangement excludes consideration of subsequent invitations, however attractive, but does not prevent you from handling your child's sudden illness in the

---

[28] For Pink, the fact that the weight of the obligation generated by a promise can depend on the gravity of its content shows that 'something else is generating the obligation beyond a will on my part to obligate myself' (Pink 2009: 408).

way you judge best (p. 90). I doubt this understanding is based on the parties' shared perception of their own individual priorities, on whether family matters more to them than friends, etc. Rather it is furnished by the social context in which they both operate. Nevertheless, the default presumption supplied by the social context can be discounted by explicit agreement amongst the parties.[29] If you say 'I'll be there whatever happens at home' in making your lunch date with me, you shouldn't even consider whether to take your child to hospital when another option is available (Finnis 1980: 309). And if you say 'I'll be there for lunch unless I hear from NN' you are now entitled to weigh the attractions of lunch with NN against those of lunch with me. In the end the solemnity of a promise depends, as much as its content, on the parties' communicated intentions.[30]

Once it has been settled how far the promisor has fallen short of respecting his promise, what determines his degree of blameworthiness? This is where the habits of recognition involved in our practice of promising come into play. The expectations theorist maintains that the stringency of a promise is fixed by the strength of the underlying promissory interest, namely the information interest. I doubt that the strength of the underlying promissory interest entirely settles the stringency of a promise. Our shared human interest in acquiring authority over the decisions of others allows for considerable variation in how seriously breach of faith is regarded within particular societies. Once we have set aside the secondary wrongs involved in breach of promise (disappointed expectations, etc.) and focused our attention on the breach of faith alone, there are no grounds for insisting that every culture must take the same attitude to breach. The underlying authority interest allows much scope for variation, and the practices of the society in question (rather than the intentions of individuals) take up the slack (pp. 162–3).

In Chapter 8, I described what is involved in an attempt to create a promissory obligation, what one must do to make a promise. In the present chapter I specified just how a successful promise changes the normative situation, how a promissory obligation constrains you. In the next chapter, I shall ask under what conditions a promise that has been offered and accepted succeeds in producing a binding promise, succeeds in creating a promissory obligation. This will complete our account of promising.

---

[29] The same is true of default presumptions about the content of a promise furnished by the social context (pp. 101–2).

[30] Very often, the parties find they sincerely disagree about what sort of consideration a particular promise was meant to exclude. Here the default presumptions provided by the social background can be invoked to resolve the matter though crucial indeterminacies may remain.

10

Which Promises Bind?

In Part II, we established that human beings have an interest in being able to impose obligations by declaration. This does not imply that all exercises of this normative power work, that every communication of an intention to hereby create an obligation succeeds in its purported aim. Can we provide an account of which declarations bind and which do not by appealing to the underlying promissory interest? Hume alleged that when thinking about such matters we draw distinctions which reflection cannot justify and he regards this as evidence of the conventional nature of promissory obligation (Hume 1978: 525). If Hume is right, we shouldn't expect our knowledge of the function of a promise to deliver a detailed account of the validity conditions of a promise. By contrast, Scanlon claims that we settle whether a promise binds by engaging in 'moral reasoning' rather than by applying the conventions of some social practice (Scanlon 1998: 310). For Scanlon, the validity conditions of a promise are determined by the underlying promissory interest.

In this chapter, I'll argue that the correct account of the function of a promise does tell us a great deal about the validity conditions of a promise.[1] In particular it tells us more than any account that appeals to our interest in information or social co-ordination. I shall not attempt a comprehensive treatment. There are many ways of invalidating a promise and I doubt the authority interest can explain them all. Some may be creatures of convention. Others are fixed by norms that have no particular connection with promising. For example, promises can turn out to be impossible to execute and at least some obstacles to performance invalidate the promise whose execution they frustrate. To determine precisely which promises such obstacles invalidate we may need to reflect quite generally on obligations it is impossible to fulfil. If so, our account of the validity conditions of a promise will not depend at this point on our theory of *promissory* obligation. But between these two extremes of local convention and general norm, the authority interest has an explanatory role to play.

---

[1] The practice of promising involves three normative powers: offer, acceptance, and release. In this chapter, I focus on the conditions that must be satisfied for the promisor's offer of a promise to bind him. Similar points apply to the other two powers.

I'll focus on three types of promise often held invalid. First, there are promises made only because the promisor was deceived on a material point. Second, there are promises made only because the promisor was put under pressure, or coerced. Third, there are promises to do something that ought not to be done. As to the first two, I agree that deception and duress often invalidate a promise and shall urge that only the authority interest theory predicts the precise conditions under which this happens. As to the third, very few promises are invalidated by their content alone, and this again is predicted by the theory.

Some authors write as if the only promises are binding promises (e.g. Prichard 1968: 169 and Searle 2001: 193). By contrast, in my mouth a promise has been made whenever a promisor has (intentionally) communicated the intention of hereby undertaking an obligation to perform and a promisee has accepted this declaration. Given my usage there are two separate questions: (a) Has a promise been made? (b) Is the promisor bound by the promise they have made? Many (perhaps most) disputes about promissory obligation concern *what* was promised rather than whether the promise binds. I have said little about how the content of a promise is fixed and this chapter will cast no further light on the matter. My excuse is that the issues raised by these disputes have nothing particularly to do with the exercise of normative power. Indeed they have nothing particularly to do with ethics. Rather their resolution calls for a theory of linguistic communication and more specifically a theory of what it is for X to communicate to Y that they have attitude A towards proposition p. With such a theory in hand we can say just when someone has communicated the intention of undertaking an obligation to make p true. We should not look to an account of promising to do this. Taking it that we know what promises have been made, I now ask which promises one must keep.

45. Wronging the promisor

There are at least three points at which deontic notions might be needed to understand promising. First, and most obviously, valid promises impose obligations to perform, obligations whose fulfilment is owed to the promisee. Second, it is widely believed that if a promise is induced by certain forms of wrongdoing (e.g. coercion or deception of the promisor) then that wrongdoing invalidates the promise.[2] Third, if doing what you promised to do would itself involve wrongdoing then, in the eyes of many, that fact casts doubt on the validity of your promise.

The first point can be restated as follows: a promise is invalid when the promisor would not wrong the promisee just by breaking their promise. An invalid promise must be distinguished from a promise that the promisor is justified in breaking.

---

[2] For some doubts about this, see (Gilbert 2006: 228–9).

Wronging someone by breaking a valid promise can be the right thing to do. One is justified in breaking a promise when for example some more weighty duty (e.g. a more important promise) turns out to conflict with it in a way that could not have been anticipated when the promise was made. The fact that one is justified in breaching is perfectly consistent with the fact that one is wronging the promisee (pp. 91–3).

Many of those who write about promises doubt whether philosophical reflection on common sense alone can tell us very much about their validity conditions.[3] I suspect at least some of these sceptics have not separated the issue of whether someone is wrong to break a promise (i.e. whether they are justified in so doing) from the issue of whether the promise is valid (i.e. whether the promisor would be wronging the promisee by breaking it). Endless considerations may bear on whether the right thing for me to do is to break my promise and perhaps there is nothing general or systematic to be said about when such a breach of promise is justified (p. 95). Nevertheless we may be able to draw some fairly definite conclusions about which promises are valid, conclusions with significant theoretical implications.

Given that a wronging like breach of promise can be justified what is the significance of its being a wronging? In Chapter 3, we discussed the deliberative significance of obligation; here I'll focus on reactions to wronging. I maintain that guilt, remorse, apology, requests for forgiveness are appropriate responses on the part of the promisor even though what they have done was justified.[4] We often feel guilty about such a breach of promise and seek the promisee's forgiveness even while continuing to believe that breaching this promise was, in the circumstances, the right thing to do. And the guilt the wronger feels here is something more than the regret a decent person feels whenever they must cause harm, or allow someone to be harmed (pp. 93–4).

None of this applies when the promise broken is simply invalid. For example, a highwayman who, finding an inadequate amount of money on his victim, forces them to promise to provide more once they are released, is not wronged when his victim fails to fulfil their promise. We might conclude from this that a decent person would not hesitate to break such a promise. But this would be a bit too quick. What, after all, is the point of extracting an invalid promise? Might it not make sense for the highwayman to hope that his victim's good character will ensure that they keep it? Must the highwayman be banking on their irrationality, or at least on their ignorance of the fact that duress invalidates a promise?

---

[3] After considering exactly when promises are invalidated by 'force or fraud', Sidgwick concludes that 'on all these points Common Sense seems doubtful' (Sidgwick 1981: 306). Sidgwick's scepticism is endorsed by (Atiyah 1981: 25). Grotius notes 'a great variety of opinions' on these points (Grotius 2005: 712).

[4] (Raz 1986: 359–66), (Thomson 1990: 93–6), and (Raz 2004: 189–93) suggest that compensation is the right reaction to breach of a justified promise but compensation is often out of place (pp. 47–8).

Adam Smith considers this very example (Smith 1976: 330–3). He affirms that such a promise is invalid 'as a matter of jurisprudence' and that 'no injury is done to the robber' by its breach. But he also says that 'whenever such promises are violated, though for the most necessary reasons, it is always with some degree of dishonour for the person who made them'. Not everyone will agree. Among those who do, some might think that this is so because the promisor would be besmirching their honour by giving in to the threat, others because of the deception involved. But whatever truth there is in these ideas, all should endorse Smith's conclusion that the highwayman's victim cannot be wronging the highwayman simply by breaching their promise. If what they do is wrong, it is wrong in some other way.

In the light of the possibility of a justified wronging, our initial observations require further elucidation. For example we supposed that certain forms of wrongdoing invalidate the promise to which they give rise.[5] Does wrongdoing here mean doing the wrong thing, i.e. behaving in a way which isn't justified? Or does it rather mean committing a wrong or, more particularly, wronging someone (p. 45)?

It is widely maintained that duress and misrepresentation invalidate a promise just where it is *wrong* to get someone to promise in that way.[6] Since employing force or fraud to get something done is at least a *prima facie* wrong whatever that something is, we can use this fact to explain why a *promise* induced by force or fraud may be invalid without obvious circularity.[7] Unfortunately those who say this do not clearly distinguish actions wrong in that they are unjustified from actions which are justified (and therefore right) but which nevertheless wrong someone. Once this distinction is made, we have two rather different proposals to consider. The first goes as follows:

---

[5] A full account of how deception and duress invalidate would explain how these invalidating conditions must be connected to the promise in order to invalidate it. I shall say only that they must induce the promise. If a highwayman's threat had nothing to do with the traveller's promise to pay, it could hardly invalidate that promise. It might also be that the threat must either excuse or justify the making of the promise. Indeed it has been suggested that we understand invalidating conditions on the model of excusing conditions (Hart 2008: 34–5 and 44–6). One problem with this idea is that the amount of force required to invalidate a promise whose breach would cause a given monetary loss is much less than the amount of force required to excuse a theft of an equivalent value. On this point, see (Durkheim 1957: 205–6) and (Scanlon 1998: 245). I shall not pursue these issues here.

[6] Fried argues that duress invalidates a contract where it 'proposes a wrong' to the promisor (Fried 1981: 97–9). See also (Altham 1985: 11–12), (Pufendorf 2003: 116), (Smith 2004: 316–23, 376–8), and (Scanlon 2008: 82–3). Thomson distinguishes doing something wrong or 'morally impermissible' from doing something that wrongs someone (Thomson 1990: ch. 3). She also maintains that duress and misrepresentation invalidate a promise specifically where they wrong the promisor (pp. 310–13). But she believes that wronging someone entails doing something wrong (p. 122) and that wrongs like coercion and misrepresentation invalidate promises because their perpetrators are 'at fault' (pp. 312–13).

[7] The fact that force or fraud is being used to induce a promise with a given content might be crucial in determining whether the victim has responded in a reasonable or else in an excusable way and so, perhaps, in determining whether his promise is valid.

The Fault Account: Promises induced by duress or misrepresentation are invalid where it is wrong to get someone to promise in that way.

Here 'wrong' means unjustified, where an unjustified action is one the agent is at fault in performing.

This proposal has at least one important virtue: it deftly handles cases in which one might think oneself justified in extracting a promise by force. Consider the parental warnings that make children promise to behave or the threats of punishment with which judges persuade malefactors to promise to reform. Though such promises are clearly extracted under duress, the point of extracting them is to put those who give them under an additional (promissory) obligation to do what they ought to do anyway. And to serve that purpose, the promises induced must be valid. The fault account can explain the validity of these promises by supposing that parents and judges are justified in using threats to obtain them.[8]

However, there is an alternative explanation of what is going on here. Perhaps the promise obtained is valid only because the threats used to extract it do not wrong the promisor *at all*, justifiably or otherwise.[9] It does seem a little odd to expect the judge to feel guilty about threatening a criminal with jail or the parent to feel remorse at warning their child that it will be confined to the house. Judges and parents are authorized to do these things. This line of thought suggests an alternative account of invalidation, namely

The Infringement Account: Promises induced by duress or misrepresentation are invalid where by getting someone to promise in that way you wrong them (i.e. you infringe some right of theirs).[10]

On this view, a promise is a more fragile thing: duress or misrepresentation invalidate a promise whenever they wrong the promisor, even where the promisee is justified in using them to extract the promise. In the next section, I'll assess the merits of these rival stories.

---

[8] Perhaps the same should be said of a promise of surrender extracted by force or fraud in the course of a just war. For discussion of surrender promises, see (Altham 1985: 10), (Scanlon 1998: 325–6), (Deigh 2002: 489–90).

[9] 'Force and fraud are in war the two cardinal virtues' (Hobbes 1994: 78). Consequently Hobbes thinks that promises made under duress in war are binding (Hobbes 1994: 86). Should we expect a decent soldier to feel that they are wronging the enemy by coercing or deceiving them in the course of a just war?

[10] It is not sufficient for invalidation that the process of inducing the promise involves a wrong to the promisor. For example, I may wrong the promisor by asking for a promise where my request constitutes an insult. But the insulted party can still fulfil my request with a valid promise provided it wasn't the insolence of the request that induced the promise. Where the promisor is shocked or intimidated by the insult, his promise may well be invalid. It is also crucial that the inducement constitute a wronging (of the promisor) and not just a wrong. For example, a judge who has been bribed can't claim that his promise to throw the case out is invalid simply because it was wrong of the promisee to induce him to promise by such means. The inducement must wrong the promisor.

46. The fragility of a promise

We are sometimes justified in using duress or deception in order to persuade a fellow adult to do something that needs to be done and which they would not otherwise do. Still to behave thus most often *is* to wrong the person coerced or misled. Can we also induce action by using the same forms of duress or misrepresentation to extract a valid promise? There is nothing in the fault account to explain why such a promise should be invalid provided the duress or misrepresentation used to obtain it is justified. And yet invalid it often is.

Take misrepresentation first. Suppose I am trying to establish an exercise routine and a friend persuades me to accompany them to the gym this evening. Both my friend and I know that I will be much better off, physically and psychologically, once this routine is established. But my friend is concealing something from me: this very evening a bar crawl is planned which would prevent me from accompanying them to the gym. My friend knows perfectly well that this is a temptation I will not resist and so, out of concern for me, they conceal the crawl and do everything they can to ensure that nobody else mentions it to me.[11] When rumours of it reach my ears, my friend reluctantly denies that there is any such crawl and gets me to promise that I will accompany them. Despite my friend's best efforts I later discover the truth and, filled with self-loathing, abandon my trip to the gym.

Clearly my friend has deceived me and it would be quite normal for them to feel guilty about deceiving. Yet if my health is in question unless I exercise, they might also feel justified in misleading me about the crawl in order to get me into the gym. Nevertheless when I do not show up, I doubt they will think that *I* have wronged *them* in breaching my promise. I may be a fool, I may be ungrateful, but I am not obliged to go to the gym simply in order to keep the promise I made them, for I made this promise only because they deceived me. They wronged me in misleading me on a material point and that wrong invalidates my promise.

In considering duress, it helps to raise the stakes a bit. Suppose I have some disease about which I feel extremely embarrassed which a course of injections is needed to treat. Without these injections, my health will be seriously damaged but I keep putting them off out of fear of the needle. I confide all this to you and as time goes

---

[11] Does such non-disclosure of material information by the promisee invalidate a promise? This is a fraught issue both within the law and beyond. It is to avoid this question that I turn the gym example into one involving outright deception. I would trace our uncertainty about when non-disclosure invalidates to our uncertainty about whether the promisee's non-disclosure wrongs the promisor. The common law imposes duties of disclosure only in rather special circumstances and so tends to uphold the validity of contracts, even where one party has kept crucial facts to himself. Civil law imposes more extensive duties of disclosure (as it does positive duties of aid) and so tends to void contracts where it was obvious to one party that the other was under a misapprehension. Both attitudes can be accommodated within the framework I am suggesting.

on you become more and more concerned about the danger to my health. Reluctantly, you threaten to break your vow of secrecy and tell people of my refusal to treat the embarrassing disease unless I begin the course of injections at once. Some would think themselves justified in making this threat but would also feel guilty because they are wronging a friend by threatening to breach a confidence. Now suppose that you have to go away suddenly and so will not be around to check whether I have actually begun the course of injections. You instead blackmail me into promising to have the injections. Here again you may be justified in doing so in the hope that I will feel obliged to keep the promise but I doubt that I would be wronging you simply by breaching it. I might be wronging you in other ways but one thing you could not complain of is breach of a promise obtained by such threats.

I conclude that the fault account cannot explain cases in which one is justified in using duress and deception in order to get someone to do something but where a promise extracted by these means would be invalid. By contrast, the infringement account is untroubled by these examples. Still the infringement account might be thought to have troubles of its own.

To see why, note that I am using 'duress' and 'misrepresentation' to cover a wide range of phenomena. Deliberate coercion or deception intended to induce the promise come immediately to mind but these terms also cover cases of negligent coercion or misstatement where the promisee did not know that they were pressurizing or misleading the promisor but ought to have known this. Furthermore, I mean to include what is often called 'innocent misrepresentation' and what might be called 'innocent duress', that is cases where the promisee had no way of knowing that they were either misleading or pressurizing the promisor. The apparent problem for the infringement account is that such duress and misrepresentation, though innocent, still puts the validity of the promise in doubt.[12]

We can illustrate the point with regards to misrepresentation by modifying the example of the would-be gym buddy. Everything is as it was except that my friend knows nothing of the bar crawl and rightly regards such a thing as extremely unlikely, so when they assure me that the rumours are groundless they are being both sincere and reasonable. Yet once it transpires that the rumours are correct, the fact that they misled me might well make me wonder whether I am still obliged to accompany them to the gym (or at least about whether I am so obliged simply because I promised). Here the fact that I was misled by the promisee and that their false assurance got me to promise is crucial. Had I refused to credit the rumours because I myself thought such a thing unlikely, the discovery that the rumours were correct

---

[12] For example, (Smith 2004: 367–8) is puzzled by the fact that innocent misrepresentation invalidates a contract in law. 'The relevant mistake is not typically serious enough, *qua* mistake, to justify setting aside the contract for this reason' and so 'absent wrongdoing' on the promisee's part it is not clear to Smith why the promisor should be allowed to breach.

and that I had based my promise on a false assumption would not release me from it. An unanticipated temptation does not invalidate a promise.

If my promise is invalid here, this is because in being misled by the promisee I have been wronged by him. It might seem strange to speak of a wrong in cases of 'innocent' misrepresentation. Even those prepared to accept the idea of a justified wrong might baulk at accusing the promisee of wronging me when he could not have known that he was wronging me. But the grounds for this reluctance are not evident.[13] It would certainly make sense for my friend to feel guilty about misinforming me on a point that clearly mattered to both of us even where his mistake was a perfectly reasonable one. He has a justification or, at least, an excuse for misinforming me but neither excuse nor justification preclude guilt. If so, my friend *has* wronged me simply by misleading me, though his behaviour is either justified or excused by the reasonable but false belief that motivated it. My promise is invalid because I was wronged when misled on a material point.[14] In cases of 'innocent duress' the promisee is in no position to know that they are putting the promisor under illicit pressure. For example, they might reasonably but mistakenly think that the gun they are waving in the promisor's face for theatrical effect is an obvious replica, a thought reinforced by the promisor's efforts to appear nonchalant. But once they discover that (as the promisor knew all along) the gun is both real and loaded, the promisee might well consider that in terrifying the promisor they wronged them and that this wrong invalidates the promise, even though their behaviour is either justified or excused by their reasonable belief.

In promising, one exercises a form of normative power. The same is true when you give someone a gift or grant them your consent. Gifts and consents can also be invalidated by duress and misrepresentation and our conclusion that the infringement account rather than the fault account provides the best treatment of promissory invalidation may be tested by asking whether the same applies to these other exercises of normative power.[15] I shall argue that it does; such an exercise of normative power is invalid where it is induced by wronging those who exercise it.

---

[13] Consider Williams's example of the driver who kills the child that runs in front of their truck (Williams 1982: 27–30). Whether or not they regard themselves as negligent, a decent person will be tormented by the thought that they *killed* a child, may appeal for forgiveness from the child's relatives, etc.

[14] We established that whilst a promisor has a specific duty to fulfil his promise, someone who makes a prediction about his own behaviour need have no duty to ensure that his prediction turns out to be true (p. 210). But if he wrongs his audience by misleading them (however innocently) does he not have a duty to put things right in so far as he can? And is that not a duty to make his prediction true (in so far as he can) whenever it threatens to be falsified? I doubt it. Merely informing your audience of your (reasonable) mistake may suffice. If you misled them in a way that was harmful you may have to ameliorate the damage or somehow compensate them for it. Occasionally it might be that the only way you can do so is to make your prediction true after all. But there is no general duty to ensure that what you say turns out to be true.

[15] The natural lawyers drew an analogy between property transfers and promises, for example (Locke 1988, Bk 2, ch. 16, sec. 186), (Pufendorf 2003, Bk 1, ch. 9, sec. 16), (Grotius 2005: 719–20).

Certain extremities justify one's seizing someone else's property or making use of it without their consent and among them are situations in which one is justified in using either force or fraud against the owner in order to gain control of their property. Still in these cases one usually wrongs the owner: a decent person will feel bad about having to behave in this way and their victim may reasonably resent it. Now one might instead use force or fraud to extract the owner's consent to one's use of their property or to persuade them to hand it over. But whatever good this indirection does, it does not remove the element of wronging. Even where one is justified in using certain forms of duress or misrepresentation to take control of someone's property, one cannot avoid wronging them altogether by first using these very means to persuade them to agree, for the consent or gift thus obtained is liable to be invalid. Promises, gifts, and consents are invalidated by force and fraud even where the perpetrator would be justified in behaving like that in order to secure the thing promised, given or permitted.

In determining whether deception or duress invalidates a promise (or a gift), it is often crucial to know whether the promisee (or recipient) was involved.[16] I leave the notion of 'involvement' here intentionally vague. The promisee is certainly involved if they coerced or misled the promisor into promising but they might also be involved in some cases where a third party set out to extract this promise by duress or misrepresentation. The crucial point is that the promisee is definitely not involved unless they are the author of the duress/misrepresentation, or had prior knowledge of it.[17]

In this section, I have argued that the infringement account rather than the fault account explains the validity of a promise and of other exercises of normative power. So what is it that promising has in common with these other phenomena which makes the infringement account true of them all? Why should the fact that the promisee has wronged the promisor by using force or fraud invalidate the promise they extract even when their extracting the promise in that way was justified? To answer this question, we must ask how exactly the obligations created by such normative powers depend on our 'free' choice.

---

[16] Hume imagines a surgeon who asks a patient for a promise of payment before they will operate to save the patient's life (Hume 1978: 525). The surgeon may have no prior obligation to operate (perhaps because they would run a serious risk of infection) and does not wrong the patient in demanding payment, even if the patient has been wrongfully injured by a third party. Once the price is agreed (and provided it is not outrageous?) both parties are committed. If the surgeon were involved in injuring the patient, the situation would be quite different.

[17] In my explicit statement of the infringement account I left it open whether duress or misrepresentation by a third party might invalidate a promise and it is unclear to me whether this is a possibility. (Thomson 1990: 312–13) and (Pufendorf 2003: 115–16), maintain that unless the promisee is involved, the wrong of coercion or misrepresentation cannot invalidate a promise made to *them*. In (Owens 2007: 305–7) I endorsed their view but I'm now less sure.

47. Voluntariness and normative interests

It is often said that choice must be 'voluntary' to be normatively significant; so far as the distribution of rights and responsibilities goes, an involuntary choice is no choice at all and choice induced by deception or duress is involuntary. At the outset, I distinguished three different ways in which our obligations might depend upon our choices, three different grades of choice-dependence for obligation (Sec. 1). With choice underwriting obligation in more ways than one, we should expect there to be several standards of voluntariness in play. I'll start by considering the notion of voluntariness appropriate to obligations with the first grade of choice-dependence, taking obligations of reciprocation as my example.

In determining where obligations of reciprocation fall, the pivotal notion is that of fairness or desert. One who does us a favour deserves a return but only because we chose to accept their favour. There may be exceptions to this—debts of gratitude that we incur regardless of our choices—but I'll focus on the standard case in which it is fair to expect a return only because one's help was accepted. In these cases, not any old choice will do. The racketeer who intimates that it would be wise for the shop owner to accept his protection acquires no right to expect a return.

Force and fraud frequently remove the obligation to reciprocate even once the favour has been accepted but the mechanism of invalidation here differs from that operating in the case of a promise. Obligations of reciprocation lack the fragility I ascribed to both promissory obligations and other exercises of normative power. Recall that in the gym buddy example, though one had no promissory obligation to go to the gym, one might still owe the deceiving buddy a debt of gratitude. This may lead one to show up anyway and also to feel obliged to help one's buddy fight his own gremlins, perhaps by similar means. So there is some obligation to reciprocate here even though deception was needed to get the offer of an accompanied trip to the gym accepted. Because the deception can be justified, a decision to accept induced by that deception still creates some obligation to reciprocate, though no specific obligation to perform. The gym buddy deserves a return, his trick notwithstanding.[18]

What is true of obligations of reciprocation is also true of other obligations with the first grade of choice-dependence like obligations of due care for expectations. We have a special responsibility for expectations we voluntarily choose to induce. Unless the expectation was engendered voluntarily, it might well be unfair to require us to fulfil it, or prevent others from relying on it. And if one chose to engender this expectation only because of force or fraud, this may cast doubt on whether one's choice was voluntary in the relevant sense. But again, it seems to matter whether the

---

[18] Might the offer alone create the debt here regardless of whether it is accepted? Certainly one should feel grateful for offers of aid but it does make big difference whether one accepts: people often decline sorely needed help simply to avoid 'being obliged' (p. 226).

force or fraud in question was justified. Having discovered my gym buddy's well-motivated deception, I remain obliged to warn him should I decide not to show up. I wouldn't feel so obliged if I thought his deception malicious or unreasonable, even though he might suffer considerable inconvenience as a result.

An expectations theorist attempts to ground our promissory obligations in our obligation to take due care of the expectations we arouse. It is plain how one who adopts this approach will go about deciding when a promise is valid. First, the promisee has an interest in not having their expectations disappointed. Second, the promisor has an interest in not being bound to performance just because of the statements they previously (and perhaps sincerely) made. Third, all of us have an interest in facilitating the provision of accurate information about how others are going to act, an interest which is served by encouraging speakers to be accurate without deterring them from speaking at all (Scanlon 1998: 302–5 and Scanlon 2003a: 244–5). The expectation theorist determines whether a given promise binds to performance by striking a balance between these three interests and any non-informational interests that may be in play. In particular, they determine when duress and misrepresentation invalidate a promise by asking whether the promisor had a fair opportunity to avoid taking on the burden of performance given the way they were misled or the pressure they were put under when they made the promise (Scanlon 2003a: 254–5, 262–8). On this approach, if the promisee was justified in using such means to extract the promise, then the promisor was not unfairly treated and the use of such means does not invalidate his promise.

Foot remarks that the role played by promises could be filled by a will-binding drug which bound one who took it to future performance (Foot 2001: 45).[19] By developing the comparison between a promise and this drug, we can test the expectation theory's approach to invalidation. *Resolve* ensures that you both decide to give up smoking and carry out this decision. Note that *Resolve* works independently of the agent's practical judgement in that *Resolve* ensures that the agent will both make and carry out the decision to give up smoking regardless of what they judge best. We have all made decisions we think we ought not to have made and stuck with decisions despite realizing that they ought to be abandoned. For example, one may have decided to take a certain trip regardless of the cost and then come to think better of it but the prospect is so pleasing that one akratically sticks with the initial plan. What *Resolve* does is to ensure that you give up smoking regardless of what you come to think about whether you ought to.

For Foot, making a promise to give up smoking is functionally equivalent to taking *Resolve*. *Resolve* is just a chemical replica of the bond created by a promise and it serves our interests in much the same way. If so, the principles governing the validity

---

[19] Like the resolve drug mentioned earlier (p. 149).

of a promise should be much the same as those governing when it is acceptable to get someone to take *Resolve*. At first sight, the comparison seems apt. Someone who took *Resolve* only because they were falsely told that smoking had been made illegal or because they were threatened with compulsory aversion therapy has not had a fair opportunity to avoid taking on the burden of performance. And so they should not be bound in that way.

Unfortunately the parallel is undermined by the very examples that make trouble for the fault account. If *Resolve* were available to us, it would sometimes be right to use force or fraud to get someone to take it. This behaviour would wrong them no doubt but the wrong might well be justified. Yet a promise extracted in such a way and in similar circumstances would not bind to performance and this fact must be a puzzle for anyone who thinks that promises matter because they assure us of the promisor's future performance. If the expectation theory is correct, why should it make any difference whether the duress or misrepresentation secures this assurance directly by inducing immediate action (whether this action be immediate performance or the taking of a performance compelling drug) or indirectly by inducing a promise to perform? If you are entitled to secure performance or deferred performance by these means, why can't you secure a valid promise of performance by these means also? Why are you unable to use promises extracted by duress or misrepresentation to ensure performance if promissory obligation exists just so that promisees can predict the future actions of promisors?

It seems that the requirement of voluntariness in the case of obligations with the third grade of choice-dependence must be understood in the way suggested by the infringement rather than by the fault account. In determining whether a promise is valid, we are not trying to decide whether the promisee *deserves* the performance of the promise. This performance may not be deserved in any case. Nor are we trying to determine whether it would be fair to require the promisor to fulfil his audience's expectations. The fair distribution of burdens is not the issue. Rather what we are asking is whether the use of duress or deception to extract the promise deprives the exercise of normative power of its distinctive value, of its ability to serve the relevant normative interests.

The normative interests at stake here are interests in controlling our normative environment. In the case of a promise there are two parties and two normative interests to be considered. The primary interest is the promisee's interest in being able to control the obligations of the promisor but no promise would be made unless promisors had a derivative interest in being able to service the authority interests of promisees by controlling their own obligations (pp. 146–7). It is this secondary interest that explains why deception and duress deprive the promise of its validity. To see how we must ask under what conditions it is in the promisor's interest to be able to control (by declaration) whether he is under an obligation to the promisee.

It is not always in our interests to be in control of things that matter to us. For example, we have no interest in being able to exercise control over our normative environment whilst drunk, hence it is no surprise that the promises and consents of drunkards lack normative significance. The same is true to a much lesser degree of choices made on the basis of false information or in various extremities. Sometimes error and desperation do deprive our choice of any value and so invalidate the corresponding exercise of normative power. But there is no general rule here. People often benefit from being in charge of their obligations, even when they are operating in difficult conditions or whilst under various illusions. Such choices may have still value—e.g. the value of self-expression, or of avoiding the humiliation of being taken care of (pp. 166-8)—a value that one couldn't attain by being allowed to make a drunken choice. Hence, unlike drunken vows, promises made on the basis of false information or in desperate circumstances may still be binding.

What of promises induced by the action of the promisee? Where a mistake is induced by the promisee or pressure applied, this may invalidate the promise, even where the mistake or the pressure are not in themselves sufficiently serious to do so. If I mistake the costs of fulfilling my promise that need not invalidate it, whilst being misled about the costs by the promisee is a different matter. And the fact that I'll suffer some injury if I don't make the promise need not invalidate it even where the threat of that injury would. We have been working on the hypothesis that to invalidate, the action of the promisor must at least amount to a wronging of the promisor. The significance of this factor is evident. For example, a promise's value as a form of self-expression or as a mark of social prestige will be undermined by the fact that it was induced by such wronging.[20] This is especially so where the perpetrator of the wronging is the very person whose interests are the primary factor in giving the promise its binding force. If I make you a promise only because you have misled me or forced me into it, my commitment is a poor expression of my values and will hardly be a source of pride. So promises induced by such wrongings lack their usual value and normative significance.

It is important that the underlying interest here be an interest in controlling the normative rather than the non-normative situation. The promisor's interest in (say) expressing himself by changing the normative situation in favour of the promisee will not be served where the promise has been given only because the promisee has flouted some of the norms governing relations between them. By contrast, the promisor's interest in being able to control the non-normative situation is not extinguished simply by the normative character of the pressure he is put under. He may retain such an interest if the motive for the pressure is benevolent and the likely impact of the decisions he consequently makes on his other interests is favourable.

---

[20] The imposition of the obligation may still have instrumental value but this form of value is not relevant to the validity of the promise (p. 149).

Thus we can explain what I called the fragility of a promise, i.e. the fact that one may be justified in getting X to ϕ by force or fraud even though one couldn't use the same means to extract a valid promise to ϕ from X. In such a case, X has a (non-normative) interest in ϕ-ing, an interest that transcends their interest in having a voluntary choice as to whether to ϕ. Therefore others are justified in forcing them to choose. But X's normative interest in controlling by declaration whether they are obliged to ϕ is distinct from their non-normative interest in controlling whether they actually do it and the validity of any promise they make depends purely on whether choosing to bind themselves under these circumstances would serve that normative interest. I have argued that it would not.

For consent, the only normative interest at stake is the consentor's interest in being able to control the obligations of those around them (pp. 181–2). The same reasoning applies: where consent is extracted by wronging the consentor, it lacks the distinctive value which gives consent its normative significance. A starving man who would be justified in stealing some bread from the bakery will still prefer to be *given* the bread. There is something he values in having the baker's consent here, something that is absent when he must steal it, however justifiably. But the starving man cannot obtain consent with that sort of value by wronging the baker. And that is because the baker will not value (for its own sake) a capacity to control what others owe him when its exercise is induced by such wrongings.

To conclude our discussion of invalidation by force and fraud, let's consider their impact on obligations with the second grade of choice-dependence, namely obligations of involvement. I have argued that these obligations exist because we have deontic interests, because being bound in this way is good for us. So the question to ask about duress and deception is whether they deprive the obligation of its value, whether such obligations are good for us in the relevant way only when they don't originate in a wrong. Should someone become my friend only because of some trick or pressure, does that deprive the friendship and its constituent obligations of their value? Given that the binding force of obligations of involvement depends on whether these obligations are valuable for their own sake—rather than on considerations of desert and fairness—they won't behave quite like obligations of reciprocation. But nor are they quite like promissory obligations. Specifically, obligations of involvement are less fragile than promises: the infringement account does not apply.

Having heard me describe the luxurious villa I have hired, the beautiful beaches, the wonderful food, and so on, you agree to go on holiday with me. A two-day train journey is required but apparently that is a price worth paying. Before setting out, you discover that I have exaggerated the delights of the holiday in order to have your company. Here, I take it, you are no longer obliged to go simply because you promised to go since I induced that promise by wronging you. Now suppose that you don't discover the deception until the journey is over. Aren't you entitled to leave at once, to move on to better accommodation or even return home? So far as any promise goes, surely you are but there may be a new consideration in play. You and I have just spent two days on a train together. We have got to know one another. Might you have acquired an obligation of friendship to overlook your annoyance and disappointment and remain in place? I'm not saying you do. My only point is that whether you are bound to stay is not settled by the fact that you were wronged in being deceived and that the friendship that has grown up between us is a direct and perhaps even an intended product of that deception. Rather, you must address the far more difficult question as to whether this new relationship lacks the distinctive value of a certain sort of friendship simply because it originated in deception. You could go either way on this issue, depending on the intricacies of the situation. You might well think: 'in misleading me he wronged me but we've become friends so I feel I've got to stay'. Whether you became involved voluntarily is indeed important (at least at the outset) to the value of the involvement and thus to the bindingness of its constituent obligations but an important consideration need not be decisive. Thus obligations of involvement are more robust in the face of force and fraud than promissory obligations.

48. Promising to do what you ought not to do

In this section, I'll consider a third and final role that the notion of wrongdoing might play in an account of the validity conditions of a promise, namely where the wrong appears in the content of the promise. Sarah, a skilful driver, is in need of a large amount of money. Some acquaintances reveal that they plan to rob a bank and offer to cut her in provided she drives the getaway car. She knows perfectly well that this is something she ought not to do, that it would be profoundly immoral but in her desperation she solemnly promises to participate. Is she obliged to participate simply in virtue of her promise? Or is the wickedness of her promise enough to invalidate it?[21] In Part I, we identified two marks of obligation and both are present. First, the fact that she promised alone would make sense of performance. Second, if

---

[21]   Many writers take it to be obvious that a wicked promise gives one no reason to perform (e.g. Altham 1985) but there is a dissenting minority. Searle maintains that logic alone takes us from the claim (a) that a promise has been made, to claim (b) that the promisor is under an obligation to perform, and thence to claim (c) that the promisor has a reason to perform (Searle 2001: 193–4). Alternatively, Gilbert regards the formation of a promise as a form of collective decision-making and she maintains that if you have decided to do something collectively that creates an obligation to do it and having such an obligation gives you a reason to do it (Gilbert 2006: 134–64 and 227–34). Searle, Gilbert, and I agree that a promise can make sense of its own fulfilment without ensuring that there is any good in its fulfilment but I explain this fact by appeal to the underlying promissory interest rather than by relying on a claim about the logic of performatives or the intrinsic normative significance of collective decisions. Consequently we disagree about the validity of promises involving duress and deception.

she were to think better of the deal and breach her promise, guilt would be apt. I'll take these points in order.

I'm assuming that Sarah would not be justified in helping to rob a bank. Even if her need of money somehow excuses her participation (and shields her against blame) it does not justify her wrongdoing. Robbing a bank is something she ought not to do and she knows it. Nevertheless it makes perfect sense for her to drive the getaway car simply in virtue of having promised. After making her promise, Sarah may decide that her associates are incompetent and that their plan is bound to fail. Though there is now nothing at all to be said for robbing the bank in her eyes, it would still be perfectly intelligible for Sarah to go through with it in fulfilment of her promise. No failure of agency or lapse of control need be involved. True, she might instead try to persuade her co-conspirators to abandon their plan (and thereby release everyone from their commitments) but should that fail, she won't walk away without compunction. That brings us to the second mark of obligation.

I regard it as obvious that a decent person will regret having to breach a solemn promise, however wicked. They won't just wish they had never made the promise; they will regret the further fact that they had to breach faith with others in order to get out of it. And they would feel this way even if they had no doubt that breach was the right thing to do. Regret might not be their dominant emotion but one coldly indifferent to such infidelity would not be admired for their *sang-froid*. We'd think they weren't taking their commitments seriously. The real question is whether something more than regret is apt, something other than the emotion one feels when one must turn down an urgent request or sacrifice a great good.

Suppose Sarah decides to renege on the deal because her conscience gets the better of her rather than because she sees the plan will never work. Sarah will not be indifferent to her breach of faith and her emotion here has a different character from that she would endure if she had, however reluctantly, refused their original request to participate, a refusal with much the same effect if made immediately before the robbery.[22] This indicates that what Sarah experiences is guilt rather than regret, a suggestion reinforced by the fact that a request for forgiveness is rather more appropriate when you've backed out of an immoral enterprise than when you simply refused to participate in it.

It may help to contrast Sarah's case with that of the victim of Smith's highwayman. As we noted, the highwayman's victim might well regret making a promise they have no intention of keeping and wish there had been some other way out of the situation. They might even feel guilty about making such a promise if this involves deceiving the highwayman; to deceive someone may be to wrong them even if the wrong is

---

[22] Compare the drug distribution example considered earlier (pp. 93–4).

amply justified. But the question before us is whether they must feel guilt at the simple fact that they will breach their promise to return with more money. This I doubt. The highwayman has not bound you into his immoral enterprise by putting a musket to your head in the way that Sarah has bound herself to her co-conspirators by freely promising to raid the bank.[23]

So what explains the validity of wicked promises? In fact there is nothing special about promises to do something wicked. The same issue is raised by all promises that you ought not to keep, that you have sufficient reason to break, whether that reason comes from self-interest or from 'morality'. When inquiring whether we can bind ourselves to do what we ought not to do, the question to ask is this: Does the promisee's interest in having authority over the promisor and the promisor's interest in being able to provide it give them a common interest in being able to offer and accept promises which bind regardless of whether the promisor would be justified in fulfilling their promise? I think so. In my discussion of deception and duress I noted that settling the validity of a promise is not a matter of deciding whether it would be fair or reasonable to require the promisor to perform or whether the promisee deserves performance all things considered. To settle the validity of a promise is not to settle whether breach of it would be justified. The same applies when we consider whether the content of a promise invalidates that promise. The simple fact that the act envisaged by the promise is of a sort that ought not to be performed does not resolve this issue.

Were the function of a promise to carry information about how the promisor is going to behave, we could work out whether the promise binds by weighing the promisee's information interest against the other interests at stake in the case. Sarah's associates do have an interest in knowing whether she'll drive the getaway car but their claims are outweighed (or even cancelled (pp. 74–5)) by those of others. As a non-normative interest, the information interest lends itself to being weighed against other interests in an effort to determine what to do. As a normative interest, the authority interest does not lend itself to being weighed in the same fashion. Since breach of promise would not constitute action against this authority interest, we can't determine whether Sarah's promise binds by weighing the authority interest against whatever reasons suggest breach. Indeed, we can't determine whether she should breach in that way either (p. 163).

Why might anyone think that a promise is invalidated by the sheer immorality of what is promised? Many maintain that genuine obligations cannot conflict. For example, Pufendorf argues that there would be a contradiction if you could bind

---

[23] (Shiffrin 2011: 160–1) suggests that guilt at breach of a wicked promise should focus on the fact that one is misrepresenting oneself as acquiring obligations one cannot in fact acquire. This suggestion won't account for the difference between the two cases, a difference which remains even if both promises are known to be invalid by the promisor but not by the promisee.

yourself to do what was unlawful and Hobbes takes a similar line.[24] Specifically, both assert that we can't be bound by conflicting promises and that the prior promise always wins out.[25] This is a mistake: although priority may count for something, prior promises don't necessarily invalidate subsequent promises. I can, even through no fault of my own, be bound to be in two different places at the same time (pp. 92–3). More generally a promise may be valid even though its fulfilment would wrong someone.

A related mistake lies behind the following principle: If you have no right to ϕ yourself, you cannot grant anyone else the right to require you to ϕ. According to this principle, a promise to do something that you have no right to do is invalid because it cannot give the promisee the right to require you to commit it. This principle has implausible implications.[26] Suppose I promise to lend you a book and then recall that the only copy is owned by someone else. That fact alone does not invalidate my promise (Thomson 1990: 314–15). I am wronging you by not providing you with the book, even though I would also be wronging the book's owner should I steal it in order to fulfil my promise. Here you have the right that I give you access to the book even though I have no right to give you the book.[27] Rights need not cohere any more than obligations.[28]

Sidgwick says that 'a promise to do an immoral act is held not to be binding' because 'otherwise one could evade any moral obligation by promising not to fulfil it, which is clearly absurd' (Sidgwick 1981: 305).[29] What does Sidgwick mean by 'evading a moral obligation'? On the one hand, he could mean 'putting yourself in a position where you are justified in breaching that obligation'. On that interpretation he is right that a wicked promise can have this effect but wrong to think there is anything absurd about this. In fact, the phenomenon has nothing particularly to do with

---

[24] (Hobbes 1991: 128) and (Pufendorf 2003: 117). The point is also implicit in Hobbes's discussion of duress at (Hobbes 1994: 86). Since he wants to ground all deontic phenomena in promise, Hobbes can't admit prior normative constraints on the exercise of the power, so neither immorality nor coercion nor deception invalidate. But he admits derivative constraints. If you've promised something to someone, you can't promise it to someone else. And if law makes coercion and deception wrong then, Hobbes allows, they do invalidate the promises they induce, law being founded on a prior promise.

[25] (Pufendorf 2003: 118) and (Hobbes 1994: 86 and 1991: 130).

[26] The principle gains support from the 'rights-transfer' model of promising to be found in Hobbes and the natural lawyers. (Watson 2009: 169–70) explicitly appeals to such a model in arguing that immoral promises are invalid. I do not endorse the rights-transfer model.

[27] True I can't make you the owner of the book unless I am already its owner (p. 192), so you acquire the right to use the book without acquiring ownership of it.

[28] Consider consent. It seems clear that your consent to my ϕ-ing is not invalid just because my taking advantage of your consent here would involve my wronging someone else, however wrongful it was of you to consent. Suppose I wish to murder my deadly rival and ask to borrow your knife for the purpose. When you consent to this, you are ensuring that, in taking your knife, I am not wronging you by stealing it, and this is so regardless of the fact that by consenting you knowingly facilitate an immoral enterprise. The case of promising may seem less clear cut because an act can make sense simply as the performance of a promise but not simply as the enjoyment of a permission. Thanks to Daniel Viehoff for discussion.

[29] For related worries, see (Altham 1985: 8–9), (Watson 2009: 172 and 178–9), and (Shiffrin 2011: 159).

promise (or even normative power). By breaking his arm I can make it the case that I am obliged to take this man to hospital and thereby ensure that I am justified in skipping today's class. On the other hand, 'evading a moral obligation' could mean 'putting yourself in a position where you have an excuse for breaching the obligation'. It would indeed be absurd if you could deflect blame for failing to give your class simply by promising to do something that would prevent your appearing. But I couldn't deflect blame in this way any more than I could by breaking the man's arm; rather the blame would focus on the way I had got myself into that position.[30] Sidgwick may have been assuming that if you are justified in doing something, then you can't be to blame for doing it but clearly an exception must be made for cases in which you are presently justified only because of some prior misstep.

Returning to the question with which we began, is any promise invalid simply in virtue of its content? One constraint on the content of a valid promise lies in the fact that it must make sense for the promisor to offer and for the promisee to accept such a promise. If there neither is nor appears to be any good in promising to ϕ, if I am not in the habit of making such promises and have no policy of so promising, etc. then I cannot promise to ϕ because I cannot intentionally communicate the intention of hereby undertaking an obligation to ϕ. Nevertheless, within the sphere of intelligible choice, one can make a binding promise to do anything that does not directly attack the promissory interest.

There are promises whose content ensures that they cannot serve the relevant promissory interests and which are thus invalid (even though their validity might be highly desirable on other grounds). For example a promise to break a promise may be invalid purely in virtue of its content (p. 202). We have also encountered someone who wished to make a promise from which it would be impossible to release him (pp. 220–1). I argued that such a promise is self-frustrating, however useful binding promises from which there was no release might be. A more familiar example is voluntary servitude, as when I agree to become your slave in return for a substantial donation to my favourite charity. A slave loses their moral personality and with it their capacity to make and receive binding promises: one can no more breach faith with a slave than with a dog. If so then slavery contracts are of doubtful validity, for how could they be grounded in the slave's interest in being able to serve the authority interests of others by making promises? In these rather special cases the perversity of what is promised renders the promise invalid but perversity or immorality as such do not.

---

[30] On the other hand a wicked command might well deflect blame, at least where I am justified in obeying it, precisely because it is not up to me to justify the command.

Conclusion

The central claim of this book is that human beings have normative interests, interests often as significant as their non-normative concerns. A life-like account of human sociality is impossible without normative interests but to establish their existence we must work in various fields and at different levels of generality. I'll close the book by briefly reviewing the course we have taken.

Suppose someone (a Stoic perhaps) denied that human beings have any interest in sensory pain and pleasure for their own sake, denied that pleasure or pain made human life go any better or worse. Suppose we wished to defend orthodoxy on this point and affirm that a life with little pain or much pleasure is, to that extent, a good life. How might we proceed? Needless to say, a proof is unavailable but there are various strategies we could employ, depending on how the Stoic's doubts are motivated.

First, we could seek to undermine the theoretical motivations for Stoicism, e.g. the metaphysics of the person that supports the claim that pain and pleasure don't directly affect us. Second, we could connect our interest in pain and pleasure to various other interests that the Stoic might be more reluctant to deny. For example, we might argue that aesthetic value depends on the possibility (and value) of enjoying the beautiful thing and that aesthetic enjoyment involves sensory pleasure (pp. 18–19). Third, we could review the character of human social life (our habits and practices) and ask how much of it would make sense on the assumption that pain and pleasure do not matter in themselves but only in virtue of their collateral effects. I dare not say how effective these moves would be against the Stoic but I hope they have been successful when used by me to address similar misgivings about normative interests.

First, I have sought to undermine a familiar rationalistic moral psychology according to which human action makes sense only in so far as it promotes some interest. That moral psychology denies habit, custom, and practice a role in motivating intentional agency and thereby obscures a form of normativity in which we have an interest. It also renders unintelligible the existence of bare wrongings, of types of action that it makes sense to avoid even though no human interest is affected by them. Most of our normative interests and all of our normative powers generate bare wrongings and would be impossible without them.

Second, I have linked our normative interests to other interests, themselves not obviously normative. For example, it is widely agreed that a life without friendship is, to that extent, an impoverished life, a life devoid of an important human good. In Chapter 4, I argued that the special value of friendship derives in part from the bonds of loyalty that it entails. The involvement of obligation in friendship is part of what makes friendship the great good that it is and the same is true of many other valuable relationships. Thus our interest in friendship evinces a normative interest, an interest in obligation for its own sake.

Third, in the course of the book, we encountered a series of social practices whose character and workings it is hard to make sense of except on the assumption that they serve a normative interest. Promising was the most closely scrutinized but our briefer consideration of request, forgiveness, and consent pointed to the same conclusion. Only normative interests can render these social phenomena intelligible.

References

Adams, R. (1999), *Finite and Infinite Goods* (Oxford: Oxford University Press).

Altham, J. (1985), 'Wicked Promises', in I. Hacking (ed.), *Exercises in Analysis: Essays by Students of Casimir Lewy* (Cambridge: Cambridge University Press), pp. 1–22.

Anscombe, E. (1981), *Ethics, Religion and Politics* (Cambridge: Cambridge University Press).

Aquinas, T. (1988), *On Law, Morality and Politics* (Indianapolis: Hackett).

Atiyah, P. S. (1981), *Promises, Morals and Law* (Oxford: Oxford University Press).

Austin, J. (1995), *The Province of Jurisprudence Determined* (Indianapolis: Hackett).

Austin, J. L. (1962), *How To Do Things With Words* (Oxford: Oxford University Press).

Ayres, I. and Klass, G. (2005), *Insincere Promises: The Law of Misrepresented Intent* (New Haven: Yale University Press).

Baron, M. (2005), 'Justifications and Excuses', *Ohio State Journal of Criminal Law* 2: 387–406.

Bentham, J. (1988), *Fragment on Government* (Cambridge: Cambridge University Press).

Bratman, M. (1979), 'Simple Intention', *Philosophical Studies* 36: 245–59.

——(1987), *Intentions, Plans and Practical Reason* (Cambridge, MA: Harvard University Press).

Darwall, S. (2007), 'Reply to Korsgaard, Wallace and Watson', *Ethics* 188: 52–69.

Davidson, D. (1980), *Essays on Actions and Events* (Oxford: Oxford University Press).

——(1984), *Inquiries into Truth and Interpretation* (Oxford: Oxford University Press).

——(2004), *Problems of Rationality* (Oxford: Oxford University Press).

Deigh, J. (2002), 'Promises Under Fire', *Ethics* 112: 483–506.

DeWaal, F. (2006), *Primates and Philosophers* (Princeton: Princeton University Press).

Downie, R. (1965), 'Forgiveness', *Philosophical Quarterly* 15: 128–34.

Durkheim, E. (1957), *Professional Ethics and Civic Morals* (London: Routledge).

——(1970), *Suicide* (London: Routledge).

Feinberg, J. (1970a), *Doing and Deserving* (Princeton: Princeton University Press).

——(1970b), 'The Nature and Value of Rights', *Journal of Value Inquiry* 4: 243–57.

——(1992), 'The Social Importance of Rights', *Philosophical Perspectives* 6: 175–98.

Finnis, J. (1980), *Natural Law and Natural Rights* (Oxford: Oxford University Press).

Foot, P. (1978), *Virtues and Vices* (Oxford: Blackwell).

——(2001), *Natural Goodness* (Oxford: Oxford University Press).

——(2002), *Moral Dilemmas* (Oxford: Oxford University Press).

Frankfurt, H. (1999), *Necessity, Volition and Love* (Cambridge: Cambridge University Press).

Fried, C. (1981), *Contract as Promise* (Cambridge, MA: Harvard University Press).

Gardner, J. and Shute, S. (2007), 'The Wrongness of Rape', in J. Gardner, *Offences and Defences: Selected Essays in the Philosophy of Criminal Law* (Oxford: Oxford University Press), pp. 1–32.

Gibbard, A. (1990), *Wise Choices, Apt Feelings* (Cambridge, MA: Harvard University Press).

Gilbert, M. (2004), 'Scanlon on Promissory Obligation: The Problem of Promisees' Rights', *Journal of Philosophy* 102: 83–109.

—— (2006), *A Theory of Political Obligation* (Oxford: Oxford University Press).

Goffman, E. (1963), *Interaction Ritual* (New York: Anchor Books).

Gordon, R. (1987), *The Structure of Emotions* (Cambridge: Cambridge University Press).

Grice, P. (1989), *Studies in the Way of Words* (Cambridge, MA: Harvard University Press).

Grotius, H. (2005), *The Rights of War and Peace*, ed. R. Tuck (Indianapolis: Liberty Fund).

Hampton, J. and Murphy, J. (1988), *Forgiveness and Mercy* (Cambridge: Cambridge University Press).

Hart, H. L. A. (1955), 'Are There Any Natural Rights?' *Philosophical Review* 64: 175–91.

—— (1994), *The Concept of Law*, 2nd edn. (Oxford: Oxford University Press).

—— (2008), *Punishment and Responsibility*, 2nd edn. (Oxford: Oxford University Press).

Hayek, F. (1960), *The Constitution of Liberty* (London: Routledge).

Hegel, G. W. F. (1991), *Elements of the Philosophy of Right* (Cambridge: Cambridge University Press).

Hieronymi, P. (2001), 'Articulating an Uncompromising Forgiveness', *Philosophy and Phenomenological Research* 62: 529–55.

—— (2004), 'The Force and Fairness of Blame', *Philosophical Perspectives* 18: 115–48.

Hobbes, T. (1991), *Man and Citizen* (Indianapolis: Hackett).

—— (1994), *Leviathan* (Indianapolis: Hackett).

Holton, R. (2009), *Willing, Wanting, Waiting* (Oxford: Oxford University Press).

Hume, D. (1975), *Enquiry Concerning the Principles of Morals* (Oxford: Oxford University Press).

—— (1978), *Treatise on Human Nature* (Oxford: Oxford University Press).

Hurka, T. (2006), 'Value and Friendship: A More Subtle View', *Utilitas* 18: 232–42.

Hursthouse, R. (1991), 'Arational Actions', *Journal of Philosophy* 88: 57–68.

James, W. (1950), *The Principles of Psychology*, Volume 1 (New York: Dover).

Kant, I. (1996), *Practical Philosophy* (Cambridge: Cambridge University Press).

Kavka, G. (1983), 'The Toxin Puzzle', *Analysis* 43: 33–6.

Kolnai, A. (1978), *Ethics, Value and Reality* (Indianapolis: Hackett).

Kolodny, N. (2010), 'Which Relationships Justify Partiality?' in B. Feltham and J. Cottingham (eds.), *Partiality and Impartiality: Morality, Special Relationships and the Wider World* (Oxford: Oxford University Press), pp. 169–93.

—— and Wallace, J. (2003), 'Promises and Practices Revisited', *Philosophy and Public Affairs* 31: 119–54.

Korsgaard, C. (1996), *Creating the Kingdom of Ends* (Cambridge: Cambridge University Press).

Langton, R. (1993), 'Speech Acts and Unspeakable Acts', *Philosophy and Public Affairs* 22: 305–30.

Locke, J. (1988), *Two Treatises of Government*, ed. P. Laslett (Cambridge: Cambridge University Press).

Mackie, J. (1980), *Hume's Moral Theory* (London: Routledge).

Marcus, R. (1996), 'More About Moral Dilemmas', in H. Mason (ed.), *Moral Dilemmas and Moral Theory* (Oxford: Oxford University Press), pp. 23–35.

Mill, J. (1991), *On Liberty and Other Essays*, ed. J. Gray (Oxford: Oxford University Press).

Milosz, C. (1990), *The Captive Mind* (New York: Vintage).

Moore, G. (1959), *Principia Ethica* (Cambridge: Cambridge University Press).

—— (1993), *Selected Essays*, ed. T. Baldwin (London: Routledge).

Morris, H. (1976), *On Guilt and Innocence* (San Francisco: University of California Press).

Nagel, T. (1995), 'Personal Rights and Public Space', *Philosophy and Pubic Affairs* 24: 83–107.

Nietzsche, F. (1968), *On the Genealogy of Morality*, in *Basic Writings of Nietzsche* (New York: Random House).

Nino, C. (1983), 'A Consensual Theory of Punishment', *Philosophy and Public Affairs* 12: 289–306.

Nozick, R. (1993), *The Nature of Rationality* (Princeton: Princeton University Press).

Oakeshott, M. (1991), *Rationalism in Politics* (Indianapolis: Liberty Fund).

O'Shaughnessy, B. (1980), *The Will*, Volume 2 (Cambridge: Cambridge University Press).

Owens, D. (2000), *Reason Without Freedom* (London: Routledge).

—— (2006), 'Testimony and Assertion', *Philosophical Studies* 130: 105–29.

—— (2007), 'Duress, Deception and the Validity of a Promise', *Mind* 116: 293–315.

—— (2008), 'Rationalism about Obligation', *European Journal of Philosophy* 16: 403–31.

Pink, T. (2009), 'Promising and Obligation', *Philosophical Perspectives* 23: 389–420.

Price, R. (1948), *A Review of the Principal Questions in Morals* (Oxford: Oxford University Press).

Prichard, H. (1968), *Moral Obligation* (Oxford: Oxford University Press).

Pufendorf, S. (2003), *The Whole Duty of Man* (Indianapolis: Liberty Fund).

Rawls, J. (1999), *A Theory of Justice*, rev. edn. (Cambridge, MA: Harvard University Press).

Raz, J. (1977), 'Promises and Obligations', in P. Hacker and J. Raz (eds.), *Law, Morality and Society* (Oxford: Oxford University Press), pp. 210–28.

—— (1979), *The Authority of Law* (Oxford: Oxford University Press).

—— (1982), 'Promises in Morality and Law', *Harvard Law Review* 95: 916–38.

—— (1986), *The Morality of Freedom* (Oxford: Oxford University Press).

—— (1994), *Ethics in the Public Domain* (Oxford: Oxford University Press).

—— (1999), *Practical Reason and Norms* (Oxford: Oxford University Press).

—— (2004), 'Personal Practical Conflicts', in P. Baumann and M. Betzler (eds.), *Practical Conflicts: New Philosophical Essays* (Cambridge: Cambridge University Press), pp. 172–96.

Reid, T. (1969), *Essays on the Active Powers of the Human Mind* (Cambridge, MA: MIT Press).

Ross, D. (1930), *The Right and the Good* (Oxford: Oxford University Press).

Rousseau, J.-J. (1987), *Discourse on the Origin of Inequality* (Indianapolis: Hackett).

—— (2004), *Reveries of a Solitary Walker* (London: Penguin).

Scanlon, T. (1998), *What We Owe to Each Other* (Cambridge, MA: Harvard University Press).

—— (2003a), *The Difficulty of Tolerance* (Cambridge: Cambridge University Press).

—— (2003b), 'Thickness and Theory', *Journal of Philosophy* 100: 275–87.

—— (2006), 'Wrongness and Reasons: A Re-examination', in R. Shafer-Landau (ed.), *Oxford Studies in Metaethics*, Volume 2 (Oxford: Oxford University Press), pp. 5–20.

—— (2008), *Moral Dimensions* (Cambridge, MA: Harvard University Press).

Scheffler, S. (1997), 'Relationships and Responsibilities', *Philosophy and Public Affairs* 26: 189–209.

—— (2004), 'Projects, Relationships, and Reasons', in R. Jay Wallace, Philip Pettit, Samuel Scheffler, and Michael Smith (eds.), *Reason and Value: Themes from the Moral Philosophy of Joseph Raz* (Oxford: Clarendon Press, 2004), pp. 247–69.

—— (2010), *Equality and Tradition* (Oxford: Oxford University Press).

Searle, J. (1969), *Speech Acts* (Cambridge: Cambridge University Press).

—— (2001), *Rationality in Action* (Cambridge, MA: MIT Press).

Shiffrin, S. (2008), 'Promising, Intimate Relationships and Conventionalism', *Philosophical Review* 117: 481–524.

—— (2011), 'Immoral, Conflicting and Redundant Promises', in J. Wallace, R. Kumar, and S. Freedman (eds.), *Reasons and Recognition: Essays on the Philosophy of T. M. Scanlon* (Oxford: Oxford University Press), pp. 155–78.

Sidgwick, H. (1981), *The Methods of Ethics* (Indianapolis: Hackett).

Simmons, A. J. (1976), 'Tacit Consent and Political Obligation', *Philosophy and Public Affairs* 5: 274–91.

—— (2001), *Justification and Legitimacy* (Cambridge: Cambridge University Press).

Smith, A. (1976), *A Theory of the Moral Sentiments*, ed. D. Raphael and A. Macfie (Oxford: Oxford University Press).

—— (1978), *Lectures on Jurisprudence* (Oxford: Oxford University Press).

Smith, S. (2004), *Contract Theory* (Oxford: Oxford University Press).

Stocker, M. (1976), 'The Schizophrenia of Modern Ethical Theories', *Journal of Philosophy* 73: 453–66.

Strawson, P. (1974), *Freedom and Resentment and Other Essays* (London: Methuen).

Thompson, M. (2004), 'What is it to Wrong Someone? A Puzzle About Justice', in M. Smith, P. Pettit, S. Scheffler, and J. Wallace (eds.), *Reason and Value: Themes from the Moral Philosophy of Joseph Raz* (Oxford: Oxford University Press), pp. 333–84.

—— (2008), *Life and Action* (Cambridge, MA: Harvard University Press).

Thomson J. (1990), *The Realm of Rights* (Cambridge, MA: Harvard University Press).

Velleman, D. (2006), *Self to Self: Selected Essays* (Cambridge: Cambridge University Press).

Wallace, J. (1993), *Responsibility and the Moral Sentiments* (Cambridge, MA: Harvard University Press).

—— (2007), 'Reasons, Relations and Commands: Reflections on Darwall', *Ethics* 118: 24–36.

Warnock, G. (1971), *The Object of Morality* (London: Methuen).

Watson, G. (2009), 'Promises, Reasons and Normative Powers', in D. Sobel and S. Wall (eds.), *Reasons for Action* (Cambridge: Cambridge University Press), pp. 155–78.

Weber, M. (1947), *The Theory of Social and Economic Organization* (New York: Free Press).

Williams, B. (1982), *Moral Luck* (Cambridge: Cambridge University Press).

—— (1985), *Ethics and the Limits of Philosophy* (London: Fontana Press).

—— (1993), *Shame and Necessity* (California: University of California Press).

—— (1995), *Making Sense of Humanity* (Cambridge: Cambridge University Press).

Wittgenstein, L. (1953), *Philosophical Investigations* (Oxford: Blackwell).

Wolf, S. (2011), 'Blame, Italian Style', in J. Wallace, R. Kumar, and S. Freedman (eds.), *Reasons and Recognition: Essays on the Philosophy of T. M. Scanlon* (Oxford: Oxford University Press), pp. 332–45.

Index

Lightning Source UK Ltd.
Milton Keynes UK
UKOW03f0628310714

236091UK00001B/1/P